THE FED AND THE FLU

PARSING PANDEMIC ECONOMIC SHOCKS

DAVID R. KOTOK

MICHAEL R. ENGLUND
TRISTAN J. ERWIN
ELIZABETH J. SWEET

Publisher
David R. Kotok

Dedication

We dedicate this book to two groups of public servants.

First, we dedicate this book to those professionals in caregiving and medical research who have confronted COVID with persistence and single-minded purpose, despite daunting obstacles. Frontline health-care professionals are to be applauded.

Second, we dedicate this book to the thousands of people who work within the Federal Reserve System. During the worldwide COVID pandemic shock, there were no major financial failures within the Fed's purview: All payments were processed on time; extensive financial and economic research was conducted; markets were calmed; the U.S. dollar-based global financial system functioned without interruption. Twelve regional Fed banks and the Board of Governors delivered continuously and quietly as the world swirled chaotically around us politically and medically.

Table of Contents

List of Tables

List of Figures

Personal Note from David Kotok

*Humanity has but three great enemies: fever, famine, and war;
of these by far the greatest, by far the most terrible, is fever.*

— William Osler

*It's only in your twenties and in your seventies
and eighties that you do the greatest work.*

— Orson Welles

I have been intrigued by the impacts of epidemics and pandemics for more than a half century. My journey began in 1966 when, as a second lieutenant in the U.S. Army, I was assigned to the 485th Preventive Medicine Unit attached to the 7th Army, Europe. We were part of the 7th Medical Brigade, whose task was to support the entire American 7th Army in Europe with field medical services, including medevac helicopter ambulance services.

The American military establishment has long understood the risk of sickness and disease. History tells us that General George Washington inoculated troops in the Continental Army against smallpox during the American Revolutionary War using a technique called variolation. Smallpox was the most virulent killer of soldiers in those days, far more dangerous than British troops.[1]

Fact is, disease has killed more soldiers throughout all wars than swords, arrows, bullets, and bombs have. American military commanders from General Washington to General Eisenhower knew this history lesson well; thus, the task of the 485th was to protect soldiers from epidemic disease.

The writing and research in this book are the culmination of over a half century's focus on disease and epidemic and pandemic events and their economic impacts. Pandemic disease, fear of disease, prevention, and treatment have long factored into economic and financial market risk alignment. An economy and its financial market function best when market agents are not sick and do not have disease risk on their minds. And while an economy can be spurred in the short term by subduing fear — a popular strategy — it cannot be fully restored as long as pandemic-caused disease, death, and disability continue to erode human health and productivity.

Years after my time with the 485th Preventive Medicine Unit, when I served as the program chair of the Global Interdependence Center (www.interdependence.org/), with the help of GIC colleagues, we expanded the scope of that nonprofit organization's dialogues beyond trade and monetary affairs. We added health issues to its lineup of rich conversations. At the time of this initiative, this shift was a major change for the GIC.

At the GIC, we subsequently organized a discussion conference about SARS, held at the Lauder Center on the campus of the University of Pennsylvania. A few years later, the GIC partnered with the College of Physicians of Philadelphia for a national conference on bird flu preparedness, a topic which has become timely again as this book goes to press. I will be forever grateful for the help and guidance of former board member and my GIC bird flu conference co-chair, Sharon Javie. Without her efforts, we would never have been able to achieve a worldwide dialogue about bird flu preparedness at that conference in Philadelphia.

Many of the lessons from SARS and bird flu and other GIC initiatives helped GIC members and their constituents to prepare for COVID. My partners and I were able to contribute N-95 masks to local healthcare workers at the start of the COVID pandemic because we had them stockpiled before COVID arrived. We did not know which virus would show up, but we did know that preventive medicine and preparedness are critical functions for a business and an individual household, and we did know that pandemics are to be expected, though we may have little warning when they begin.

The GIC continues its programming on health issues through today. It has held multiple conferences on disabilities thanks to the efforts of former GIC board member Stephanie Mackay. Another project at GIC has been to examine the issue of long COVID and what it means in economic terms as well as how medical science will deal with millions of new victims of post-viral disease originating with COVID infections. The information can be found on the GIC website at www. interdependence.org/.

For more than two years, I published through Cumberland Advisors numerous reports on COVID developments and their economic implications. A linked list of these writings, along with other resources, can be found on the book website: thefedandtheflu.com.

The COVID shock is one of the largest pandemic-related economic shocks in modern history. As such, it provides us with the most recent and best data for analysis of the economic effects from pandemics as those impacts unfold. Much, of course, has been written about the disease aspects of COVID, but just as there is still more to learn about a constantly mutating virus with insidious and lasting impacts on multiple systems of the human body, there is also more to learn about short- and medium-term economic impacts of the COVID pandemic and other pandemics. As we contend with the ongoing march of COVID variants through our midst, we can also learn from history. Pairing the lessons of the present and the past with regard to pandemics and their impacts on societies and economies is the focus of this book, with a particular nod to the new role of the U.S. Federal Reserve during COVID.

---

1. Andrew Lawler, "How a Public Health Crisis Nearly Derailed the American Revolution," *National Geographic,* April 16, 2020, https://www.nationalgeographic.com/history/article/george-washington-beat-smallpox-epidemic-with-controversial-inoculations.

Introduction:

Why Write This Book

"Study history, study history"

— Winston Churchill

Pandemics impact wages, the labor force, supply chains, inflation, financial transactions, and interest rates, amid other economic factors. This book focuses on the economic factors that are influenced by pandemic shocks, relying on evidence from antiquity to modern times.

The chapters that follow are inspired and shaped by a prestigious research study of pandemic shocks published in June of 2020 by the Federal Reserve Bank of San Francisco (FRBSF). In their working paper "Longer-Run Economic Consequences of Pandemics," authors Òscar Jordà, Sanjay R. Singh, and Alan M. Taylor, three economists at the University of California at Davis, posed the question, "What are the medium-to-long-term effects of pandemics? How do they differ from other economic disasters?" They examined the macroeconomic impacts of pandemic shocks using data available for Europe spanning the last 700 years, starting with the Black Death in Europe during the 14th century. Jordà, Singh, and Taylor chose to analyze nineteen pandemics estimated to have resulted in 100,000 or more deaths, from the Black Death in the 14th century to the Asian flu of 1957–1958.[1]

They found that the natural rate of interest declines after every pandemic. They define that conclusion in terms of the framework originated by economist Knut Wicksell in 1898.[2] Their study establishes a prospective decline of 1.5%–2% in the real natural rate of interest over the medium term (10–20–30–40 years). According to the authors' conclusions, this remarkable outcome followed every single pandemic. They tested their findings with and without the Spanish flu and COVID pandemics included. In both iterations the findings were the same. Thus, history suggests that pandemic shocks are truly different from other kinds of shocks, such as wars, in this and other ways.

The San Francisco Fed working paper is a must-read for any serious student of pandemic shocks and their effects on economics and financial markets. When I read the paper in the summer of 2020, I was inspired and intrigued. What if the historical inquiry were expanded beyond the 19 European pandemics that Jordà, Singh, and Taylor examined? Would available evidence, however fragmentary, regarding other epidemics or pandemics reaching back into antiquity, align with their findings? What can be learned from 20th century pandemics that have unfolded after the Fed was created in 1913? How has the Fed's role evolved during the COVID period? And what have we learned since Jordà, Singh, and Taylor wrote in June 2020, as we have lived the remarkable history of a new pandemic?

Readers should view this book as building upon the foundation of the FRBSF authors' excellent effort. They are the pioneers, and they are building on and adding to other work in the Fed that has focused on the natural rate of interest.[3]

My co-authors and I are adding further observations after studying their work, appreciating its importance, delving further into the history of epidemics and pandemics, and watching all that has happened since June of 2020. In Part One, we take a closer look at their evidence, their process, and their findings and establish our template for examining epidemics and pandemics beyond the 19 included in the paper.

In Part Two we examine seven epidemics and pandemics from the distant past stretching from ancient Mesopotamia to the Bronze Age Levant to classical Greece and then Rome to the medieval Black Death in Europe. While we do not have the quality and quantity of data that Jordà, Taylor, and Singh had from the Bank of England for later European epidemics and pandemics, we do find evidence and indications of the economic and societal impacts of long-ago plagues; and we can see how those impacts, as best we can determine them, align with the findings of the FRBSB economists.

In Part Three we turn to the modern era, the creation of the Fed, and three of the pandemics that have occurred since the Federal Reserve Bank of New York opened its doors on November 16, 1914, with the mission of preventing disastrous banking panics and financial crashes. We trace how the Fed's understanding of pandemic economic shocks has evolved, paving the way for a nimble response during the COVID crisis.

In Part Four we look at the lessons of the COVID-19 pandemic, many of which are foreshadowed in epidemic and pandemic events across thousands of years of history. We do so even as we recognize that the dust has not settled in terms of how people view the lessons COVID has had to teach and that many readers may draw quite different conclusions. We humbly present our own findings and cite the research behind them for readers' consideration. They are an offering to the future, and they include assessments of the economic implications of more versus fewer deaths and cases of disability. We wish we could be around in fifty or a hundred years, once the fog of humanity's war with this new pathogen has cleared, to assess the medium-term impacts of the COVID pandemic and to update or revise the lessons we have painstakingly derived here, but that will be a task for others.

Part Five, compiled and annotated by Mike Englund, is a COVID pandemic economic chart book that covers the period of the COVID-19 public health emergency and national emergency, which officially ended on May 11, 2023, though endemic COVID continues to circulate. Diverse charts capture the many dimensions of the initial COVID pandemic economic shock and recovery. We offer them recognizing that what the world might have been today had the pandemic never happened remains an unattainable counterfactual and not a future we can recover, as the world now proceeds without the contributions of those who have died and despite the toll that pandemic-related disabilities continue to take on productivity and quality of life, lifetime earnings, and patterns of consumption.

---

1.   Òscar Jordà, Sanjay R. Singh, and Alan M. Taylor (2020), "Longer-Run Economic Consequences of Pandemics," Working Paper 2020-09, Federal Reserve Bank of San Francisco, https://doi.org/10.24148/wp2020-09.

2.   Knut Wicksell, *Interest and Prices: A Study of the Causes Regulating the Value of Money* (Jena: Gustav Fischer, 1898), 19.

3.   Listed below are selected Fed papers that address the natural rate of interest:

Thomas M. Humphrey (1990), "Wicksell's Monetary Framework and Dynamic Stability," Working Paper No. 90–07, Federal Reserve Bank of Richmond, https://www.richmondfed.org/publications/research/working_papers/1990/wp_90-7.

Thomas A. Lubik and Christian Matthes (2015), "Calculating the Natural Rate of Interest: A Comparison of Two Alternative Approaches," Economic Brief, Federal Reserve Bank of Richmond, https://www.richmondfed.org/-/media/richmondfedorg/publications/research/economic_brief/2015/pdf/eb_15-10.pdf.

Richard G. Anderson (2005), "Wicksell's Natural Rate," *Economic Synopses*, No. 6, Federal Reserve Bank of St. Louis, https://files.stlouisfed.org/files/htdocs/publications/es/05/ES0506.pdf.

John Williams (2003), "The Natural Rate of Interest," FRBSF Economic Letter 2003-32, Federal Reserve Bank of San Francisco, https://www.frbsf.org/economic-research/publications/economic-letter/2003/october/the-natural-rate-of-interest/.

François Velde (2022), "A Model of Economic Activity in San Francisco During the 1918 Influenza Epidemic," Working Paper 2022-04, Federal Reserve Bank of Chicago, https://www.chicagofed.org/publications/working-papers/2022/2022-04.

PART 1

Economic Implications of Pandemics

"History is not the past but a map of the past,
drawn from a particular point of view,
to be useful to the modern traveller."

— Henry Glassie, U.S. historian (1941–)

Chapter 1

A Study of 19 Pandemics

Òscar Jordà, Sanjay R. Singh, and Alan Taylor characterized in their abstract the undertaking they documented in their San Francisco Fed Working Paper, "Longer-Run Economic Consequences of Pandemics":

> We study major pandemics using the rates of return on assets stretching back to the 14th century. Significant macroeconomic after-effects of pandemics persist for decades, with real rates of return substantially depressed, in stark contrast to what happens after wars. Our findings are consistent with the neoclassical growth model: capital is destroyed in wars, but not in pandemics; pandemics instead may induce relative labor scarcity and/or a shift to greater precautionary savings.[1]

Their research relied on Paul Schmelzing's marvelous staff working paper, published by the Bank of England in 2020, on the history of interest rates in Europe, "Eight Centuries of Global Real Interest Rates, R–G, and the 'suprasecular' decline, 1311–2018."[2] Fortunately for the San Francisco Fed paper's authors, historical interest rates covering seven centuries have been compiled at the Bank of England Repository, as have other data series.[3] There were other substantial data sources also available to them. Using these sources, Jordà, Singh, and Taylor looked at long-term debt contracts for voluntary loans made to "executive political bodies" and derived real interest rates from these by weighting the real interest rates by GDP shares. They used the Bank of England data for France, Germany, the Netherlands, Italy, Spain, and the UK, along with data on real wages from Clark (2007) and data on real GDP per capita from Thomas and Dimsdale (2017).[4]

That extraordinary dataset made it possible for the three UC Davis economists to examine interest rate shocks from previous pandemics from the 14th century onward, and it drove their choices of events to study. There are not equivalent data sets going back that far from other parts of the world, so they concentrated on Europe and, in later periods, the U.S. They started with the Black Death, which killed one third or more of the population of Europe during the 14th century.

Òscar Jordà (a senior policy advisor in the Economic Research Department of the Federal Reserve Bank of San Francisco), Sanjay Singh (a senior economist in the Economic Research Department of the Federal Reserve Bank of San Francisco), and Alan M. Taylor (a research associate at the National Bureau of Economic Research who has since joined the faculty at Columbia) were seeking data and records to try to find a consistent economic reaction function to pandemics; and, most importantly, they were searching for an economic metric to estimate what that economic reaction is when pandemics disrupt life and business as usual. They were looking for a common outcome from other pandemics that would enable a forward-looking expectation after the COVID pandemic shock runs its full course.

Figure 1 from the paper lists the nineteen major pandemic events they analyzed. Their inclusion criterion was that an epidemic had to have resulted in at least 100,000 deaths, according to estimates.

Nineteen major pandemic events from the past with at least 100,000 estimated deaths

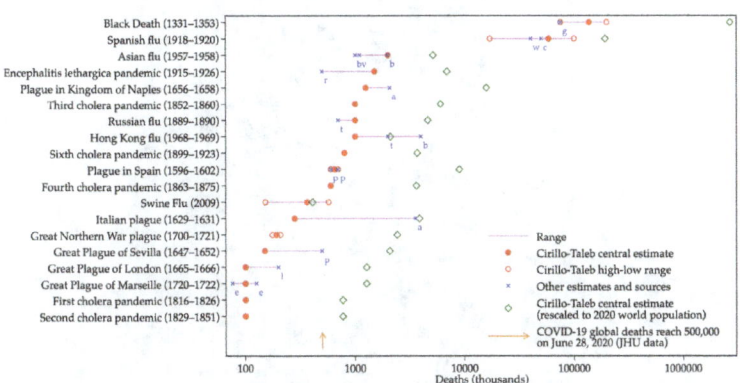

Notes: The main data are taken from the recently published study of Cirillo and Taleb (2020). See the references therein. Additional estimates of pandemic mortality are taken from: (g) George M. Gould and Walter L. Pyle. 1896. *Anomalies & Curiosities of Medicine.* New York: Bell; (w) Wang-Shick Ryu. 2017. *Molecular Virology of Human Pathogenic Viruses.* Amsterdam: Academic Press. (c) CDC. https://www.cdc.gov/flu/pandemic-resources/1918-pandemic-h1n1.html; (b) *Encyclopaedia Britannica;* (v) Cécile Viboud et al. 2016. Global Mortality Impact of the 1957–1959 Influenza Pandemic; *Journal of Infectious Diseases* 213(5):738–45; (r) R.T. Ravenholt and W.H. Foege. 1982. 1918 influenza, encephalitis lethargica, parkinsonism. *Lancet* 2(8303):860–864; (a) Alfani and Murphy (2017); (t) Paul V. Targonski and Gregory A. Poland. 2017. Influenza. In *International Encyclopedia of Public Health,* 2nd ed., edited by William C. Cockerham. Amsterdam: Academic Press. (p) Stanley G. Payne. 1973. *A History of Spain and Portugal.* Madison, Wisc.: University of Wisconsin Press. (l) James Leasor. 1962. *The Plague and The Fire.* London : George Allen and Unwin. (e) Cindy Ermus. 2015. The Plague of Provence: Early Advances in the Centralization of Crisis Management. *Arcadia* (9). [Arcadia Collection: Disaster Histories.]

Figure 1.1 Nineteen major pandemic events from the past with at least 100,000 estimated deaths, Òscar Jordà, Sanjay R. Singh, and Alan M. Taylor (2020), "Longer-Run Economic Consequences of Pandemics," Working Paper 2020-09, Federal Reserve Bank of San Francisco.

Like many other pandemic researchers, the authors used deaths as their filtering metric for establishing a pandemic's severity. But the authors took a critical next step. They utilized an established economic theory to derive a common economic estimate of a medium-term economic outcome from a pandemic. That way they could compare pandemic shocks in different time periods over the course of 700 years. To do that, they used what is known by economists as "the natural rate of interest."

The concept of the natural rate of interest was originated by Swedish economist Knut Wicksell over a century ago. Wicksell, for whom a research center is now named, visualized that there was an interest rate which would reflect equilibrium among different economic elements.

Figure 1.2 Knut Wicksell, Okänd bildupphovsman,1928,
CC Attribution-Share Alike 4.0 International license.

Here is the authors' definition:

> [T]he real natural rate of interest is the level of real
> returns on safe assets which equilibrates an economy's
> savings supply and investment demand — while
> keeping prices stable. This latent equilibrium variable
> can therefore serve as a useful barometer of medium-
> term fluctuations in economic dynamism.[5]

The Hutchins Center at Brookings explains the concept this way:

> The natural rate of interest, also called the long-run
> equilibrium interest rate or neutral real rate, is the

rate that would keep the economy operating at full employment and stable inflation.[6]

The natural real interest rate is an interest rate adjusted for inflation. Wicksell explains, "There is a certain rate of interest on loans which is neutral in respect to commodity prices, and tends neither to raise nor to lower them."[7] If an interest rate is neutral over a generation, whether in Ancient Greece or medieval Europe or in 21st-century Iowa, for example, a piece of land or a bag of grain will cost the same amount, adjusted for inflation, as it did 20 or 30 years before.

(For a technical discussion of the estimation of the natural rate, see the Federal Reserve Bank of New York's online resource: "Measuring the Natural Rate of Interest." For a global view of the natural rate, see Jeffery D. Amato [2005], "The role of the natural rate of interest in monetary policy," BIS Working Papers No 171.)

As they traced the impacts pandemics have had on the natural real interest rate and other economic indicators, Jordà, Singh, and Taylor importantly distinguished among the short term, medium term, and long term. Their focus was on the medium term. They wrote:

> In the very long run, from century to century, the natural rate may drift slowly for technological, political, or institutional reasons. But over a horizon of around 10–20 years, medium-term deviations will dominate. Economic theory presumptively indicates that pandemics could be felt in transitory downward shocks to the natural rate over such horizons: investment demand is likely to wane, as labor scarcity in the economy suppresses the need for high investment. At the same time, savers may react to the shock with increased saving, either behaviorally as precautionary motives mount in bad times (cf. Malmendier and Nagel,

2011), or simply to replace lost wealth used up during the peak of the calamity."[8]

They traced both the well-known gradual decline of the natural rate and a decline in annual volatility from the Middle Ages to the present. Of that lessening of volatility from year to year, they observed,

> Beyond measurement error, that noise also reflects wild fluctuations in harvests, armed conflict, and other events to which pre-industrial societies were exposed to a much greater degree versus today. With industrialization and modern finance, those fluctuations diminished considerably.[9]

The conclusion about "diminished" fluctuations was articulated by the authors *before* Vladimir Putin's forces invaded Ukraine in February of 2022, commencing the Russo-Ukrainian war, and before the ongoing conflict between Israel and Hamas exploded into a brutal war in Gaza in October of 2023. Given these developments, we are not so sure about this conclusion when we now see the largest land war in Europe since World War 2 and the war in the Middle East between Israel and Hamas, Houthis (Yemen), Hezbollah (Lebanon), and possibly Iran. Both conflicts have widened since they began and pose risks of broadening further. There are many other war-related risks in the world, including the obvious tensions in the South China Sea, given China's designs on Taiwan, and in the Caribbean, given Venezuela's designs on the Essequibo region in neighboring Guyana. Other risks linked to wars include shortages of oil, gas, and food, resulting in scarcity and higher prices.

The authors have shown that there is a response of the natural rate of interest to a pandemic, spanning about 40 years:

Pandemics have effects that last for decades. Following a pandemic, the natural rate of interest declines for years thereafter, reaching its nadir about 20 years later, with the natural rate about 150 bps lower had the pandemic not taken place. At about four decades later, the natural rate returns to the level it would be expected to have had if the pandemic had not taken place. These results are staggering and speak of the disproportionate effects on the labor force relative to land (and later capital) that pandemics had throughout the centuries. It is well known that after major recessions associated with financial crises, history shows that real safe rates can be depressed for 5 to 10 years (Jordà, Schularick, and Taylor, 2013), but the responses here display even more pronounced persistence.[10]

The degree to which the natural rate of interest fell in the wake of a pandemic varied from more pronounced effects in France, Italy, and Spain to much smaller ones in Germany and the UK. The trend was a constant, though there were variations. Jordà, Singh, and Taylor saw these differences as reflecting "among other explanations, the timing of the pandemics across countries, the relative exposure of each country to the pandemic, the relative size of the working population, and how industrialized one economy was relative to another."[11]

In addition to precipitating a decline in the real natural rate of interest in the medium term, pandemics also had other effects. Looking at long-term data available for England, Jordà, Singh, and Taylor found that labor scarcity following a pandemic resulted in a cumulative rise in real wages averaging 15% over a 40-year period. Real GDP per capita rose, too, while debt sustainability increased.[12]

The authors contrasted the medium-term impacts of pandemics with those of wars. Wars, unlike pandemics, resulted in a rise of the real natural rate, while wages were reduced slightly for a time and then returned to baseline. Instead of rising, GDP per capita dropped slightly for a couple of decades and then muddled back above baseline, but, again, only slightly, and far below real GDP per capita 40 years out from a pandemic.[13]

Jordà, Singh, and Taylor selected data to separate the economic consequences of war (more debt and inflation pressures, which raise the natural interest rate) from the economic consequences of pandemics (higher savings rates leading to a decline in the natural rate of interest). While this exercise is key to understanding the differing economic trajectories charted by these two different types of disasters, history is replete with examples of wars and pandemics being intertwined. In our opinion, war, disease, and money are all first cousins in the same family of economics and finance.

Writing in June of 2020, the three economists added a specific warning to their conclusions drawn in the early months of the COVID pandemic. In financial market parlance we would call their caveats the "this time is different" risk.

> There may be at least three factors that could possibly attenuate the decline of the natural rate predicted by our analysis, but their presence and magnitude is uncertain and unknowable until therapies to fight COVID-19 are more developed. First, the death toll of COVID-19 relative to the total population might be smaller than the worst pandemics of the past, but we cannot know for sure at this point. Second, COVID-19 primarily affects the elderly, who are no longer in the labor force and tend to save relatively more than the young, so the demographic channels could be altered, although a recent pickup in infections is now affecting younger

individuals. Third, aggressive counter-pandemic fiscal expansion will boost public debt further, reducing the national savings rate and this might put upward pressure on the natural rate, even though our analysis suggests that this expansion of public debt should be easier to sustain in the long-run.[14]

This book was completed four years later, and the results suggest that their warning was prescient. All three factors they identified have played out in worst outcomes since and in a way that contributes to the decline of the natural rate rather than attenuating it (though always amid other forces going into the medium term).

First, the official global death toll from COVID places this pandemic's cumulative death toll among the top 10 pandemic-related mortality events in recorded history.[15] As of July 2024, the official COVID death toll worldwide had exceeded 7 million people.[16] The unofficial estimate of excess deaths during the COVID pandemic, however, numbered about 18 million people for 2020–2021 alone, according to an IHME study, "Estimating excess mortality due to the COVID-19 pandemic: a systematic analysis of COVID-19-related mortality, 2020–21."[17] The total excess mortality precipitated by a pandemic event is a key factor determining the magnitude of a pandemic's economic implications. Causes of deaths recorded on death certificates are not.

Second, COVID-19 continues to impact working-age adults, children, and adolescents, as well as the elderly. It is also causing systemic health impacts and, among some, temporary or permanent disability that continues to erode the global labor force. The FRBSF study did not mention long COVID disability because the post-acute sequelae of COVID infections and their persistence were not yet apparent during the first few months of the COVID pandemic. We were only beginning to hear, in those days, of people whose symptoms were not resolving.

We can now estimate that for every COVID death, there are between 6 and 20 (center point estimate 11) temporarily or permanently, partially or fully disabled long COVID victims.[18] The General Accounting Office estimated in 2022 that between 7.7 million and 23 million Americans were victims of long COVID.[19] While preparing this book, I have interviewed a number of them.

Last, in the U.S., fiscal support for relief from the pandemic has dried up because of deadlocked American politics. This political failure in a pandemic is nothing new. Throughout this book, readers will find some of the worst examples of governance threaded through the history of pandemic and epidemic response. Today's COVID-shocked world is only a continuation of what preceded in other epidemics and pandemics.

There is far more to a pandemic and its economic outcomes than the pathogen that infects people. Knowing the enemy is not enough. Bringing science to bear and having the tools to mitigate a pandemic, as it turns out, is not enough, either. As we assess the economic impacts of pandemics through history and likely impacts from the COVID pandemic going forward, we need a concept of a pandemic broader than one that is specific to epidemiology and public health. In an authoritative dictionary of epidemiology, a pandemic is defined as "an epidemic occurring worldwide, or over a very wide area, crossing international boundaries and usually affecting a large number of people."[20]

Human beings are not agents in this definition. The epidemic pathogen is the agent, and it is geographical spread that distinguishes a pandemic from an epidemic. People are merely the victims.

Other definitions of pandemics throw in the word *novel,* because human beings have not yet acquired immunity to protect them against novel viruses. Referencing flu pandemics, the CDC explains, "An influenza pandemic is a global outbreak of a new influenza A virus. Pandemics happen when new (novel) influenza A viruses emerge which are able to infect people easily and spread from person to person in an efficient and sustained way."[21] Again, the pathogen is the agent, and people are the infected. Their agency — their role in managing the spread of a pandemic — is not reflected here.

In contrast, Paul Offit, Maurice R. Hilleman Chair of Vaccinology at the University of Pennsylvania Perelman School of Medicine and Director of the Vaccine Education Center at the Children's Hospital of Philadelphia, injects human agency into his concept of a pandemic. For Offit, a pandemic period is defined by shifts in human behavior in response to the geographical spread of a new disease. Of the COVID pandemic, Offit asserts, "It's an end when we decide it's an end. It's an end when we decide we're to go about living, working, and playing the way we normally did, and then the pandemic's over."[22]

By this definition, the COVID pandemic is "over" for many who have returned to life as they knew it before the outbreak in Wuhan at the close of 2019, though it is not over for others — the immuno-compromised, those who have underlying conditions that make them especially vulnerable, the 100,000 who are projected to die of COVID each year going forward, and those who develop serious new health issues after a COVID infection.

Offit's approach to calling the end of a pandemic asserts human agency into the equation but downplays the ongoing agency of the continuously mutating virus. The SARS-CoV-2 virus that drove the COVID pandemic continues to exact a human and an economic toll, and deaths and rising disability resist our power to banish the problem from our lives with words.

Neither of these two ways of conceptualizing pandemics accounts for the fateful interaction between a deadly and/or disabling pathogen and people. In his book *Doom: The Politics of Catastrophe*, historian Niall Ferguson characterizes a pandemic in terms that best capture the dynamics of agents, actions, and outcomes when he writes: "A pandemic is made up of a new pathogen and the social networks that it attacks. We cannot understand the scale of the contagion by studying only the virus itself, because the virus will infect only as many people as social networks allow it to."[23]

Ferguson's more comprehensive understanding of a pandemic is vital to parsing a pandemic's economic impacts, which vary widely in different places. It highlights the role of human behavior and of our chosen or virtually forced interactions with a pandemic pathogen. A pathogen knows exactly nothing of politics and religion, human preferences and emotions and habits, nothing of information or disinformation, ignorance or understanding, good governance or poor governance. It knows nothing of human morality or a lack thereof.

Instead, given innumerable rolls of the evolutionary dice, a virus merely gains the ability to infect human bodies efficiently, given as many opportunities as we afford it to do so. The pathogen itself is not the only determinant of pandemic outcomes, either in terms of human health or the health of economies. Instead, pandemic outcomes, economic and otherwise, reflect complex interactions between a new pathogen and human behavior in any given population. Human beings, meanwhile, weigh health risks with all else that they value or depend on, and their choices collectively and individually impact outcomes for others and for societies and their economies.

It is this understanding of pandemics that we find validated by the distant past, the recent past, and the present; and we'll return to its implications in Part 4: Pandemic Lessons and Observations.

The San Francisco Fed working paper "Longer-Run Economic Consequences of Pandemics" provides us a starting point for taking stock of what we know about pandemics and the economic fallout from them, reflected in the real natural interest rate, the changing labor force, wages, and more. After years wading through the COVID pandemic, it is tempting to dive immediately into all that we have seen so far and to look to what lies ahead. But it is important to look backward first. Anyone who once studied the Bush administration's 2005 "National Strategy for Pandemic Influenza" or more recently the Obama-era

"Playbook for early response to high-consequence emerging infectious disease threats and biological incidents," has rediscovered the truth behind German military strategist Helmuth von Moltke's words of wisdom: "No battle plan survives contact with the enemy."[24]

In their 2020 working paper, Òscar Jordà and fellow UC Davis economists Sanjay Singh and Alan Taylor, have laid out a template, a model, for examining pandemics and their economic impacts through history, to the extent that surviving evidence permits.

---

1.   Òscar Jordà, Sanjay R. Singh, and Alan M. Taylor (2020), "Longer-Run Economic Consequences of Pandemics," Working Paper 2020-09 (abstract), Federal Reserve Bank of San Francisco, https://doi.org/10.24148/wp2020-09.

2.   Paul Schmelzing (2020) "Eight Centuries of Global Real Interest Rates, R–G, and the 'Suprasecular' Decline, 1311–2018," Staff Working Paper No. 845, Bank of England, https://www.bankofengland.co.uk/-/media/boe/files/working-paper/2020/eight-centuries-of-global-real-interest-rates-r-g-and-the-suprasecular-decline-1311-2018.pdf.

3.   Ryland Thomas and Nicholas Dimsdale (2017), "A Millennium of UK Data," Bank of England OBRA dataset.

4.   Jordà Singh, and Taylor, "Longer-run economic consequences of pandemics," 5.

5.   Jordà, Singh, and Taylor, "Longer-run economic consequences of pandemics," 4.

6.   David Wessel and Peter Olson, "The Hutchins Center Explains: The Natural Rate of Interest," Brookings, https://www.brookings.edu/blog/up-front/2015/10/19/the-hutchins-center-explains-the-natural-rate-of-interest/.

7.   Knut Wicksell, *Interest and Prices,* trans. R.F. Kahn (London: Macmillan, 1936), 102.

8.   Jordà, Singh, and Taylor, "Longer-run economic consequences of pandemics," 4.

9.   Jordà, Singh, and Taylor, "Longer-run economic consequences of pandemics," 7.

10. Jordà, Singh, and Taylor, "Longer-run economic consequences of pandemics," 7.

11. Jordà, Singh, and Taylor, "Longer-run economic consequences of pandemics," 9.

12. Jordà, Singh, and Taylor, "Longer-run economic consequences of pandemics," 13.

13. Jordà, Singh, and Taylor, "Longer-run economic consequences of pandemics," 13–14.

14. Jordà, Singh, and Taylor, "Longer-run economic consequences of pandemics," 17.

15. "List of Pandemics and Epidemics," Wikipedia, last edited July 28, 2024, accessed August 4, 2024, https://en.wikipedia.org/wiki/List_of_epidemics_and_pandemics.

16. "WHO Coronavirus (COVID-19) Dashboard," World Health Organization, accessed June 5, 2024, https://data.who.int/dashboards/covid19/cases?n=c.

17. Covid-19 Excess Mortality Collaborators, COVID-19 Excess Mortality, "Estimating Excess Mortality Due to the COVID-19 Pandemic: A Systemic Analysis of COVID-19-related Mortality, 2020–2021," *The Lancet* 399, no. 10334 (2022): 1513–36, https://doi.org/10.1016/

S0140-6736(21)02796-3. See also, "The Pandemic's True Death Toll," *The Economist*, October 25, 2002, https://www.economist.com/graphic-detail/coronavirus-excess-deaths-estimates.

18.   To obtain these figures, we took high and low estimates of long COVID prevalence as of 2022 and applied those against one million excess U.S. deaths from COVID. Estimates were drawn from three sources, as follows:

> "Science & Tech Spotlight: Long COVID," GAO-22-105666, Mar 02, 2022, last accessed June 5, 2024, https://www.gao.gov/products/gao-22-105666.

> Philippa Dunne, Melissa Smallwood, and Emily Taylor, "Long COVID Impact on Adult Americans: Early Indicators Estimating Prevalence and Cost," April 2022, Solve Long COVID Initiative,https://solvecfs.org/wp-content/uploads/2022/04/Long_Covid_Impact_Paper.pdf.

> Katie Bach, "New data shows long COVID is keeping as many as 4 million people out of work," August 24, 2022, Brookings, https://www.brookings.edu/research/new-data-shows-long-COVID-is-keeping-as-many-as-4-million-people-out-of-work/.

19.   "Science & Tech Spotlight: Long COVID," GAO-22-105666, Mar 02, 2022, accessed June 5, 2024 https://www.gao.gov/products/gao-22-105666.

20.   John M. Last, ed., *A Dictionary of Epidemiology*, 4th edition (New York: Oxford University Press, 2001).

21.   "Pandemic Influenza," CDC, last accessed June 5, 2024, https://www.cdc.gov/flu/pandemic-resources/index.htm.

22.   "Boosters On," This Week in Virology (TWiV) episode #917, July 10, 2022, Paul Offit interview with Vincent Racaniello, Dickson Despommier, Rich Condit, and Kathy Spindler, https://youtu.be/xXJ2Y2ARMvU.

23.   Niall Ferguson, *Doom: The Politics of Catastrophe* (New York: Penguin Press, 2021), 5. Kindle edition.

24.   Andrew Marshall, "No Plan Survives Contact with the Enemy," Boot Camp & Military Fitness Institute, Feb 28, 2016, https://bootcampmilitaryfitnessinstitute.com/military-and-outdoor-fitness-articles/no-plan-survives-contact-with-the-enemy/.

PART 2

Ancient and Medieval Plagues

"History is a vast early warning system."

— Norman Cousins, American journalist (1915–1990)

Chapter 2

Back to the Bronze Age
An Epidemic in the Kingdom of Mari,
(circa 1775 BCE)

The god spreads infection in the upper district. I passed in a hurry.

— Asqudum, servant of the King of Mari, writing to the king

Historical Overview

In 1933, at a place in Eastern Syria called Tell Hariri, members of a Bedouin tribe mourned the loss of a tribe member. As they began to dig a grave, they found that the spot was already occupied — by an ancient statue without a head. That was how the ancient city of Mari was discovered.[1]

Following that accidental find, French archeologists would, over succeeding decades, excavate a strategically planned circular city on the western bank of the Euphrates, situated in a bend of the river, not far from Syria's present-day border with Iraq.

The fortified Mesopotamian city, built between 3000 and 2900 BCE, was situated as a trade hub that helped to link the Levant region on eastern shore of the Mediterranean Sea and Sumer to the southeast. Mari became a major center for the smelting of bronze and copper. One canal bisected the circular, fortified city to shorten the trip by river and to bring traffic and trade into the city for the price of a toll. Another canal provided irrigation to fields for growing crops in surrounding fields, making an otherwise unwelcoming place a suitable spot for a thriving city. Built on an incline, Mari featured a complex drainage system to carry water away in case of flooding.[2]

This regional capital city would go through three different incarnations under three different peoples over its 1200-year history before the Babylonian king Hammurabi defeated Mari's last king, the Amorite Zimri-Lim, burning his 250-room palace in 1761 BCE and largely destroying the city. The map below depicts the region during this period.

Figure 2.1 The Kingdom of Mari, Attar-Aram Syria. Modified map originally made by Sémhur, Wikimedia Commons, CC BY-SA 4.0.

Zimri-Lim's extensive library contained more than 25,000 clay tablets, written in Akkadian and dating from the last 50 years or so of the city's existence. The tablets contained administrative and economic records as well as letters. Since they were clay, they were not destroyed by the fire. And among the more than 25,000 clay tablets found there, some recount an epidemic in the area circa 1775 BCE.[3]

Figure 2.2 Cuneiform clay tablets from the Amorite Kingdom of Mari, Gary Todd, Wikimedia Commons, CC0 1.0.

Epidemic

No details in the tablets could help medical historians today to pinpoint the pathogen that caused the epidemic in the Kingdom of Mari thousands of years ago, but the painstaking inscriptions do indicate how people responded to and understood the plague, and some suggest impacts with economic implications.

First, those responsible for the letters and reports framed a disease outbreak and its eventual end as acts of God. Kibri-Dagan of Terqa, noting an outbreak in the district of Kulhitum, reported to the king, "God has set himself to devour beast and humans. In one day, two to three men died."[4] Once an epidemic had run its course in a particular place and that place had been purified by diviners, another writer concluded, "God is now done with the land."[5]

This language attributing epidemics to divine will did not play into fatalistic resignation, however, at least not for the king and his administrators. They also understood that disease was spread in some way by contact and offered advice in keeping with that understanding. The diviner Asqudum, a strategic advisor, wrote to the king:

> The god spreads infection in the upper district. I passed
> in a hurry. And my lord must give instructions, and
> inhabitants of any cities that are infected must not
> enter cities that are not infected. I am afraid they will
> infect the land, all of it. And if there will be a campaign
> of my lord to the upper district, my lord must stop in
> Terqa. He must not move on to Saggaratum. The land
> is infected.[6]

Even in 1775 BCE, it seems, governments attempted to control the spread of disease through travel restrictions, and epidemics shaped discussion around policy and military action. The last king of Mari appears to have shared Asqudum's understanding of disease transmission and how it might be controlled. When risk of infection reached the palace in the form of an infected woman named Nanna, Zimri-Lim warned Queen Šiptu to take precautions:

> I have heard "Nanna has an infection (simmum).
> Since she is often at the palace, it will infect the many

women who are with her. Now give strict orders: No
one is to drink from the cup she uses; no one is to sit
on the seat she takes; no one is to lie on the bed she
uses, lest it infect the many women who are with her.
This is a very contagious infection![7]

The king and his adviser had concluded that the pathogen responsible for the epidemic spread through contact with an infected person
or with things an infected person had touched. This seems to have
been the extent of observational medical knowledge brought to bear,
however. In Mari, the tablets make evident, there were no doctors
armed with medical knowledge that might alter the course of an infection. According to Zimri-Lim's emissary Yasim-El, reporting on his
diplomatic mission to Andarig, a diviner's medical advice amounted
to, "Things look bad — pray."[8]

Across the Kingdom of Mari, the epidemic struck in particular
places for limited time periods — it was not happening everywhere
all at once, and the severity of disease and numbers of resulting fatali-
ties varied. People died quickly after falling ill, in a handful of days.
Reports stated that families died together, and many corpses had to
be dealt with. Some households that served the king had no one left
to manage them, such that someone had to be sent to handle the situation.[9] No doubt, transfers of wealth ensued.

In Dunnum, 20 people died in a couple of days. There was "a heap
of dead" — "a devouring of God" terrifying enough that people fled
the city for the mountains, just as 21st-century city dwellers fled to
rural areas during COVID.[10] Economic implications for Dunnum can
be inferred as travelers and residents avoided the place.

As during COVID, essential workers fell ill and lost their lives.
High numbers of deaths among "domestics, the weaver women, prisons,
and cultivators" appear to have disrupted households and economic
activity. In the case of the cultivators, worker losses appear to have

impeded the harvest, creating grain deficits though the crops were growing well, and delayed the transport of grain due for taxes, which were, under the circumstances, deemed burdensome by those who had to pay them.[11]

Ritual purification of places ensued following an outbreak, though we do not know what such a "cleansing" entailed, except that there was not any Lysol.

Of these immediate effects — the loss of individual lives and what they might have continued to contribute to the society and the economy, the movement of populations to avoid disease, the transfers of wealth, the shifts in the trajectories of economic activity and perhaps policy during outbreaks — some assuredly played into lasting impacts that no one was tasked or equipped to measure. There can be no study now of the medium-term economic impacts of the epidemic in Mari: War, destruction, and regime change less than a decade later would close the chapter on Zimri-Lim's kingdom and the extraordinary city of Mari.

---

1.   Wolfgang Heimpel, *Letters to the King of Mari* (University Park, PA: Eisenbrauns, 2003), 3. Google Books.

2.   Henry Curtis Pelgrift, "Mari," *World History Encyclopedia*, 2016, https://www.worldhistory.org/mari/.

3.   "Mari, Syria," Wikipedia, last accessed June 7, 2024, https://en.wikipedia.org/wiki/Mari,_Syria.

4.   "ARM 3 61," in *From the Mari Archives, An Anthology of Old Babylonian Letters*, ed. Jack M. Sasson (Winona Lake, Indiana: Eisenbrauns, 2015), 333–34. Google Books.

5.   "ARM 26 263," *From the Mari Archives*, 334.

6.   ARM 26 17," *From the Mari Archives*, 196.

7.   "ARM 10 129," *From the Mari Archives*, 331.

8.   Yasim-El wrote to his king:
I have been seriously ill since the beginning of the year. In fact, both servants of my lord died. Just now, my illness has gotten worse. I have had omens taken a couple of times by a diviner about my illness. The omens about me are grave. I was advised this: "Go and kiss the foot of the gods, and thus strengthen your body. If it pleases my lord, my stay in Andarig. ... My lord should send Ḫaššum. If I get stronger, I would want to go kiss

the foot of my lord, offer sacrifices to my gods, then at the end of five days go back to Andarig. I fear that my illness might worsen and that I might no longer be able to serve my lord. Yasim-El, ARM 26 403, *From the Mari Archives,* 332.

9. *From the Mari Archives,* 334–35.
10. ARM 26 259, *From the Mari Archives,* 274.
11. ARM 26 265, *From the Mari Archives,* 279.

Chapter 3

Late Bronze Age Plague in the Levant
(circa 1350 BCE – 1300 BCE)

Historical Overview

As the Bronze Age neared its close hundreds of years after the Amorite king Hammurabi reduced Mari to a tiny Babylonian settlement, ancient records point once more to outbreaks of epidemic disease. (Such plagues were undoubtedly more common than surviving records are.) Clay tablets from the administrative records of Egyptian pharaohs late in the 18th Dynasty and, some years later, the plague prayers of an anguished Hittite king, Mursili II, provide glimpses into a regional epidemic that spanned decades and kingdoms, along with some of its economic impacts.

Egypt was ruled during this period by Amenhotep III (1390–1352 BCE); Amenhotep IV (1352–1336 BCE), who renamed himself Akhenaten, and his Queen Nefertiti; a female pharaoh called Neferneferuaten (perhaps Nefertiti) (1337–1334[?] BCE) and a shadowy figure named Smenkhkare (1334–1333 BCE), whose identity is debated; and finally by Akhenaten and Nefertiti's son Tutankhamun (1332–1322 BCE).[1]

Akhenaten was a religious revolutionary who reinterpreted a thousand years of Egyptian mythology and an extensive pantheon to ultimately elevate one god as the only god — the sun god (literally the sun disk), Aten. The better to make a new beginning and leave the old behind (along with internal political resistance), he relocated from the great city of Waset (known as Thebes to the Greeks) to build a new city, Akhet-Aten, "the horizon of Aten." The place is now known as Amarna, after the el-Amarna plain, where laborers built Akhenaten's city.[2] Akhet-Aten would be built and abandoned in the space of fifteen years; and Egypt's new monotheistic religion (the first known to history) would not outlast by long Akhenaten himself, as his enemies tried to chisel his name out of history, his face off his coffin, and his religion from memory.

Figure 3.1 Akhenaten (Amenhotep IV), courtesy of Gérard Ducher, Wikimedia Commons, CCA-SA 2.5.

A remarkable cache of records found in the ruins of Akhenaten's palace provides reports of disease outbreaks in several cities whose leaders corresponded with one pharaoh or another. While Akhenaten and Nefertiti were devoted to the worship of Aten above all and to their own identities as embodiments of Aten, in the secular dimension of their lives Akhenaten inherited, administered, and maintained through his life an enormous kingdom, encompassing vassal states, including Canaan and Syria, and more loosely allied buffer states that lay between Egypt and potential aggressors. Egypt dealt with powerful neighbors Babylon, Assyria, Mitanni, and Hatti.

A repository of mostly administrative letters, known as the Amarna letters, affords glimpses into the relationships and transactions between various other states and Egypt. The letters date from the latter part of the reign of Amenhotep III and span the reign of his son Akhenaten through the first year of the reign of Tutankhamun. At that point, the son of Akhenaten and Nefertiti moved the Egyptian court back to Waset (Thebes) and changed his name from Tutankhaten (a name honoring his father's god, Aten, the sun disk) to Tutankhamun (a name honoring Amun-Re, the traditional sun god venerated by his grandfather Amenhotep III, among other gods in the Egyptian pantheon). Tutankhamun left the Amarna letters behind in the move to Waset, and they were lost to history until they were rediscovered in 1887 AD.[3]

A small subset of the Amarna letters reference disease outbreaks and the impacts that those outbreaks had on the labor force, production, the movement of goods, and more. Those letters will be our initial focus, along with archeological evidence, and later, the plague prayers of the Hittite king Mursili II.

As we sift through evidence of a regional epidemic captured in the Amarna letters, though, we will start not with Egypt but with a prominent city-state in Canaan — Megiddo, known in Greek as Armageddon.

Figure 3.2 The Ancient Near East c. 1350 BCE (the world of the Amarna letters), courtesy of Ian Mladjov. On Mladjov's map, we have labeled Egypt, Megiddo, and Canaan as identified in this chapter.

Megiddo

> *"And he gathered them together into a place called in the Hebrew tongue Armageddon."*

— Revelation 16:16, King James Version of the Bible

A personal note from David Kotok:

I remember standing on the excavation wall in Megiddo when I was part of a national conference and tour of Christians and Jews. Next to me was a Protestant clergyman of deep religious faith. He was trembling. I asked him if he was all right. He whispered to me: "This is the place where it ends." He held his hand up high above his head and showed me how high the blood will be.

I asked him respectfully, "Are you sure that is how high?"

"Yes" he said. "That is how high." He was certain of his faith. The image is as clear to me today as it was decades ago when I stood at the archaeological dig in Megiddo, the site of Battle of Armageddon prophesied in the Book of Revelation.

Figure 3.3 Tel Megiddo, courtesy of Avram Graicer via Wikimedia Commons, CC BY-SA 3.0.

When we first mined the internet for the ancient epidemics we would target to research, we happened upon Wikipedia's extensive list, which featured a plague at Megiddo (now in Israel, then in Canaan) as the earliest documented epidemic, circa 1350 BC.[4]

It turned out that the epidemic reported at Megiddo was not the earliest for which we have useful records, nor did it happen in isolation as the Bronze Age edged toward its close.

Megiddo was a wealthy, important city in Canaan, overlooking the Valley of Jezreel. Its proximity to the Way of the Sea, a major North-South trade route, meant that whoever controlled the city also held sway over a narrow pass across Mount Carmel that afforded Egypt access to cities to the north and then along east-west routes to Asia Minor and Mesopotamia. Over the city's long history, its strategic location inevitably embroiled Megiddo in conflicts as various forces contended for control of those key trade routes.[5]

Eric Cline, a George Washington University professor of ancient history and archeology, spent ten seasons as a field archeologist at Megiddo and has written extensively about the dig there. He describes two treasure troves that appear to have been buried during the late

Bronze Age, likely when or shortly before the Stratum VIIA city was destroyed in the century that followed a plague reported to the Pharoah in a letter composed on a clay tablet. The hoards, one found in a pit dug into an older level of the city and one found in a buried jar, speak to the wealth to be found in Megiddo — objects of gold, serpentine, lapis lazuli, and ivory.[6] These artifacts, hastily buried in the palace at Megiddo, primarily reflect the city-state's ties to Egypt; but further digging revealed additional palace rooms replete with hundreds of ivories that are truly international in origin, with motifs that have been identified as "Hittite, Mycenean, Egyptian Ugaritic, Canaanite, and Assyrian."[7] Both Megiddo's wealth and its trade connections are affirmed by these artifacts.

Figure 3.4 Female sphynx plaque, Megiddo, Stratum VIIA, Late Bronze IIB, 1300–1200 BCE, ivory, courtesy of Daderot, Wikimedia Commons, CC0 1.0.

In *The Cities That Built the Bible*, Robert Cargill concluded, "Megiddo was identified as the location of the end of the world because it had been the epicenter of armed conflict throughout Israel's history."[8] The area was so vigorously contested through its history that, just to have a reliable source of water, Megiddo's residents were compelled to dig a tunnel 80 feet underground to carry water into the city from a spring in a cave outside the city. They concealed the cave with a great rock.[9]

Among the Amarna letters are five that Biridiya, the mayor of Megiddo, wrote to the pharaoh of Egypt, whose vassal city he was charged to guard. They take the form of cuneiform characters inscribed in clay tablets in Akkadian, the diplomatic language of that era.[10] Since the Amarna letters are not dated and the pharaoh to which each was written is not identified by name, we cannot trace, with all the precision we would like to obtain, the progression of the epidemic through time and across the Levant; however, William Moran, translator and editor of *The Amarna Letters,* concludes that Biridiya's letters are among the earlier ones in the collections, likely written during the reign of Amenhotep III.[11]

Conflict and the defense of the city is a predominant theme in Biridiya's communications, as is the provisioning of troops and workers on behalf of Egypt's vassal city-state. In one letter, el Amarna (EA) 244, however, pestilence joins Biridiya's two-legged enemy, a Canaanite named Lab'ayu (or Labaya), ruler of Shechem (also known as Sakmu), among Megiddo's troubles. In that letter, Biridiya pleads for a garrison of 100 men to help defeat the aggressor Lab'ayu and laments to the pharaoh that his city is not only being beset by Lab'ayu but is also being consumed by pestilence, death, and dust. He writes:

> May the king, my lord, know that since the return (to Egypt) of the archers, Lab'ayu has waged war against me. We are thus unable to do the plucking (harvesting), and we are unable to go out of the city gate because of Lab'ayu.

When he learned that archers were not coming out, he immediately determined to take Magidda (Megiddo). May the king save his city lest Lab'ayu seize it. Look, the city is consumed by pestilence, by … [symbols are unclear, translated as "dust and death" in Davies]. So may the king give a garrison of 100 men to guard his city lest Lab'ayu seize it. Look, Lab'ayu has no other purpose. He seeks simply the seizure of Magidda.[12]

The letter ends with an appeal for the Pharoah to send a garrison of Egyptian troops to help Biridya defend the city. (Later letters confirm that Lab'ayu, who also wrote letters to the pharaoh protesting his loyalty to Egypt, failed in his attempt to overrun Megiddo.)

Figure 3.5 One of the Amarna letters from Biridiya (EA 245), courtesy of Osama Shukir Muhammed Amin, Wikimedia Commons, CC BY-SA 4.0.

We have a reference to an epidemic in Megiddo. Notably, for Biridiya, disease seemed a concern secondary to an enemy at the gate. Both at once, however, constituted a dire situation. An outbreak of epidemic disease spiked a disease burden that was already high in a time when life was much shorter than it is now. The pestilence inside the gates weakened Megiddo's ability to defend itself against the enemy just outside, and the inability to harvest threatened the city.

But is there evidence of economic impacts as a result of the epidemic that Biridiya reported in Megiddo? Archeology, unfortunately, cannot offer a sufficient answer.

In *The Archeology of the Land of Israel*, archaeologist Yohanan Aharoni discussed the excavations at Megiddo and other crossroad cities that were the major trade routes during that late Canaanite period. He noted that the pottery at a stratum consistent with the Amarna letter dates is of the types used in trade from places as far away as Cyprus or Mycenae.

Aharoni offered this observation: "One must also remember that the pottery from every stratum is principally associated with its culmination, and one cannot expect whole vessels, except those in tombs, to derive from phases during which there was no heavy destruction of the city. Therefore, it is probable that in most of the towns, occupation continued, but in the first phase there is no evidence of significant public building projects, and the mighty Hyksos fortifications continued to serve for local defense."[13]

Arahoni reasons that the lack of new building suggests a time of economic stagnation in Megiddo during the two-century time frame that included the Amarna period, but there is not a way to dial in a timeline precisely enough to enable conclusions about the economic impacts of an epidemic there, though it is possible that population loss could have resulted in a time when new building simply was not necessary.

Megiddo is, however, not the only place where a pestilence was reported during the Amarna years. Both Near Eastern historian Graciella Gestoso Singer and physician and medical historian Philip Norrie have taken pains to map a much broader epidemic in the Levant, thanks to the historical records that the Amarna letters supply.[14]

Cyprus

The King of Alašiya (thought by many scholars to be modern Cyprus) would also report to the pharaoh a time of plague. The dating of the series of seven letters from the king of Alašiya to the pharaoh is uncertain, so it remains unclear which pharaoh the king addressed.[15]

Alašiya was an important source of copper for Egypt during the Amarna period. In letter EA 36, the king of Alašiya apologized for sending only 500 talents of copper as a greeting gift, with a deadly infectious disease outbreak as the explanation for the apparent shortfall: "Behold, the hand of Nergal is now in my country; he has slain all the men of my country, and there is not a (single) copper-worker." (Nergal was the Mesopotamian god of death to whom plagues were attributed, though it is possible that another plague god was referenced here.[16]) Notably, 500 talents of copper was a lot of copper — about 14.1 tons — 2.5 times more than is mentioned in any other letter and far, far more than makes sense in this context. [17] We have to ask, why would the king of Alašiya apologize for sending such an extraordinary quantity of copper, with a plague as an excuse?

Here we confront a textual issue. There is, in fact, no unit of measure identified in the original text, though translators have long supplied the unit *talents*. Georgia Papadopoulou, who has studied the metal trade in the Eastern Mediterranean in the Late Bronze Age, has argued that talents are the wrong unit of measure to insert here. She observes that the word *talent* is not omitted in other texts of the time, but that the word *shekel* often was, because it was "the commonly used weight unit in commerce." She concluded that 500 shekels, not

500 talents, is the correct translation. If so, the greeting gift that the King of Alašiya sent to the pharaoh of Egypt, would have amounted to around 10 pounds of copper — an amount a king might have to apologize for to a pharaoh.[18]

The much smaller amount of copper — the smallest mentioned in the Amarna letters, rather than the largest, if Papadopoulou is correct (and we think she is) — reflected the toll that an epidemic took on workers in copper mining and refining. Promising to send more copper, the king asked for silver, an ox (probably a figurine), sweet oil, an augur specializing in reading omens, and payment owed by Egypt for timber. The king went on to report that the plague had also preyed on his own family: "There was a young wife of mine that now, my brother, is dead."[19]

The economic evidence in this letter, though scant, suggests that the number of deaths among workers — in this case copper workers — significantly affected copper production capacity in Alašiya at the time. The impact of the epidemic would not have been limited to copper production, but only the copper shortfall was relevant here.

Byblos (EA 362)

Two additional references to epidemic outbreaks in Canaan also appear in the Amarna letters, one in Gubla (Byblos) and the other in Sumur. Both Gubla and Sumur were port cities situated on the east coast of the Mediterranean Sea north of Megiddo, and both letters were written during the time that a king named Rib-Hadda ruled Gubla. Moran concludes that Rib-Hadda's rule comes after the death of Lab'ayu of Shechem, who had besieged Megiddo, so we can place these two epidemic reports sometime after the plague at Megiddo.[20]

As king of Byblos, Rib-Hadda wrote many letters to Akhenaten, and many of them were pleas for support in defending Gubla from aggressors. In EA 362, he urged the pharaoh to send archers immediately to defend the city, to keep it from falling to his enemies. In making the request, he countered an enemy claim that there was an infectious disease outbreak that might sway the pharaoh against sending the archers. He vows, "There is no pestilence in the lands. It has been over for a long time."[21] We have here an acknowledgment that Byblos, like Alašiya and Megiddo, experienced an epidemic outbreak. And if the disease was still circulating, Rib-Hadda was not about to admit it, lest the pharaoh not send the archers.

Sumur (EA 96)

EA 96 is a snarky letter written by a frustrated general of Sumur, expressing a message for Rib-Hadda in Byblos, requesting asses that he had clearly requested before, to no avail, along with men, to guard the city of Sumur. Sumur was under Rib-Hadda's guardianship at the time — until Sumur fell to Rib-Hadda's enemy Abdi-Ashirta. After a perfunctorily polite greeting, the general turned abruptly to the matter of the asses he expected the king to produce: "As to your saying, 'I will not permit men from Sumur to enter my city. There is a pestilence in Sumer,' is it a pestilence affecting men or one affecting asses? What pestilence affects asses so that they cannot walk? But watch out! Do the asses belong to the king or not? Properties of the king are not lost; indeed, their owner seeks them out...."

The general considered the pestilence in Sumur to be no excuse for Rib-Hadda's failure to send men and asses for the city's defense, and he objected to an anticipated excuse, that asses were afflicted, too. That said, both the report regarding an active outbreak in Sumur and the one regarding a previous outbreak in Byblos/Gubla evidence concern on the part of those who governed about how disease might be transmitted from one place to another. We can infer that rulers did not want to send their troops where a disease outbreak was happening, lest they bring a plague home with them when they returned.

When we tally the implications of the epidemic reports from Megiddo, Alašiya, Byblos, and Sumur, we see indications, once again, that epidemic outbreaks impacted workers, production, trade, and perhaps even decisions about where to send troops — or asses.

Egypt

Back in Egypt, while power struggles played out in vassal cities in Canaan, Akhenaten and Nefertiti ruled as embodiments of the sun god Aten, scenes from their lives unfurled in murals weighted with symbolism affirming their divinity. One particularly spectacular event — a show of glory and power — may have precipitated the personal griefs that the pharaoh and the queen would experience when plague came to Amarna. In the 12th year of Akhenaten's rule, people from all over Egypt's known world — North Africa, the Middle East, and the Mediterranean — visited Amarna to pay tribute to Akhenaten and Nefertiti.[22] Panoramic scenes painted on the walls of the tombs of two Amarna officials depict Akhenaten and Nefertiti sitting on their royal sedan chair. The caption tells us, "In order to receive the tribute of Syria and Kush, the West and the East, all foreign lands assembled on one occasion — even the islands in the midst of the sea — presenting tribute to the king on the great throne of Akhet-Aten for the receiving of the gifts of every foreign land, so that the breath of life might be given to them."[23]

John and Colleen Darnell have vividly described the scene in which the tributes were presented, as representatives converged from Nubia, Libya, the eastern Mediterranean, Crete, and Punt bearing their gifts of ivory, incense, cattle, leopards, and gold.[24] The tribute ceremony was an extraordinary event. But was it also a superspreader event? A year or two later, three of Akhenaten and Nefertiti's six daughters would die in short order.[25] Was there a connection between the tribute ceremony and a disease outbreak in Amarna? Egyptologists Gabriela

Singer and Aidan Dodson suspect, as we do, that the historic gathering not only brought together nations and treasures but might also have transmitted epidemic disease. Singer quotes Dodson: "Between Years 12 and 17, the Queen mother Tiye, Akhenaten, the Great Royal wife Nefertiti, and the princesses Meketaten, Meritaten Setepenra, and Neferneferura were dead."[26]

Now, there are no death certificates to record causes of death for these people, and this was an age when child mortality was high and average lives were short, even for those who survived childhood. A small minority reached old age, but the average male did not live to age 30, while the average woman might live into her mid-30s.[27] Without details regarding how the royal children died, while we can speculate about the possibility of an epidemic at Amarna, it is not the historical records that can yield further evidence. We need to hear instead from the dead.

Of the cemeteries identified at Amarna, the most interesting one is the North Cemetery, which differs from the others surrounding the city in several respects. First, 43% of the graves contain more than one body — an unusually high percentage. These are simple pit graves, sometimes dug wider than usual to accommodate multiple bodies, but often one body is interred on top of another. The usual artefacts buried with the dead are much scarcer in this cemetery — many people buried here took nothing with them into the afterlife, and the dead are young — ages 7–25.[28]

Their bodies evidence malnutrition and hard lives — some had already developed arthritis; others had spinal injuries suggesting dangerous, hard work, perhaps at a quarry not far away.[29]

The multiple bodies in single graves suggest the possibility and even the probability of an epidemic. The conditions in the workers' village would certainly have been conducive to disease. Both cat fleas and human fleas have been found there, identified by archeologist Eva Panagiotakopulu, who studies fossilized insects. Panagiotakopulu argues that the fleas, along with Nile rats known to be present in the region during the period, and a description in an earlier Egyptian medical text of an illness that generated a bubo all suggest that *Yersinia pestis,* the bacteria that causes the bubonic plague, could have been a contender as the culprit for an epidemic outbreak that would have had gravediggers making space for multiple bodies at once in Amarna.[30]

Genetic evidence confirming the presence of now-extinct strains of bubonic plague, along with typhoid, has been found in the bones of bodies buried in Crete centuries earlier, around 2000 BCE, so we know that the Eastern Mediterranean had experienced both of these pathogens. Indeed, bubonic plague has been found across Eurasia as far back as the Neolithic period.[31]

The presence of malaria, tuberculosis, dysentery, and smallpox at Amarna reflect both the heavy disease burden people contended with and the poor, crowded living conditions they dealt with, which would have made any epidemic worse.[32]

The evidence for a plague in the years following the tribute ceremony is compelling but admittedly not ironclad. However, we can say this: If there had been no epidemic in Egypt, an epidemic would not have been transmitted, as seems to have been the case, some fifteen years after the tribute ceremony, by Egyptian prisoners of war (or perhaps the tiny insect hitchhikers they carried) to the Kingdom of Hatti.[33]

As we step back to consider the broader political and religious ramifications of the deaths that occurred at Amarna and a possible epidemic, Dodson draws an inference that would be hard to counter: The deaths in the royal family and across the region had to have called into question the notion that Akhenaten's political regime and revolutionary religion embodied divine will. Radical change would follow.[34]

In a time when a pestilence was reflexively blamed on a perceived offense against a god (or multiple gods), we can readily imagine what conclusions Egyptians might have drawn, from royal deaths and the deaths of others in Amarna, about a bold new religion that had elevated the sun disk, Aten, above all other gods — gods who were no longer acknowledged or worshiped by the pharaoh and his queen or openly by anyone else. It seems a no-brainer that an epidemic outbreak in the latter years of Akhenaten's reign would have cemented opposition to his religious revolution and sent people scurrying back to the old gods and especially to the older sun god, Amun-re. An epidemic curse might well help to explain why Akhenaten's and Nefertiti's faces were chiseled out of their images with such vehemence and their monuments demolished. Certainly, the chapels in the workers' village at Amarna suggest that Akhenaten's workers, in private, still continued to worship the old gods even as they toiled to construct his city and the tombs where the royal family would ultimately rest, intent on immortality. The Amarna Project website describes them:

> The sanctuaries of these chapels were brick benches, evidently for the support of images. The chapels were decorated with painted designs and scenes, and with a certain amount of carved stonework. Mention of the Aten is notably absent. In its place were traditional designs and references to familiar deities. The initial explanation was that the chapels belong to the short interval after the death of Akhenaten. The placement of the shrines, however, implies that they were integral to the village layout and belong within the reign of Akhenaten.[35]

Perhaps in these rooms Akhenaten's workers prayed to the older Egyptian gods to lift the curse of a plague among them.

We see in the case of Amarna the very real possibility that an epidemic may have played a role in intensifying the rejection of a religious revolution and in political change as the Amarna period ended with Akhenaten's son Tutankhamun's leading Egypt back to the worship of the old gods.

The Hittite Empire

The epidemic in the Kingdom of Hatti would come years later, after Tutankhamun's death in Egypt, and after the young pharaoh's widow, Ankhesenamun, sent an extraordinary letter to the king of Hatti, Suppiluliuma, requesting one of his sons as her new husband and promising to make that son ruler of Egypt. That letter came as quite a surprise to the Hittite king.

After all, the Kingdom of Hatti, to the north, was not among Egypt's allies either in the time of Akhenaten or his heir Tutankhamun. In his time, Akhenaten would launch a failed military mission against the Hittites, designed to secure the city of Kadesh, which was vital to the control of a north-south corridor that was, in turn, vital to Egypt's control in Syria-Palestine.[36] Control of Kadesh was also a goal of Tutankhamun's Egyptian Asiatic campaign, which was underway when he died without an heir, and later for Ramses II.

When Suppiluliuma did not take Ankhesenamun's first letter seriously, she wrote again, protesting her sincerity. In the end, Suppiluliuma complied, sending his son Zannanza to marry the former pharaoh's widow.

But Tutankhaman's widow was apparently not the only person in the royal court with a plan. Zannanza was killed en route apparently; and when Suppiluliuma learned of his son's death, heartbroken, he launched an attack on Amqa, an Egyptian territory. The attack violated a treaty between Hatti and Egypt, a treaty that the Hittites deemed to have been forged by the Storm-god of Hatti. Suppiluliuma's forces brought Egyptian prisoners of war back to Hatti, and with them, it appears, the epidemic disease that had afflicted Egypt.[37]

Suppiluliuma's son and successor, Mursili II, would spend years composing prayers to this Hittite god and that one and then to all known gods at once, seeking relief from the plague. He would tell the story of the breaking of the treaty and the coming of the plague with the prisoners of war, but he would blame the plague not on disease transmission but on his father's transgressions, among them the breaking of the treaty, for which he sought forgiveness.

Mursili II's prayers concerning the plague have been collected and translated by the late Tel-Aviv University historian and Hittitologist, Itamar Singer. From those prayers emerges a picture of the scope and duration of the epidemic in Hatti and its distressing impacts. They also offer a poignant portrait of a man trying to reason on behalf of his country with seemingly implacable gods. Mursili lost both his father, Suppiluliuma, who died in 1330 BCE, and his older brother, Arnuwanda II, in the epidemic.[38]

In No. 8, "Mursili's Hymn and Prayer to the Sun-goddess of Arinna," after praising the goddess in the invocation, Mursili begins to plead with his deities:

> Oh gods, what is this that you have done? You have allowed a plague into Hatti, and the whole of Hatti is dying. No one prepares for you the offering bread and the libation anymore. The plowmen who used to work the fallow fields of the gods have died, so they do not work or reap the fields of the gods. The grinding women who used to make the offering bread for the gods have died, so they do not [make] the god's offering bread any longer.
>
> The cowherds and shepherds of the corrals and sheepfolds from which they used to select sacrificial cattle and sheep are dead, so that the corrals and

sheepfolds are neglected. So it has come to pass that the offering bread, the libations, and the offering of animals, have stopped.[39]

The economic devastation is clear — death has struck, among others, the plowmen, the women who ground the grain, cowherds and shepherds, with clear implications for the food supply, though Mursili focuses first on those impacts that might be of greatest interest to the Sun-goddess: the offerings the people would otherwise be making to her if the plague were not raging. (Hint, oh Sun-goddess, take the pestilence away.)

The letter also captures the role that the epidemic played in weakening Hatti against its enemies. Mursili, ever resourceful, proposed an alternate set of disease victims — Hatti's enemies:

> Turn the plague, the hostility, the famine, and the severe fever towards Mittanni and Arzawa. Rested are the belligerent lands, but Hatti is a weary land. Unhitch the weary one, and hitch up the rested one.[40]

Mursili's prayers suggest that plague threatened the balance of power in the Levant. Mursili confirms that a plague-weakened Hatti was also in danger of losing control of lands it had already conquered:

> Moreover, those lands which belong to Hatti, the Kaska land — they were swineherds and weavers — Arawanna, Kalasma, Lukki, and Pitassa, have declared themselves free from the Sun-goddess of Arinna. They discontinue (the payment of) their tributes and began to attack Hatti. In the past, Hatti, with the help of the Sun-goddess of Arinna, used to maul the surrounding lands

like a lion…. But now, all the surrounding lands have begun to attack Hatti…. To those enemy lands give severe fever, plague, and famine.[41]

In No. 13, Mursili's fourth prayer to the assembly of the gods, the king implores more than thirty Hittite deities to end the plague and promises to restore a temple and the statue of a god whose worship has been neglected. But then, after a section of missing text, he questions how he can do what he has promised, given the march of death through his country:

> Or should I have restored it for the gods, my lords, from my land, or from my infantry and chariotry? If I should indeed reestablish the gods, since now the members of my household, land, infantry and chariotry keep dying, by what means should I reestablish you, O gods? … O gods, have mercy on me again because of this reason! Turn towards me! Send the plague away from the land! Let it subside in the towns where people are dying, and let the plague not return to the towns in which it has subsided![42]

The epidemic, which does not seem to have surged everywhere all at once, eroded the strength of the Hittite kingdom not for a year or for five years, but, according to Mursili's third plague prayer, for twenty years. Mursili laments the long siege of disease:

> People kept dying at the time of my father, at the time of my brother, and now since I have become priest of the gods, they keep on dying in my time. For twenty years now people have been dying in great numbers in Hatti. Hatti has been very badly damaged by the plague.[43]

We suspect that twenty years may not have been the end of the ordeal. For the Hittite Kingdom, the impacts reported by Mursili were profound: depopulation, famine, the disruption of governance, defense, and the ability to maintain an empire and the revenue that taxes and tributes would have otherwise delivered. Every human activity would have been disrupted, including the usual volume of trade.

We do not see in Mursili's prayers any indication of rudimentary medical understandings of disease transmission or how it might have been stopped or slowed, though we saw inklings of these understandings in Mari and in the Amarna letters. Both the coming of a plague and its ending were, for Mursili, doings of the gods alone. Whether a solely theological approach to addressing plague, sans other mitigations, protracted the epidemic period and level of suffering in Hatti relative to the plague experience in Egypt or Megiddo or Byblos, we lack the historical evidence to say.

Conclusion

In mapping the evidence for a widespread rolling epidemic in the Levant in the Late Bronze Age, we owe a considerable debt to Philip Norrie, a family physician who still makes house calls in Sydney, Australia, and who lectures as a member of the medical faculty at the University of New South Wales. His keen interest in the role that epidemics have played in history led him to write *A History of Disease in Ancient Times*. We owe a similar debt to Gabriela Gestoso Singer for her paper "Beyond Amarna: The 'Hand of Nergal' and the Plague in the Levant." Both Norrie and Singer, citing Papadopoulou and others, identify the bubonic plague as a pathogen potentially responsible for the epidemic outbreaks captured in the historical remnants of information that we have.[44] However, other pathogens have been suggested, as Norrie catalogs, including tularemia (rabbit fever), smallpox, and tuberculosis.[45] As he considers the Bronze Age collapse, Norrie sees no good reason to single out one pathogen as if there were only one around at the time capable of causing disease and death on an epidemic scale: bubonic plague, smallpox, and tularemia were all capable of causing widespread epidemics, and dysentery, poliomyelitis, tuberculosis, measles, influenza, anthrax, and malaria were all in play and capable of causing more localized outbreaks.[46]

Norrie concludes, as some archeologists have begun to do, that epidemic disease likely conjoined with other shocks as Bronze Age civilizations stumbled and finally collapsed more than a century after the Amarna letters were consigned to the ruins of Akhenaten's palace at Akhet-Aten. The widely recognized horsemen of the Bronze Age apocalypse include volcanic eruptions, earthquakes, climate change, years of intense drought, famine, and attacks by invaders called simply "the Sea Peoples" (because historians still debate over who they were and the world needs a name for them). But these were almost certainly accompanied by the erosion of human capital and societal and economic capacity wrought by epidemic diseases that tended to break out wherever human populations lived in close quarters.[47]

Risk analyst Luke Kemp and historian and archeologist Eric Cline, examining the Bronze Age collapse from a systemic risk perspective, have argued that the metaphor of a "perfect storm" is too simple (and perhaps too abrupt):

> Instead, there are good reasons to view the Bronze Age Collapse as a systems disaster in which certain shocks reinforced others, rather than being unrelated. It was, in the language of systemic risk, more likely to be, and perhaps more accurately described as, a case of 'synchronous failures.'[48]

They concluded that the "interconnectedness" of Bronze Age civili-

zations, given shocks that compounded and reinforced each other, served as "a conduit for chaos."[49]

The chance historical records that we have concerning epidemic disease in the Late Bronze Age are sparse, but evidence from the Amarna letters and the prayers of Mursili II hint at the role epidemic disease may have played. The effects of epidemics in ancient societies, as best we can reconstruct them from scant records, align with the effects of more recent pandemics where there are economic records to flesh out the story and provide fodder for mathematical analysis.

1.   John Coleman Darnell and Colleen Manassa, *Tutankhamun's Armies: Battle and Conquest During Ancient Egypt's Late Eighteenth Dynasty* (Hoboken: John Wiley & Sons, 2007), xxiv. (Dates are best estimates rather than certainties.)

2.   Darnell and Manassa, *Tutankhamun's Armies,* 19–30.

3.   Priscilla Scoville, "Amarna Letters," *World History Encyclopedia* (November 6, 2015), https://www.worldhistory.org/Amarna_Letters/.

4.   "List of Epidemics," Wikipedia, accessed January 9, 2023, https://en.wikipedia.org/wiki/List_of_epidemics.

5.   Robert Cargill, *The Cities That Built the Bible* (San Francisco: Harper Collins, 2017), 104. Kindle edition.

6.   Eric Cline, *Digging Up Armageddon: The Search for the Lost City of Solomon* (Princeton: Princeton University Press, 2020), 247–248.

7.   Cline, *Digging Up Armageddon,* 250–253.

8.   Cargill, *The Cities That Built the Bible,* 99.

9.   Cargill, *The Cities That Built the Bible,* 102–103.

10.   Graham Davies, *Cities of the Biblical World: Megiddo* (Grand Rapids: Eerdmans, 1986), 59–60.

11.   William L. Moran, editor and translator, *The Amarna Letters,* (Baltimore: Johns Hopkins University Press, 1992), xxxvi–xxxvii.

12.   Moran, *The Amarna Letters,* 298–299. See also Graham Davies, *Cities of the Biblical World: Megiddo* (Grand Rapids: Eerdman's, 1986), 60.

13.   Yohanan Arahoni, *The Archeology of the Land of Israel,* Anson F. Rainey, trans. (Philadelphia: Westminster Press, 1978), 118.

14.   Graciela Gestoso Singer, "Beyond Amarna: The 'Hand of Nergal' and the Plague in the Levant, Ugarit Forschungen 48 (2017): 223–47; and Philip Norrie, *A History of Disease in Ancient Times: More Lethal Than War* (Sydney: Palgrave Macmillan, 2016).

15. Moran, *Amarna Letters,* xxxv.

16. Moran, *Amarna Letters,* 107–108.

17. Georgia Papadopoulou, "'Now I have sent you 500 (talents) of copper': the Amarna Letter EA 35 from the King of Alašiya to the King of Egypt," *Athens University Review of Archaeology,* 1:61–67 (2018): 64.

18. Papadopoulou, "'Now I have sent you 500 (talents) of copper,'" 65.

19. Moran, *Amarna Letters,* 107–109.

20. Moran, *Amarna Letters,* xxxv–vi.

21. Moran, *Amarna Letters,* 360.

22. John Coleman Darnell and Colleen Darnell, *Egypt's Golden Couple: When Akhenaten and Nefertiti Were Gods on Earth* (New York: St. Martin's Press, 2022), 232. Kindle Edition.

23. Norman de Garis Davies, *The Rock Tombs of el Amarna* 3, plate 13 (Boston: Egypt Exploration Society, 1941), quoted in Darnell and Darnell, *Egypt's Golden Couple,* 233.

24. Darnell and Darnell, *Egypt's Golden Couple,* 233.

25. Darnell and Darnell, *Egypt's Golden Couple,* 254.

26. Aidan Dodson, "Akhenaten (Amenhotep IV)," in R. Bagnall, K. Brodersen, C. Champion, et al., *The Encyclopedia of Ancient History* (Oxford: Blackwell Publishing, 2012), 2. Cited in Singer, "Beyond Amarna: The Hand of Nergal," 235.

27. Grigorios I. Kontopoulos, "Getting Old in Ancient Egypt," *The Ancient Near East Today,* 6, no. 4 (April 2018), https://www.asor.org/anetoday/2018/04/Getting-Old-In-Ancient+Egypt.

28. Anna Stevens, "Death and the City: The Cemeteries of Amarna in Their Urban Context," *Cambridge Archeological Journal* 28, no. 1. Cambridge University Press (September 25, 2017), https://www.cambridge.org/core/journals/cambridge-archaeological-journal/article/death-and-the-city-the-cemeteries-of-amarna-in-their-urban-context/DBD79DE7272127369D22 A805525D3D08.

29. See Mary Shepperson, "Did children build the ancient Egyptian city of Amarna?" *The Guardian,* June 06, 2017, https://www.theguardian.com/science/2017/jun/06/did-children-build-the-ancient-egyptian-city-of-Amarna-, and Alaa Shahine, "Study shows life was tough for ancient Egyptians," Reuters, March 30, 2008, https://www.reuters.com/article/us-egypt-archaeology-study/study-shows-life-was-tough-for-ancient-egyptians-idU.S.L2886575820080330.

30. Cameron Walker, "Bubonic Plague Traced to Ancient Egypt," *National Geographic* (March 10, 2004), https://www.nationalgeographic.com/science/article/bubonic-plague-traced-to-ancient-egypt.

31. Michelle Starr, "Extinct Pathogens Ushered the Fall of Ancient Civilizations, Scientists Say," Science Alert, August 6, 2022, https://www.sciencealert.com/thousands-of-years-ago-plague-may-have-helped-the-decline-of-an-ancient-civilization.

32. Gabriela Gestoso Singer, "Beyond Amarna," 242.

33. Aidan Dodson, *Amarna Sunset: Nefertiti, Tutankhamun, Ay, Horemheb, and the Egyptian Counter-Reformation* (New York and Cairo: American University in Cairo Press, 2009), 17. Kindle Edition.

34. Aidan Dodson, *Amarna Sunset,* 26.

35. "Workmens' Village, The Amarna Project, https://www.amarnaproject.com/pages/amarna_the_place/workmans_village/index.shtml.

36. Darnell and Manassa, *Tutankhamun's Armies,* 172–175.

37. Darnell and Manassa, *Tutankhamun's Armies,* 184–186.

38. Itamar Singer, *Hittite Prayers.* Writings from the Ancient World, 11 (Atlanta: Society of Biblical Literature, 2002).

39. Itamar Singer, 52.

40. Itamar Singer, 52.

41. Itamar Singer, 52–53.

42. Itamar Singer, 65–66.

43. Itamar Singer, 56.

44. Graciela Gestoso Singer, "Beyond Amarna," 237–240.

45. Norrie, *A History of Disease in Ancient Times,* 88–96.

46. Norrie, *A History of Disease in Ancient Times,* 96.

47. Sonja Eliason and Bridget Alex, "Plague was around for millennia before epidemics took hold — and the way people lived might be what protected them," The Conversation, November 6, 2019, https://theconversation.com/plague-was-around-for-millennia-before-epidemics-took-hold-and-the-way-people-lived-might-be-what-protected-them-120316.

48. Luke Kemp and Eric H. Cline, "Systemic Risk and Resilience: The Bronze Age Collapse and Recovery." In *Perspectives on Public Policy in Societal-Environmental Crises: What the Future Needs from History*, Izdebski, A., Haldon, J., Filipkowski, P., eds. (Springer, 2022): https://doi.org/10.1007/978-3-030-94137-6_14.

49. Kemp and Cline, "Systemic Risk and Resilience."

Chapter 4

Greece: The Plague of Athens
(430 – 429 BCE)

Historical Overview

The Plague of Athens erupted, as contagious diseases often do in the context of war, wherever people are living in crowded conditions. The epidemic, perhaps a form of typhus, was not limited to Athens — it afflicted many other locales as well — but it was intense in the city, claiming an estimated quarter of the population in 430–429 BCE and a third of the population in total. Its economic and societal impacts are almost inextricably intertwined with those of the Peloponnesian War. But the story of how Athens fared in the wake of both the plague and the war begins long before. We might argue that it begins in 479 BCE as Athens lay in ruins.

Under Xerxes I, Persian forces invaded not once but twice and burned and destroyed the city before Athens and its allies, including Sparta, finally defeated them. When Athenians who had evacuated to Salamis returned, they would survey the ruin of their city. Homes were burned. The agora — that place of open assembly where Athenians bought and sold at the market, worshiped at shrines and temples, discussed events and ideas, saw their cases tried and their coins minted, and gathered to debate and vote in the world's first known democracy — was ransacked. In the Acropolis complex, atop the rocky hill overlooking the city, the old Parthenon, the first sanctuary for the statue of Athena Parthanos (Athena the Virgin), was destroyed while still under construction, along with, at least partly, the temple of Athena Polias, with its ancient, deeply revered olivewood statue of the goddess of wisdom, and the shrine of Athena Nike (Athena and Nike, the goddess of victory, rolled into one). Pediment sculptures of two lions killing a bull and Herakles wrestling a sea serpent, along with numerous freestanding figures, including those of Athena herself, were hacked into pieces with axes and hammers, heads and limbs lopped from bodies. And in the rubble lay the remains of those Athenians who had stayed behind to defend the city's sacred sites.[1]

Among the Athenians who returned to survey their ruined city was 15-year-old Pericles, who would come to lead Athens for three decades as a persuasive voice of reason and one of 10 elected generals, or *strategos*. As a leader, he projected for his city his high ideal of Athenian character and heroism. We can only imagine the thoughts and feelings that must have tumbled through a teenage Pericles's mind in 479 as he saw torched walls, rubble, and broken statuary. We may imagine that his life's purpose came into focus. In 472, he would sponsor for the annual festival of Dionysus a production of Aeschylus's trilogy *The Persians,* the centerpiece of which was a play focused on the Athenian navy's defeat of Xerxes' forces at Salamis as divine retribution for Xerxes's hubris. Pericles performed as the choragus.[2]

Whatever the Persians had desecrated, the Athenians ultimately decided to bury, as they did their dead. For 13 centuries, these artefacts would not see the light of day. For 30 years, the Acropolis would remain in ruins as a testament to the destruction that the Persians had wrought, before Athens decided to rebuild.

Figure 4.1 Debris from the ransacked Acropolis (1866) with Moschophoros, Athena, and "Kritios Boy," courtesy of Barker Newhall Photographic Collection, Chalmers Library, public domain.

In the decades that followed the end of the Persian Wars, Athens purposed to ensure that the city would not be destroyed again by the Persians (or anyone else). It had the means. The year 483 had brought the discovery of immense silver-lead deposits at Laurion, about 30 miles from Athens. Mines developed there and manned by thousands of slaves produced immense wealth for the city-state. The silver from the mines had already funded the expansion of the Athenian Navy to 200 triremes by 480, when Athenian forces proved victorious at Salamis. The next step was to better protect the city itself

The construction of an impregnable wall around Athens was followed with the construction of long walls that spanned the distance between the city and the Port of Piraeus, nearly four miles away. As long as the Athenian navy could defend the port, the city would now be safe from siege.

In 478, the Delian League, an alliance of Greek city-states, was founded, and that alliance fell increasingly under the hegemony of Athens until its treasury was moved from Delos to Athens in 453 and member states paid Athens 3%–6% of imperial GDP in tribute in exchange for the protection afforded by the Athenian navy. Though there were rebellions, there were also economic benefits in terms of conditions that enabled the growth of trade.[3] The Delian league included some 300 cities, among them Halicarnassus, Rhodes, Chois, and Lesbos. The rest of Greece, fearing that it would soon be forced into becoming subsidiaries of Athens, formed its own alliance, the Peloponnesian League. This alliance, led by Sparta, would include other major powers such as Corinth, Delphi, and Thebes.[4]

Democracy, though limited to Athenian male citizens only, evolved under the leadership of Pericles, who, while not its founder, would become its champion. Athens began the work of building a new Parthenon, as a first step in an ambitious building program at the Acropolis, the ruins of which we know today.

Figure 4.2 Pericles, courtesy of Jastrow (2006),
Museo Pio-Clementino, Muses Hall, via Wikimedia Commons, public domain.

Athens became an empire in the fifth century BCE, as Josiah Ober has detailed; and trade flourished across the Aegean as the Athenian navy, funded in part by annual tribute payments from members of the Delian League, protected sea routes from the Persians and from pirates. The Port of Piraeus and the agora in Athens provided a sizable regional market, with a 2% tax on imports and exports. The Athenian owl (each coin worth four silver drachmae) provided a standard, stable currency; weights and measures were standardized; and the Athenian mint, which produced 12–24 million silver drachmae per year, ensured market liquidity. Ober concluded that all these developments lowered transaction costs, incentivizing both exchanges and specialization.[5]

Athenians prospered. Military wages were good, and booty won on campaigns supplemented them. The building program in Athens employed many, from architects to quarrymen to highly skilled stone masons to carpenters and unskilled laborers. Citizens and foreigners and slaves working on the Parthenon and other projects all received the same wages, "well above the subsistence level that was the pre-modern norm."[6] When subject states decided that they were better off without the protection of Athens and rebelled, the lands that the Athenian military seized were divided among Athenians, providing them opportunities to oversee landholdings personally or to collect rents, perhaps from the original owner of the land, who was reduced to sharecropping. Athenian mining and industry flourished.[7]

In fifth-century Athens, according to Sidney Homer, interest rates on personal (or "normal") loans averaged 10–12%, loans secured by real estate 8–12%, and loans to industry and commerce averaged 12%–18%. Temple loans, secured by land and sought mostly by individuals, carried an interest rate of 10%. In the fifth century, that rate was considered comparatively low. Interest rates charged for the "sea loans" that financed merchant voyages were higher than loans made for other purposes, reflecting greater risks at sea.[8] Usually, noncitizen traders financed their voyages by borrowing money from citizen lenders.[9]

Athens and the Delian League became so powerful as a result of efforts to defend, rebuild, and triumph after the Persian wars that Sparta and the Peloponnesian League came to perceive the Athenian military and economic juggernaut as a growing threat. Distrust between the two Greek city-states and their allies turned to enmity and, in 431 BCE, enmity to war. The evolution of sentiment and history that led from the Persian Wars, in which Athens and Sparta had fought as allies, to the Peloponnesian War, in which they fought as enemies, is a convoluted one, captured by Thucydides in his groundbreaking history of the war.

War Erupts

In 431 BCE, what had been a long cold war ended as Sparta and the Peloponnesian League declared war against Athens and its Delian League. The long war entailed not only a conflict between Greek city-states and their allies but also a conflict between political ideologies, with Athens and its allies representing democracy (for male citizens of Athens, that is) and Sparta and its allies representing oligarchy, in a war that would decide the future of Greece.

Pericles recognized that the power of the Athenian alliance lay in the Athenian navy, and that the Delian League was outmatched in a land war by the Spartan, Corinthian, and Theban armies. With the Peloponnesian army advancing, Pericles decided that the Athenians should avoid an open field battle and employ a fortress strategy instead, leaving Attica, the surrounding agricultural region around Athens, mostly undefended. No existing weapons of war could enable the Spartans to breach the walls of Athens, Pericles reasoned; and food and other necessities could be imported through the port of Piraeus. The Athenian treasury at the beginning of the war contained 11,000 talents, each representing 57 lbs. of silver. Athens could afford to sustain itself, and the well-funded Athenian navy could launch attacks against members of the Peloponnesian League while defending the port and imports and exports. Surely, Sparta and its Peloponnesian alliance would see the futility in waging a long war they could not win: That outcome was only logical. Athens could simply outlast the enemy's will to wage a futile war.[10]

Pericles did not issue commands the way modern generals do, however. He had to *persuade* Athenian citizens that his plan would work; and he did, just as he had persuaded them on so many other matters, such as the building program, over preceding decades. In general, he did it so well that Thucydides observed, "So it came about that what was in name a democracy was in practice government by the foremost man."[11] And so Athenians who lived outside the city walls sent their livestock off to the island of Euboea for safekeeping and moved into the city, bringing what essentials they could and leaving their fields, vineyards, olive groves, and homes behind, at the mercy of the Spartans and their allies. It was a hard thing to do.

Athens was a crowded place when enemy forces came calling in Attica for annual spring or summer sieges that lasted up to 40 days — the number of people living within the city walls tripled (from perhaps 300,000 to 900,000), resulting in overcrowding and squalor. Refugees from the surrounding countryside occupied every corner of the city, from its temples to the shrines of heroes to the towers of the city walls and eventually the long walls that stretched from Athens to the port and every vacant spot in Piraeus.[12] Waging a war by not actually fighting on the ground was not a popular strategy among Athenians who watched, from atop the city walls, their crops and property destroyed.

Renowned historian of Greek democracy Donald Kagan, who, like Thucydides, admired Pericles on many counts, faulted him on this one thing: Pericles was a man who believed in reason above all, and he did not sufficiently reckon with the kinds of long-burning human emotions that fuel the conflagration of war.[13] The Spartans and its

Peloponnesian League did not give up because that was the logical thing to do; and the Athenians chafed at a strategy that, however logical, required that they restrain their anger and desire to defend Attica.

In a funeral oration that Pericles delivered that first winter to honor the first Athenians to die in the war, Pericles upheld the high ideals of a democratic society and the character and behavior of its citizens, upon which the success of a democracy and a war depend.

> We enjoy a form of government that does not emulate the institutions of our neighbours; indeed we ourselves are more often the model for others than their imitators. Democracy is the name we give to it, since we manage our affairs in the interests of the many not the few; but though everyone is equal before the law in the matter of private disputes, in terms of public distinction preferment for office is determined on merit, not by rank but by personal worth; moreover, poverty is no bar to anyone who has it in them to benefit the city in some way, however lowly their status. A spirit of freedom governs our conduct, not only in public affairs but also in managing the small tensions of everyday life, where we show no animosity at our neighbours' choice of pleasures, nor cast aspersions that may hurt even if they do not harm. Although we associate as individuals in this tolerant spirit, in public affairs fear makes us the most severely law-abiding of people, obedient to whoever is in authority and to the laws, especially those established to help the victims of injustice and those laws which, though unwritten, carry the sanction of public disgrace.[14]

We note that Pericles, at least according to Thucydides, our only source for the speech, endeavored not only to affirm the superiority of Athenian democracy, but also to articulate a model for citizens' behavior in a trying time. Tolerance of others was critical when people were living almost on top of one another, and adherence to both the law and the unlegislated norms of virtue would be critical to ensure the cohesion of a city under stress, the success of the democracy that Athens aspired to be, and the success of Pericles's war strategy of rational restraint.

Plague Strikes the City

However unpopular Pericles's strategy became as Attica fell under attack, it backfired on an enormous scale in the summer of 430, when a different foe invaded the densely populated city — not the enemy Athens had prepared for but a deadly pathogen instead. Experts have long debated what pathogen might have caused the virulent plague in Athens (a form of typhoid fever might be a candidate), but no firm conclusions have ever been reached.[15]

Thucydides refrains from blaming the epidemic on the gods, as many in Athens did; or on the Peloponnesians poisoning rainwater tanks, as others did; or even on squalid conditions caused by population density within the city walls, as still others did. He opted instead simply to report events as they occurred, writing, "For my part I will say what it was like as it happened and will describe the facts that would enable anyone investigating any future outbreak to have some prior knowledge and recognise it."[16] His approach aligns with that of the Greek physician Hippocrates, who was around 30 years old and living in Athens when the plague struck. Though no surviving texts from Hippocrates mention the plague, Hippocrates believed and taught that diseases derived from natural causes (an imbalance of the four humors) rather than divine whims. Given this paradigm, he observed symptoms closely in an attempt to diagnose a malady and prescribe a treatment. As Kagan explains, Ionian philosopher Anaxogoras, who lived in Athens as a metic, or resident alien, had taught since Pericles's youth that natural events resulted from natural causes rather than from supernatural intervention. Such teachings handed some Athenians, including his avid student Pericles, a rational and naturalistic lens through which to see the world as an alternative to a religious and superstitious lens perpetually inclined to attribute fortune and misfortune to the favor or disapproval of various anthropomorphic gods. (Pericles's personal perspective on the plague we do not have.)[17]

Thucydides and others described the course of the disease in horrifying detail, and Thucydides reports having been infected himself. The disease brought a raging fever and "a thirst that could not be quenched." First, eyes became red and swollen and tongues and throats inflamed and bloody. Hard coughing followed, and the skin erupted with pustules and ulcers. The skin felt hot, like fire, such that victims could not bear clothes against their skin and longed to plunge into cool water for relief.[18] Some did. The burning became internal as well as external. In its later stages, the disease caused intense diarrhea. Some who survived all those symptoms lost their fingers, toes, genitalia, or eyes to necrosis.[19] Others lost their memories and did not know either their friends or themselves. Many died after a week of intense suffering, as did birds or dogs that scavenged on corpses.

A City's Faith Shaken

Whatever pathogen caused the Plague of Athens, it is hard to imagine an infectious disease capable of causing more intense suffering. The scale of suffering and the logistics of dealing with so many of the sick and the dead undermined the societal norms Pericles had celebrated in his funeral oration. Many who were healthy feared taking care of the sick, having observed, as Thucydides did, that those who provided care often fell ill. Survivors of the plague, on the other hand, were able to care for others without incurring a second serious bout of illness. Elaborate funeral rituals fell by the wayside as corpses accumulated throughout the city and bodies were unceremoniously thrown on the funeral pyres that others had constructed for their own dead.

Thucydides described the changes of perspective and behavior that the plague wrought: "Overwhelmed by the disaster people could not see what was to become of them and started losing respect for the laws of god and man alike."[20] Property changed hands as people died, and patterns of consumption changed with the onslaught of grief and the barrage of reminders of how fleeting life could be:

> It was the plague that first led to other forms of lawlessness in the city too. People were emboldened to indulge themselves in ways they would previously have concealed, since they saw the rapid change in fortunes — both for those who were well off and died suddenly and for those who originally had nothing but in a moment got possession of the property of these others. They therefore resolved to exploit these opportunities for enjoyment quickly, regarding their lives and their property as equally ephemeral. No one was eager to add to their own hardships for supposedly fine objectives, since they were uncertain whether they would die before achieving them. Whatever gave immediate pleasure or in any way facilitated it became the standard of what was good and useful. Neither fear of the gods nor law of man was any restraint: they judged it made no difference whether or not they showed them respect, seeing that everyone died just the same; on the contrary, no one expected to live long enough to go on trial and pay the penalty, feeling

that a far worse sentence had already been passed and was hanging over their heads, and that it was only reasonable to get some enjoyment from life before it finally fell on them.[21]

Athenian exceptionalism had incurred a heavy blow as a traumatized population scrambled for answers as to why the plague might have befallen the city. Hippocrates's focus on the four humors (rather than the gods) as the cause of ailments generally and Thucydides's unwillingness to identify divine displeasure as the cause of the plague together mark an important moment in history, but no tipping point in popular opinion had as yet been reached. Both Thucydides and, later, historian Diodorus Siculus confirmed that the overwhelming majority of Greeks still believed in divine wrath as cause for catastrophe. Writing sometime between 30 and 60 BCE, Diodorus described one extraordinary measure Athenians went to in order to right a perceived offense against Apollo in hopes of ending the Plague of Athens. Since the birthplace of Apollo was said to be Delos, that island had become a sacred site for the worship of the deity. Athenians were led by an oracle to believe that plague stemmed from Apollo's anger, sparked by a desecration of the island.

> The Athenians, however, because the disease was so severe, ascribed the causes of their misfortune to the deity. Consequently, acting upon the command of a certain oracle, they purified the island of Delos, which as sacred to Apollo and had been defiled, as men thought, by the burial there of the dead. Digging up, therefore, all the graves on Delos, they transferred the remains to the island of Rheneia, as it is called, which lies near Delos. They also passed a law that neither birth nor burial should be allowed on Delos. And they also

celebrated the festival assembly, the Delia, which had
been held in former days but had not been observed
for a long time.[22]

Their solution, to remove all buried corpses from the island and
then to revive the Delia festival in honor of Apollo, did not, of course,
succeed in abating the plague. Thucydides mentions this peculiar
episode of corpses relocated from Delos but does not explain why they
were removed.[23] He reports instead two other foreboding prophecies
that Athenians seized upon. Old men remembered a prophecy that
foretold, "A Dorian war shall come and with it plague."[24] The adjec-
tive *Dorian* referred to the people who settled in particular areas of
Greece that included the Spartans, Corinthians, and Peloponnese,
such that the Peloponnesian War seemed to them a fulfillment of
that prophecy. Thucydides notes that "There was some disagree-
ment among them as to whether the word used by the men of old
was not 'plague' but 'famine,' but in the present circumstances the
view naturally prevailed that it was 'plague,' as people matched their
memories to their sufferings."[25]

Translation of ancient Greek to English is daunting. We wanted to know
more about the word *plague*. So we asked a personal friend, Ray Perez, for some
help. Ray is a scholar who teaches ancient Greek. He provided the following
language lesson about the word *plague*:

The word that Thucydides uses is νόσος [nosos] ... the same
word that Homer uses as sent by Apollo onto the Greeks at
the beginning of the Iliad. Thucydides does not view it as
divine-sent, but says that it came from the mid-East by way
of Ethiopia, before he launches into a detailed description
of its symptoms, etc. The word νόσος is not uncommon:

it is generally used in Homer, Hesiod, and the tragedians for "disease." Sophocles even uses it of eros; Plato says that the greatest νόσος, or affliction, is άνοια (lack of thinking/ thoughtlessness).

Along with νόσος, he also uses νόσημα for "plague." Obviously a closely related word. Looking at various authors, they both seem to mean, in general, a disease of animals or plants or humans. It is several times described as god-sent, and/or as something that an individual can "fall into" (and by extension, an affliction of passion or of vice). Thucydides also uses a third term: λοιμός (loimos). The Athenians called to mind a saying of their ancestors: "A Doric war will come, and at the same time a λοιμός" (2, 54) [sort of a double whammy]. This word occurs once in Homer. Shortly after he uses νόσος in the opening of the Iliad to describe what will occur, he details how Apollo shoots his arrows for nine days, starting with the mules and dogs. Then, after the pyres of the men burn thick, Achilles addresses the army and refers to the situation as a λοιμός (1, 61). Hesiod says that for one man's hubristic actions, Zeus will sometimes punish a whole city with famine and λοιμός. (Op., 243). Herodotus says that Crete was at one point desolate because the men and their flocks suffered a λοιμός (7, 171). In Aeschylus' "Persians," Darius wonders aloud whether it is a "thunderbolt of λοιμός" that has utterly destroyed them (Pers. 715). Plato uses both νόσος and λοιμός to reference the Athenian plague (Smp., 201d). So, there seems to be a good deal of overlap with these terms: god-sent, sudden onset, can be used to describe a contagion among men or animals. However, it appears that λοιμός is used only of a plague-like episode.

Even more demoralizing in a time of war was a prophecy claiming that the god was, from the start of the war, on the Spartans' side, not the Athenians':

> There were those who also recalled an oracle given to the Spartans when the Spartans asked the god whether they should go to war and he answered that victory would be theirs if they fought with all their might and promised that he would himself take their side. They therefore supposed that what then happened was the fulfilment of the oracle, and indeed the plague did begin straight after the invasion of the Peloponnesians; and although it did not get into the Peloponnese to any significant extent, it invaded Athens in particular and after that other densely populated areas elsewhere.[26]

The fact that plague did not afflict the enemy, too, appeared to confirm the dire prognostication. As the plague raged, it seemed to many that Athena, the patron goddess, protector of the city, had abandoned them, while the wrath of Apollo seemed insatiable.

Pericles, meanwhile, held to his position that most Athenians needed to stay within the city walls; and he launched a naval attack on the Peloponnese. An attempted siege of Potidaea failed when the plague claimed 1050 of 4000 Athenian hoplites sent to aid in that mission and also infected the forces that had initially led the siege attempt.[27]

The trauma wrought by the plague shook the faith of Athenians — in Athena's favor, which they had believed that they enjoyed and merited; in the value of the kinds of virtuous behavior that Pericles had celebrated in his funeral oration; and in the political leadership that had brought them to this point. It was not the Spartans whose will to persevere was doused by the futility of attempting to seize Athens itself; it was the Athenians' whose resolve began to crack because of the plague, to the extent that some tried to approach the Spartans, seeking peace.

While Athenians believed they had lost their favored relationship with the gods, we may be sure that Pericles, in his turn, grieved that they had lost their relationship with reason and virtue. Pericles was variously blamed by his fellow citizens for the war they had supported, the destruction in Attica, and the overcrowding that contributed to the severity of the plague. In a speech reported by Thucydides, Pericles reasoned with thousands gathered at the Agora, warning them, "In your distress at your domestic misfortunes you are sacrificing our common security...."[28] He then acknowledged not only the hardships of war but also the blow that the plague was inflicting on the people's will to persevere:

> What has happened is that you were persuaded to go to war when you were still unscathed but you regret it now that you are suffering harm, and with your resolve weakened you have come to think my policy wrong because each of you is already experiencing the suffering while no one can yet see evidence of the benefit; and now that you have been visited by this great disaster — with very little warning — you lack the strength of mind to persevere with the policy you decided on. The spirit is crushed when something so sudden, unexpected and so completely unaccountable comes along; and that is what has happened to you, especially as regards the plague. Nevertheless, since you come from a great city and were brought up in a way of life worthy of her, you must willingly endure even the worst misfortunes and do nothing to eclipse your fame. After all, people feel as justified in blaming someone who is too faint-hearted to live up to the reputation

he already enjoys as they do in hating someone who is arrogant enough to grasp at a reputation he does not deserve. You must therefore put aside private sorrows and concentrate on securing our common safety.[29]

Pericles reminded his audience of Athenian naval superiority and urged them to recover their courage, which should be based not on mere hope but on the strong position Athens still maintained in the war.[30] Encouraged (and with no peace terms offered by the Spartans, anyway), Athenians took Pericles's advice and resolved to continue the fight. But after Pericles led a siege of the town of Epidaurus, an offensive ultimately doomed by plague losses among the Athenian forces, Athenians voted to fine Pericles and strip him of his command. The amount of the fine was significant — Plutarch noted that some accounts stated it to be 15 talents and others 50. For perspective, a single talent paid an entire trireme rowing crew of 200 for a month.[31] Meanwhile, the plague continued to churn through the population. It claimed Pericles's sister and his two sons, leaving him no legitimate heirs and, according to Plutarch, plunging him into a season of grief. Not long after, however, Athens voted Pericles back into office, having found him to be the polis's most skilled commander. There was no way around the war, and the now-chastened Pericles was, the city deemed, still the best man to lead Athens' defense.

Fate, however, intervened. The plague's death toll in Athens was colossal. It is estimated that 70,000 to 100,000 people perished during the first two years of the plague — as mentioned, around 25% of the populace.[32] In 429, Pericles himself, at the age of 65, joined their number. Athens would now have to rely on other military leaders, whatever their foibles.

The plague was not limited to Athens — Thucydides points to reports that it emerged "out of Ethiopia beyond Egypt, and then spread into Egypt and Libya and into most of the territory of the

Persian King."[33] Livy describes a pestilence in Rome in 433–432 BCE, afflicting both people and cattle. Farming was impacted to the point that, fearing famine, the city arranged to import grain from Etruria, Cumae, and perhaps Sicily. We have no description of the symptoms of that epidemic to match the detail that Thucydides provided, so there is no evidence to confirm that the epidemic in Rome was caused by the pathogen that resulted in the Athenian plague, but it seems quite possible that the microorganism responsible was the same.[34] Wherever no related prior infection had conferred immunity to the plague that hit Athens, populations were vulnerable, and they were most vulnerable where people were crowded together.

Whatever their bearing on who lost and won, the ramifications of the plague were immense in a time of war. The fallout was psychological (as we have seen), military, and economic. But did the plague contribute to the defeat of Athens in 404, a generation later? It is impossible to say whether that outcome might have been different had the plague not penetrated the city's defenses where Spartan forces could not, but we can conclude that Athens was not the stronger for its losses wrought by disease and war. Greece as a whole was more fragmented and weaker going into the future as a result of the Spartans' successful campaign to curb Athenian power and ambitions. It would ultimately be more vulnerable to the Roman Empire's forces than it might have been otherwise.

War and Plague: Intertwined Economic Impacts

The economic picture in the wake of both the war and the plague is complex. Athens' efforts to shore up its economic base, its regional power, and its defenses after the Persian Wars actually protected the city from some of the typical short-term economic impacts of a virulent plague. Its vast empire and the Port of Piraeus meant that the city had already prepared for agricultural disruptions by importing grain from its allies. Until shipping routes were disrupted later in the war, Athens had a secure food supply.

It also had a sizable dislocated rural labor force as of the summer of 431, as those who had made their living growing grain or making wine or harvesting olives or raising livestock could no longer do so. Those people were looking for a means to earn a living in the city or were serving in the Athenian military. So the initial demographic shock would have impacted the labor market differently than it would have done in peacetime. When plague and war culled its forces, the city could also turn to its allies to supply rowers, well-armed hoplites, and peltasts, who were lightly armed with javelins and shields but often lacked armor.

Following the war, too, Athens was spared destruction of the city. Moreover, Athenians were not enslaved. Agriculture across Attica could recover — annual crops could be planted; new grape vines could grow; and stumps of olive trees would sprout new branches and soon bear olives again. New generations of the herds moved to Euboea were brought back again.[35]

The Athenian fleet had been destroyed in the war (to be built again in remarkably short order), and the walls that had protected Athens for so long were demolished following. The Corinthians and the Thebans wanted to plunder and destroy the city, as well, but the Spartans refused. Athens had contributed too much to the cause of Greece in the Persian Wars, they felt. Pulling the plug on its once-mighty empire, the Delian League, and curbing its imperial ambitions seemed enough. Besides, thoroughly crippling this seat of power and commerce would have been both economically and militarily unwise, given other potential aggressors. The Spartans apparently sought not a destroyed Athens and a power vacuum but an Athens whose overweening ambitions as an empire capable of posing a threat had been curbed.

This course ultimately meant that the regime the victors put in place did not last. The city itself came through the plague and the war with much of its infrastructure still intact, though its population had been dramatically reduced by both the plague and the long war. Athens had long attracted metics, residents who were by birth citizens of some other polis, and the city would continue to do so. Slavery filled in labor gaps. But the population of Athenian citizens, i.e. males whose parents were both Athenians by birth, could not be rapidly replenished, and that fact is worth remembering as we look at the limited data we have from the time.

Economists and historians have been able to paint with a broad brush key economic changes across Greece from the fifth century BCE to the fourth, given what evidence we have, which is in many aspects too spotty to tell a story. It is harder to sort specifics for the short and medium term following the Plague of Athens, and it is likewise a challenge to extricate economic impacts of the plague from the economic impacts of the Peloponnesian War. The two shocks, one concluding in a handful of years and the other stretching for decades, intertwined in terms of their effects. But that is how history works. What we can say is that the plague claimed around a third of the population of Athens early on, while another quarter of Athenian citizens (males) had been lost by war's end. The Delian League was gone; the Athenian treasury was empty and its fleet sunk — but the city itself stood positioned to mount a recovery.

Wages

If we look at the course of the Peloponnesian War, however, which extended well into the medium term following the pandemic, we can infer how the plague compounded the economic impacts of the war, given the immense demographic hit, which equaled or exceeded that of the war, at least among the male citizens of Athens. In no way does this chapter offer scope for a blow-by-blow account of the war, but it is possible to succinctly trace certain inflection points, how Athens handled the economic vicissitudes of war and plague, and how wages, at least in some instances, were affected. The following table, drawn variously from the work of William Loomis, Thomas Martin, and Alec Blamire, is the tool we have chosen for doing this.[36]

Historical context and wages in Athens, 450–330 BCE

Estimated population in 431 – 60,000 adult male citizens, 300,000+ total residents (Ober, 205)
Estimated population in 404 – 25,000 adult male citizens

450–431: Athenian Power on the Rise	
Historical Context	**Wages**
• Delian League tribute revenues flow to the treasuries of Athena and other gods in Athens (perhaps 600 talents per year in total). • Persia is no longer a threat. • Silver mines of Laurion, which had enabled Athens to build the fleet that defeated the Persians, supply up to one million ounces of silver per year. • Long walls are built to defend city and port access. • Athenian fleet is expanded.	• Sparse data suggests a rise of as much as 50% for public wages. • Welfare payments for widows and orphans and the disabled are two obols per day.

431–412: Plague Strikes a Confident City at War	
Historical Context	**Wages**
• Peloponnesian War begins in 431; Athenian treasury contains 9,700 talents; 1000 talents are held in reserve. • Plague breaks out in 430 and rages into 429, kills 25% of population, then reemerges 427. Total deaths estimated at one third of the population. • Pericles dies of plague in 429 at 65. • In 428, the eisphora property tax (a measure taken only in extenuating circumstances) is imposed on wealthy Athenians, with metics paying more than citizens do. A levy is collected from allies. • Tribute assessment is more than doubled in 425, and the eisphora discontinued. • The treasurers of Athens, the Hellanotamiai, borrow from the Athenian treasury (temple of Athena) every year until 422 to cover costs. The interest rate on these loans is lowered after 426. (See discussion following). • In 415, Spartan forces capture the silver mines of Laurion, which are then abandoned by the 20,000 slaves who worked them.	• Public wages for soldiers and sailors remain stable at one drachma per day. • When the war seems to be going well, wages for 6000 Athenian male citizens who serve as dikasts (jurors) is increased from two obols to three obols in 425, suggesting a labor shortage occasioned by both plague and war. • Welfare payments in place since 480 are cut from two obols to one obol per day.

413–403: Athens under Duress	
Historical Context	**Wages**
• In 413, the Sicilian Expedition ends in disaster, with immense human and financial costs. • The same year, Spartan forces occupy Dekeleia, disrupting the grain supply chain from Euboea to Athens. • The annual tribute is replaced with a 5% levy on sea trade. • In 411, Athens dips into its 1000-talent reserve. • An oligarchic coup overthrows democracy in Athens, but the oligarchs are replaced at the insistence of the Athenian navy. Democracy returns in 410. • In 410, in the restored democracy, a new diobelia dole provides assistance for Athenians without means. Fragments suggest that the tribute system may have been reinstated. • In 406, eight statues of Nike are melted down for their gold, and the dole is cut to one obol per day. • An emergency gold currency is minted in 406/7, followed by an emergency silver-plated bronze currency for local retail transactions. Some Athenians keep private hoards. • The treasuries of other gods and the treasury of Athens are merged.	• In 412, wages for soldiers and sailors are cut by half, from one drachma to three obols per day. • In 411, pay is eliminated for most public officeholders. • In 409–407, construction of the Erechtheion, which began in 420, pays one drachma/day to all workers regardless of skill level. (The Erechtheion project entailed the restoration of the Acropolis after its partial destruction in the Persian Wars and the construction of a place of worship honoring multiple gods worshipped by Athenians.) This public works project would have celebrated Athenian identity, expressed religious devotion to various gods Athenians worshipped, and afforded a measure of economic stimulus, including jobs, for the city during wartime.

- The dole is paid in grain rather than obols as of 405–404.
- In 404, the Athenian navy is defeated, and the war ends. The long walls between Athens and Piraeus are destroyed.
- The Corinthians and Thebans call for the destruction of the city, but Sparta insists on sparing it.

403–323: Athens Recovers	
Historical Context	**Wages**
<ul><li>Rule by the "Thirty Tyrants," imposed by Sparta in 403, falls apart in less than a year.</li><li>Athens reconstitutes its democracy.</li><li>The debt to the temple of Athena is written off, and temple treasuries are no longer utilized for public finance.</li><li>In 400, an emergency eisphora tax helps to pay the costs of the war against the Thirty Tyrants.</li><li>The city completes the rebuilding of its walls by 393 and builds a new fleet.</li><li>The silver mines at Laurion return to production in the 390s and reach peak production mid-century.</li><li>The bronze currency is demonetized in the 390s.</li><li>Trade expands again, as does production of goods in Athens.</li><li>Financial management and budgeting in Athens evolve.</li></ul>	<ul><li>In 403–402, cavalrymen and mounted archers take a 1/3 pay cut.</li><li>Wages rise broadly in the 4th century, but evidence is not sufficient for a decade-by-decade account of the changes. Travel allowances for Athenian ambassadors are doubled from the previous century, from one to two drachmas per day. Pay doubles for stone inscribers, from one to two drachmas per day, and appears to rise sharply for esteemed teachers.</li><li>Pay of one obol per day is instituted in 403 for those who attend the ekklesia, the democratic decision-making assembly, which requires a quorum of 6000 male Athenian citizens. With a sharply reduced population in the city, Athenian citizens who live in the countryside need to be able to attend. Pay increases to</li></ul>

• Athenian owls are recalled and reminted in 353, netting a windfall for the state. • Macedon becomes an empire threatening the power of Athens. • Poor harvests around 330 impact food supply and drive inflation, which until this point remained very low. • The classical period ends in 323 with the death of Alexander the Great and the fragmentation of the Macedonian empire.	three obols per day by around 393 and to six obols by the 330s (a time of inflation). • Labor shortages are a fact of life through the fourth century. Real wages gradually rise, as calculated by how much wheat a daily wage can buy.

Table 4.1 Historical context and wages in Athens, 450–330 BCE

We can see from the multi-page table above that Athens maintained public wages well above the subsistence level as long as possible into the teeth of the war, and the loss of Athenian citizens to plague and war spurred rises in pay for public roles that only male citizens could fill. The ranks of Athenian males had to recover the slow way, as children were born, and not the quick way, with imported labor from across the region. Athens was better able to fill labor force needs when those positions could also be filled by slaves, metics, or mercenaries. Public wages associated with building projects served alongside the dole for poor Athenians to provide for Athenians' needs and to forestall a more serious economic crisis. Defeat in 403 and civil war following meant a time of real hardship for the city-state, reflected in reduced public wages and a reduced welfare program; but as Athens recovered and began to thrive again, real wages rose. It is not the case that we have enough evidence to speak of the wage trends for many professions (artists, priests, prostitutes, doctors, or inscribers, for instance) — the data is far too spotty.[37] But we do have evidence for the public positions cited in the chart. For Athenians, given labor shortages in the city and across Greece, real wages rose from the fifth century BCE to the fourth, and wages were already well above subsistence levels in the fifth. Barry O'Halloran, basing calculations on the broader work of Walter Scheidel, estimates that rise in terms of how much wheat a daily wage could buy:

> For most ancient and medieval economies, real income expressed as wheat equivalent has been estimated at 4–6 litres per day. In Athens, however, labourers received wages of 8–9 litres during the late 5th century which rose to 13–16 litres per day by the late 4th century.[38]

In fact, real wages in Athens matched or bettered those in other prosperous pre-modern economies. They compare, for example, with those in Holland from the 16th through the 18th centuries. Wages in Holland during this prosperous period, expressed as wheat wages, ranged from 10–17 liters per day.[39] The increase in real wages over a century seems dramatic. Still, from the 430s forward, the annual wage inflation rate in Athens appears to have been a modest 1%–2%, resulting in a doubling across 70 years.[40] Real wages in Athens dipped at the end of the war, when Athens had to get back on its feet economically and financially; but beyond that period they demonstrated the response that typically follows a demographic hit caused by an epidemic: They gradually rose.

Defeat and Economic Recovery

To finance the Peloponnesian War, Athens borrowed enormous amounts from the temple of Athena. As Alec Blamire has noted, the terms of those loans would change after the plague, as war-related expenses mounted. The annual interest rate was reduced from 6% as of 433–432 to 1.2% during the 426–426 financial year.[41]

This interest-rate reduction on war-related loans to the state or in some instances to the generals who led particular campaigns reduced the total debt that Athens would have otherwise owed to the temple treasury, though in the end the action Athens took was more drastic than the lowering of rates.

After Athens' defeat in 404, Sparta put in place a conservative oligarchy to rule the city, dubbed the Thirty Tyrants. Their rule would last only a bloody eight months as they purged their opposition, killing around 1500 people. Athenians who were determined to retake their formerly democratic city fled, regrouped some distance north at Phyle, gathered forces, and overthrew the city's oppressors in 403.

A divided Spartan leadership ultimately decided that maintaining the tyrants' control in Athens and Attica was not worth the effort.[42] The fact that Sparta did not maintain control of Athens would be crucial for its economic recovery. Sparta's austerity and its isolationist economic model, ultimately reliant on the fact that it had land fertile enough for agriculture adequate for its needs (an advantage Athens did not have), enabled it to turn inward from far-flung trade in a way that Athens could not afford to do. Its landed elite were well-positioned to maintain their wealth and to keep a vast labor force bound to working the land and a conscripted hoplite army doing the fighting. While Sparta espoused equality among its citizens (who were a shrinking minority of the population), some were, to borrow from Orwell's *Animal Farm,* "more equal than others." But it was far-flung trade that fed Athens and could serve, in the wake of war and plague, to fuel its economy.

Athens restored its democracy in 403 and then refined it. The city's leadership "wrote off" the debt to Athena and reorganized its finances so as not to borrow again from the temple treasury. State financial resources, once one big pot of money, were organized after the Peloponnesian War into categories that allowed budgeting to be overseen by the appropriate spending authorities.[43]

As Sidney Homer notes in *A History of Interest Rates,* despite all the financial strain, the city did not debase its primary currency, the highly regarded Athenian owl, the way Rome would later do its currency.[44] However, leaders in Athens did take extraordinary measures during the course of the war. When silver was scarce late in the war, in 406, the city melted down eight gold statues of Nike and other gold objects from the Parthenon to mint a gold currency necessary for military expenses. A second emergency currency was introduced a year later for domestic use only, to enable people to buy and sell everyday essentials. Those coins were silver-coated bronze — a token currency. They served a temporary purpose and did not circulate forever as a debased currency: Athens was able to demonetize them in the 390s.[45] And over time, the new democratic government would replace the sacred Parthenon treasures that had been melted down for gold coins.

Athens used a variety of short-term measures to navigate the economic blows dealt by plague and war: the lowering of the interest rate the temples charged the state, temporary substitute currencies, additional levies and tribute assessments as circumstances required, and even a debt cancellation instrumental in speeding the city's recovery. Though the city went through a difficult period after its defeat by Sparta, replete with hardships depicted in Greek theater, it ultimately recovered remarkably quickly, rebuilding its walls, its fleet, and trade.[46] Ironically, it did so initially with some funding help from Persia, a cautious ally intent on keeping Spartan ambitions in check — at least until the 380s, when it became clear that Athens was making a bid to recover an empire.[47] Athens would cobble together for a time an anti-Spartan league, though not one that ever created the flow of wealth to the Athenian treasury that the Delian League had — no tribute payments were allowed, by agreement.

A New Means to Prosperity: Markets, not Empire

In broad terms, the fourth century BCE in a decentralized Greece was a volatile one. The balance of power across Greece remained fluid over the course of the century. Sicily fell into decline, and Sparta's power and influence waned after its defeat by Thebes in the Battle of Leuctra in 371, while Thebes expanded its influence, founding Messene, a new, fortified capital for the Messenians, strategically positioned to deter Spartan expansion.[48] Despite the shifting geopolitical scene across Greece, however, trade networks, which operated independently of states, managed to thrive; and markets grew. In *The Rise and Fall of Classical Greece,* historian Josiah Ober aptly described the fourth century as a "shifting collage" that resulted from millions of people and groups collaborating, competing, and specializing in pursuit of opportunity.[49]

Fourth-century Athens prospered. Greek culture and exports gained new geographical reach. While 238 hoards have been found dating from the fifth century, that number grew to 564 in the turbulent fourth century, and the number of coins found in them tripled.[50] While Ober concedes that people tend to hoard money when turbulent times pose elevated risk, evidence of investment and growth during the first half of the fourth century BCE indicates that Athens and Greece as a whole contrived to recover and to prosper, raising per capita GDP. Imported labor (mostly slaves, for classical Athens was, like Sparta, a slave-dependent society), agricultural products, and raw materials flowed into the region, while Greek manufactured goods and expertise were sought far beyond its borders.[51]

Athens was faced after the Peloponnesian War and the demise of the Delian League with the challenge of reinventing its financial model and its means to achieve prosperity. Though mining resumed at Laurion after the war, with its production peaking in the middle decades of the century, payments from Delian League members no longer contributed to the treasury at Athens. Then the second Athenian League fell apart in a two-year conflict between Athens and its allies. (Athens lost, in 355.) In 354–353, partly in an effort to ensure the integrity of its currency, Athens recalled all Athenian owls to be reminted in a new style that would be easy to identify, and it collected minting fees for doing that. Those fees, amounting to either 3% or 5% before reminting expenses were deducted (the figure in the text might be either number), produced a large one-time windfall at a time when that was urgently needed to revive Athens' hopes of restoring its empire.[52]

Athens was, at the time, once again facing financial hardship. Writing in 355, the Athenian philosopher, historian, and general Xenophon lauded the commercial infrastructure and opportunities Piraeus and Athens offered — "unrivalled amenities and advantages," including a safe harbor and opportunities to make return journeys with ships laden either with goods or with Athenian silver. At that critical moment, the aging strategist encouraged further investment in Athens as a commercial center and trade as a means to greater revenue. In his pamphlet "On Revenues" (or "Ways and Means"), Xenophon acknowledged the value of the infrastructure that Athens already offered merchants — meeting places, houses, public lodging, and stores — and proposed funding a further expansion of such facilities. No doubt, the ideas expressed in "On Revenues" both reflected and furthered conversations in Athens about the revenue that new investments designed to foster the growth of trade could bring to the state.[53] In the decades that followed Athens's defeat and the end of its imperial ambitions for the second Athenian League, annual state spending would rise from the dust of 0 in 354 to 50 talents in 340 to 200 talents in the 330s.[54] State activity, as described by Ober, indicates that Athens followed through with at least some of Xenophon's suggestions:

> The democratic government continued to function throughout the period in question; fortifications, dockyards, and warships were built; important new public buildings were erected for a variety of civic

purposes; the safety net of government-supported social welfare was expanded.[55]

While imports and exports incurred a 2% tax and traders paid other transport, port, and market taxes as well, being able to buy and sell a wide array of goods from near and far made participating in the vast regional market assembled at Athens and Piraeus profitable and as safe and convenient as possible. Those coming to sell also found every possible thing to buy.[56] The indirect taxes on trade helped to fund the state's needs in the absence of tribute revenues. Trade was not organized by the state; nor was mining. But Athens and Piraeus profited from both in the form of taxes that were not so high as to squelch opportunity.

In the market where sellers and buyers converged, Athenian approvers assured sellers, both Athenians and noncitizens alike, that coins proffered by buyers were indeed authentic, with the correct silver content. Ober observed that Athens began to "open up" to become an even more attractive commercial and cultural center. Where the law and contract disputes were concerned, constitutional changes ensured that non-Athenians enjoyed a more level playing field with citizens. In the previous century, citizens had enjoyed a significant advantage in court proceedings.[57] After plague and war had claimed the lives of well over half of its male citizens, Athens needed more than ever what noncitizens could contribute. Other changes reflected that realization, too. Though such actions were still unusual and constituted exceptions to laws that remained unchanged, more metics were granted by popular vote the privilege to own land in Attica *(enktesis),* and some few noncitizens who had made extraordinary contributions to the state were made citizens. Taxes imposed on metics were more often forgiven in the fourth century, too.[58]

As Ober observed, just as Athens opened up in matters of trade, investments, and even citizenship, the city also demonstrated an openness to divergent ideas, making it an ideal home for the philosophical schools of Plato, Aristotle, and Isocrates, which drew students from near and far. The city cultivated expertise in many arenas, including the military and finance, and exported that expertise.[59]

Through skillful and innovative management, financial and otherwise, Athens secured an income stream for the state sufficient for ambitious public and military projects as substantial as those in the age of Pericles. Moreover, better wages for officials, workers employed on state projects, and the military, along with higher payments to the poor and to orphans, helped to limit income inequality that war and plague had widened and thus to promote economic growth as Athens refined its financial and monetary balancing act.[60]

Lending and Interest

Athenian lenders continued to provide the short-duration sea loans essential for trade across the Black, Aegean, and Mediterranean seas. Interest rates for maritime loans remained in line with those in the previous century. As noted previously, these loans commanded higher interest rates than land loans did (in the fourth century up to 30%), but they did not have to be paid back if the ship never made it to port. It was the lender who took the risk in hopes of a considerable profit. Rates were higher when risk was higher.[61]

A small number of wealthy metic bankers, the wealthiest among them a former slave, provided a growing array of sophisticated banking services. Sidney Homer catalogs these: The *trapezitai*, as they were called, loaned money so that merchant ships could sail, laden with their valuable cargoes. They lent money on real estate and on items people brought to pawn. They made loans, secured and, increasingly, unsecured, to states and individuals. They kept their books, changed one currency for another, took deposits, kept careful financial records, made payments, and dealt with checks, money orders, and letters of credit.[62]

That said, when we speak of bankers and banking in classical Athens, we should not infer all that banking entails today. M.I. Finley has reminded us that there were no credit ratings beyond reputation and word of mouth. People did not handle their money in the way that we do today, with some cash in our wallets but most of our money deposited in a bank. Instead, Finley notes, people kept most of their coins at home or in hoards that they buried for safekeeping.[63] Banks enabled them to get loans or to put their money to work in some way.

Though most "land loans" were personal in nature, for "consumptive purposes," Darel Tai Engen has argued, "it is hard to deny that the evidence of productive lending and borrowing from banking practices, numerous maritime loans, and even temple loans in the classical period constitute something more than just exceptions to the rule."[64] Productive loans became much more common in the fourth century than they had been in the fifth.[65]

"Land loans" were generally made between one individual and another. When a personal loan was secured by a parcel of land or a house, a stone inscribed with basic information about the loan was placed as a marker on the property. No central authority and no bank kept a record of such things. The stone markers, called *horoi*, served as a notice to all that a loan had been made for which the property was security. Most land loans were made for a short term, commonly one year, though sometimes for five years or longer.[66]

There was no bustling real estate market to speak of in classical Greece; there were no real estate agents who dealt in land sales or 15- or 30-year mortgages.[67] (Scholars debate, however, whether certain *horoi* might have reflected loans to buy land.) However, land did change hands, and more so in the fourth century than the fifth. It changed hands as people died and others inherited property; it changed hands as one man's debt and need to sell became a wealthier man's opportunity. Over the course of the Peloponnesian War, when people were torn from the plots of land that were the foundation of their way of life, a deep connection was loosened; and land was viewed more often than before as a commodity and a means to profit, at least in the immediate vicinity of Athens. Absentee landlords who put farmland under others' management became more common, though there had certainly been absentee landlords before.[68] In the fourth century more often than in the fifth, landowners (citizens) borrowed against their land and utilized their money more often for productive purposes.[69]

For "normal loans," interest rates did not change after the plague and the war but remained at 10–12% through the fourth century. Loans secured by real estate remained mostly between 8% and 12% but with instances at 16%–18% around the difficult period of 400 BCE (with an additional instance in 469), while the interest rate charged by temples for loans remained at 10%.[70]

San Francisco Fed economists Jordà, Singh, and Taylor found in their study of 19 European pandemics and epidemics that wars and pandemics exert opposite pressures on the real natural rate of interest. They captured these forces in the chart below:

(a) *Response of European real natural rate*

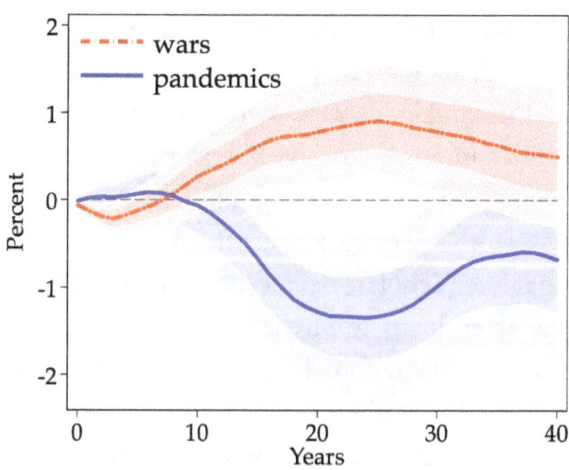

Figure 4.3 Response of the European real natural rate, Jordà, Singh, and Taylor, "Longer-Run Economic Consequences of Pandemics," page 11, figure 3 detail.

What their findings and the limited data set of loans known to have taken place in Athens suggest is that the Plague of Athens and the Peloponnesian War together went some distance toward canceling each other out with regard to their influence on the real natural rate of interest. Overall, interest rates for many types of loans, in real and nominal terms, did not change significantly enough to move the ranges found in the previous century. Maritime loans that funded trade were, however, subject to exorbitant rates and functioned in some ways like a form of insurance.

Now, what did the Plague of Athens have to do with the outcomes we have noted for Athens in the fourth century, extending beyond the medium term into the longer term? The story of the Peloponnesian War and the Plague of Athens intertwines, and one cannot be teased out from the other. Microbes have proven over and over again through history to be wild card foes with which peoples at war must contend, and they are thoroughly capable of tipping the balance in human affairs. In economic terms, the demographic hit delivered by the plague and the war together (with the plague responsible for more than half of lives lost), later combined with the cost of the war and with defeat, pushed Athens in the medium term to raise or institute pay for jobs that only male citizens were by law qualified to do. Recovery was expedited after the war because the city itself was not destroyed as it had been after the Persian Wars. Over the course of the fourth century, demographic changes and the city-state's changed geopolitical circumstances provided incentives for Athens to revise its financial model (particularly after events made clear by mid-century that there was no road back to empire for Athens) and to open opportunity more equitably to noncitizens, whose participation in the Athenian economy had become significantly more important to funding the prosperity, programs, and projects of the state and to providing a standard of living far above subsistence levels across Attica.

The lesson for monetary policy from the history of Athens is profound. Athens did not permanently debase its currency. Their substitution of a silver-coated bronze drachma was temporary, and they restored the coin's full silver content after the war. Their substitution of gold for silver was likewise temporary. Athenian authorities demonstrated their commitment to sound money with actions. Sidney Homer characterized their resolve and its result:

The Athenians took every precaution to maintain the integrity of their famous "owls." Even in times of tragic national disaster, when the treasury was empty and Attica occupied by an enemy, Athens refused to debase this silver coinage. As a consequence, the Athenian "owl" became current in all markets and an article for export. It remained a most acceptable currency throughout the Mediterranean for 600 years, long after the disastrous defeat of Athens in the Peloponnesian War, 431–404 B.C. This tragic event, immortalized by Thucydides and mourned to this day by lovers of human excellence, was not a turning point in the financial history of Greece.[71]

---

1. Rachel Kousser, "Destruction and Memory on the Athenian Acropolis," *The Art Bulletin* 91, no. 3, (September 2009 (263–82): 264–265, https://www.jstor.org/stable/40645507. See also Josiah Ober, *The Rise and Fall of Classical Greece* (Princeton: Princeton University Press, 2016), 191–192. Kindle edition.

2. Donald Kagan, *Pericles of Athens and the Birth of Democracy* (New York: MacMillan, 1991), 36–37.

3. Josiah Ober, *The Rise and Fall of Classical Greece* (Princeton: Princeton University Press, 2016), 201. Kindle edition.

4. Mark Cartwright, "Delian League," *World History Encyclopedia*, March 4, 2016, https://www.worldhistory.org/Delian_League/.

5. Ober, *Rise and Fall of Classical Greece*, 202–204.

6. Ober, *Rise and Fall of Classical Greece*, 204–205.

7. Ober, *Rise and Fall of Classical Greece*, 204.

8. Sidney Homer and Richard Sylla, *A History of Interest Rates* (Rutgers: Rutgers University Press, 2005), 95. For the distinctions between land loans and maritime loans, see Edward E. Cohen, "Athenian Finance: Maritime and Landed Yields," *Classical Antiquity* 8, no. 2 (October 1989): 207–223.

9.   Darel Tai Engen, "The Economy of Ancient Greece," *Economic History Association* (July 31, 2004), https://eh.net/encyclopedia/the-economy-of-ancient-greece/.

10. Kagan, *Pericles of Athens and the Birth of Democracy*, 228–232.

11. Thucydides, *Thucydides: The War of the Peloponnesians and the Athenians,* ed. Jeremy Mynott, Cambridge Texts in the History of Political Thought (Cambridge: Cambridge University Press, 2013), 130. Kindle Edition.

12. Thucydides, *The War of the Peloponnesians and the Athenians*, 2.17, 101.

13. Kagan, *Pericles of Athens and the Birth of Democracy*, 243–245.

14. Thucydides, II.37, 111-112.

15. For a succinct run-down of that long debate, see John Horgan, "The Plague at Athens, 430-427 BCE," *World History Encyclopedia* (August 24, 2016), https://www.worldhistory.org/article/939/the-plague-at-athens-430-427-bce/.

16. Thucydides, *The War of the Peloponnesians and the Athenians*, 2.48, 118.

17. Kagan, *Pericles of Athens and the Birth of Democracy*, 23.

18. Thucydides, *The War of the Peloponnesians and the Athenians*, 2.49, 2–8.

19. Titus Lucretius, *De Rerum Natura*, 6.1221–1230.

20. Thucydides, *The War of the Peloponnesians and the Athenians*, 2.52.3, 122.

21. Thucydides, *The War of the Peloponnesians and the Athenians*, 2.53.1–4, 122.

22. Diodorus Siculus, *Library,* 12.58.6–7.

23. Thucydides, *The War of the Peloponnesians and the Athenians*, 1.8, 7.

24. Thucydides, *The War of the Peloponnesians and the Athenians*, 2.54.3, 122.

25. Thucydides, *The War of the Peloponnesians and the Athenians*, 2.54.1–3, 122.

26. Thucydides, *The War of the Peloponnesians and the Athenians*, 2.54.4, 122.

27. Thucydides, *The War of the Peloponnesians and the Athenians*, 2.47.58, 124.

28. Thucydides, *The War of the Peloponnesians and the Athenians*, 2.60.4, 125.

29. Thucydides, *The War of the Peloponnesians and the Athenians*, 2.61.2–4, 125.

30. Thucydides, *The War of the Peloponnesians and the Athenians*, 2.62.5, 127.

31. Cecil Torr, "Triremes," *The Classical Review* 20, no. 2 (March 1906): 137.

32. Robert J. Littman, "The Plague of Athens: Epidemiology and Paleopathology," *Mount Sinai Journal of Medicine* 76, no. 5 (Oct 2009): 456–67.

33. Thucydides, 2.48.1, 118.

34. Effie Coughanowr, "The Plague in Livy and Thucydides," *L'Antiquité Classique,* 54 (1985): 152–158, https://www.jstor.org/stable/41657158.

35. A. French, "Economic Conditions in Fourth-Century Athens," *Greece and Rome* 38, no. 1 (April 1991): 24–40.

36. Sources for the table are William T. Loomis, *Wages, Welfare Costs and Inflation in Classical Athens* (Ann Arbor: University of Michigan Press, 1998), chapter 15; Thomas R. Martin, "An Overview of Classical Greek History from Mycenae to Alexander," digitized at perseus.tufts.edu and excerpted from *Ancient Greece: From Prehistoric to Hellenistic Times* (New Haven: Yale University Press, 2013), chapters on the Peloponnesian War and its aftermath; and Alec Blamire, "Athenian Finance, 454–404 BC," *Hesperia: The Journal of the American School of Classical Studies at Athens* 70, no. 1 (Jan.–March 2001) 99–126.

37. William T. Loomis, *Wages, Welfare Costs and Inflation in Classical Athens* (Ann Arbor: University of Michigan Press, 1999). All extant references to wages are gathered herein.

38. Barry O'Halloran, *The Political Economy of Classical Athens: A Naval Perspective,* Mnemosyne Supplements, History and Archaeology of Classical Antiquity, 425 (Boston: Brill, 2019), 264. See also Walter Scheidel, "Real Wages in Early Economies: Evidence for Living Standards from 1800 BCE to 1300 CE," *Journal of the Economic and Social History of the Orient* 53, no. 3 (2010): 425–462.

39. Ober, *The Rise and Fall of Classical Greece,* 95.

40. O'Halloran, *The Political Economy of Classical Athens,* 133.

41. Alec Blamire, "Athenian Finance, 454–404 BC," *Hesperia: The Journal of the American School of Classical Studies at Athens* 70, no. 1 (Jan-March 2001): 99–126, 108.

42. Christopher Planeaux, "The Thirty Tyrants," *World History Encyclopedia*, November 13, 2015, https://www.worldhistory.org/The_Thirty_Tyrants/.

43. Blamire, "Athenian Finance," 123.

44. Sidney Homer and Richard Sylla, *A History of Interest Rates (Rutgers: Rutgers University Press, 2005), 79,* 322. Kindle Edition.

45. Blamire, "Athenian Finance," 121–123.

46. French, "Economic Conditions in Fourth-Century Athens," 24.

47. French, "Economic Conditions in Fourth-Century Athens," 36.

48. Ober, *Rise and Fall of Classical Greece,* 223, 231.

49. Ober, *Rise and Fall of Classical Greece,* 223.

50. Ober, *Rise and Fall of Classical Greece,* 83.

51. Ober, *Rise and Fall of Classical Greece,* 248–249.

52. John H. Kroll, "The Reminting of Athenian Silver Coinage, 353 B.C.," *Hesperia: The Journal of the American School of Classical Studies at Athens* 80, no. 2 (April–June 2011): 229–259.

53. Xenophon. *Ways and Means,* Book. Chapter 3. Marchant, Bowersock. Perseus Digital Library, last accessed June 6, 2024, https://www.perseus.tufts.edu/.

54. Ober, *The Rise and Fall of Classical Greece,* 244.

55. Ober, *The Rise and Fall of Classical Greece,* 244.

56. Engen, "The Economy of Ancient Greece."

57. Ober, *The Rise and Fall of Classical Greece,* 244.

58. Ober, *The Rise and Fall of Classical Greece,* 245.

59. Ober, *The Rise and Fall of Classical Greece,* 247.

60. Ober, *The Rise and Fall of Classical Greece,* 243–252.

61. Engen, "The Economy of Ancient Greece."

62. Homer and Sylla, *History of Interest Rates,* 84.

63. Moses I. Finley, "Land, Debt, and the Man of Property in Classical Athens," *Political Science Quarterly* 68, no. 2 (June 1953): 249–268, 265–266.

64. Engen, "The Economy of Ancient Greece."

65. Homer and Sylla, *History of Interest Rates,* 79.

66. Homer and Sylla, *History of Interest Rates,* 86.

67. Finley, "Land, Debt, and the Man of Property in Classical Athens," 261.

68. French, "Economic Conditions in Fourth-Century Athens," 27.

69. G. Glotz, *Ancient Greece at Work: An Economic History from the Homeric Period to the Roman Conquest* (New York: Routledge, 2003), 237–239. Kindle Edition.

70. Homer and Sylla, *A History of Interest Rates,* 89; G. Glotz, *Ancient Greece at Work,* 243. See also the discussion of the term "mortgage" in Moses I. Finley, *Studies in Land and Credit in Ancient Athens: The Horos Inscriptions, 500–200 B.C.* (Rutgers: Rutgers University Press, 1985), XV–XVIII. Google Books.

71. Homer and Sylla, *A History of Interest Rates,* 79–80.

Chapter 5

Rome: The Antonine Plague
(165–189 CE)

Three Roman Pandemics: An Introduction

The long history of the Roman Empire was punctuated by three pandemics that imposed severe demographic and economic shocks: the Antonine Plague (165–189 CE), the Plague of Cyprian (250–270 CE), and the Plague of Justinian (541–542 CE, with regional outbreaks thereafter until the middle of the eighth century). The Antonine Plague unfolded during the rule of the last of the "five good emperors," Marcus Aurelius Antoninus and his co-emperor, in a period previously stable and prosperous that provides records sufficient for capturing much of the economic damage the pandemic shock caused.

Less than a century later, well before population numbers had recovered, the Plague of Cyprian hammered the empire again, during a tumultuous time historians have dubbed the "third century crisis," a period marked by unstable leadership, a sharply devalued currency, rampant inflation, civil war, invasions, and adverse changes in climate. The Plague of Cyprian may have claimed more lives than the Antonine Plague did. Surviving historical evidence is sparser from the chaotic third century than it is from the second, but we can draw conclusions from what data we have about the economic shock that resulted from the pandemic in concert with all the other troubles of the time. History does not craft controlled experiments, and Rome's third century "perfect storm" is instructive for all its entangled complexities, including a pandemic, and their intermingled consequences.

When the Cyprian Plague subsided, Rome enjoyed a respite of more than two centuries from epidemic-level infectious diseases, though the usual microbial suspects continued to rein in life expectancies. In the meantime, a Roman Empire too vast to manage was divided in 286 by Diocletian into a Western Empire and an Eastern Empire with its capital in Constantinople. The Western Empire, besieged and weakened, would crumble in the fifth century; its last emperor, Romulus Augustus, was deposed by the Germanic King Odoacer in 486. The ambitious sixth-century Byzantine emperor Justinian, ruling from Constantinople, aimed to reconquer the Western Empire; instead, the pandemic named for him, which erupted in 541–542, halved the population, wrought economic devastation, and laid to waste Justinian's dreams of restoring the glory of Rome.

Walter Scheidel has outlined three factors that enabled Rome to amass its vast empire in the first place. First, Rome had an intensely militaristic society and an extraordinarily high military participation rate, far higher than that among surrounding peoples. Second, the size of its population, in combination with its high military participation rate, afforded immense — indeed overwhelming — military strength. We must add that Rome was particularly good at integrating the conquered into this militaristic model (and the Roman tax structure) while leaving space for a considerable degree of local control, such that its military strength grew with its empire for centuries. Third, during Rome's expansionary phase, Roman leadership would be characterized by what Scheidel terms *integrity*, which he defines as "the degree of cohesiveness among the decision-making ruling class and more generally the stability of the polity."[1] By the time of the Plague of Cyprian, that cohesiveness had given way to rivalries and divisions, along with leadership instability. Three pandemics would deliver demographic shocks of varying magnitudes, weakening the overall military and economic strength of the empire. With this broad picture in mind, we turn to the first of the three Roman pandemics: the Antonine Plague.

The Antonine Plague: Historical Overview

The decades leading up to the Antonine Plague were a time of prosperity and growth for the empire. In Roman Egypt, where the papyri record is plentiful, real wages rose, outpacing rising real land prices and rents. The population of Roman Egypt topped 5 million or so.[2] The empire's population had peaked at perhaps 75 million people.[3] On the eve of the Antonine Plague, the Roman Empire stretched across three continents, defended by an army of close to a half million men.[4] What evidence we have (from Roman Egypt) suggests that the Roman economy had achieved growth over the preceding century even on a per capita basis, and wages were slowly rising.[5] Roman roads knit the empire together, facilitating trade; and trade traffic by sea appears to have hit a peak, judging by the number of shipwrecks found dating from the second century.[6]

Across the empire, it was a time of relative peace. Territorial expansion continued, but more slowly than it had before; and the structure of the empire still reflected the integrity of leadership that Scheidel has noted as one key to its success. In *The Fate of Rome*, Kyle Harper characterized that military and political cohesiveness in the second century: In short, control of the military that served the vast Roman Empire was still centered in the city of Rome. Its commanders came from its privileged senatorial class, who were represented by an emperor who rose among their ranks.[7]

In short, the heart of the Roman Empire was still Rome itself in those days. The empire's economy depended, as it had for centuries, on its conquered territories as a widening source of revenue drawn from booty and tribute, taxation of new citizens, taxes on trade, and vital resources from food to pottery, cloth, and metals, to slaves. Rome's economic model depended on its ability to conquer and tap new sources of wealth and simultaneously to protect lands and peoples it had already subjugated, a dual challenge that was destined to become increasingly difficult both fiscally and logistically.[8] Some historians believe that the Antonine Plague altered the trajectory of Roman history, weakening the empire and nudging it toward its eventual fall. Certainly, the epidemic correlated with the beginning of the Roman Empire's economic decline.[9]

A Reversal of Fortune: Plague Strikes

During the reign of co-emperors Verus and Marcus Aurelius, in 165 CE, as Aurelius contemplated new conquests in Central Europe, a deadly plague struck. It would last for a full fifteen years and then return, evidence suggests, in 189 CE to ravage Rome again. Before it had run its course, it would claim the life of Verus in 169 CE and, 11 years later, the life of Marcus Aurelius.[10] The Antonine Plague is believed to have been caused by a pox virus (most likely an ancient and now-extinct strain of smallpox). Its victims suffered chills, fever, vomiting, thirst, blackish diarrhea, and a scarring rash of black and purple pustules. The course of the disease lasted two or three weeks.[11] The epidemic is estimated to have killed 5–10 million people. Though estimates vary dramatically regarding the percentage of the population that perished, mid-range estimates fall between 10% and 20%.[12]

According to Roman historian and soldier Ammianus Marcellinus, the plague originated during the sack of Parthia by the Roman army, led by co-emperor Verus.

When this city was stormed by the generals of Verus

Caesar (as I have related before), the statue of Apollo Comaeus was torn from its place and taken to Rome, where the priests of the gods set it up in the temple of the Palatine Apollo. And it is said that, after this same statue had been carried off and the city burned, the soldiers in ransacking the temple found a narrow crevice; this they widened in the hope of finding something valuable; but from a kind of shrine, closed by the occult arts of the Chaldaeans, the germ of that pestilence burst forth, which after generating the virulence of incurable diseases, in the time of the same Verus and of Marcus Antoninus polluted everything with contagion and death, from the frontiers of Persia all the way to the Rhine and to Gaul.[13]

Alternatively, it was said to "have arisen in Babylonia, when a pestilential vapor escaped from a golden casket that a soldier happened to smash open in the temple of Apollo. From there, it spread over Parthia and the whole world."[14] That origin story would drive attempts to appease an angry god. According to another theory, this time from Greece, the plague was believed to have been spread via witchcraft. Instructions to destroy the voodoo dolls of witches to end the plague were issued in both Saris and Ephesus and likely other Greek cities as well.[15]

Setting aside the supernatural accounts of the origin of the plague, however, the disease appears to have been brought back to Rome by Verus's army returning from a campaign in the east, in what is now Iraq. In terms of how widespread the Antonine Plague was, we know from archeological evidence that the Oracle of Claros was consulted on how to ward off the plague. A total of 16 inscriptions have been found detailing the oracle's instructions, which included erecting statues of Apollo and conducting animal sacrifices. These inscriptions have been found in Italy and Greece and as far away as Asia Minor, Spain, Morocco, Egypt, Ukraine, Britain, and Germany. This evidence indicates that there was indeed a widespread pandemic, and that populations were desperate enough that advice from the oracle was sought from across the Roman Empire.[16]

An archeological survey of London gives us an idea of the population loss that occurred in that far-flung Roman city during the plague. Studies by archaeologists of Roman London, or *Londinium*, as it was called, show a large contraction of the city during the period of the Antonine Plague, either because people fled or because they died. Dating to sometime in the 160s CE, a layer of dark earth can be seen over a large part of London, indicating the abandonment and degradation of thatched buildings.[17]

Seeking Deliverance

Romans sought deliverance from suffering and death through every means. They resorted to the help of doctors; they appealed to the gods; and they clung to the promises of at least one self-proclaimed deliverer. None of these avenues of action worked in the absence of medical understanding as to how the pandemic pathogen was transmitted or what treatments could better chances of survival. Roman medical knowledge proved utterly unable to quell the pox. The Greek historian Herodian recounted physicians' failed advice:

> At the direction of their doctors, those who remained in Rome filled their nostrils and ears with fragrant oils and used perfume and incense constantly, for some said that the sweet odor, entering first, filled up the sensory passages and kept out the poison in the air; or, if any poison should enter, it would be neutralized by the stronger odors. The plague, however, continued to

rage unchecked for a long time, and many men died,
as well as domestic animals of all kinds.[18]

This approach to prevention and treatment reflected the miasma
theory, supported by the most famous physician of the period, Galen,
which held that the air itself was contagious, and a foul smell would
indicate that disease was present. If a stench in the air signaled contagion, the remedy was to stay away from the infected and the smell
of rotting flesh and death. This preventative measure could have been
effective had people kept a few feet from the sick, since smallpox was
transmitted via large droplets in the air. But it was the notion that
masking the odor of sickly breath or blood-tainted diarrhea with a
sweet smell would protect an uninfected person from contagion that
proved to be flawed. Sweet odors did not prevent or cure disease.

Since medicine remained powerless, many turned to the gods as
the only possible salvation. In particular, the Romans went to great
lengths to appease the god Apollo, whose wrath they believed had
been provoked when Roman soldiers desecrated a temple of Apollo
on their campaign in the East. Oracles, including the oracle of Apollo
and the sibyls, were consulted for a cure. Most prescribed the erec-
tion of statues of Apollo and animal sacrifices to appease that god's
anger. These measures, however, did not quell Apollo's vengeance
and stop the pestilence — at least until the pox virus that actually
caused the plague had endowed enough survivors with immunity to
end pandemic-level disease. (In the case of smallpox, if an infection
does not kill, it confers immunity. The same cannot be assumed of all
pathogens — coronaviruses, for instance.) Ultimately, many Romans
would believe that "Apollo the Healer" was ultimately responsible for
ending the Antonine Plague, and that belief would figure into the
Roman Empire's response to the Plague of Cyprian in the next century.

From the Antonine Plague period, we also see an early instance of
an unprincipled individual who saw opportunity in others' desperation

and peddled misinformation for his own ends. Because misinformation and fraud cost lives whenever better information might otherwise save them, and with economic consequences, this extraordinary early instance is worth a brief retelling of the tale.

Glycon was an unusual false prophet and cult leader — the puppet star of a ventriloquist act orchestrated by the charlatan Alexander of Abonoteichus, an ancient town in Asia Minor. Alexander declared himself the descendant of Perseus, a demi-god, and prophesied the coming of the reincarnation of the healing god Asclepius.[19] According to Lucian of Samosata, who was sufficiently irked by Alexander's unprincipled exploits to write a damning account of them, Alexander summoned the town to the temple to witness the birth of the new Asclepius. When he had gathered an audience, he dug an egg out of the ground (carefully placed there prior) and opened it to reveal a snake, the symbol of Asclepius, the Greco-Roman god of medicine.

Figure 5.1 Mid-second century statue of Glycon, the false prophet who claimed to offer a cure, courtesy of Angel M. Felisimo via Wikimedia Commons, CC BY 2.0.

The next day, awed villagers returned to see the healing snake god again. Meanwhile, the snake, whom Alexander introduced as Glycon, had grown immensely since its emergence the day prior and was now quite large. Alexander had meticulously crafted a snake hand puppet; and by means of a ventriloquist's act, Glycon the puppet snake prophesied the future and offered all sorts of advice to those who came to visit.[20] A new cult was hatched, and its popularity would spread from Asia Minor to the Greek mainland and then to Italy itself. Glycon's puppet master, Alexander, was both a fraud and, Professor Stephen Kent of the University of Alberta believes, a malignant narcissist, grandly claiming that he could offer protection from all sorts of ills.[21] Lucian reported what followed:

> No sooner did Alexander get Italy in hand than he began to devise ever more ambitious projects, and sent oracle-mongers everywhere across the empire warning the cities to be on their guard against plagues and conflagrations and earthquakes; he promised that he would himself afford them infallible aid so that none of these calamities should befall them. There was one oracle which he dispatched to all the nations during the pestilence; it was just a single line of verse: 'Phoebus, the god unshorn, keepeth off plague's nebulous onset.'

> This verse could be seen everywhere, written over doorways as a charm against the plague; but in most cases it had the opposite result to that intended. By some chance it was those very houses on which the verse was inscribed that suffered the worst. I don't mean that they were stricken specifically on account of the verse, but by some chance or other that's what happened. Perhaps the residents neglected the usual precautions because of their confidence in the oracle

and so carelessly didn't help the oracle in combating the disease. They just trusted the syllables to defend them and 'unshorn Phoebus' to drive the plague away with his arrows.[22]

The lies spread by Alexander (who preferred to remain unshorn, himself) through Glycon, Lucius suggested, led to the deaths of many followers. The promulgation of the false protection was so widespread that one of Glycon's amulets of protection against the plague was found in the Thames River in London.[23] Despite the failure of Glycon's charm to ward off the disease and death, the cult retained its believers and power even fifty years after Alexander's death.

Economic Ruination

When smallpox struck the Roman world, reports ensued of both livestock and people succumbing to the plague. These reports were followed not long after by desperate straits, described here by the Roman priest and historian Paulus Orosius:

> A plague which broke out over many provinces followed and so laid waste all Italy that everywhere country estates, fields and towns were left without a cultivator or inhabitant and gave way to ruins and forests.[24]

A tragic but frequent theme in epidemics is echoed here again — that those who gather and grow food, essential to life itself, have fallen and can no longer provide the sustenance necessary to support society. The attrition among farmers was lamented the loudest, for quickly following their deaths came food shortages that led to starvation and food price inflation. Herodian reported how hunger resulted not only from the pestilence but also from a misstep in governance on the part of Marcus Aurelius (here called Cleander):

> The plague, however, continued to rage unchecked for a long time, and many men died, as well as domestic animals of all kinds. Famine gripped the city at the same time…. Responsible for it was a Phrygian named Cleander (Marcus Aurelius), one of the slaves offered for sale by the public auctioneer for the benefit of the state…. Because of his wealth and wantonness, Cleander coveted the empire. He bought up most of the grain supply and put it in storage; he hoped in this way to get control of the people and the army by making a generous distribution of grain at the first sign of a food shortage, anticipating that he would win the support of the people when they were suffering from a scarcity of food.[25]

Marcus Aurelius had purchased the bulk of the food supply so that he might dole it out to the masses in times of need and thus appear a hero. But this tactic backfired tremendously when the plague struck. The food and grain shortage that the emperor could not adequately address was a calamity felt most keenly by the poor.

A tax record from Roman Egypt in the territory of Fayuum shows that even twenty years after the outbreak of plague, agriculture was still attempting to recover. The state expected to collect taxes on a total of 814,862 artabas of wheat. (An artaba is an Egyptian unit of measurement roughly equivalent to a bushel.) The record, however, stated that taxes had been paid on only 223,581 artabas.[26] A shocking 73% of the taxes expected on grain had not been paid.

Death did not target specific trades, of course; it swept over the entire society. The plague killed slaves, soldiers, construction workers, architects, engineers, doctors, smiths, bankers, traders, shopkeepers, fishermen, sailors, and miners. All of the trades and professions that kept an advanced society running would have suffered labor shortages to one degree or another. That said, of particular concern for the Roman imperial war machine was the depletion of its armies due to plague. When Germanic tribes breached Rome's borders in 167 CE, Marcus Aurelius resorted to a series of extraordinary measures to replenish the ranks needed to push the invaders back:

> The pestilence was still raging at this time; he both zealously revived the worship of the gods and trained slaves for military service — just as had been done in the Punic war — whom he called Volunteers, after the example of the Volones. He armed gladiators also, calling them the Compliant, and turned even the bandits of Dalmatia and Dardania into soldiers. He armed the Diogmitae, besides, and even hired auxiliaries from among the Germans for service against Germans. And besides all this, he proceeded with all care to enroll legions for the Marcomannic and German war. And lest all this prove burdensome to the provinces, he held an auction of the palace furnishings in the Forum of the Deified Trajan, as we have related, and sold there, besides robes and goblets and golden flagons, even statues and paintings by great artists.[27]

The situation warranted drastic action to supplement Rome's military capacity. Slaves, gladiators, criminals, and Germanic mercenaries were all recruited into service. That soldiers could not be paid without selling the fineries of the imperial palace more than suggests serious economic struggles and the depletion of the Roman treasury.

Another profession deserves particular attention, that of the miner. The plague was devastating to miners and mining, and thus to the economy as a whole. Many of the Roman mines in Hispania (Spain) ceased operations with the coming of the plague. In Dacia (modern Romania) a wax tablet was found in a Roman gold mine that confirmed that in 167 CE the number of miners had dwindled from 54 to 17, their deaths being due to plague.[28] Miners would have been ready victims of contagion, of course, in the cramped quarters of a mine.

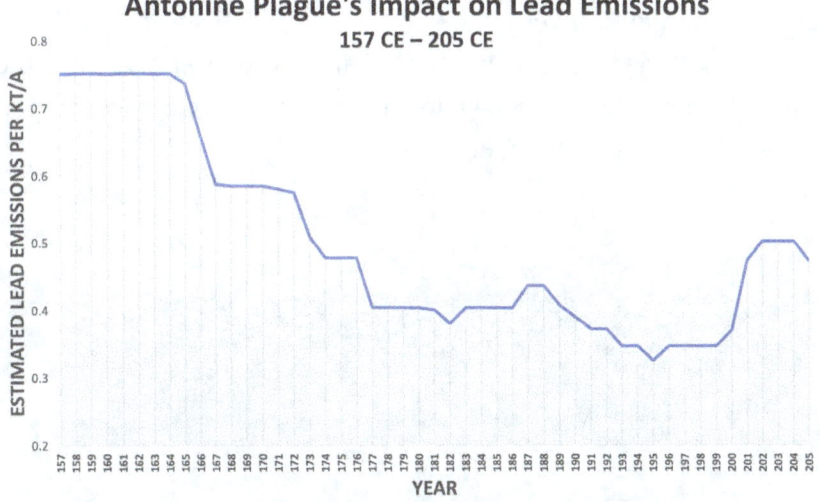

Figure 5.2 The Antonine Plague's impact on lead emissions
(Data source: J.R. McConnell, et al, "Lead pollution recorded in Greenland ice indicates European emissions tracked plagues, wars, and imperial expansion during antiquity").

The data that demonstrates the consequent reduction in mining comes from a surprising source: an ice cap in Greenland. In Greenland there is an ice cap that is 3km deep, and the study of this ice cap and its layers has given scholars a way to accurately determine the level of lead pollution for a 3,000-year period. The dating determined in the Greenland ice core project shows that lead pollution from mining drops precipitously in the year 166. Lead pollution reflecting mining production would not return to pre-Antonine Plague levels for another six centuries, according to the data. In mining, lead most often co-occurs in silver mines and can be used as a measurement of the mining of silver.[29] Figure 5.2 displays the precipitous drop in mining during the Antonine period, including the smaller drop in mining during the Plague of Cyprian.

Lead emissions dropped a surprising 56% during the period, correlating with an immense reduction in mining activity. Data from the Greenland ice core project also coincides with a further debasement of the amount of silver in the currency during the period. The denarius went from 80% silver in 155 CE down to 67% silver by 180 CE. The weight of the coins also began to change: The silver content of the Roman denarius fell from 3.4g down to 3.2g by 180 CE and dropped to a weight of 2.8g in 187 CE.[30]

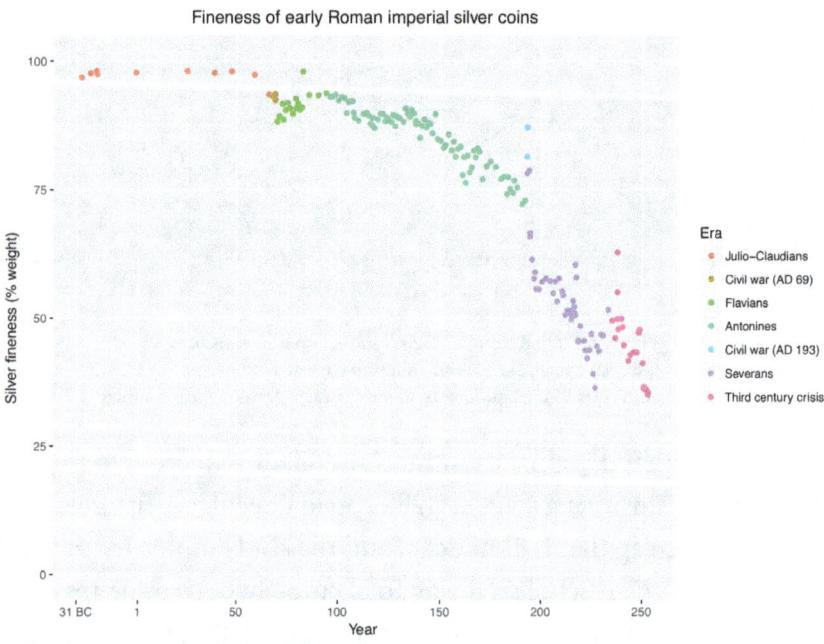

Figure 5.3 The drop in the weight of silver in Roman coins, courtesy of Nicolas Perrault III, CC0, via Wikimedia Commons.

Though debasement of the currency had preceded the pandemic, it would accelerate in the pandemic's wake. We can say with reasonable certainty that a silver shortfall is due at least in some measure to the population reduction in the period and its impact on mining. The substantial decline in mining operations across the empire would have led to shortages and almost certainly to significant price increases of lead, iron, tin, copper, arsenic, mercury, gold, and silver.

The shortages of these metals could have impacted prices for items made from these metals, from luxury items such as jewelry and statues to more essential items such as swords, armor, agricultural tools, and metal cookware. On the other hand, there were fewer people left; and the goods that had belonged to the dead were passed along to their heirs, increasing wealth per capita and reducing demand.

It was not until 200 CE, 35 years after the onset of the plague, that lead emissions began to recover, reflecting the resumption of silver mining on a broader scale. This reduction does not occur in minor plagues; but in the Plague of Cyprian, the Plague of Justinian, and later the Black Death, we see the same precipitous drop in mining.

For some time, historians have fiercely debated how significant the plague during the Antonine period was — and thus how dramatic its economic impact would have actually been. Though the historical evidence from which we can draw conclusions is limited, Walter Scheidel, a professor of classics and history at Stanford, has studied references to wages, the price of land leases, and commodity prices in Roman Egypt during the period before, during, and after the Antonine Plague, cobbling data together from the 22,000 papyri extant from the time. Though the Egyptian papyri, which survived many centuries in a dry climate, cannot fill in the picture for the Roman Empire as a whole, Scheidel's findings point to the Antonine Plague's economic impact in Roman Egypt and perhaps beyond.[31]

Scheidel's own aim was to work from the economic impacts to conclusions about what proportion of the population likely died in the Antonine Plague. The scattered evidence that exists about the plague, however, does not lead historians to a consensus about the death rate. Instead, it leads to vigorous debate. The debate aside, the evidence we have points to the development of labor shortages occasioned by the widespread plague.

Relative to the cost of everything else in Roman Egypt, annual rents for wheat fields increased during the second century until the Antonine Plague years and then fell in real terms in the third century. Those rents generally included taxes that would be owed. The number of leases for which references can be found also fell.[32] Scheidel explained, "Nominal cash rents and land prices failed to rise nearly as strongly as the prices of various consumer goods and the price of labour, thereby dropping in real terms."[33] Rises in real rents and land prices lagged real wages because demand for land weakened with a demographic shock.

The price of wine, olive oil, and slaves roughly doubled in the third quarter of the second century CE. The price of donkeys nearly tripled. Since a slave cost between four and five times what a donkey did, the higher value of donkeys suggests their increasingly vital role as work animals in a time when human laborers were in short supply. Moreover, Scheidel found that real agricultural wages appeared to be higher in the third century, with wage increases outstripping increases in the costs of wine, oil, and wheat — everything except donkeys.[34]

Some villages saw significant decreases in the number of taxpayers, though it is not possible to sort how many people in those villages may have died and how many may have left instead, either to avoid disease or to avoid rising taxes, for which villages were made collectively responsible by Rome.[35]

The sample sizes that Scheidel had to work with are small — there are no more than a couple hundred references for each economic category, scattered across many years, well beyond a timeframe we would define as the medium term. But the shifts we see from the second century to the third suggest that a labor shortage had developed following the Antonine Plague, and no other explanation fits the story that the surviving data outlines.

It is, of course, impossible to generalize what might have happened from one place to the next, from Roman Egypt to Rome itself or anywhere else. More dense population centers likely took a harder hit than sparsely populated rural areas did, since smallpox (or a similar pox virus) would have spread by respiratory transmission more successfully where population density was greater.

Writing of the Antonine Plague's economic impact, Greco-Roman historian William V. Harris noted the damage that must have occurred as the plague tore through towns, creating gaps in the human expertise that had enabled the emergence of a middle class and a Roman economy rich in specialization. In the wake of the plague, the Roman economy transitioned to "a much more run-of-the-mill pre-modern agrarian structure."[36] The ranks of an affluent middle class thinned, and metal working fell into a decline — both impacts that seem at least partially attributable to the plague.[37]

The plague was not, it must be noted, the only crisis that Rome had to contend with. Military crises arose in various provinces during the period of the Antonine Plague. Fiscal pressure on the empire and on the military increased. Military losses would have included losses resulting from the conflicts that affected up to a third of Rome's provinces added to losses resulting from pandemic disease.[38]

Mentions of starvation do not occur during insignificant plagues; indeed, archaeological records also do not show partial abandonment of cities and towns in minor plagues. It is also worth pointing out that minor disease outbreaks were a near constant in the ancient world. We see in the records lesser plagues being mentioned a couple of times at most; the abundance of primary source evidence alone on the Antonine Plague sets it apart from minor plagues and unequivocally places it amongst the worst plagues of ancient history, along with the two other Roman pandemics that followed.

1.   Scheidel, Walter. *Escape from Rome: The Failure of Empire and the Road to Prosperity*, The Princeton Economic History of the Western World (Princeton: Princeton University Press, 2019), 103. Kindle edition.

2.   Kyle Harper, "People, Plagues, and Prices in the Roman World: The Evidence from Egypt," *The Journal of Economic History*, 76, no. 3, (2016): 807, https://doi.org/10.1017/S0022050716000826.

3.   Kyle Harper, *The Fate of Rome: Climate, Disease, and the End of an Empire*, The Princeton History of the Ancient World 2 (Princeton: Princeton University Press, 2017), 29–30. Kindle edition.

4.   Harper, *Fate of Rome*, 27.

5.   Harper, *Fate of Rome*, 33.

6.   Luigi Oddo, "Revisiting Roman Economic Growth: Predatory Policies, Self-Sustaining Strategies, and the Limits of Neo Institutional Economics," International Economics (December 4, 2023): 25, https://www.iei1946.it/article/993/revisiting-roman-economic-growthpredatory-policies-self-sustaining-strategies-and-the-limits-of-neo-institutional-economics.

7.   Kyle Harper, *Fate of Rome*, 27.

8.   Oddo, "Revisiting Roman Economic Growth," 9.

9.   John Horgan, "Antonine Plague," *World History Encyclopedia* (May 2019), https://www.worldhistory.org/Antonine_Plague/.

10.   John Horgan, "Antonine Plague."

11.   John Horgan, "Antonine Plague."

12.   Kyle Harper, *Fate of Rome*, 108; Kyle Harper, "People, Plagues, and Prices in the Roman World: The Evidence from Egypt," *The Journal of Economic History*, 76(3) (2016): 803–839, https://doi.org/10.1017/S0022050716000826.

13.   Ammianus Marcellinus, *Rerum Gestarum*, 22.6.23–24.

14.   "*Life of Verus*," *Historia Augusta*, I, trans. David Magie, Loeb Classical Library 139 (Cambridge, MA: Harvard University Press, 1921), 8, http://penelope.uchicago.edu/Thayer/E/Roman/Texts/Historia_Augusta/Lucius_Verus*.html.

15.   Fritz Graf, "An oracle against pestilence from a western Anatolian town," *ZPE 92* (1992): 268–269.

16.   Christopher Jones, "Ten Dedications 'To the gods and goddesses' and the Antonine Plague," *JRA* 18 (2005): 293–301.

17.   Dominic Perring, "Two Studies on Roman London. Population decline and ritual landscapes in Antonine London," *JRA* 24, no. 2 (2011): 249–82.

18.   Herodian, *History of the Roman Empire*, 1.12.1–2. Trans. Edward C. Echols. *Herodian of Antioch's History of the Roman Empire*, 1961, https://www.livius.org/sources/content/herodian-s-roman-history/herodian-1.12/.

19.   Lucian, *Alexander the False Prophet*, trans. A.M. Harmon, Loeb Classical Library, 10–11, https://www.tertullian.org/rpearse/lucian/lucian_alexander.htm.

20.   Lucian, *Alexander the False Prophet*, 12–15.

21.   Stephen A. Kent, "Narcissistic Fraud in the Ancient World: Lucian's Account of Alexander

of Abonuteichos and the Cult of Glycon," *Ancient Narrative* 6 (2007): 77–99), https://skent.ualberta.ca/wp-content/uploads/2014/06/Glycon-narcissism-cult.pdf.

22. Lucian, *Alexander the False Prophet*, 36.

23. Lucian, *Alexander the False Prophet*, 59–61.

24. Paulus Orosius, *Seven Books of History Against the Pagans, Book VII,* trans. Roy J. Deferrari (Washington, DC: Catholic University of America Press, 1964), 309.

25. Herodian, *History of the Roman Empire*, 1.12.1–4.

26. Peter van Minnen, "P. Oxy. LXVI 4527 and the Antonine Plague in the Fayyum," *Zeitschrift für Papyrologie und Epigraphik* 135 (2001), 175.

27. *Historia Augusta: The Life of Marcus Aurelius,* 21.6–8.

28. Russu, I. I. (1975). Inscriptiile Daciei Romane, 1: Introducere Istorica si Epigraphica Diplomele Militare & Tablitele Cerate. Bucuresti.

29. J. R. McConnell, A.I. Wilson, Airenzo M. M. Stohl, N.J. Chellman, S. Eckhardt, E.M. Thompson, A.M. Pollard, and J.P. Steffensen (2018), "Lead pollution recorded in Greenland ice indicates European emissions tracked plagues, wars, and imperial expansion during antiquity," *Proceedings of the National Academy of Sciences of the United States of America 115*, no. 22: 5726–31, https://www.pnas.org/doi/full/10.1073/pnas.1721818115.

30. Christopher Howgego, Kevin Butcher, Matthew Ponting, and Volker Heuchert. "Coinage and the Roman Economy in the Antonine Period: the view from Egypt" (2013), Working Paper, Oxford: Oxford Roman Economy Project, University of Oxford, 8, http://oxrep.classics.ox.ac.uk/docs/Howgego2010.pdf.

31. Walter Scheidel, "A Model of Demographic and Economic Change in Roman Egypt after the Antonine Plague," *Journal of Roman Archaeology* 15 (2002): 97–114, https://doi.org/10.1017/S1047759400013854.

32. Scheidel, "A Model of Demographic and Economic Change in Roman Egypt," 101–102.

33. Scheidel, "A Model of Demographic and Economic Change in Roman Egypt," 107.

34. Scheidel, "A Model of Demographic and Economic Change in Roman Egypt," 103–104.

35. Scheidel, "A Model of Demographic and Economic Change in Roman Egypt," 97.

36. William V. Harris, "The Great Pestilence and the Complexities of the Antonine-Severan Economy," *L'Impatto Della "Pete Antonia"* (2012), 336–337.

37. Harris, "The Great Pestilence and the Complexities of the Antonine-Severan Economy," 332.

38. Harris, "The Great Pestilence and the Complexities of the Antonine-Severan Economy," 332.

Chapter 6

Rome: The Plague of Cyprian
(249–262 CE or 270 CE)

Figure 6.1 Jules-Élie Delaunay, "The Plague in Rome" (1869),
Minneapolis Institute of Art, Public Domain.

Historical Overview

After the Antonine Plague, Rome's respite between pandemic shocks proved painfully short — less than a century. The Plague of Cyprian, reported to have originated in Ethiopia, erupted across the Roman Empire amid a series of mounting calamities known as the third century crisis, a multifaceted nightmare from which the Romans would never fully recover. The crisis was a convergence of events that decimated the Roman economy. First, the empire had to contend with repeated invasions from peoples to the north. Second, the period of 235 to 284 CE saw warring generals usurping one another to become emperor. This period, known as the time of the Barracks emperors, would bring constant civil war and military coups that damaged civil infrastructure and resulted in leadership too short-lived to combat crises effectively. The average lifespan of an emperor during this period was two years.[1] Third, once-favorable climate conditions that had guaranteed abundant harvests during the heyday of the Roman Empire had segued to more erratic conditions. In the mid 240s, precipitation proved insufficient to cause the seasonal flooding of the Nile, upon which a large portion of the crops that fed Rome depended.[2] Reduced harvests appear to have doubled grain prices and would have sharply eroded tax revenue out of Egypt.

A Deadly Torment of Flux and Fire

Amid all these challenges, in 249 CE, a new epidemic disease advanced across the empire. The bishop Cyprian (who was later executed by the Romans for his Christian faith) provided posterity with a description of its dire symptoms:

> This trial, that now the bowels, relaxed into a constant flux, discharge the bodily strength; that a fire originated in the marrow ferments into wounds of the fauces; that the intestines are shaken with a continual vomiting; that the eyes are on fire with the injected blood; that in some cases the feet or some parts of the limbs are

taken off by the contagion of diseased putrefaction; that
from the weakness arising by the maiming and loss of
the body, either the gait is enfeebled, or the hearing is
obstructed, or the sight darkened; — is profitable as
a proof of faith.[3]

The disease remains almost as mysterious to us as it would have
been to the Romans. No mention is made of pustules or a rash, so it
is unlikely that the Plague of Cyprian was caused by new outbreaks
of smallpox. Historian Kyle Harper has suggested that the symptoms
that Cyprian and other witnesses describe most closely align to a
viral hemorrhagic fever of some kind — perhaps a filovirus (Ebola
is an example), but no confirmation is possible. A highly pathogenic
pandemic influenza is another possibility, though a less compelling
one.[4] The scant historical record affords us only scattered glimpses of
the pandemic's impacts, but surviving accounts agree regarding the
immense suffering and loss dealt by the plague.

The population in Alexandria, Egypt, plunged by more than 60%,
though how many died versus how many fled would be impossible
to determine.[5] The port city, which once boasted a population of half
a million people, was reduced to 190,000 during the plague.[6] It was
impacted not only by plague but also by erratic climate conditions
and consequent food supply issues along with other infectious diseases. An account from the period, from a Christian named Dionysis,
recorded by the bishop and church historian Eusebius, notes how the
city had suffered droughts and outsized floods by turns, along with
"continual epidemics" that had thinned its numbers and weakened
the young so that they seemed old even prior to the horrific plague
described by Cyprian.[7]

The pandemic spanned two decades and claimed the lives of two
emperors. At its peak, Rome itself, according to one historian, saw 5000
deaths per day — a figure, if not exact, still suggestive of the magnitude

of the disaster.[8] The plague's ultimate death toll is lost to time, but given what evidence we do have, a death toll of between 10% and 25% of the populace seems to historians a reasonable estimate. We know from contemporary reports that it is unlikely to have been lower. In terms of the plague's geographical spread, Kyle Harper mapped 13 sites in Southern Europe, North Africa, and the Middle East, at varying distances inland from the shores of the Mediterranean, where probable indications of outbreaks can be found. The pandemic appears to have penetrated populations across the Roman Empire and well beyond.[9]

The Economic Shock

The economic devastation from plague amid seemingly endless imperial coups combined with war and climate change-driven fluctuations in harvests was predictably immense. Beset by rebellions, invasions, unfavorable weather, and plague, the empire saw the price of goods escalate by 100% amid a full-blown monetary crisis.[10] But only in Roman Egypt does scattered evidence noting prices, rents, and wages survive, enabling observations about economic trends there and presumably across the empire, into which the region was by this time fully integrated.

Nominal wheat prices in Roman Egypt had doubled after the Antonine Plague, in tandem with the debasement of the currency, which only accelerated after the Plague of Cyprian. The range of nominal wheat prices stretched higher during the Plague of Cyprian and proved highly volatile and variable from place to place during the century that followed. That said, Harper noted that "the nominal price of silver rose faster than the nominal price of grain in this inflationary phase (something like a 25,000x increase vs. an 8,000x increase)," such that the trend for real wheat prices across the fourth century was deflationary.[11]

It is not possible to speculate about land prices in the medium

120

term after the Plague of Cyprian in that region simply because there is a century-long gap in the papyri record on land sales following. Scant records in the latter half of the fourth century and the fifth century show both nominal and real land prices recovering as the population did.[12]

Land rents paid in kind (services and goods such as a portion of the harvest), though challenging to compare for a number of reasons, began to fall after the Antonine Plague. The trend continued after the Plague of Cyprian, at least until the second half of the fourth century saw a partial recovery in rents in kind, though rents appear, from surviving records, to have dipped lower again more than a century before the Justinianic Plague halved the population. The caution here is that evidence is quite limited; the discovery of other stashes of papyri could potentially change the sketchy picture we have. Cash rents were rarer than rents paid in kind, and there is simply no data for them following the Plague of Cyprian until the second half of the fourth century, long after the plague ended.[13] Interestingly, however, co-emperors Valerian (253–260) and Gallienus (Valerian's son, 253–268) ruled in 260 that landowners could not raise rents when existing leases were "tacitly" renewed.[14] That ruling hints, it occurs to us, at possible inflationary pressures on rents at the time, resulting from the continuing devaluation of money.

Evidence for wages paid for agricultural labor comes from estate records, often records that encompass a span of years from a single estate. In a context of runaway inflation, real wages, calculated as an annual wheat wage, fell after the Plague of Cyprian following a demographic shock and amid ongoing political, military, and monetary turmoil. The demographic hit impacting the labor supply failed to create wage price pressures sufficient to outpace inflation amid market disruptions and demand curtailed by population loss.

We know little of interest rates on loans secured by land during the third century — far less than we know about interest rates in the first century BCE and the first century CE, when rates were volatile. We do know that the legal limit for such loans remained at 12% until the fourth century, when it was raised by Diocletian to 12.5%.[15]

The third century calamity was so colossal that it entirely reordered Roman society. As a result of its scarcity, food had become so important that it was no longer those in the city but the land-owning elite that held the power. In addition, poverty produced by this catastrophe was now so rampant that it produced the origin of serfdom. Many were reduced to such poverty that they gave up their rights as free citizens and tenant farmers to become a new class of people, the *coloni*, or serfs, and work on the agricultural estates.[16] That many traded their freedom to work on the land of a noble speaks to how monumental the economic destitution was. In the early fourth century, Constantine would tether the *coloni* to the jurisdictions in which they were listed on the tax rolls.[17]

By the third century, extensive Roman trade networks linked by sea and by Roman roads stretched across Europe as far north as Britain and well into Northern Africa. Those trade routes provisioned cities and armies, facilitated the collection of taxes and rents, and enabled the movement of goods such as pottery that are well documented in the archeological record, as well as cloth, spices, wine, and even marble.[18] But swift debasement of the currency during the third century crisis, in conjunction with the Plague of Cyprian, undermined trade and trade networks in the second half of the third century.

Roman money became less useful as a store of value and a medium of exchange; and the labor supply, along with demand, fell in tandem with the demographic shock. Local production of basic needs and bartering became key strategies for obtaining life's essentials. In the western portion of the empire, great cities dwindled in population and importance, and towns shrank.[19] The eastern portion of the empire appears to have suffered less and recovered more quickly.

In the wake of the plague, the Greenland ice core project once again shows us a large dip in lead pollution, just as occurred with the Antonine plague.[20]

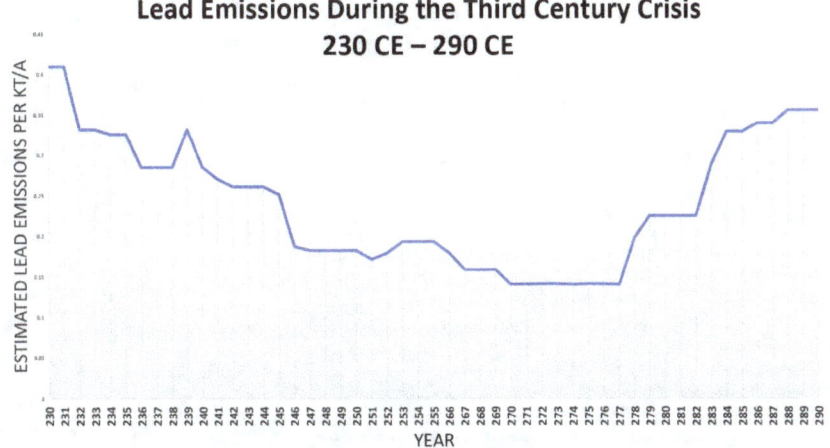

Lead Emissions During the Third Century Crisis
230 CE – 290 CE

ESTIMATED LEAD EMISSIONS PER KT/A

YEAR

Figure 6.2 Third century crisis effect on lead emissions
(Data source: J.R. McConnell, et al, "Lead pollution recorded in Greenland ice indicates European emissions tracked plagues, wars, and imperial expansion during antiquity").

The third century crisis saw a reduction of lead pollution, and thus of mining, of an astonishing 57%. This curtailment of mining corresponded with an acceleration in the debasement of the Roman currency after the plague, though the reduced silver supply from mining was only one factor in the runaway inflation and currency debasement that followed.

This time, however, debasement became so severe that the mainstays of the Roman monetary system, the sesterce (one-fourth denarius) and the denarius became extinct. The denarius was temporarily replaced by the antoninianus, introduced in 215 CE. Although the new coin was supposed to be worth two denarii, it possessed, even at the beginning, the silver content of only 1.5 denarii.[21] When mining activity stagnated midcentury, the silver content of the new coin only continued to decrease. In just two decades' time, these coins had nearly zero silver content, which made them easy to forge and rendered them practically useless.[22] The chart below shows the precipitous drop in their silver content.

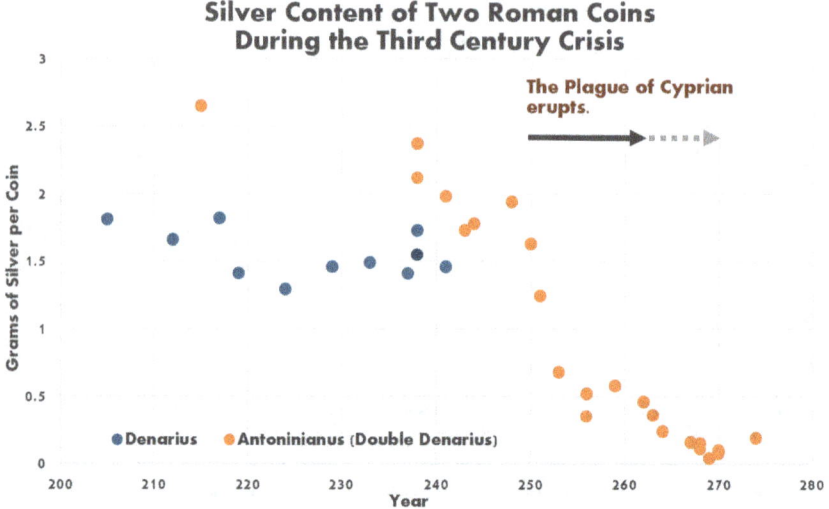

Figure 6.3 The weight of silver in the Roman denarius and the Roman antoninianus during the third century. The antoninianus, or "double denarius" had twice the nominal value of the denarius (Data source: Tables 6.1 and 6.2 in Kenneth Harl, *Coinage in the Roman Economy, 300 BC to AD 700* [1996], pages 127, 130).

In his *History of Interest Rates,* Sidney Homer summarized the trajectory of monetary debasement in Rome:

> During the first century A.D. the metal content of Roman coins was reduced about 25%, and during the second century A.D. it was reduced substantially more. Silver coins were reduced to the status of token coins. In the third century A.D. monetary inflation on a grand scale accompanied a succession of revolutions and civil wars. These later centuries have left us little information on credit and finance. The chaotic fifty years before Diocletian, 284–305 A.D., were, in the

opinion of Tenney Frank, the period when Rome fell.
There was anarchy and looting. Provincials lost faith
in Rome. Industry and trade disintegrated, and even
the Latin speech decayed.[23]

There is a pattern in Rome that did not exist in Athens. The Romans debased their currency again and again. The city-state of Athens, on the other hand, did so only for a short time when silver was in short supply, but it quickly restored the monetary value of its coinage to the pre-Peloponnesian War, pre-plague level. The monetary crisis in Rome, on the other hand, lasted for decades. Between 260 and 330 CE no evidence of banks survives.[24] Rome would not recover financial stability until reforms were undertaken by Diocletian (284–305 CE) and then Constantine (305–337 CE). Diocletian in 295 implemented wage and price controls, increased taxes on land and individuals, introduced a gold currency, and raised the ceiling on interest rates. Currency reforms under these two emperors included new gold coins, and over time gold replaced discredited and debased Roman silver, stabilizing the currency. Diocletian's wage and price controls failed, but new tax revenues put the empire on stronger financial footing, and a gold currency came to anchor a recovering Roman economy in the fourth century.[25] Undoing the damage of dramatic currency debasement took a long time.

The Fall of Olympus

Beyond economics, pandemics drive societal change of one kind or another, with varying implications. The Plague of Cyprian proved to be a factor in a turning point, not only for Rome, beset by a hydra of a third century crisis, but also for an old faith and a new one. A radical new fringe faith — Christianity — would come to supplant the gods of Olympus, who would within a generation or two relinquish their role as active players in human affairs and retreat into the world of myth and ruin.

In 249 CE, the popular Roman general Decius (proclaimed emperor by his troops) defeated Philip, then emperor of Rome, in the Battle of Verona. Early in his short rule, the pestilence that Cyprian has described spread across the empire. As the epidemic raged, the new antoninianus was stamped with Apollo the Healer's image as early as 251 CE, likely in hopes that even Roman money itself could demonstrate devotion to a god whose favor was coveted in a time of disease and death.[26]

Seeking the favor of the gods for the well-being of the empire (along with demonstrations of loyalty), Decius, in the first year of his rule, commanded all within the empire to sacrifice an animal and provide proof of the act by means of a papyrus certificate.[27] An exception was made for Jews, as had been the practice since the reign of Julius Caesar; but a newer sect, the similarly monotheistic Christians, was not exempted. The sacrifice was not optional, and Christians who declined to undertake it were imprisoned or killed.

Historians debate Decius's intentions with regard to the Christians. In an age of polytheism, sects that worshiped this god or that one with particular devotion little minded making a sacrifice to another god or to all of them at once. But the Jews and the Christians operated under a different set of beliefs altogether. Was Decius out to eliminate the Christians? Was he worried chiefly about the favor of the gods? Was he seeking to stop the plague? (The appearance of Apollo the Healer on coinage would align with that last possibility.) Extant evidence — we have only papyrus certificates from Roman Egypt, not the edict itself — cannot settle that question. We are left to infer that freedom from the pestilence was sought with every other auspicious blessing. Decius would rule for a scant two years before he, in turn, died alongside his son and co-emperor in a battle against the Goths.

When the plague brought disease and death, some Romans blamed the pestilence on the Christians and their stubborn refusal to honor the old gods, who might have stayed the plague. Harper reminds us of the Roman perspective: "After all, the Christians' refusal to sacrifice was not only an act of defiance; it imperiled the protection of the gods in the face of the enveloping disaster."[28]

Christians, predictably, saw the situation in an entirely different light. The 13th book of the Oracula Sibyllina, written between 264–267 CE, prophesied the end of Rome amid all the tribulations of the third century crisis, plague included; and many Christians expected the end of the world foretold in the Book of Revelation.[29] The Roman priest and historian Paulus Orosius opined that the plague was God's punishment of the Roman people for their genocide of the Christians (and that God ultimately allowed the empire to be overrun by surrounding tribes).[30]

The persecution that unfolded under Decius and his successors did not squelch Christianity; instead, the Plague of Cyprian and ensuing persecution contributed to its growth. Early Christians, committed to an ethos of love, with their faith fixed on salvation after death, were willing to care for the sick as others were not — and to risk death doing it. Because basic nursing care enhanced chances for survival among the afflicted, Christians were credited for saving lives (though many lost their own and counted that martyrdom), and conversions resulted.[31] The Christian writer Dionysis, quoted in Eusebius's history, claimed a striking contrast between how Romans and Christians reacted to the new disease:

> But when both we [Christians] and they [followers of the old religion] had been allowed a tiny breathing-space [following war and famine], out of the blue came this disease, a thing more terrifying to them than any terror, more frightful than any disaster whatever, and as a historian of their own once wrote: 'the only thing

of all that surpassed expectation.' To us it was not that, but a schooling and testing as valuable as all our earlier trials; for it did not pass over us, though its full impact fell on the heathen ....

Most of our brother-Christians showed unbounded love and loyalty, never sparing themselves and thinking only of one another. Heedless of the danger, they took charge of the sick, attending to their every need and ministering to them in Christ, and with them departed this life serenely happy.... The best of our brothers lost their lives in this manner, a number of presbyters, deacons, and laymen winning high commendation, so that death in this form, the result of great piety and strong faith, seems in every way the equal of martyrdom. With willing hands they raised the bodies of the saints to their bosoms; they closed their eyes and mouths, carried them on their shoulders, and laid them out; they clung to them, embraced them, washed them, and wrapped them in grave-clothes. Very soon the same services were done for them, since those left behind were constantly following those gone before.

The heathens behaved in the very opposite way. At the first onset of the disease, they pushed the sufferers away and fled from their dearest, throwing them into the roads before they were dead and treating unburied corpses as dirt, hoping thereby to avert the spread and contagion of the fatal disease; but do what they might, they found it difficult to escape.[32]

Kyle Harper has outlined, as he sees them, the secrets to the early church's success:

> Christianity's sharpest advantage was its inexhaustible ability to forge kinship-like networks among perfect strangers based on an ethic of sacrificial love. The church boasted of being a "new ethnos," a new nation, with all the implications of shared heritage and mutual obligation. Christian ethics turned the chaos of pestilence into a mission field.[33]

Some years after Decian's death in 251, the emperor Valerian would again demand that the Christians make animal sacrifices to the Roman gods. This time the persecution was systematic. Valerian ordered the execution of the Christian clergy, resulting in the deaths of Pope Sixtus II and countless others, including Cyprian himself.[34] Valerian would confiscate all property of Christians; and if they still refused to convert, they were tortured and exterminated.[35] Many, of course, went into hiding. Ultimately, Valerian was captured in the Roman war with Persia, and the Persian King Shapur I personally oversaw his execution. Upon Valerian's death in 260, his son and successor, Gallienus, halted the persecution of Christians, at least for a time.[36] The Romans had attempted to end the plague in the usual manner, with empire-wide sacrifices, ceremonies, and prayers to the gods. Exterminating Christians did not work, either. The failure of the old gods to save Rome awakened many to the possibility that they were in fact, not real. Christianity, despite the genocide, had not only survived but was rapidly growing. By the end of the third century, perhaps as much as 20% of the population of Roman Egypt (where papyri survive with evidence of Christian names) had converted.[37]

Across history, from the ancient past to the present, we find that pandemics have tended to undermine faith in the authorities of a given age, whether political or religious, when those authorities cannot forestall disease-driven disaster. Pandemics open new space for alternative voices asserting claims of authority, as happened with the radically new religion of Christianity. Equally prominent in societal responses to the Plague of Cyprian were the perennial beliefs that (1) the gods (whether plural or singular) must be angry, and (2) some human party and their transgressions or omissions must be responsible for the damage and the suffering actually dealt by opportunistic microbes, which were then unknown actors. Interestingly, even today, in an age when viruses and bacteria have been identified and their activity broadly understood, these ancient notions about the suffering caused by infectious diseases persist.

The Western Empire Succumbs

While the third century crisis and the Plague of Cyprian did not turn out to be "the Apocalypse" that eyewitnesses of the time thought it might be, it was an apocalyptic time by any measure. Evidence suggests that the Roman Empire mounted a remarkable if fleeting recovery, though the Western Roman Empire would fall to invading forces in the century that followed, as climate change stirred migrations from the east. But before that time, in the fourth century, restored stability enabled economic recovery and stabilization of the currency at last.[38]

The ancient world was changing, and the medieval age was taking shape. We cannot say how much of the debacle can be attributed to the plague, as many forces of calamity beset Rome at once. What can be said is that the plague in combination with civil war, foreign invasions, and climate change forever altered the destiny of Rome's empire and thus the future of Europe. Not many decades later, in 313 CE, Emperor Constantine the Great would convert to Christianity; and in

330 CE, he would move the capital of the Roman Empire from withering Rome to the eastern part of the empire. The city of Byzantium, renamed Constantinople, would become the new heart of an Eastern Roman Empire that would endure for another thousand years. In 380 CE, Emperor Theodosius would officially change the religion of the empire to Christianity; and roughly a hundred years later, Rome would be sacked and conquered by the Germans, in 476 CE. The lost western empire was not forgotten, however. The emperor Justinian, who reigned from 527 to 565 CE, purposed to recover the west and restore the glory of the old Roman Empire. But that was when the first known pandemic caused by the bacterium *Yersinia pestis* precipitated a pandemic catastrophe of even greater magnitude than Rome had suffered before.

---

1. Mary T. Boatwright, Daniel J. Gargola, Noel Lenski, and Richard J.A. Talbert, *The Romans: From Village to Empire* (London: Oxford University Press, 2004), 428.

2. Kyle Harper, *The Fate of Rome*, The Princeton History of the Ancient World 2 (Princeton: Princeton University Press, 2017), 134. Kindle.

3. Cyprian, *De Mortalitate*, 1.14. Cyprian, *"De Mortalitate"* in *Ante-Nicene Christian Library: Translations of the Writings of the Fathers,* trans. Ernest Wallis (Edinburgh: T&T Clark, 1885), 472, https://www.ewtn.com/catholicism/library/on-the-mortality-or-plague-de-mortalitate-11412.

4. Harper, *Fate of Rome*, 141–143.

5. Harper, *Fate of Rome*, 140–141.

6. Harper, *Fate of Rome*, 140–141.

7. Eusebius, *The History of the Church*, Andrew Louth, ed., translated by G.A. Williamson (New York: Penguin, 1990), 235–236. Kindle.

8. Vedran Bileta, "The Invisible Enemy: The 4 Worst Pandemics of the Ancient World," *The Collector,* August 31, 2021, https://www.thecollector.com/worst-pandemics-of-the-ancient-world/.

9. Harper, *Fate of Rome*, Map 12. Indications of Plague of Cyprian, 139.

10. Kyle Harper, *Fate of Rome*, 148.

11. Kyle Harper, "People, Places, and Prices in the Roman World: The Evidence from Egypt," *The Journal of Economic History* 76, no.3 (September 2016): 820.

12. Harper, "People, Plagues, and Prices," 820–822.

13. Harper, "People, Plagues, and Prices," 828–831.

14. Walter Scheidel, "Chapter 6: Contract Labor," in *The Cambridge Companion to the Roman Economy*, ed. Walter Scheidel (New York: Cambridge University Press, 2012), 118. Kindle edition.

15. Sidney Homer and Richard Sylla, *A History of Interest Rates*, 4th edition (Hoboken: Wiley, 2005), 101, 104–105.

16. Christopher Mackay, *Ancient Rome: A Military and Political History* (New York: Cambridge University Press, 2004), 298.

17. "The Reforms of Diocletian and Constantine," in "Byzantine Empire: The Empire to 867," *Britannica*, last updated Jul 5, 2024, https://www.britannica.com/place/Byzantine-Empire/The-6th-century-from-East-Rome-to-Byzantium.

18. Andrew Wilson, "Chapter 14: A Forum on Trade," in *The Cambridge Companion to the Roman Economy*, ed. Walter Scheidel, 289–90.

19. Paul Erdkamp, "Chapter 12: Urbanism," in *The Cambridge Companion to the Roman Economy*, ed. Walter Scheidel, 244–245.

20. J. R. McConnell, A.I. Wilson, Airenzo M. M. Stohl, N.J. Chellman, S. Eckhardt, E. M. Thompson, A.M. Pollard, and J.P. Steffensen (2018), "Lead pollution recorded in Greenland ice indicates European emissions tracked plagues, wars, and imperial expansion during antiquity," *Proceedings of the National Academy of Sciences of the United States of America* 115, no. 22: 5726–31.

21. Kyle Harper, *The Fate of Rome*, 128.

22. Daniel Hoyer, "An Overview of the Numismatic Evidence from Imperial Roman Africa," *ISAW Papers* 13 (2018): 19. http://dlib.nyu.edu/awdl/isaw/isaw-papers/13/.

23. Sidney Homer and Richard Sylla, *History of Interest Rates*, 104.

24. Sitta von Reden, *The Cambridge Companion to the Roman Economy*, ed. Walter Scheidel, 271.

25. See Ann Kordas, Ryan J. Lynch, Brooke Nelson, and Julie Tatlock, "7.3 The Roman Economy: Trade, Taxes, and Conquest," in *World History, Volume 1: to 1500* (Rice University, OpenStax, 2023), and "The Reforms of Diocletian and Constantine," in "Byzantine Empire: The Empire to 867," *Britannica*, https://www.britannica.com/place/Byzantine-Empire/The-6th-century-from-East-Rome-to-Byzantium.

26. Harper, *Fate of Rome*, 154.

27. J.B. Rives, "The Decree of Decius and the Religion of the Empire," *The Journal of Roman Studies* 89 (1999): 135, https://www.jstor.org/stable/300738.

28. Harper, *Fate of Rome*, 154.

29. *Oracula Sibyllina*, 13.133–42.

30. Orosius, *Seven Books Against the Pagans*, 7.22, Internet Archive.

31. Harper, *Fate of Rome*, 155–156.

32. Eusebius, *History of the Church*, 237. Kindle.

33 Harper, *Fate of Rome*, 156.

34. "Valerian: Roman Emperor," *Encyclopedia Brittanica*, last modified April 12, 2024, https://www.britannica.com/biography/Valerian-Roman-emperor.

35. Paul Middleton, *The Wiley Blackwell Companion to Christian Martyrdom* (New York: Wiley-Blackwell, 2020), 48.

36. Charles Pietri. "Prosecutions" in Phillipe Levillain, *The Papacy: An Encyclopedia*, Vol. 2 (London: Psychology Press, 2002), 1156.

37. Harper, *Fate of Rome,* 155.

38. Harper, *Fate of Rome,* 155.

Chapter 7

Eastern Roman Empire: The Plague of Justinian
(541–542 CE, recurring outbreaks through 750 CE)

The Plague of Justinian, which engulfed the Byzantine Empire and stretched beyond, is interwoven with a history so complex that we need to trace the outlines of an entire tapestry of events to contextualize our understanding of the plague's economic impacts. Justinian, who ruled the Eastern Roman Empire from 527 CE to 565 CE, devoted his reign to restoring the grandeur of the empire. In the years before bubonic plague gripped the Byzantine Empire, he spent immense sums from the treasury on the construction of wonders and monuments, including the Hagia Sophia, which remained the world's largest building until 1520. Much of the rest he spent to procure an army that would see the liberation of Rome in 538 CE and eventually the reconquest of much of the Western Roman Empire. Justinian's accomplishments are impressive. Historian Kyle Harper summed them up in *The Fate of Rome*:

> Between his accession in AD 527 and the advent of plague in AD 541, Justinian made peace with Persia, reattached vast stretches of the western territories to Roman rule, codified the entire body of Roman law,

overhauled the fiscal administration, and executed the grandest building spree in the annals of Roman history. He survived a perilous urban revolt and tried to forge orthodox unity in a fractious church, through his own theological labors. By AD 540, only his religious policy could be deemed unsuccessful.[1]

Bent on rooting out corruption, Justinian instituted reforms and reorganized the provincial system, upsetting the status quo and vested interests and thus stirring opposition. And for all the glory, conquest, and construction he undertook, there proved a tremendous cost — a cost in the form of poverty and a neglect of some of the most basic infrastructure.

Figure 7.1 Mosaic of Justinian I, San Vitale, Ravenna, courtesy of Petar Milošević (2015), CC BY-SA 4.0.

Justinian's reign was chronicled by the Byzantine scholar Procopius. In his eight-volume *History of the Wars*, Procopius detailed Justinian's military triumphs, along with other notable events; and in another volume, *On Buildings*, Procopius recounted all the wondrous buildings and other infrastructure that Justinian commissioned, from roads, bridges, and aqueducts to hospitals and churches across the Eastern Empire.

In the officially commissioned imperial history, however, Procopius did not write what he actually thought about Justinian and his wife, Theodora. But when he had finished the *History of the Wars*, he resolved that the whole truth as he saw it (he strongly disliked Justinian) should not be lost to history. He wrote the *Secret History*, a work chronicling what he judged to be Justinian's disastrous mismanagement of the economy. That work details Procopius's own assessment of the monumental economic impact of Justinian's wars of reclamation, and it would remain a secret until after Justinian's death.

The Price of Glory

To fund wars and wonders, Justinian had resorted to taxing the populace heavily. His governors drained the resources of Greece and Egypt. To reap revenue, Hephaestus, the governor of Egypt, not only canceled the government's feeding of the needy but attempted to entirely control the market of goods himself.[2]

> He started by bringing all the shops in the city under a 'monopoly', forbidding any other merchant to carry on this business, and making himself the one and only retailer. Then he began selling commodities of every kind, fixing their prices, it goes without saying, by the authority of his office, so that the city of Alexandria, where hitherto even the very poorest had found every-

thing cheap enough to buy, was brought down to starvation level. They felt the pinch most of all through his manipulation of the bread supply; for he kept all the purchasing of grain from Egypt entirely in his own hands, allowing nobody else to buy so much as a single bushel: in this way he controlled the supply of bread and the price of a loaf to suit his own convenience. So he soon amassed unheard of wealth himself, and at the same time satisfied the demands of the Emperor in this matter.[3]

Even in Constantinople itself, according to Procopius, people suffered as Justinian focused on reclaiming the empire; and that priority, for a time, took precedence over restoring the city's water supply.

The city's aqueduct had broken and was carrying only a fraction of the usual quantity of water into the city. But Their Majesties took no notice and would not spend a penny on it, though there was always a great crowd of people round the fountains with their tongues hanging out, and all the public baths were closed. Yet he lavished money inexcusably on buildings along the shore and other senseless erections, littering all the suburbs with them.[4]

A lack of water for both drinking and bathing plagued the most populous city in Europe and along with food shortages made life in the city difficult for many. The effect in Constantinople was enormous.

Only two things, then, in the way of food and drink were left to those who were utterly destitute and wholly without means — bread and water; and the Emperor, as I have already made clear, employed both of these to make life impossible for them, by making the one much more costly, the other quite unobtainable.[5]

High taxes, heavy-handed treatment of debtors, and the negative impacts of reforms and the downsizing of the civil service on the wealth and power of nobles generated opposition to Justinian's rule; and when trouble erupted in connection with hotly contested chariot races supported by two teams that doubled as proto-political parties, the blues and the greens, a full-on revolt in Constantinople, known as the Nika Riots, erupted in the Hippodrome in 532 CE. This revolt was crushed by Justinian, who ordered the army to massacre all 30,000 of the rioters, mostly greens.[6] There was never again another uprising against the rule of Justinian.

It would be after the Nika riots that Justinian acted to undertake public works in Constantinople and to secure the city's water supply by repairing the aqueduct, which had likely been damaged in an earthquake, and by rebuilding the Basilica Cistern, a magnificent structure with 336 columns that still stands today a few hundred feet southwest of the Hagia Sophia. Procopius would describe this and other important public works in his later work *On Buildings*.[7] But as the building projects took shape and Justinian's army reasserted control over lands previously a part of the Roman Empire, hunger and poverty plagued many.

One Comet, Two Volcanoes, the Shrouded Sun, and a Flea

The impoverishment of the people was unfortunately only the beginning of the horrors that befell the empire and the rest of Europe, and a comet would be understood by many as the harbinger of a coming apocalypse. The comet was likely Halley's Comet, which would have made its return trip past the earth in the 530s CE. Extraterrestrial material found in the Greenland ice, dated to this time, indicates that fragments of the comet struck the earth somewhere in the north.[8] Elsewhere, two massive volcanic eruptions, one in late 535 or early 536 and one in 539 or 540 expelled massive amounts of sulfur dioxide into the atmosphere, where particles would remain for two or three years in each instance, creating a heavy, lasting veil of haze that partly obscured sunlight.[9] The analysis of tree rings by dendrochronologists in the Yamal Peninsula confirmed that the period suffered from extreme climate change.[10] What followed was the most significant climate cooling event in the last 2,000 years of human history. Accompanied by the striking of the comet, frequent earthquakes and volcanic eruptions produced a volcanic winter and an ash cloud that enveloped Europe, lowering summer temperatures by around three or four degrees Fahrenheit.[11] Michael the Syrian described what happened in 536:

> The sun became dark and its darkness lasted for one and a half years, that is, eighteen months. Each day it shone for about four hours, and still this light was only a feeble shadow. Everyone declared that the sun would never recover its original light. The fruits did not ripen, and the wine tasted like sour grapes.[12]

The calamity produced a world without sun — and thus a world without adequate harvests. The starving already taking place reached new levels. Cassiodorus described the impacts of the dimmed light, late frosts, and drought:

> The Sun, first of stars, seems to have lost his wonted light, and appears of a bluish colour. We marvel to see no shadows of our bodies at noon, to feel the mighty

vigour of his heat wasted into feebleness, and the phenomena which accompany a transitory eclipse prolonged through a whole year.... We have had a winter without storms, a spring without mildness, and a summer without heat. Whence can we look for harvest, since the months which should have been maturing the corn have been chilled by Boreas? How can the blade open if rain, the mother of all fertility, is denied to it? These two influences, prolonged frost and unseasonable drought, must be adverse to all things that grow. The seasons seem to be all jumbled up together, and the fruits, which were wont to be formed by gentle showers, cannot be looked for from the parched earth.[13]

The resulting famine became so dire that the Bishop of Milan reported instances of cannibalism.[14] The volcanic winter lasted for a full eighteen months, and from the darkness and the cooler temperatures it brought, another disaster emerged, a pandemic caused by the bacterium *Yersinia pestis,* the plague that would later cause the medieval Black Death.

The cooling period and the disease that followed were, in fact, linked. The flea that carries the plague becomes active in a narrow temperature range between 59 and 68 degrees. The cooler period that lasted until around 550 provided it the opportunity to expand its range as the black rats that were its hosts sailed on ships and hid in carts that clattered across the empire on Roman roads. Without that period of climate cooling, the flea would have stayed put and the plague with it.[15] The Justinian Plague is an early reminder that climate change can create new opportunities for pathogens to find new human networks to infect.

Death Arrives

Figure 7.2 Josse Lieferinxe (1477–1497), Saint Sebastian pleading for the life of a gravedigger afflicted with plague during the 7th-century Plague of Pavia, Italy, public domain.

The bacterium *Yersinia pestis* is responsible for one of the deadliest illnesses in human history. The Plague of Justinian, like the medieval Black Death, originated in China and spread to Europe, Africa, and the Middle East via the Silk Road.[16] *Y. pestis* made its way from the port city of Pelusium in the Nile Delta inland across Egypt, eastward to Palestine, and then westward to Syria and Mesopotamia. It reached Alexandria and then, in 542 CE, Constantinople, where massive grain tributes — 240 metric tons from Egypt alone — were stored in immense warehouses that provided harborage and boundless sustenance for rats, which reproduce to the limits of their food supply. As plague gripped the city, deaths in Constantinople came to top 10,000 per day, according to Procopius. The plague swept across Persia, southern Arabia, Palestine, Syria, Asia Minor, Italy, North Africa, Gaul, Spain, and the British Isles. It penetrated even rural Bavaria.[17]

The disease would come in three forms, depending on how it was contracted. If the pathogen was breathed in, pneumonic plague would result. It would affect the lungs and result in a bloody discharge from the mouth and nose. If the disease was contracted via an infected flea bite, bubonic plague developed, accompanied by buboes, or swollen lymph nodes, that would burst, emitting a bloody discharge. Gangrene would often occur in the fingers, arms, feet, lips, and toes. The plague could also develop into septicemic plague when the infection entered the bloodstream. This form of the infection would result in bleeding beneath the skin, rotting of flesh, vomiting of blood, and a profusion of blood from every body cavity.[18]

During the Black Death in the Middle Ages, both pneumonic and septicemic plague had a mortality rate of 100%; only the bubonic form, with a roughly 60% mortality rate, offered any hope of survival.[19] We cannot be certain that an earlier strain of *Y. pestis* would have had the same mortality rate seen during the later Black Death period; however, the first-hand reports we do have recount a horrendous toll, which may have been more dire in the cities than in the countryside. Kyle Harper has estimated that the population of the Roman world plunged by half.[20]

As an imaginative exercise, consider that should a pandemic of similar virulence and scope happen today, the U.S. population would plummet to what it was in 1953. Though an estimate of the size of the demographic decline caused by the Justinianic Plague and succeeding outbreaks is the stuff of best guesses rather than hard data, archeological evidence of abandoned towns corroborates the heavy death tolls reported by witnesses of the time, such as Procopius, John of Ephesus, and Gregory of Tours.

Fevered Dreams

Among the symptoms suffered by those infected with the plague were hallucinations, the living nightmares experienced in delirium, as Procopius reported:

> Apparitions of supernatural beings in human guise of every description were seen by many persons.... Now at first those who met these creatures tried to turn them aside by uttering the holiest of names and exorcising them in other ways as well as each one could, but they accomplished absolutely nothing, for even in the sanctuaries where the most of them fled for refuge they were dying constantly. But later on they were unwilling even to give heed to their friends when they called to them, and they shut themselves up in their rooms and pretended that they did not hear, although their doors were being beaten down, fearing, obviously, that he who was calling was one of those demons. But in the case of some the pestilence did not come on in this way, but they saw a vision in a dream and seemed to suffer the very same thing at the hands of the creature who stood over them, or else to hear a voice foretelling to them that they were written down in the number of those who were to die.[21]

For many witnesses, death swarmed through the streets with demons and devils. The belief that the devil and demons were disseminating the plague made the pandemic seem even more apocalyptic. Often, the devil was believed to have been set loose upon the people by God as punishment for their sins.[22] Because, according to Ezekiel 28:15–18, Lucifer was cast out of heaven and down to earth, a falling star of sorts, the appearance of the comet preceding the plague seemed later to have been a portent.

Justinian and Theodora were not spared from rumor and blame. Justinian had ordered the slaughter of civilians in the Nika Riots. Those who hated him deemed him the cause of the plague as well. It was rumored that Justinian and Theodora were, in fact, "man-demons," or "blood-thirsty demons," intent on the destruction of the human race.[23] It was said that Justinian's mother had been raped by an incubus, and from this unholy union Justinian was born.[24] Another rumor held that Justinian was in fact possessed and that witnesses had oddly seen his head disappear on multiple occasions and then return to his body.[25] For Theodora's part, she was rumored to have been trained by witches from an early age and to be, herself, a practitioner of the dark arts.[26] Procopius, in his *Secret History*, theorized that the disasters of Justinian's reign, the plague included, reflected God's displeasure with the emperor.

> During his control of the Empire, numerous disasters of various kinds occurred, which some attributed to the presence and artifices of his evil genius, while others declared that the Divinity, in detestation of his works, having turned away in disgust from the Roman Empire, had given permission to the avenging deities to inflict these misfortunes.[27]

It is not unusual for a political leader to be blamed for a plague or other misfortunes. In Justinian's case, it was inevitable, given the suffering and opposition his policies had stirred and the religious worldview of the time. Regardless of the century, people incorporate new developments, including pandemics, into the narrative lenses through which they already see the world.

Devastation

The lamentations of death from firsthand witnesses of the Justinian Plague are poignant and unforgettable. Deaths may have numbered between 25 and 30 million or more, though estimates have long been debated. William Rosen situated the plague in its critical moment in the history of the Eastern Roman Empire:

> The Plague of Justinian, to give both pandemic and emperor their names, killed at least twenty-five million people; depopulated entire cities; and depressed birth rates for generations precisely at the time that Justinian's armies had returned the entire western Mediterranean to imperial control and only decades before Muhammad's followers emerged out of Arabia to conquer Egypt, Palestine, Syria, Libya, Persia, Mesopotamia, and Spain.[28]

The plague would not buckle the empire, but it dealt a serious blow. The effect on the size of the military after the plague testifies to the attrition. The poet and historian Agathias reported in his histories the state of the Byzantine army in 558–559 CE:

> The Roman armies had not in fact remained at the desired level attained by the earlier Emperors but had dwindled to a fraction of what they had been and were no longer adequate to the requirements of a vast empire. And whereas there should have been a total effective

fighting force of six hundred and forty-five thousand men, the number had dropped during this period to barely one hundred and fifty thousand.[29]

The 77% reduction among Byzantine soldiers reflects the magnitude of the impact that the Plague of Justinian had on Byzantium. The hollowing out of the army enabled the Huns to pillage near Constantinople. Remarkably, though, Justinian's army, despite its reduced size, managed to repulse attempts at invasion.

A falloff in tax revenue came with the demographic toll the plague imposed. Given labor shortages, rising wages made it difficult for Justinian's generals to recruit soldiers from the provinces, even in rural areas, such that the Roman army came to depend to an ever-greater degree on foreign mercenaries.[30] Classics Professor Athanasios Fotiou has outlined the plight of soldiers in Justinian's armies, whose pay had not risen for two centuries:

> Rations and pay given to the men serving in Justinian's armies remained practically at the same level since the fourth century; during Justinian's later period, pay frequently fell into arrears; no pensions were given to retired, disabled or killed soldiers unless, according to Procopius, they had a long active service.[31]

Imperial efforts aimed to maintain sufficient revenue — tax collection rather than tax relief continued amid the pandemic. Taxes were based on assets, not income. A law that long predated the plague required the living to pay taxes due on the arable lands of their deceased neighbors. That law became an extraordinary burden during a plague event, but Justinian would delay repealing it until 544 CE.[32]

Despite the plague, Justinian managed to resume his efforts to reconquer Italy and to mount a campaign against Persia and, within a decade, Spain.[33] Justinian's pandemic response was actually quite limited in scope, in keeping with the empire's usual way of operating. There were no steps taken to prepare for the coming of the pandemic and no warnings issued, though reports of plague elsewhere long preceded its arrival in Constantinople. To be fair, there were no known public health measures to take.

Responses were individual: Some people locked themselves away in their homes, while others broke pitchers in the street believing the noise might scare death away.[34] Most public services were the province of the cities, which operated on smaller budgets during the pandemic, economizing on public entertainment and publicly paid salaries.[35] In Constantinople, the dole for the poor — a universal basic income of sorts — met with disruptions when adequate food supplies failed to reach the capital after the plague broke out there, but the dole was restored in full within a few years. Five years later, the amount per person exceeded what it had been before, likely in part because there were fewer people to feed.[36]

The Greenland ice core study that showed precipitous declines in mining activity during the Antonine and Cyprian plagues also found a decrease in mining when the Western Roman Empire collapsed and then once again during the Justinianic Plague.[37] Whatever the state of mining production, unlike his predecessors, Justinian did not choose to debase the currency. (The Byzantine Empire used coins of gold, silver, and bronze.) He did, however, make some adjustments, rolling back a monetary reform that had, in 538, increased the weight of bronze coins used for commerce, replacing those coins with somewhat smaller and lighter ones (though not as light as before the reform). The move kept the value of that Roman coin from changing during the crisis.[38]

Death on a prolific scale temporarily disrupted an economy already strained in service of Justinian's imperial agenda. In an agrarian society, the deaths of farmers impacted planting and harvests. The descriptions from Byzantium, Italy, France, Egypt, the Middle East, and even far-flung Britain are all the same. So many deaths had brought agricultural devastation; crops could no longer be collected; and livestock had also died in tremendous numbers.

Like farming, much other economic activity slowed or stopped during an outbreak. The bishop John of Ephesus described the situation in Constantinople:

> Buying and selling ceased and the shops with all their worldly riches beyond description and moneylenders' large shops (closed). The entire city then came to a standstill as if it had perished, so that its food supply stopped. There was nobody to stand and do his job, with the result that food vanished from the markets, and great tribulation ensued, especially for the people prostrate with exhaustion from illnesses. Only a few were strong (enough) to bring to any bazaar anything worth one obol, but if they wished they took a dinar for it. Thus everything ceased and stopped.[39]

During the height of an outbreak, shops in Constantinople closed. Those able-bodied vendors who still brought food to the market charged six times the normal price. (One dinar was worth roughly 6 obols.) The shortage of food and its exorbitant prices led to further starvation. The bishop portrayed a world in which economic activity of all kinds paused during an outbreak:

> Work of every description ceased, and all the trades were abandoned by the artisans, and all other work as well, such as each had in hand. Indeed, in a city which was simply abounding in all good things starvation almost absolute was running riot. Certainly, it seemed a difficult and very notable thing to have a sufficiency

of bread or of anything else; so that with some of the sick it appeared that the end of life came about sooner than it should have come by reason of the lack of the necessities of life.[40]

The Byzantine capital found itself, like many other places, overrun with corpses, the grim harvest of *Y. pestis*. Justinian addressed the problem by paying for the removal of the corpses himself. This dangerous task found a few volunteers, but the magnitude of the job was so large that Justinian was forced to pay a king's ransom to any individual who was able to carry a corpse. He appointed a minister named Theodoros to deal with disposing of the dead. Theodoros began by enticing people to bring out their dead and bury them in ditches:

> He placed by the pits men holding gold and encouraging the workmen and the common people with gifts to carry and to bring up (corpses), giving five, six and even seven and ten dinars for each load.[41]

Justinian had to pay between five and ten dinars for every cart of extracted corpses. According to John of Ephesus, in some cases the pay of a grave digger during the crisis could reach a wage of 100 dinars.[42] When the number of bodies to be buried exceeded the number that the living could bury, even in mass graves, Theodoros resorted to the extraordinary measure of having Justinian's soldiers fill with corpses the towers spaced along the wall around the outskirts of Constantinople.[43] Even that turned out not to be a satisfactory solution, as the smell of death wafted back into the city. Eventually the dead were taken to outlying areas instead for burial.[44]

The plague resulted in significant labor shortages generally. In 544 CE, wages that had doubled or tripled their pre-plague levels spurred

Justinian to issue an edict to attempt to control them. The edict characterized demands for higher pay as avarice.

> The visitation of traders and artisans and husbandmen and sailors have yielded to a spirit of covetousness and are demanding prices and wages two or three times as great as they formerly received. We therefore forbid all such to demand higher wages or prices than before. We also forbid contractors for building and for agricultural and other works to pay the workmen more than was customary in old days.[45]

Edict or no edict, in the medium term and beyond, agricultural wages, for one, inevitably rose because fewer hands could be hired (or bought); and over time farming methods became more efficient to compensate. In Egypt, the breadbasket of the empire, for example, the wages of unskilled laborers continued to grow. As shipments of grain from Egypt remained vital to the empire and fewer workers were on hand to perform the work, the wages of agricultural laborers grew substantially. By 570 CE, the daily wheat wage became 7.7 liters of wheat per day; by 700 CE this form of payment had escalated to 13.4 liters of wheat per day. The wages of farmers would not return to pre-plague levels until nearly 800 CE.[46] Though demand for food had obviously dropped given fewer mouths to feed, the size of the demographic shock outweighed that reduced demand to keep real wages higher than they had been before. Despite the bump, however, real wages never again reached the peak they had achieved in the mid-second century.[47]

Over time, innovation helped to address the agricultural labor shortage. By the year 600 or so, the moldboard plow had been invented in China and adapted in Europe for heavier soils. Horses pulled the plow, and a "three-crop rotational system" that included the oats needed to feed those horses replaced the practice of leaving a field fallow every other year, netting a gain in efficiency.[48] William Rosen points out that the agricultural revolution in response to the labor shortage helped to set the stage for a population boom once the plague ceased its periodic recurrences in the middle of the eighth century.[49]

Higher wages were not limited to those in agriculture. As economic historians Şevket Pamuk and Maya Shatzmiller observed, wage and price evidence for Egypt beginning in the eighth century indicates that "the purchasing power of the wages of urban unskilled workers in Egypt during the eighth and ninth centuries was much higher than those in Egypt during the Hellenistic and Roman eras."[50]

Meanwhile, as of the eighth century, wheat prices in Egypt remained low relative to wages, and demand for Egyptian wheat had dropped.[51] The same is true for wine. Ancient trash heaps at an archeological site in Gaza offer evidence of the collapse of the Gaza wine trade with the Plague of Justinian. Before the pandemic, sweet wine from Gaza was in demand across Byzantium and even as far away as Britain. Fully 25%–50% of the seeds dating prior to the plague in those eleven trash heaps were grape seeds. But over the two centuries that followed the arrival of *Y. pestis,* the percentage of grape seeds fell to 5%–14%, depending on the trash heap. Other evidence suggests a return to subsistence farming and the abandonment of some sites. Furthermore, trash collection fell off in some cities, and the construction of new irrigation dams ceased.[52]

In Roman Egypt, where a limited number of papyri records survive, the Plague of Justinian seems to have driven cash rents for land lower, as we might expect, because of lower demand given fewer people. Land rents were also paid in kind, however, and those data points remain roughly in line with those that had come before, though at least one was unusually high. There is simply not enough data on land sales (which are hard to compare in any case) to enable any conclusion regarding land prices before and after the arrival of *Y. pestis.*

We also lack records of loan agreements to document variations in interest rates before and after the Plague of Justinian. What we do have is a record of Byzantine interest rate policy. The legal limit for interest rates on loans of various kinds was reduced by Justinian in 534, in his Codex, and those new legal limits remained in place until the ninth century. Justinian reduced the old 12.5% interest limit, which he deemed exorbitant, to between 4% and 8% depending on the type of loan. Yes, interest rates were lower after the plague, but Justinian's action predated the arrival of the plague by years.[53]

As Pamuk and Shatzmiller have pointed out, the data we do have from the Byzantine world is consistent with a significant demographic decline that did not reverse until the latter half of the eighth century, when *Y. pestis* receded, and birth rates outpaced death rates again.[54] The demographic hit assuredly varied from place to place. For example, Egypt and Syria, evidence suggests, suffered a sharper and longer-lasting population decline than Iraq did.[55] Cities likely endured higher rates of illness and death than some outlying areas did, though there were probably exceptions; and where and when and how hard plague hit and hit again remained a function not only of human networks but of environmental conditions. There would have been variations in local and regional levels of economic impact that we will never be able to map for lack of evidence.

The bubonic plague held the world in its necrotic grasp for 210 years. Economic and demographic recovery was stifled by plague's return no fewer than 18 times, on average every 11 years or so, until the year 750 CE.[56] When we think of the medium term following a pandemic (10–40 years, say), keep in mind that in many places recurrences of plague would reset that timeline over and over. Consequently, our focus has to extend beyond what would have, in a far more succinct pandemic, constituted the medium term as examined by Jordà, Taylor, and Singh in the paper that inspired this book. For instance, Walter Scheidel noted that, while plague debuted in Egypt in 541 CE, recurrences followed there as a part of larger outbreaks across the Eastern Mediterranean in 551–552, 567–568, 573–574, 590–591, 599, and thereafter in Egypt specifically in 607–608, 619, 672–673, 689–690, 714–15, 724, 732–735, and 743–744 before a respite of six centuries ensued.[57]

To what degree did the sixth century debut of plague change the trajectory of an empire? In the end, we cannot precisely measure its impact amid other factors. History is always the result of many variables in play. Justinian's rule did not fall apart after the plague struck. And though he caught the plague himself, he recovered to rule until 565, when he died in his bed in his 80s. The empire did not fall apart, despite the harrowing depopulation it suffered. Trade would recover — granaries would be filled again, and shops would reopen. But the pandemic shock and its many aftershocks amounted to a mechanism of erosion that took multiple forms — demographic, economic, and military. In *Escape from Rome,* Scheidel summarized how things went for a weakened Byzantine Empire beset both by repeated outbreaks of *Y. pestis* and by adversaries mounting ongoing territorial challenges:

> Between the mid-sixth century, the high-water mark of reconquest, and the early eighth century, [the Eastern Empire's] territory shrank by about 60 percent, from 1.5 million to 600,000 square kilometers. Effective army strength halved from around 150,000 men in the 550s to 80,000 by the 770s. Fiscal attrition was even more severe: state revenue fell by four-fifths or more between the mid-sixth and the early eighth century. The reason that the latter exceeded the loss of territory and military strength by so much may be sought in the

fact that the lost provinces had also been among the richest. A more generalized economic decline coupled with the demographic consequences of the plague also contributed: archaeological evidence points to de-urbanization and the contraction of surviving urban sites, as well as a dwindling of trade in bulk goods.[58]

Justinian's dreams of a restored Roman Empire eventually succumbed to military campaigns launched by formidable adversaries — the Lombards, the Slavs, the Avars, the Visogoths, the Sasanians, and the Arabs. We are left to wonder whether things might have gone differently had a bacterium not infected a flea that hitchhiked on a rat that stowed away for a bumpy ride down a Roman road where grass now grows between half-buried stones.

Plague would, of course, return in force in 1341 and kill half the population of Europe, returning in waves for a further 324 years. *Yersinia pestis* has left a scar on humanity deeper than any other pathogen has before or since. Fortunately, plague pandemics are now relegated to the pages of history books. Though cases still occur today, modern antibiotics given early in the course of an infection deliver victims from the worst this pathogen can do, whereas various treatments attempted in Justinian's day — from cold water to spells, charms, prayers, physicians' formulations, or a bit of red clay blessed by a saint — never did.[59]

1.	Harper, *The Fate of Rome: Climate, Disease, and the End of an Empire* (Princeton: Princeton University Press, 2017), 203. Kindle edition.
2.	Procopius, *The Secret History,* trans. G.A. Williamson (London: Penguin Books, 1965), 175.
3.	Procopius, *Secret History,* 174.
4.	Procopius, *Secret History,* 171.
5.	Procopius, *Secret History,* 172.
6.	Mike Dash, "Blue versus Green: Rocking the Byzantine Empire," *Smithsonian Magazine,*

March 02, 2012, https://www.smithsonianmag.com/history/blue-versus-green-rocking-the-byzantine-empire-113325928/.

7. "Constantinople's Byzantine Basilica Cistern Reopens after 5 Years of Restoration Works (Photo Gallery)," July 30, 2022, The Archeologist: Civilizations of the World, https://www.thearchaeologist.org/blog/constantinoples-byzantine-basilica-cistern-reopens-after-5-years-of-restoration-works-photo-gallery.

8. Mike Wall, "How Halley's Comet Is Linked to a Famine 1500 Years Ago," NBC News, December 19, 2013, https://www.nbcnews.com/sciencemain/how-halleys-comet-linked-famine-1-500-years-ago-2d11776548. See also Dallas H. Abbott, Dee Breger, Pierre E. Biscae, John A. Barron, Robert A. Juhl, and Patrick McCafferty, "What Caused Terrestrial Dust Loading and Climate Downturns between A.D. 533 and 540?" The Geological Society of America, Special Paper 505 (2014), https://www.researchgate.net/publication/266375665_What_Caused_Terrestrial_Dust_Loading_and_Climate_Downturns_Between_533_and_540_AD.

9. See the conclusions of Abbott et al, "What Caused Terrestrial Dust Loading and Climate Downturns between A.D. 533 and 540?" on page 13 and Sarah Zielinski, "Sixth-Century Misery Tied to Not One, But Two, Volcanic Eruptions," *Smithsonian Magazine,* July 8, 2015, https://www.smithsonianmag.com/science-nature/sixth-century-misery-tied-not-one-two-volcanic-eruptions-180955858/.

10. Sarah Zielinski, "Sixth-Century Misery Tied to Not One, But Two, Volcanic Eruptions," *Smithsonian Magazine,* July 8, 2015, https://www.smithsonianmag.com/science-nature/sixth-century-misery-tied-not-one-two-volcanic-eruptions-180955858/.

11. Zielinski, "Sixth-Century Misery Tied to Not One, But Two, Volcanic Eruptions."

12. Michael the Syrian, Chronicle 9.26.796, *Chromigne de Michelle Syrien, Parriarche Jacobite d'Anrioche 1,* ed. and trans, J. B. Chabot (Paris: Ernest Leroux, 1899), 220–21.

13. Cassiodorus, *The Letters of Cassiodorus,* trans. Thomas Hodgkin (Project Gutenburg Ebook, 2006), 519–520.

14. *The Book of the Popes: To the Pontificate of Gregory I,* trans. Louis Ropes Loomis (New York: Columbia University Press, 1916), 149.

15. William Rosen, *Justinian's Flea: The First Great Plague and the End of the Roman Empire* (New York: Penguin Books, 2007), 200. Kindle edition.

16. G. Morelli, Y. Song, C.J. Mazzoni, M. Eppinger, P. Roumagnac, D.M. Wagner, M. Feldkamp, B. Kusecek, A.J. Vogler, Y. Li, Y. Cui, N.R. Thomson, T. Jombart, R. Leblois, P. Lichtner, L. Rahalison, J.M. Petersen, F. Balloux, P. Keim, T. Wirth, J. Ravel, R. Yang, E. Carniel, and M. Achtman. "*Yersinia pestis* genome sequencing identifies patterns of global phylogenetic diversity," *Nature Genetics* 42, no.12 (2010):1140–3.

17. Harper, *Fate of Rome,* 224–227.

18. "Plague," Mayo Clinic, April 20, 2023, https://www.mayoclinic.org/diseases-conditions/plague/symptoms-causes/syc-20351291.

19. Anna Rovid Spickler, "Plague," Iowa State University, 6, https://www.cfsph.iastate.edu/Factsheets/pdfs/plague.pdf.

20. Harper, *The Fate of Rome,* 263.

21. Procopius, *History of the Wars,* 2.22.10–11.

22. Zachariah of Mitylene, *The Syriac Chronicle,* trans. F.J. Hamilton (London: Methuen & Co, 1899), 313.

23. Procopius, *History of the Wars,* 12.18.

24. Procopius, *History of the Wars,* 12.18.

25. Procopius, *History of the Wars,* 12.20–23.

26. Procopius, *History of the Wars,* 22.26.

27. Procopius, *Secret History,* Chapter 18, https://www.pallasweb.com/deesis/the-secret-history-of-procopius.html.

28. Rosen, *Justinian's Flea,* 3.

29. Agathias, *The Histories,* trans. Joseph D. Frendo (New York: Walter de Gruyter & Co., 1975), 148.

30. Athanasios Fotiou, "Recruitment Shortages in Sixth-Century Byzantium," *Byzantion* 58, no. 1 (1988), 66–67, https://www.jstor.org/stable/44171039.

31. Fotiou, "Recruitment Shortages," 71–72.

32. Procopius, *Secret History,* 20:23, trans. Peter Sarris (London: Penguin Books, 2007).

33. Merle Eisenberg and Lee Mordechai, "The Short- and Long-Term Effects of an Early Medieval Pandemic," in *Perspectives on Public Policy in Societal-Environmental Crises,* Risk, Systems and Decisions series, eds. A. Izdebski, J. Haldon, and P. Filipkowski (New York: Springer, Cham, 2022), 298, https://doi.org/10.1007/978-3-030-94137-6_19.

34. Eisenberg and Mordechai, "The Short- and Longo-Term Effects of an Early Medieval Pandemic," 294–296.

35. J.A.S. Evans, *The Age of Justinian: The Circumstances of Imperial Power* (New York: Routledge, 1996), 164.

36. Eisenberg and Mordechai, "The Short- and Long-Term Effects of an Early Medieval Pandemic," 298.

37. Joseph R. McConnell, Andrew Wilson, Andreas Stohl, Monica M. Airenzo, Nathan J. Chellman, Sabine Eckhardt, Elisabeth M. Thompson, A. Mark Pollard, and Jørgen Peder Steffensen (2018), "Lead pollution recorded in Greenland ice indicates European emissions tracked plagues, wars, and imperial expansion during antiquity," *Proceedings of the National Academy of Sciences of the United States of America 115,* no. 22: 5726–31.

38. Eisenberg and Mordechai, "The Short- and Long-Term Effects of an Early Medieval Pandemic," 297.

39. John of Ephesus, *Chronicle* fragment, in Joshua the Stylite, *Pseudo-Dionysus of Tel-Mahre,* trans. Witold Witakowski (Liverpool: Liverpool University Press, 1996), 80–81.

40. Procopius, *History of the Wars 1,* trans. H.B. Dewing, Loeb Library of the Greek and Roman Classics, (Cambridge: Harvard University Press, 1914), 471.

41. John of Ephesus, "John of Ephesus Describes the Justinianic Plague," translated by Roger Pearse. Posted May 10, 2017, https://www.roger-pearse.com/weblog/2017/05/10/john-of-ephesus-describes-the-justinianic-plague/. See Joshua the Stylite, *Pseudo-Dionysius of Tel-Mahre,* trans. Witold Witakowski. (Liverpool: Liverpool University Press, 1996), 94. This work contains the surviving fragment of the chronicle written by John of Ephesus.

42. John of Ephesus, "Chronicle" fragment, in Joshua the Stylite, *Pseudo-Dionysius of Tel-Mahre,* trans. Witold Witakowski (Liverpool: Liverpool University Press, 1996), 94.

43. Rosen, *Justinian's Flea,* 215.

44. Eisenberg and Mordechai, "Short- and Long-Term Effects of an Early Medieval Pandemic," 297.

45. Justinian, *Novella,* 122.

46. Walter Scheidel, "Real Wages in Early Economies: Evidence for Living Standards from 1800 BCE to 1300 CE," *Journal of the Economic and Social History of the Orient* 53, no. 3 (2010): 453, http://www.jstor.org/stable/20789801.

47. Kyle Harper, "People, Places, and Prices in the Roman World: The Evidence from Egypt," *The Journal of Economic History,* 76, no.3 (September 2016): 828.

48. Rosen, *Justinian's Flea,* 263–264.

49. Rosen, *Justinian's Flea,* 264–265.

50. Şevket Pamuk and Maya Shatzmiller, "Plagues, Wages, and Economic Change in the Islamic Middle East, 700–1500, *The Journal of Economic History* 74, no. 1 (2014), 211–215, https://www.cambridge.org/core/journals/journal-of-economic-history/article/plagues-wages-and-economic-change-in-the-islamic-middle-east-7001500/3A99790607F69D1D7 802907D21455A54.

51. Pamuk and Shatzmiller, "Plagues, Wages, and Economic Change in the Islamic Middle East," 215.

52. Kiona Smith, "Ancient trash heaps reveal the Plague of Justinian's economic toll," *Ars Technica,* July 27, 2020, https://arstechnica.com/science/2020/07/ancient-trash-heaps-reveal-the-plague-of-justinians-economic-toll/.

53. Sidney Homer and Richard Sylla, *A History of Interest Rates,* Fourth Edition (Hoboken: Wiley, 2005), 112–115. Kindle edition.

54. Pamuk and Shatzmiller, "Plagues, Wages, and Economic Change in the Islamic Middle East," 215.

55. Pamuk and Shatzmiller, "Plagues, Wages, and Economic Change in the Islamic Middle East," 213.

56. Samuel Cohn, Jr., "Epidemiology of the Black Death and successive waves of plague," *Med. History Supp.* 2008, 27:74–100, https://www.ncbi.nlm.nih.gov/pmc/articles/PMC2630035/.

57. Walter Scheidel, "Real Wages in Early Economies: Evidence for Living Standards from 1800 BCE to 1300 CE," *Journal of the Economic and Social History of the Orient,* 53, no. 3 (2010): 457, https://www.jstor.org/stable/20789801.

58. Walter Scheidel, *Escape from Rome: The Failure of Empire and the Road to Prosperity,* The Princeton Economic History of the Western World (Princeton: Princeton University Press, 2019), 136–137. Kindle edition.

59. Rosen, *Justinian's Flea,* 212–213.

Chapter 8

The Black Death
(1346–1353 CE, with recurrent outbreaks into the 18th century)

Figure 8.1 Michael Wolgemut, The "danse macabre" from The Nuremberg Chronicle (Nuremberg: 1493), via Wikimedia Commons, public domain.

The Black Death is both the most familiar and the most devastating of all pandemics, an unparalleled season of annihilation and one that every high school student, simultaneously fascinated and repelled by tales of rats and fleas and buboes, learns about in world history class. The first and most devastating outbreak lasted for seven years, from 1346 to 1353. According to various estimates, between 30% and 60% of Europe's population died during this initial outbreak.[1] A 2010 estimate of mortality in England, based on an extensive database, put the figure at almost 50% in that country.[2] Any deep dive into primary sources from the period makes 50% seem a more believable figure than 30%. Precise estimates of mortality have long been debated and will continue to be.

This part everyone knows, at least in general terms. But the outbreaks did not end. Over the course of the next five centuries, plague epidemics popped up whenever and wherever conditions favored the reproduction of the bacterium *Yersinia pestis* and its spread among hosts that lacked immunity.

The Black Death is also the first pandemic for which economists Jordà, Singh, and Taylor had data to enable them to study, with some precision, rates of return on assets. The Black Death provides some of history's starkest set of lessons regarding the human and economic implications of a highly pathogenic pandemic.

The plague was long believed to have originated in Asia, likely China, and moved by way of the Silk Road into the Middle East. In Europe, the story went, it was spread via Mongols of the Golden Horde, who besieged the Genoese port city of Caffa in 1346, catapulting plague-ridden bodies from their own army over the city walls into the city itself to infect the populace, an act of biological terrorism that would cause apocalyptic levels of death.[3] This grim account of diseased corpses launched into the city is no longer universally accepted by historians, though the plague can indeed be traced as far as Central Asia, the heartland of the Mongol Empire. Some scholars even reconsider the rats and the fleas and implicate marmot meat enjoyed by the Mongols instead. Historian James Belich has eyed the trade routes traveled by caravans of camels that bedded down by night on soils disturbed by Kazakh great gerbils that could, like black rats, be carriers of plague-infected fleas.[4] For the purposes of this chapter, however, we are going to refrain from taking sides on the debate, which is tangential to our purpose in this chapter and this book.

In any case, once the plague reached Genoa, it followed the Genoese back from Asia Minor to Italy and spread from there to consume the rest of Europe and parts of North Africa. Primary sources do not, however, suggest that it also ravaged China or India at the time.[5] (That would happen centuries later, in the third plague pandemic.)

Catastrophe

The scale of the human catastrophe caused by the bacterium *Yersinia pestis* is difficult to fathom. Agnolo di Tura, a shoemaker and tax collector, recounted the horror of the Black Death in Siena.

> The mortality began in Siena in May (1348). It was a cruel and horrible thing; and I do not know where to begin to tell of the cruelty and the pitiless ways. It seemed to almost everyone that one became stupefied by seeing the pain. And it is impossible for the human tongue to recount the awful thing. Indeed, one who did not see such horribleness can be called blessed. And the victims died almost immediately. They would swell beneath their armpits and in their groins and fall over dead while talking. Father abandoned child, wife husband, one brother another; for this illness seemed to strike through the breath and sight. And so they died. And none could be found to bury the dead for money or friendship. Members of a household brought their dead to a ditch as best they could, without priest, without divine offices. Nor did the death bell sound.

And in many places in Siena great pits were dug and piled deep with the multitude of dead. And they died by the hundreds both day and night, and all were thrown in those ditches and covered over with earth. And as soon as those ditches were filled more were dug. And I, Agnolo di Tura, called the Fat, buried my five children with my own hands. And there were also those who were so sparsely covered with earth that the dogs dragged them forth and devoured many bodies throughout the city. There was no one who wept for any death, for all awaited death. And so many died that all believed that it was the end of the world.... And those that survived were like persons distraught and almost without feeling. And many walls and other things were abandoned, and all the mines of silver and gold and copper that existed in Sienese territory were abandoned as is seen; for in the countryside . . . many more people died, many lands and villages were abandoned, and no one remained there. I will not write of the cruelty that there was in the countryside, of the wolves and wild beasts that ate the poorly buried corpses, and of other cruelties that would be too painful to those who read of them .... The city of Siena seemed almost uninhabited for almost no one was found in the city.[6]

Every source reports the same horror — the countryside filled with dying animals and city streets emptied of the living but full of the dead. People fell ill and died within two or three days. Varied accounts report that between 30% and 80% of the population in an impacted town or city was dead, that there was no hope, that all was lost. Lamentations penned across many nations voiced the grief of those who had lost their wives, their husbands, their children.

Government Responses

Because the mechanism of spread for the plague — infected fleas carried by black rats (though perhaps not exclusively by that host) — was not recognized at the time (and would not be until the 1890s), efforts to save lives were thwarted. But people assuredly tried. In Italy, the city of Pistoia was the first to implement quarantine measures, in 1348. Aware that the plague was currently raging in Pisa and Lucca, Pistoia's government issued an ordinance imposing an enormous penalty of 500 pence for anyone trying to enter into the city from those locations.[7] The city forbade anyone from entering into the homes of the diseased, even during funerals. Only family members of the dead were exempt from this new law.[8] As the first to implement quarantine protocols, leaders in Pistoia seem to have been aware that certain unhygienic practices might contribute to plague. In this, they were on the right track, as fleas typically laid their eggs in old clothing or bedding. The city's 1348 statute stated that no one was permitted to bring old cloth, linen, or old bedding into the city on pain of the exceptionally high penalty of 200 pence. Any such cloth, if discovered, was to be burnt.[9]

As early as 1350, the city of Milan built outside the city walls a plague hospital — a pesthouse — where the infected and those who were caring for them could be quarantined. Milan's measures were especially strict (three houses were walled shut with their infected occupants at one point), and the mortality suffered there remained comparatively low during the 14th century — under 15%.[10] In 1374, Milan required the removal of anyone deemed infected.

> We wish that each person who displays a swelling or tumor shall immediately leave the city, castle or town where he is and take to the open country, living either in huts or in the woods, until he either dies or recovers.[11]

Milan also required anyone who cared for these victims to wait 10 days after the death of the victim before returning to human society.[12]

Other cities during later outbreaks implemented quarantine laws of their own to attempt to stay the plague. The measures were, however, implemented late and failed to keep the plague at bay. Many cities eventually implemented a forty-day quarantine and attempted to keep travelers from entering the city.

Over ensuing decades and centuries, the Black Death and its reappearances would lead to the rise of plague boards and boards of public health in towns and cities, as municipalities attempted to protect their citizens from the ravages of plague and other infectious diseases. Anne-Emanuelle Birn, co-author of the *Textbook of Global Health*, described the long trajectory of those developments:

> Spurred on by more stringent sanitary enforcement during plague years, concepts of cleanliness and sanitation gradually took hold in Europe's cities. Through increasingly forceful legislation and public awareness, announced via the printing press (c. 1440) and town criers, urban centers began to approach the hygienic standards reached by the Roman Empire more than a millennium earlier. Influenced by neo-Hippocratic ideas on the link between health and 'airs, waters and places,' health boards and many local governments took on more rigorous control of street cleaning, disposal of dead bodies and carcasses, public baths, and water maintenance. By the 18th century, cities began to employ, fitfully, a new environmental engineering approach to epidemic disease, which emphasized preventive actions including improved ventilation, drainage of stagnant water, street cleaning,

reinternment, cleaner wells, fumigation, and the burial of garbage.[13]

Public health advancements reflected learning from encounters not only with *Y. pestis* but other stern teachers. But back in the mid-14th century, as the Black Death ravaged cities and smaller communities, measures that may have saved some failed to save many more.

No Remedy

The efforts of the medical community to stop the plague or treat victims proved futile. Galen's miasma theory of infected air did at least make people wary of being near others that were infected; but balancing the four humors that Hippocrates had imagined — blood, yellow bile, black bile, and phlegm — proved as useless as ever. Bloodletting was attempted, and buboes were lanced, all to no avail. The thinking was that removing the bile or disease would cure the victim, but the practice served only to spread the disease. Piercing the skin could introduce *Y. pestis* into the bloodstream, causing septicemic plague. According to one record, after a bubo had been lanced, a curative tonic comprised of lily, carrots, celery, and human feces would be placed on the wound, introducing additional infection risk.[14]

Ineffective and even harmful "cures" reflected humanity's plight in a time when pathogens were not understood and treatments remained a shot in the dark. Some doctors prescribed mercury and arsenic.[15] One cure involved eating emeralds and other green gemstones.[16] Some believed the feces of a falcon could cure plague, while others thought the ingestion of the gall bladder of an ox to be a guaranteed remedy.[17] Four thieves vinegar was another popular concoction. Made of vinegar or wine and medicinal herbs and spices, the formulation was said to have enabled four thieves to plunder the homes of the dead without contracting the plague.[18]

Folk cures proved less deadly, in many instances, than professional medical treatment did. Some advised the sick to strap a live chicken to a bubo so that the infection would leave them and enter the chicken (as if the plague were a sort of demon that might be happy to move house if given a chicken as an option).[19] From the preposterous to the dangerous, no treatment mitigated the plague.

The medical community, however, did offer one potentially useful piece of advice — to flee as far as possible from anyone and anywhere that was infected. Many people of means did indeed flee, and some survived. But just as many refugees unwittingly brought the plague with them.

A Faith Tested

The Black Death posed an equally formidable challenge for the Catholic church. Fervent prayer did not stop the Black Death any more than desperate medical interventions did. In the province of Canterbury in England, as advised by King Edward III, a concerted effort was made to organize prayer. The Prior of Canterbury issued directions in a September 1348 letter to the Bishop of London:

> Bishops and others in priests orders should celebrate masses and should organise, or have organised, sermons at suitable times and places, along with processions every Wednesday and Friday; and should perform other offices of pious propitiation humbly and devoutly, so that God, pacified by their prayers, might snatch the people of England from these tribulations, of his grace show help to them and, of his ineffable pity, preserve human frailty from these plagues and mortality.[20]

But as people continued to die and the clergy were especially hard hit, given their ministry to the sick and dying, the spiritual authority of the Church was eroded; and alternative religious responses arose independently, gaining in popularity.

Many believed the plague to be the fulfillment of prophecies in the apocalyptic Book of Revelation, for the first judgment of God was said to be a plague of sores: "The first angel went and poured out his bowl on the land, and ugly, festering sores broke out on the people who had the mark of the beast and worshiped its image."[21]

When Genoese ships made landfall in Sicily at Messina, bearing death, rumors of the supernatural proliferated. Michele Da Piazza wrote of the events in his chronicle on the years 1347–1361:

> For demons appeared in the city, having changed themselves into the shape of dogs, and they inflicted much harm on the bodies of the Messinese. Struck numb with terror, no one dared leave their homes. Nevertheless, by the general agreement of all and following the wishes of the archbishop of Messina, the citizens resolved to devoutly process around the city while chanting litanies. And as the whole populace of Messina was entering the city, a black dog carrying a drawn sword in its paw appeared among them; growling, it rushed the crowd and broke silver vessels, lamps, and candelabra that were on the altars, and shattered various other kinds of things. At this sight, everyone all at once fell flat on their faces, half-dead with fear. But after a while the men recovered and got up, and they saw the dog leave the church, but no one dared follow it or approach it.[22]

St. Agatha as well as Mother Mary herself were also believed to have made appearances at Messina to attempt to stay the plague; but disease and death prevailed, and many Messinese fled their city and spread the disease everywhere they went.[23]

As the plague spread across Europe, heretical sects and cults rose in popularity, offering their own answers. Doomsday prophets preached that the end of days was at hand, and the figure of Antichrist gained prominent attention. Rumors circulated that he had already been born. A letter from William of Blofield to a Dominican friar at Norwich reflects the rumors that were stirring among the people.

> There are various prophets in the regions around Rome, whose identity is still secret, who have been making up stories like this for years. They say that this very year, 1349, Antichrist is aged ten, and is a most beautiful child, so well educated in all branches of knowledge that no one now living can equal him.[24]

The doomsday prophets were usurped in importance, however, by the rise of the Flagellants, or the Brotherhood of the Cross, who mutilated themselves seeking atonement for sin, hoping to appease God's wrath. The movement, which had emerged in the 13th century in response to an epidemic in Perugia, gained prominence during the Black Death. Adherents processed from town to town beating themselves in spectacular form. They preached that their self-inflicted penance would save themselves and others from the plague (though they were, in fact, likely enough to carry the plague with them). The Catholic Church, however, had long held that forgiveness of sin came from confession and prayer — never from self-mutilation. As Pope Clement VI learned more about the movement, he found the methods and the teachings of the Flagellants not only disturbing but also a threat to Christianity and condemned the Flagellants and their heresies in 1349.[25]

Figure 8.2 Francisco de Goya (1808), "Los disciplinantes" or "procession of Flagellants,"
via Wikimedia Commons, public domain.

More disturbing than the behavior of the Flagellants and far more problematic was the age-old human propensity for blaming those perceived as the "other" for suffering. Antisemitism, which had long festered in Europe, erupted into genocidal proportions during the plague. Many people believed that the Jews were somehow responsible for the Black Death. One popular conspiracy theory held that Jews were intentionally poisoning wells. It was alternatively believed that everyone was being punished by God simply for the existence of the Jews, or, just as problematically, that because this was the end of the world, the Jews had to be destroyed before Christ's return.[26]

A chronicle from 1349 by a Franciscan friar in Franconia recounted the allegations against the Jewish people.

> Some say it was brought about by the corruption of
> the air; others that the Jews planned to wipe out all
> the Christians with poison and had poisoned wells

and springs everywhere. And many Jews confessed as much under torture: that they had bred spiders and toads in pots and pans, and had obtained poison from overseas.[27]

Antisemitic paranoia was so strong that Germans in some towns blocked up wells and springs so that no one could drink the water or use it for cooking. Residents relied on rainwater they collected instead.[28] Pogroms carried out against Jewish communities engulfed Germany and spread into France and Austria as well.[29] Jews were most often burned, either alive at the stake or in their own homes set aflame after they were walled in by their neighbors. Based on an overwhelming body of evidence, the death toll may have reached the tens of thousands.

For its part, the Catholic Church was wholly against the wanton murder of the Jews. Pope Clement VI made several decrees that Jews should not under any circumstances be harmed. After lamenting the killings and the accusations of poisoning against the Jews, the pope commanded: "We order you by apostolic writing... not to dare to capture, strike or kill any Jews."[30] Regrettably, massacres of Jews continued despite the pope's attempts to stop them.

In their study of the economic and societal implications of the Black Death, Remi Jedwab, Noel Johnson, and Mark Koyama found that there was a significant "protective effect" for Jewish populations in cities where skilled Jews served important functions as bankers, merchants, and doctors. Where Jews were the only moneylenders in town, for example, the Jewish community was safer. Where there were alternatives for such essential services, persecution was more intense. Prior antisemitism in a given area was also predictive of behaviors during the Black Death.

The vicious pogroms not only needlessly destroyed innocent lives; they also squandered human capital — and inevitably with economic consequences. Jews tended to be better represented among the more highly educated and skilled, so communities bent on their elimination lost what their Jewish neighbors had been contributing to society and to the local economy. Across Europe, fully half of Jewish communities in Europe were wiped out, either because their residents were killed or because they were run off. Over the longer term, communities that carried out pogroms paid a high price for succumbing to some of humanity's darkest impulses. Jedwab, Johnson, and Koyama observed, "Indeed, cities that committed pogroms during the plague bore the cost of this for centuries, as their population grew 30% slower each century than did those cities that protected their Jewish communities."[31]

As for the Catholic Church, its powerlessness against the monumental burden of suffering and death wrought by the Grim Reaper now known as *Yersinia pestis* numbered among the factors that undermined its authority in the late Middle Ages. Alternative sects continued to emerge — the Lollards and Hussites among them — as the world stepped closer to the Protestant Reformation.[32]

The Economic Toll of the Black Death

The Middle Ages in Europe had, in the three centuries preceding the arrival of the Black Death, seen at least a doubling of its population. Towns and cities had grown. Life was good for the nobility, given the rights of liege lords, and hard for the peasantry because laborers were many and wages were low. Land prices and rents, on the other hand, were high, as arable land was in high demand. To feed the burgeoning population, marginal lands had been converted to grain production. Bad weather and periodically poor harvests sometimes resulted in famines felt most keenly among the peasantry.[33] On the other hand, though locally produced goods were sold through weekly markets and shops, international trade had expanded to move luxury goods and more. Better roads, better ships, and canals had made long distance transport somewhat more efficient. By the mid-14th century, however, there were pressures for change, especially with regard to political and institutional realities that constituted obstacles for the growth of trade and innovation.

The demographic collapse and economic disruption precipitated by the arrival of the Black Death drove short-term calamity but also structural economic and societal changes that would play out not only over the medium term but across ensuing centuries. So many Europeans died of plague that entire communities disappeared. England lost 1300 villages over the 150 years following the initial outbreak. Isolated Dutch and French farms were abandoned, as were remote villages in Italy and across Germany, where anywhere from one fifth to two thirds of villages disappeared, depending on the region, as plague survivors found reason to migrate in search of opportunity.[34]

The Greenland ice core study, which validated the Antonine and Cyprian plagues as major events, shows the Black Death to have been a monumental pandemic. The average pollution of lead in the ice for the 38 years prior to the plague was 140.31 ng/L during the plague years. This measure dropped by 86.6% to an average of 18.82 ng/L from 1340 to 1371 before beginning to recover. In 1352, the pollution would drop to the lowest point in human history, 0.42 ng/L.[35] This amount of lead pollution in the ice points to this being the least amount of mining conducted in the 3500-year record of the lead pollution study. Mining would not recover to pre-Black Death levels until the year 1500 CE, a full 164 years after the outbreak in 1336.[36]

The most affected industry, however, was agriculture. Medieval Europe was still an ancient economy based greatly upon farming: 90% of the population were agricultural workers or peasants.[37] The booming population in Europe had for generations kept wages low for peasants, and the high population had also kept prices for goods and rent for housing high.

The plague delivered an immense economic shock in the short

term. The shortage of laborers and the subsequent inflation of wages and the prices of products and services is well documented in Europe. When the plague struck, as people fell ill and died, work of all kinds was disrupted, as were markets, so both prices and wages were impacted. As Jedwab, Johnson, and Koyama note in their immensely valuable comprehensive review of research on the Black Death's economic and societal impacts, nominal wages rose sharply as the plague raged; but inflation outstripped those wage gains initially because supply disruptions inflated prices even more sharply. In hard-hit England, then, real wages fell by 20% in 1348–49, while GDP dipped by 6%. In Spain, real wages fell by 9% and per capita GDP by 3.3%.[38]

By contrast, in Florence, Italy, which had incurred an immense death toll and thus faced an even greater labor shortage than England or Spain had seen, surviving unskilled workers actually saw their real wages surge by 87% from 1348 to 1350, while skilled workers earned 27% more in real wages. Given the disruption of work and trade, however, per capita GDP still fell compared to the period prior to the plague, by about 1.5%.[39] Contemporary historian Matteo Villani complained that minor artisans were demanding three times the wages they had earned before the plague and that serving girls demanded a minimum of 12 florins a year while some commanded a salary of 24 florins per year, an enormous wage for a lower-class position by historical standards.[40]

In England, data points to a tremendous inflation in the short term, persisting into the 1370s. The price of grain and drink rose by roughly 55%, according to the British Library of Political and Economic Science.[41] Robert Allen, who created a consumer price index for England spanning the Middle Ages to the early 20th century, found a 27% increase in that index from 1348 to 1350.[42]

At first, the increase in wages could not account for the price increase in goods, but in the medium term — the next fifty years or so — real wages soared because of the scale of the labor shortage.[43]

The average laborer in Southern England would see daily wages rise from 1.5 pence to 4 pence by 1420 before stabilizing at that rate until 1550. The skilled craftsman would see the same trend as wages escalated from 2 pence to 6 pence by 1420 before stabilizing at 6 pence until 1550.[44]

A class-conscious William Dene remarked upon wage inflation in his *Historia Roffensis,* chronicling the situation in Rochester, England.

> Such a shortage of workers ensued that the humble turned up their noses at employment, and could scarcely be persuaded to serve the eminent unless for triple wages. Instead, because of the doles handed out at funerals, those who once had to work now began to have time for idleness, thieving and other outrages, and thus the poor and servile have been enriched and the rich impoverished. As a result, churchmen, knights and other worthies have been forced to thresh their corn, plough the land and perform every other unskilled task if they are to make their own bread.[45]

The labor shortage created a situation where two thirds of the agricultural land in the kingdom, according to Dene, lay abandoned and uncultivated.[46] Surviving peasants in the area rebelled against working unless they were paid far higher wages, and it was rumored among the disgruntled who had to pay those wages that Gog and Magog were supernaturally corrupting the peasants.[47]

The plague shook the foundations of a hierarchical society that viewed particular roles for each class as a part of the divine order. In a time when death might be just around the corner, those whose lot it had been to toil in the fields reconsidered their options, and the old order was upended. For a time, Dene reported, workers from threshers to craftsmen could afford better diets than some of the gentry could. Meanwhile, with farm labor both scarce and expensive, much of the harvest was left in the fields.[48] It is important to note that, given significant work interruptions during outbreaks, the higher wages of the working class did not equate to annual incomes that increased by the same percentage. In England, meanwhile, the nobility saw their incomes erode by 20% from 1347 to 1353.[49]

The short-term economic effects of the Black Death were similar outside of Europe. Egypt was most affected. Ahmad Ibn Al-Maqrizi, writing in the year 1349, informed us that the deaths were so many that soldiers tasked with ensuring the harvest promised agricultural workers as much as half the crop if they agreed to work the land. Often, they found few ploughmen available to work (some had fallen dead with their hands guiding the plow behind a team of oxen), and so the soldiers had to attempt to cultivate the land and bring in the harvest themselves, loading the grain on their horses. They were too few in number and too ill-equipped to complete the job. During this time, only half of the arable lands produced a full harvest. In the administrative district of Nay and Tanan (north of Cairo), a total of 1,557 acres of farmland was left completely abandoned. In many cases, the clothes and household goods of the dead were sold off, so that prices for those products fell by 20%. Artisans found themselves dealing with the disposal of corpses rather than practicing their crafts.[50]

At Aysut (south of Cairo), 6000 individuals typically paid property tax; but once the plague struck, only 106 individuals could pay the tax.[51] In Aysut alone, then, less than 2% of the populace was able to pay taxes. The loss of revenue for the city of Aysut was tremendous. A loss of revenue in taxes would have affected every afflicted territory across Europe and Asia.

In Italy, the City of Florence took drastic action to recoup lost revenue from unpaid taxes. Municipal officials in 1348 stole the inheritances and estates of the deceased for a gain of 375,000 gold florins.[52] Milan, in 1374, issued a similar law that stated:

> All the goods, both movable and immovable, shall
> be put to the use of the lord's treasury. The goods of
> anyone who carries the epidemic from another place
> shall likewise be put to the use of the lord's treasury,
> and no restitution shall be made.[53]

Governments were desperate to make up for lost tax revenue, even, in some instances, at the expense of a plague victims' heirs.

Governments, predictably, also strove to curb the rise in nominal wages. England's 1349 Statute of Laborers succeeded for a decade or so in keeping the lid on wages. A 1351 statute in France regulated both wages and prices.[54] Over the medium term, however, real wages per capita rose sharply over what they had been before 1348. Jedwab, Johnson, and Koyama show real wages in 1400 substantially higher in England, Italy, and Spain than they had been before bubonic plague arrived in Messina.

Agriculture was transformed because of the Black Death. The old regime simply could not be sustained when landowners were competing for labor. They found ways around the laws. St. Edmund's, for instance, provided seasonal rewards and shares of coveted grains as a means of attracting agricultural workers.[55] Though marginal land could be left fallow because there were many fewer mouths to feed, nobles would have no choice but to open their coffers to keep their agricultural estates running. By the 1360s, wages had grown by an astonishing 60%. Despite attempts to control wages, a lord that failed to pay the wages demanded would quickly witness his fields abandoned, so the need forced individual landowners to find ways around the wage laws. Peasants began to seek out the best wage available (even if a fine was involved) and for the first time had some control over their own destinies. Many found better opportunities in cities.

The nobility, on the other hand, initially lost revenue during the

Black Death economic shock as the masses made gains. With a dramatically reduced population to feed, demand for grain fell after the initial pandemic shock, and grain prices dropped rather than climbed, as did the price of land. Over the decades that followed the initial demographic shock, however, less grain was required to feed fewer mouths; and fewer hands were available for planting, harvesting, and processing. Many landowners grazed sheep on their lands instead or diversified crops to include fruits, vegetables, hops, hemp, and flax — all less labor-intensive options than grain.[56]

As historian James Belich has pointed out, though there were fewer hands to do the work, plague survivors had more resources available to them — "carts, wagons, horses, oxen, mules, boats, ships, barns, and granaries."[57] With more resources per capita and fewer hands to do the work, innovations ensued; and various regions began to specialize with regard to agricultural products and goods made from them. While people in many places continued to grow most of their own food, Sicily's grain exports accelerated during the last quarter of the century, while the Baltic region exported timber; manors in Suffolk grew barley for beer; northern regions cultivated hops and flax for linen; more southerly places grew olives, grapes, fruit, cotton, and silk; the uplands of Bavaria grazed cattle and dairy goats; and Castile vastly increased its production and exports of fine merino wool.[58]

In England, the growing wool supply played into the production and trade of less-expensive woolen cloth, while Flemish and Italians began to specialize more in luxury textiles to better compete. English lords slowly shifted away from hands-on management of their lands and from shorter leases of 4–6 years to leases of 10, 20, or 30 years. By 1425, most had handed over the management of their lands to lessees. The leases provided a fixed income for the landowners while tenants kept profits beyond the fixed cost of their leases.[59]

Peasants, meanwhile, enjoying their new economic status, relied less on grain in their diets and could afford meat and other luxuries. While an increase in discretionary income across the board was enough to change consumption patterns and drive a growth in trade, the gains for most were "modest," as Belich described them:

> A few trinkets, a pound or two of meat a week, a larger hut, and sewing your clothes from purchased cloth rather than also spinning and weaving it yourself, was an improvement, but not much by some standards. It varied over time and space. France and other regions experienced devastating warfare over much of the later fourteenth century, delaying the onset of relative prosperity. The Catalan economy declined, at least in relation to neighbouring Valencia. There was a major recession in England in the mid-fifteenth century. Famine still struck, though less often than before the Black Death.[60]

However, to all who remembered how things used to be, the contrast between wages and prices before and after the Black Death remained dramatic. According to Henry Knighton, a canon who wrote his chronicle in Leicester, England, in the 1390s, even the priestly class, whose numbers had been more sharply reduced than those in other occupations, more than doubled the income they required to serve a parish. He noted that, prior to the plague, a parish could hire a priest for 4 or 5 marks; but since the plague, a parish could scarcely find a priest to perform duties for as little as 20 marks. Moreover, in the wake of the Black Death, many who took to the priestly orders were illiterate and untrained.[61] Knighton also reported price inflation occurring in basic goods: "All essentials were so expensive that something which had previously cost 1d was now worth 4 or 5d."[62]

The ruling elite had, of course, launched early on a legal offensive to put the peasants back in their place and to reduce wages or alternatively to tax them more heavily than previously. The Statute of Laborers, which had attempted to fix maximum wages and which ultimately failed to keep them fixed, was a primary driver of the Peasants' Revolt in England in 1381. Although the revolt was crushed, peasants had made large gains that would be the beginning of the end for serfdom. In France, a major peasant revolt occurred in 1358, led by the Jacquerie. Revolts occurred through the 1360s and 1370s in Italy. Samuel Cohn has tallied 621 of them across Europe over the course of the 75 years that followed the initial pandemic shock.[63] In Western Europe, because of the loss of so many laborers, surviving peasants were, for the first time in their existence, important. They used these circumstances to demand higher wages; and if they didn't get those wages, they would simply ignore the fact that they were legally bound to a lord's land and seek employment elsewhere. The lower classes were gaining newfound freedom as opportunities abounded in major urban centers, a trend that would continue over centuries until serfdom was abolished. In Eastern Europe, the story was different: Urban areas were smaller and offered fewer opportunities, while agriculture predominated. In Eastern Europe serfdom expanded over the longer term; and as cities in Western Europe grew, the divergence widened.[64]

Per capita GDP was another story. The initial hurdle was the loss of human capital and expertise, which had to be compensated for over time as skilled workers could be replaced. Over the medium term, per capita GDP rose in England, but it rose and fell in Italy, beginning to regain ground and overtake pre-plague per capita GDP only toward the end of the century. In Spain per capita GDP jagged more downward than upward between 1350 and 1400 and approached pre-pandemic levels only briefly in the early 1550s before it slumped again.[65]

Given a situation where lives were lost but property other than some portion of livestock was not destroyed, per capita money supply increased. In the decades following the massive demographic and economic shock dealt by the Black Death, consumption rose, particularly in Italy, bolstered by people's desire to enjoy life, as precarious as it was, while it lasted. In 15th century Europe, while mining was still recovering, demand for luxury goods from Asia drove an outflow of money sufficient to result in occasional shortages of silver and gold, dubbed by some historians the Great Bullion Famine.[66]

The wealth obtained by peasants was so substantial that some were able not only to upgrade their diets but also to discard their humble workaday attire and dress like nobles in luxury clothing. The increasing share of wealth held by the lower classes was so upsetting to nobility that laws were passed to control what peasants could wear and even what they could eat. A 1363 statute in England, for example, ordered peasants not to wear gold and silver jewelry, expensive clothes, or fur. It also forbade them from indulging in luxury foods.

> Those given cloth for their clothing or stockings shall have cloth worth less than 2 marks a cloth and use no cloth of a higher value, whether purchased by them or otherwise, and shall use nothing of gold or silver, embroidered, decorated, or of silk.[67]

Such laws regulating dress based on status had predated the plague, but they became far more common after the Black Death changed the balance of economic power. Drawing upon the work of Alfani (2021), Scheidel (2017), and Picketty (2017), Jedwab, Johnson, and Koyama summarized the shift in wealth share:

> Evidence suggests that the plague reduced inequality (Alfani, 2020) and was a "great leveler" (Scheidel, 2017). For example, Alfani (2017) shows that the wealth share of the richest 10 percent in Europe was 65–70 percent in

the early 14th century and decreased to about 50 percent by 1450, implying a drop of 15–20 percentage points.[68]

The economic equation also changed for women. As Belich has explained, once fewer people were producing their own cloth and grinding their own grain, women had more time to work for wages. Real wages for women appear to have risen after the Black Death, as they had for men, though pay differentials remained significant. The Florentine silk industry depended on their labor along with that of children. Women also brewed ale in England and distilled brandy in Germany, but when they were successful enough, men tended to take over their enterprises and their profits.[69] Belich, considering the sweep of history, summed up the way of things, evident not only after the Black Death but over and over again:

> This seems a recurrent dynamic in gender history: women respond to a sudden mega-shift in circumstances, whether a great plague or a great migration to a labour-starved frontier, by increasing their economic centrality. Men then rein in women's gains.[70]

The Black Death further shaped the medieval trade and craft guilds that undergirded and facilitated economic activity in the Middle Ages. As it ravaged populations, the plague culled their memberships, requiring that they open to an influx of trainees and ultimately replace-ments. In many places, this process would happen more than once as later plague epidemics ensued. They attracted new journeymen and apprentices from the countryside, stimulating migration from rural areas and shortening the training period required for journeymen; but they also served as gatekeepers to the professions they represented, tending to reserve opportunities, when possible, for the families of existing members, masters of their professions. Traditionally, they had endeavored to keep a lid on the wages they paid and to optimize members' incomes. They acted, too, to control the quality of the goods members produced, for the reputation of the entire guild. The merchant guilds were influential enough to keep rulers seeking revenue in check. If rulers decided to seize money and goods from foreign merchants, merchant guilds proposed to boycott their kingdoms, undermining their access to goods.[71] Guilds enforced their monopolies and lobbied their local governments for privileges.[72]

In the medium and longer term after the Black Death, the guilds accelerated their rise, importance, and prosperity, with merchant guilds tending to enjoy higher standing and greater wealth. This prosperity remains apparent today in impressive and even magnificent surviving guild halls graced in the 16th century and later by exquisite stained-glass windows. In vibrant blues and reds and golds, such windows often portray well-dressed guild members sitting around a great table, with their names and coats of arms arrayed above and below, a dog gnawing a bone in the foreground, and everyday scenes depicting work or other activities fitted into the corners.[73]

The guilds served other functions, too. When the plague gutted extended families and the networks of support that families provided, the guilds took on something more of this role for survivors. Religious guilds rose with the Catholic doctrine of purgatory, the idea being that these groups could, maintaining virtuous lives for maximum results, pray their members out of purgatory and into heaven faster. Even secular guilds adopted some religious roles.

In the wake of the Black Death, the guilds rose to their heyday. Jedwab, Johnson, and Koyama offered evidence quantifying this rise, from the Ogilvie Guilds Database:

> During the periods 1200–1299 and 1300 to 1399 there
> are 1,080 and 943 observations on guilds respectively.
> For the period 1400–1499, however, the number of

observations increases by about 75% to 1,753. In the 16th century, there are 2,814 observations. While these data are certainly not a random sample, the marked increase in guild activity after the Black Death is difficult to ignore.[74]

Gary Richardson has summed up the role of the guilds:

> For nearly two centuries after the Black Death, guilds dominated life in medieval towns. Any town resident of consequence belonged to a guild. Most urban residents thought guild membership to be indispensable. Guilds dominated manufacturing, marketing, and commerce. Guilds dominated local politics and influenced national and international affairs. Guilds were the center of social and spiritual life.[75]

It would be the Protestant Reformation in the 16th century that would ultimately undermine the power of the guilds and outlaw their religious functions. But after the Black Death, the guilds did much to lend stability, create conditions favorable to business, maintain quality, and afford the products and the trade networks that contributed to economic recovery and growth.

The demographic collapse caused by the Black Death resulted in lower real interest rates over time, as Jordà, Singh, and Taylor found to be the case not only in the Black Death but also in the other 18 deadly pandemics and epidemics they studied. Stephan R. ("Larry") Epstein from the London School of Economics mapped the dynamics of that shift in chapter 3 of his book *Freedom and Growth: The Rise of States and Markets in Europe, 1300–1750*. The century preceding the Black Death saw economic growth in Europe constrained by wars and their costs, by heavy dependence on labor-intensive grain production as commodity and sustenance, by harvests that sometimes failed and by resulting hunger, and by the working features of feudal society that impeded the growth of trade and innovation and raised the risk of borrowing. The demographic collapse caused by the Black Death changed the balance of economic power and led in western Europe over succeeding decades to further urbanization, given the demand for labor and greater mobility of the peasantry. Before the Black Death, the jurisdiction of a lord or a town was designed to return rents and other income streams, not to facilitate cost-effective trade; and jurisdictions were many — transporters of goods encountered tolls along roads and at bridges, and transportation costs in general were high. (It made economic sense to trade items such as wine, fine cloth, or spices across great distances but not everyday staples that could be produced locally.)

The Black Death accelerated what would probably have happened anyway: Sovereignties were consolidated in struggles for territorial expansion (a means of extending wealth), and markets in the resulting larger jurisdictions grew larger and became more integrated; higher GDP per capita in some regions (Northern Italy and England, for instance) fueled consumption and enabled innovation and regional specialization both in rural areas and in towns; trade barriers fell as consolidation occurred; and trade became more integrated, trimming costs. Return on capital improved. As financial markets matured, legal systems evolved to better hold borrowers, whether monarchs or republics or individuals, accountable for repaying debts. As all this happened, opportunity grew and risk fell, and borrowing costs fell with lower risk.[76] Epstein described the dramatic shift:

> Probably the most remarkable evidence of structural improvements after the Black Death comes from the collapse in public and private interest rates. The decades after the Black Death saw a major change of trend in

European interest rates, which set in motion a gradual decline in the real cost of capital that lasted up to the eighteenth century. Interest rates paid by larger monarchies dropped from 20–30 per cent before the Black Death to 8–10 per cent in the early sixteenth century, and from 15 to 4 per cent in the more advanced Italian, German and Netherlands cities over the same period. The development is particularly striking because it took place at a time of increasing warfare and of increased political and commercial insecurity.[77]

Epstein likewise noted a decline in interest rates for individuals.

The fall in the expected rates of return and cost of capital for individuals was nearly as impressive. The cost of capital in England declined from a rate of 9.5–11 per cent which had prevailed between 1150 and 1350, to 7 per cent in the half century after the Black Death and to only 4.5 per cent by the late fifteenth century; proportionally similar gains occurred elsewhere in Europe. By the second half of the fifteenth century, Europeans were enjoying a huge 'free lunch' consisting of a more than doubling in the amount of capital available per person. The effect will have been a massive substitution of capital for labour.[78]

In a 2022 NBER working paper, Kenneth S. Rogoff, Barbara Rossi, and Paul Schmelzing investigated long-maturity real interest rates spanning the 14th century through 2021. They found the Black Death to be one of two "structural breaks" (along with the triple 1557 defaults of Spain, France, and the States General) in real interest rate trends that "can be plausibly linked to major combined political-economic shocks — but not per se to institutional innovations (such as the founding of central banks), sovereign default events alone, or foreign exchange (FX) regime changes — and generally fail to be associated with major monetary policy events...."[79] Global real interest rates had risen through the first half of the 14th century and rose further immediately after the first immense mortality event but then began to fall in the medium term and beyond over the next 700 years, an average of 1.6 basis points per century.[80]

Jordà, Singh, and Taylor examined the singularly enormous economic impacts of the Black Death in their 2020 paper on the medium-term impacts of pandemics and epidemics; but when they crunched numbers and created charts to generate findings that appear to apply to pandemics in general, they omitted two especially destructive outliers — the Black Death and the 1918 pandemic (which we will discuss in Part 3). They wanted to be sure that these two exceptionally deadly pandemics did not obscure or distort the impacts of others. They noted, however, that "the Black Death induced labor scarcity in the European economy and pushed real wages up. In equilibrium, this went hand in hand with lower returns to capital."[81] Citing two papers by Gregory Clark, they summarized:

> This shock left England with a 25% to 40% drop in labor supply, a roughly 100% increase in real wages, and a decline in rates of return on land from about 8% to 5% (Clark, 2007, 2010). But it is an open question how representative the macroeconomic responses in the case of the Black Death are of large pandemics in general.[82]

Snarled supply chains, initially rampant inflation, labor short-ages, and resulting higher wages and prices (along with attempts to manage these), segued over time to lower prices (for land especially, since demand for food crops had been slashed with the size of the population) and to lower borrowing costs in the medium term and beyond. Increased mobility, institutional changes, and lower trade costs ultimately led to innovation and economic growth in an era no longer bound to the manorial system. In short, the medieval world had to reinvent itself in the wake of the plague. It could not return to the past but had to find its way forward in a radically changed world. To borrow an image from Leonard Cohen, it was precisely through the gaping cracks that the plague had hammered into the old world that light illuminating new possibilities would emerge.

To say that is assuredly not to weigh the evidence and draw the conclusion that a deadly plague was, on balance, a positive development. It was a horrific, cataclysmic development that delivered immeasurable griefs and an enormous economic shock with lasting repercussions.

Positive economic results unfolded specifically when certain changes occurred. When a modest increase in per capita income for the many afforded enough discretionary income to drive new demand, that increase encouraged expanded trade, and trade grew. When institutional changes and political changes made long-distance trade less costly, trade accelerated, and economies recovered. When means, opportunity, mobility, creative problem-solving, strategic collaboration, and specialization emerged as the tools at hand to achieve success, a middle class rose; and the world edged away from feudalism, which relied on the subjugation of a huge peasant class, toward capitalism. When more work needed doing than there were hands to do, innovations resulted, whether a better plow or greater use of work animals or a printing press to replace an army of scribes or a greater array of iron tools or sailing ships propelled by winds rather than men toiling at oars. When greater accountability for honoring property rights and paying debts drove the risk of borrowing down, interest rates fell with diminished risk and greater certainty of achieving returns on investments. These were, in fact, the mechanisms that helped a decimated population find its way forward.

Some historians have argued that many changes were poised to happen even if the plague had not arrived. We cannot argue that counterfactual. The cataclysm caused by the Black Death simply meant that *there was no going back to what had been before, no matter who was deeply invested in doing so: Demographic changes precluded that option.*

Aftershocks

As for *Y. pestis,* that Grim Reaper, the plague continued to stall a demographic recovery for the better part of 150 years, and it would be joined by the likes of influenza, typhus, and smallpox. The first outbreak of plague had been the most devastating time of death in world history; but for centuries after, the plague returned intermittently in both Europe and the Middle East. Major outbreaks struck in 1360–63, 1374, 1400, 1438–39, 1456–57, 1464–66, 1481–85, 1500–03, 1518–31, 1544–48, 1563–66, 1573–88, 1596–99, 1602–11, 1623–40, 1644–54, and 1664–67.[83] After the plague's initial onslaught in Europe, the return of Y. *pestis* would mostly take the form of incredibly deadly but localized outbreaks. Some of the most devastating recurrences took place in the years 1360–1363, which saw lead emissions from the Greenland ice core study fall to the second lowest level ever recorded. Emissions that had already seen the largest drop on record with the initial outbreak of the Black Death plunged even further. An 83% drop occurred in these years, from 4.6 ng/L down to 0.8 ng/L.[84] This was not the only reoccurrence large enough to be visible in the geological record. After the mining sector recovered from the initial pandemic, major recurrences in the years 1438, 1456 and 1464 saw lead emissions drop by 98% down to 2.9 ng/L.[85]

In the 1970s, J.N. Biraben found written evidence of at least 5,659 outbreaks in Western Europe from 1500 to 1749.[86] This figure represents outbreaks in towns but underrepresents rural outbreaks, and it is not geographically comprehensive, but it does point to the extent to which bubonic plague remained a fact of life — and, all too often, death.[87] Some of these localized eruptions of plague would prove just as fatal as the original outbreak. Venice lost half its population in a 1553 outbreak and another third of its population in a 1567 plague epidemic. Milan would suffer a similar blow in 1629. In the same outbreak, known as the Italian Plague, fair Verona lost 61% of its population.[88] The 1656 Plague of Naples claimed the lives of half the population in the City of Naples and around a third across the kingdom.[89] A similar horror struck the English capital in 1665: Around 20% of the populace died in the Great Plague of London.[90] The Great Northern War, which lasted from 1700–1721, would see a major outbreak of plague across Europe that in some cities would kill over half the people. The Great Plague of Marseille in 1722 killed approximately half the people of Marseille and Toulon.[91]

Plague outbreaks caused by *Y. pestis* would recur into the eighteenth century in Europe and then surface to cause a third plague pandemic in China in the 19th century, which spread to India and beyond. In China and India *Y. pestis* again caused millions of deaths — but only hundreds in parts of the world where the deadly bacterium had culled humanity again and again over preceding centuries. When we speak of the economic impacts of the Black Death, then we are not speaking only of the impacts of a pandemic of succinct duration, such that there is a neat short-term, medium-term, and long-term set of outcomes driven only by a single, succinct demographic collapse. In human history, all-at-once-and-done pandemics have not been the rule of thumb. Each pathogen capable of causing a pandemic or epidemic does so in concert with other factors, and the whole concatenation — from microorganism to vectors to environmental conditions to human systems and effective or ineffective responses — results in a different trajectory and timeline of disease and death.

1.   John Kelly, *The Great Mortality* (New York: Harper Collins Publishers, 2005), 11–12.
2.   James Belich, "The Black Death and European Expansion," Faculty of History, University of Oxford, 2014, last accessed June 7, 2024, https://www.history.ox.ac.uk/black-death-and-european-expansion.
3.   Gabriele de Mussis, "Historia de Morbo," in Rosemary Horrox, *The Black Death* (Manchester: Manchester University Press, 1994), 17.
4.   James Belich, *The World the Plague Made: The Black Death and the Rise of Europe* (Princeton: Princeton University Press, 2022), Chapters II and III. Kindle edition.
5.   George D. Sussman, "Was the Black Death in India and China?" *Bulletin of the History of Medicine* 85, no. 3 (Fall 2011): 319–355, https://muse.jhu.edu/article/456167/pdf.
6.   William M. Bowsky, *The Black Death: A Turning Point in History?* (New York: Holt, Rinehart and Winston, 1971), 13–14.
7.   "Gli Ordinamenti Sanitari del Comune di Pistoia contro la Pestilenza del 1348," A. Chiappelli, ed., Archivio Storico Italiano, series 4, (1887), in Horrox, *The Black Death*, 195.
8.   "Gli Ordinamenti Sanitari del Comune di Pistoia contro la Pestilenza del 1348," in Horrox, *The Black Death*, 195.
9.   "Gli Ordinamenti Sanitari del Comune di Pistoia contro la Pestilenza del 1348," in Horrox, *The Black Death*, 195.
10.   Joshua R. Mark, "Medieval Cures for the Black Death," *World History Encyclopedia*, April 15, 2020, https://www.worldhistory.org/article/1540/medieval-cures-for-the-black-death/.
11.   "Rerum Italicarum Scriptores XVIII, Milan, 1731, col. 82," Chronicon Regiense, ed. and L. A. Muratori, in Horrox, *The Black Death*, 203.
12.   "Rerum Italicarum Scriptores XVIII, Milan, 1731, col. 82," Chronicon Regiense, ed. and L. A. Muratori, in Horrox, *The Black Death*, 203.
13.   Anne-Emanuelle Birn, "How Did the Plague Impact Health Regulation?" *OUPblog, Oxford University Press*, March 20, 2018, https://blog.oup.com/2018/03/plague-impact-health-regulation/.
14.   Roger French, *Canonical Medicine: Gentile da Foligno and Scholasticism* (Boston: Brill Publishing, 2001), 293.
15.   French, *Canonical Medicine*, 291.
16.   French, *Canonical Medicine*, 308.
17.   French, *Canonical Medicine*, 309–310.
18.   Mark, "Medieval Cures for the Black Death." (Recipes abound.)
19.   Erik A. Heinrichs, "The Live Chick Treatment for Buboes: Trying a Plague Cure in Medieval and Early Modern Europe," *Bulletin of the History of Medicine* 91, no. 2 (Summer

2017): 210–232, https://muse.jhu.edu/article/66548

20. Letter from the Prior of Christchurch, Canterbury to the Bishop of London, September 28, 1348, "Terribilis," in Horrox, *The Black Death*, 114.

21. Rev 16:2 NIV.

22. Michele da Piazza, "Chronica," in Horrox, *The Black Death*, 38.

23. Michele da Piazza, "Chronica," in Horrox, *The Black Death*, 36–38.

24. Robert E. Lerner, "The Black Death and Western European Eschatological Mentalities," *American Historical Review* LXXXVI (1981): 552.

25. Toke, Leslie, "Flagellants," in *The Catholic Encyclopedia 6, ed. Charles George Hebermann, et al.* (New York: Robert Appleton Company, 1909), http://www.newadvent.org/cathen/06089c.htm.

26. Horrox, *The Black Death*, 110.

27. J. G. Meuschen, ed., *Hermanni Gygantis, ordinis fratrum minorum, Flores Temporum seu Chronicon Universale ab Orbe condito ad annum Christi MCCCXLIX* (Leiden, 1750), 138–139.

28. J. G. Meuschen, ed., *Hermanni Gygantis, ordinis fratrum minorum, Flores Temporum seu Chronicon Universale ab Orbe condito ad annum Christi MCCCXLIX*, 139.

29. J. F. Boehmer, ed., *Fontes Rerum Germanicarum*, 4 vols., Stuttgart, 1843–68, IV 68–71.

30. S. Simonsohn, ed., *The Apostolic See and the Jews vol 1 Documents: 492–1404* (Toronto: Pontifical Institute of Medieval Studies; Studies and Texts 94, 1988), 373.

31. Remi Jedwab, Noel D. Johnson, and Mark Koyama, "The Economic Impact of the Black Death," *Journal of Economic Literature* 60, no. 1 (March 2022): 147–148, https://www.aeaweb.org/articles?id=10.1257/jel.20201639. (The 2020 version is online at https://www2.gwu.edu/~iiep/assets/docs/papers/2020WP/JedwabIIEP2020-14.pdf. All references, however, are to the 2022 version.) See also Noel D. Johnson and Mark Koyama, *Persecution and Toleration: The Long Road to Religious Freedom* (New York: Cambridge University Press, 2019), 111–117.

32. Johnson and Koyama, *Persecution and Toleration*, 118.

33. David Routt, "The Economic Impact of the Black Death," *Economic History Association*, July 20, 2008, https://eh.net/encyclopedia/the-economic-impact-of-the-black-death/.

34. Routt, "Economic Impact of the Black Death."

35. Alexander F. More, et al, "Next-generation ice core technology reveals true minimum natural levels of lead (Pb) in the atmosphere: Insights from the Black Death," *GeoHealth* 1, no. 4 (May 2017): Supplementary Evidence Data Set S3, https://agupubs.onlinelibrary.wiley.com/doi/full/10.1002/2017GH000064.

36. J. R. McConnell, A.I. Wilson, Airenzo M. M. Stohl, N.J. Chellman, S. Eckhardt, E. M. Thompson, A.M. Pollard, and J.P. Steffensen (2018), "Lead pollution recorded in Greenland ice indicates European emissions tracked plagues, wars, and imperial expansion during antiquity," *Proceedings of the National Academy of Sciences of the United States of America* 115, no. 22: 5726–31.

37. Kelly, *The Great Mortality*, 17.

38. Jedwab, et al., "The Economic Impact of the Black Death," 141–142.

39. Jedwab, et. al, "The Economic Impact of the Black Death," 143.

40. Kelly, *The Great Mortality*, 284.

41. John H. Munro, "Before and after the Black Death: money, prices, and wages in fourteenth-century England," University of Toronto, Department of Economics, April 2004. Troels Dahlerup and Per Ingesman, *New Approaches to the History of Late Medieval and Early Modern Europe. Historisk-filosofiske Meddeleser 104* (Copenhagen: Royal Danish Academy of Sciences and Letters, 2009), 350.

42. Robert Allen, "The Great Divergence in European Wages and Prices from the Middle Ages to the First World War," *Explorations in Economic History* 38, no. 4 (October 2001): 411–47, cited in Jedwab, et al., "The Economic Impact of the Black Death," 143.

43. Jedwab, et al., "The Economic Impact of the Black Death," 142.

44. H. P. Brown and S. A. Hopkins, *Perspective of Wages and Prices* (London: Methuen, 1981), 3.

45. William de la Dene, "Historia Rofensis," in Horrox, *The Black Death*, 70.

46. William de la Dene, "Historia Rofensis," in Horrox, *The Black Death*, 72.

47. William de la Dene, "Historia Rofensis," in Horrox, *The Black Death*, 70–73.

48. William de la Dene, "Historia Rofensis," in Horrox, *The Black Death*, 70–73.

49. Routt, "The Economic Impact of the Black Death."

50. Ahmad Ibn Ali al-Maqrizi, "A History of the Ayyubids and Mamluks," in *The Black Death: The Great Mortality of 1348–1350,* ed. John Aberth, second edition (Boston: Bedford Publishing, 2017), 70–71.

51. al-Maqrizi, "A History of the Ayyubids and Mamluks," in *The Black Death*: Aberth, 71.

52. Kelly, *The Great Mortality*, 111.

53. Chronicon Regiense, ed. and L. A. Muratori, "Rerum Italicarum Scriptores XVIII, Milan, 1731, col. 82," in Horrox, *The Black Death*, 203.

54. Jedwab, et al., "The Economic Impact of the Black Death," 143.

55. Routt, "The Economic Impact of the Black Death."

56. Routt, "The Economic Impact of the Black Death."

57. Belich, *The World the Plague Made*, 88.

58. Belich, *The World the Plague Made*, 88–89, 91.

59. Routt, "The Economic Impact of the Black Death."

60. Belich, *The World the Plague Made,* 103.

61. John of Reading, "Chronica Johannis de Reading et Anoymi Cantauriensis 1346–1367," in Horrox, *The Black Death, The Black Death*, 78–79.

62. John of Reading, "Chronica Johannis de Reading et Anoymi Cantauriensis 1346–1367," in Horrox, *The Black Death*, 80.

63. Samuel K. Cohn, *Lust for Liberty: The Politics of Social Revolt in Medieval Europe, 1200–1426, Italy, France, and Flanders* (Cambridge: Harvard University Press, 2006), 228; cited in Belich, *The World the Plague Made,* 98.

64. Jedwab, et. al., "The Economic Impact of the Black Death," 162–164.

65. Jedwab, et al., "The Economic Impact of the Black Death," 142.

66. Jedwab, et al., "The Economic Impact of the Black Death," 145.

67. "Sumptuary Legislation, 1363. Statues of the Realm I, 380," in Horrox, *The Black Death*, 340.

68. Jedwab, et al., "The Economic Impact of the Black Death," 153.

69. Belich, *The World the Plague Made,* 97.

70. Belich, *The World the Plague Made,* 98.

71. Gary Richardson, "Medieval Guilds," Economic History Association, March 16, 2008, https://eh.net/encyclopedia/medieval-guilds/.

72. Jedwab, et al., "The Economic Impact of the Black Death," 165.

73. Virginia Raguin, "Windows on the Working Class," *Different Visions: New Perspectives on Medieval Art* 10 (2023): 1–31, https://differentvisions.org/wp-content/uploads/sites/1356/2023/09/Windows-on-the-Working-Class.pdf.

74. Jedwab, et al., "The Economic Impact of the Black Death," 165.

75. Gary Richardson, "Medieval Guilds."

76. Stephan R. Epstein, *Freedom and Growth: The Rise of States and Markets in Europe* (New York: Routledge, 2001), Chapter 3: "The Late Medieval Crisis as an Integration Crisis," 69–110.

77. Epstein, *Freedom and Growth,* 95.

78. Epstein, *Freedom and Growth,* 95.

79. Kenneth S. Rogoff, Barbara Rossi, and Paul Schmelzing, (2022), "Long-Run Trends in Long-Maturity Real Rates 1311–2021," Working Paper 30475, National Bureau of Economic Research, 4, https://www.nber.org/system/files/working_papers/w30475/w30475.pdf.

80. Rogoff, et al., "Long-Run Trends in Long-Maturity Real Rates 1311–2021," 12.

81. Jordà, Singh, and Taylor, "Longer-Run Economic Consequences of Pandemics," *The Review of Economics and Statistics* 104, no. 1 (January 2022): 166–175.

82. Jordà, et al., "Longer-Run Economic Consequences of Pandemics," 166. The authors cite two papers by Gregory Clark: "The long march of history: Farm wages, population, and economic growth, England 1209–1869," *Economic History Review* 60, no. 1 (2007): 97–135; and "The macroeconomic aggregates for England, 1209–2008," *Research in Economic History* 27 (2010): 51–140.

83. Jo N. Hays, *Epidemics and Pandemics: Their Impacts on Human History* (Denver: ABC CLIO, 2005), 46. Kindle edition.

84. More, et al., "Next-generation ice core technology," Supplementary Evidence Data Set S3.

85. More, et al., "Next-generation ice core technology," Supplementary Evidence Data Set S3.

86. Jean-Noël Biraben, *Les hommes et la peste en France et dans les pays Europeens et Mediterranees* (Berlin: De Gruyter Mouton, 1975), 363–374.

87. Joris Roosen and Daniel R. Curtis, "Dangers of Noncritical Use of Historical Plague Data," *Emerging Infectious Diseases* 24, no. 1 (January 2018): 103–110, https://www.ncbi.nlm.nih.gov/pmc/articles/PMC5749453/.

88. Hays, *Epidemics and Pandemics,* 103.

89. Guido Alfani, "Plague in Seventeenth-Century Europe and the Decline of Italy: An Epidemiological Hypothesis," *European Review of Economic History* 17 (June 2013): 417.

90. "The Great Plague of London, 1665," Contagion: Historical Views of Diseases and Epidemics, CURIOSity Collections, Harvard Library, last accessed June 7, 2024, https://curiosity.lib.harvard.edu/contagion/feature/the-great-plague-of-london-1665.

91. Hays, *Epidemics and Pandemics,* 136–137.

PART 3

Three Modern Pandemics and the U.S. Federal Reserve

Introduction

I n Part 3, we examine how the Federal Reserve, since its formation
in 1913, has dealt with pandemics and their economic impacts.
What we find is a central bank whose role has, over the years, expanded
beyond its narrow initial focus on preventing a repeat of the Banking
Panic of 1907. As it has evolved, the Fed has come to understand the
economic shocks that pandemics deliver, and it has come to embrace
a broader role in ensuring financial stability and shielding the U.S.
economy from the worst that a global onslaught of infectious disease
can do.

Six pandemics have swept the globe since the Fed was formed.
The 1918–1922 H1N1 influenza pandemic (dubbed the Spanish flu)
is estimated to have killed 25–50 million people globally, including
some 675,000 people in the United States. Though the Fed worked
with the Treasury to finance the war effort in World War I through
the sale of Liberty Bonds, it did not act specifically to mitigate the
economic impacts of the 1918 pandemic. It functioned as a reserve
bank for banks alone, not directly for individuals or businesses hit
hard by pandemic disruptions. Its support for the financial health
of the country during a pandemic shock remained limited and
indirect — merely a function of its original vision for protecting
the banking system.[1]

The 1957–1958 H2N2 influenza pandemic (dubbed the Asian flu)
killed between one and two million people worldwide. Between 70,000
and 116,000 Americans died, according to CDC estimates. While the
Asian flu saw the first effort in the U.S. to develop a vaccine designed
to offer protection against a novel pandemic flu strain, it was not
the occasion for a paradigm shift in the Fed's thinking, under the

leadership of William McChesney Martin, Jr., about its role in pandemic response.

The same would be true in 1968, when a vaccine arrived too late to do much good against what was probably a mutated strain of the 1957 flu. The 1968 H3N2 influenza pandemic (dubbed the Hong Kong flu) is estimated to have killed one to four million people globally, including more than 100,000 in the United States.

The long-burning HIV/AIDS pandemic, which first erupted in 1981, killed 36 million people globally through 2022, according to CDC estimates, including more than 700,000 people in the U.S.[2] That pandemic, often termed an epidemic because its most damaging impacts have been concentrated in particular regions and particular populations, hitting especially hard among gay men and minorities, drove high medical costs and more than quadruple those costs in mortality-related productivity losses.[3] The President's Emergency Plan for AIDS Relief (PEPFAR), launched by the George W. Bush administration in 2003, marked a whole-of-government response in an effort to bring the AIDS epidemic under control and to strengthen global health systems and global economic security.[4] The program is estimated to have saved 25 million lives. Brookings estimates that the funding also resulted in a 13% rise in employment among men in sub-Saharan Africa relative to control countries who did not receive PEPFAR funding.[5] Because the HIV/AIDS pandemic did not impact everyone everywhere all at once the way an influenza pandemic does, it is easy to forget the lessons the world learned from the effectiveness of PEPFAR.

Again, however, HIV/AIDS was not a pandemic in which the Fed found reason to act. The economic costs and losses were high but incurred over years; and in the U.S. they fell short of an economic shock of sufficient magnitude to require monetary policy intervention. They have more in common with the burden-of-care costs and productivity losses that long COVID will continue to entail, as a drag on the economy and the labor market. We believe that the world will be in a better position to assess the comparisons between the two afflictions and their economic consequences within the next few years.

The 2009 H1N1 influenza pandemic was dubbed *swine flu* at the time because it contained a reassortment of genetic material from the human H1N1 influenza virus and swine and avian influenza viruses. Though the highly contagious virus spread swiftly around the world, thanks to air travel, and infected perhaps 20% of the global population, its case fatality rate was relatively low. Statistical models suggest that the 2009 pandemic killed between 284,500 and 575,400 people globally.[6]

The COVID-19 pandemic, caused by the SARS-CoV-2 virus, swept the world in 2020 and had claimed almost seven million lives as of September 2023, including 1.13 million in the U.S., according to Our World in Data.[7] By the spring of 2021, the pandemic was an "everyone everywhere all at once" shock. By that point, post-1918 and post-1957 Fed studies and other works had grokked the economic impacts that past pandemics had delivered. The Fed and its leaders had realized that epidemics and pandemics were economic shocks and sources of financial shock. Pandemic shocks impaired the ability of market agents to make payments on their debt. They changed the capital nature and structure of finance, and they impacted the labor force. The Fed had adopted a broader role in supporting the financial stability of the country; it had expanded its lending facilities; and it had the SARS scare, the H5N1 bird flu threat, and the Great Financial Crisis under its belt. When news out of China in January 2020 made clear that the world was in for a pandemic shock of major proportions, the Federal Reserve had evolved and broadened its role, and it had grappled with the enormity of the financial shock that the new, as yet unnamed virus would deliver to the global and national economy.

In Part 3, we will examine, alongside the evolution of the Fed, three of the five pandemics that have occurred during the existence of the central bank of the United States — the 1918 Spanish flu, the 1957 Asian flu, and COVID–19. We will not revisit the 1968 H3N2 flu pandemic, comingled as it was with the Vietnam War and reflecting much the same approach as the 1957 pandemic did, the slower-burning AIDS/HIV pandemic, or the comparatively mild 2009 H1N1 pandemic.

But before we turn to the creation of the Federal Reserve and the flu pandemic that followed four years later, we need to construct a bridge from the past to the modern era. We must consider how the practice of medicine was being transformed from traditional beliefs and practices passed from doctor to apprentice into a research-based science as the modern age dawned, enabling advances in public health and extending human longevity. Only when we see clearly where we have come from in the long war between people and pathogens can we fully grasp why we do not want to turn back the clock with regard to scientific advancements in medicine and public health. Knowing the past is vital to navigating the future. And that is, in fact, precisely the work that the Fed would embrace, with regard to pandemics and economics, in the years before COVID-19 broke out in Wuhan, China.

---

1. Tim Sablik, "The Fed's Emergency Lending Evolves," *Econ Focus,* Federal Reserve Bank of Richmond, 2020, https://www.richmondfed.org/publications/research/econ_focus/2020/q2-3/federal_reserve.
2. "Statistics Overview," HIV Surveillance Report: Diagnoses of HIV Infection in the United States and Dependent Areas 2020, Centers for Disease Control and Prevention, last reviewed May 24, 2022, https://www.cdc.gov/hiv/statistics/overview/index.html.
3. Angela Hutchinson, Paul Farnham, Hazel Dean, Donatus Ekwueme, Carlos del Rio, Laurie Kamimoto, Scott Kellerman, "The HIV/AIDS Epidemic in the United States: The Basics," KFF, June 07, 2021, https://www.kff.org/hivaids/fact-sheet/the-hivaids-epidemic-in-the-united-states-the-basics/.
4. "PEPFAR," HIV.gov, updated September 15, 2023, https://www.hiv.gov/federal-response/pepfar-global-aids/pepfar/.
5. Jeremy Barofsky, Neeraj Sood, and Zachary Wagner, "PEPFAR funding associated with an increase in employment among males in ten Sub-Saharan African countries," Brookings,

June 9, 2015, https://www.brookings.edu/articles/pepfar-funding-associated-with-an-increase-in-employment-among-males-in-ten-sub-saharan-african-countries/.

6.   Kara Rogers, "Influenza Pandemic (H1N1) of 2009," *Britannica*, Last Updated December 1, 2023, https://www.britannica.com/science/influenza/additional-info#history.

7.   Edouard Mathieu, Hannah Ritchie, Lucas Rodés-Guirao, Cameron Appel, Charlie Giattino, Joe Hasell, Bobbie Macdonald, Saloni Dattani, Diana Beltekian, Esteban Ortiz-Ospina and Max Roser "Coronavirus (COVID-19) Deaths," Our World in Data, September 21, 2023, https://ourworldindata.org/COVID-deaths#what-is-the-cumulative-number-of-confirmed-deaths.

Chapter 9

The Modern Era Dawns

Figure 9.1 Louis Pasteur in his lab, Chronicle / Alamy Stock Photo.

In the centuries that followed the Black Death, bubonic plague continued to cause periodic outbreaks, most notably in the Italian plague of 1629–1631, but even into the 18th century. In fact, the first 8 of the 19 pandemics and epidemics that economists Òscar Jordà, Sanjay Singh, and Alan Taylor investigated were caused by plague. Remember that their study relied upon interest rate records maintained by the Bank of England, so their list was geographically circumscribed by the reach of those records. Further, estimates of deaths had to exceed 100,000 people in order for an epidemic to be included. Cholera made their list five times, and influenza another five times. Below, the list has been reordered chronologically.

Black Death (1331–1353)
Plague in Spain (1596–1602)
Italian plague (1629–1631)
Great Plague of Seville (1647–1652)
Plague in Kingdom of Naples (1656–1658)
Great Plague of London (1665–1666)
Great Northern War plague (1700–1721)
Great Plague of Marseille (1720–1722)
First cholera pandemic (1816–1826)
Second cholera pandemic (1829–1851)
Third cholera pandemic (1852–1860)
Fourth cholera pandemic (1863–1875)
Russian flu (1889–1890)
Sixth cholera pandemic (1899–1923)
Spanish flu (1918–1920)
Encephalitis lethargica pandemic (1915–1926)
Asian flu (1957–1958)
Hong Kong flu (1968–1969)
Swine Flu (2009)

In addition, smallpox, malaria, typhus, typhoid fever, and yellow fever all continued to afflict humanity. But as centuries passed, key advancements equipped humanity with new weapons in the age-old fight against disease. Vaccination, germ theory, and an emphasis on hygiene began to save lives and lengthen lifespans. Medicine grounded in scientific research gained prominence and scored new victories against pathogens.

Smallpox and the World's First Vaccine

It was the fight against smallpox, the disease that likely caused the Antonine Plague in Rome back in 165 CE, that led to vaccination as a means for blunting the worst harms that contagious diseases could cause. Smallpox, also known as the red plague or speckled monster, had harassed populations for centuries, as far back as the Bronze Age, often killing between 20% and 60% of those it infected.[1] Ramses V, who ruled Egypt from 1150 BCE to 1145 BCE, bears the smallpox pock marks on his mummified face.[2] Two millennia later, Abraham Lincoln was beginning to feel symptoms of a smallpox infection when he delivered the Gettysburg Address less than a month before he was assassinated at Ford's Theater. He became quite ill, much to the concern of those around him, but recovered.[3] Though Lincoln was only lightly scarred, many who managed to survive the disease were left horrifically disfigured, and one third of survivors were blinded as well.[4]

One defense against smallpox, variolation, or inoculation, had been practiced from at least as far back as the early 17th century in Thessaly and Macedonia.[5] The Greeks scratched infected material from a pock into the skin of an uninfected person, producing a smallpox infection that in most cases would be much less severe than a naturally acquired one. Inoculation was also practiced in North Africa among Arab cultures, in Turkey, and in Wales. Jacob Pylarinius, a physician in Turkey, reported in 1716 that the practice of inoculation had been introduced by a Greek woman to Constantinople as early as 1660.[6] The early practice was described in detail by the travelling Frenchman A. De La Motraye, who witnessed the operation on the north shores of the Black Sea.

The manner of inoculating the pock was thus: She took

three needles flattened together, and pricked first the Pit of the Stomach; secondly, directly over the Heart ; thirdly, the Navel; fourthly, the Right Wrist ; and fifthly, the Ankle of the Left Foot, till the blood came; at the same time she took some Matter from the Pocks of the sick Person, and applied it to the bleeding Parts.[7]

The variolation technique involved significant risk, however: Around 2% of those who were inoculated died, and an inoculated person was contagious for a short period of time, so occasionally an outbreak resulted.[8] But, on the whole, those who dared to undergo inoculation dramatically bettered their odds of surviving an unmitigated exposure to smallpox. Simply put, a 1-in-50 chance of death beat a 1-in-3 chance of death hands down.

There are reports of inoculation also being used in China and India. The Chinese form of inoculation, in which fluid from pustules or bits of dry scabs were introduced to the body through the nose, is believed to have existed since the mid-16th century.[9] Regardless of who first developed inoculation, though, it is the Greek version, with needle pricks in a circle, that proliferated in Western medicine.

When smallpox erupted across Europe to become a leading cause of death in the 18th century, inoculation grew in popularity as a means of preventing severe illness, disfigurement, and death. The practice was adopted quickly by royal and noble families eager to ward off the horror.

As the protective practice spread in the West, it was met with stiff resistance in France; but the British eventually accepted inoculation, and the results were telling during the American Revolution. In 1775, the British colony of Boston was besieged by smallpox; unsurprisingly, the inoculated British army was unaffected by the outbreak, while the colonists were ravaged.[10] With the approval of the Continental Congress, General George Washington ordered in 1776 that all members of the Continental Army be inoculated against smallpox.[11] Washington understood that an army intent on victory could not afford to lose its soldiers to preventable disease.

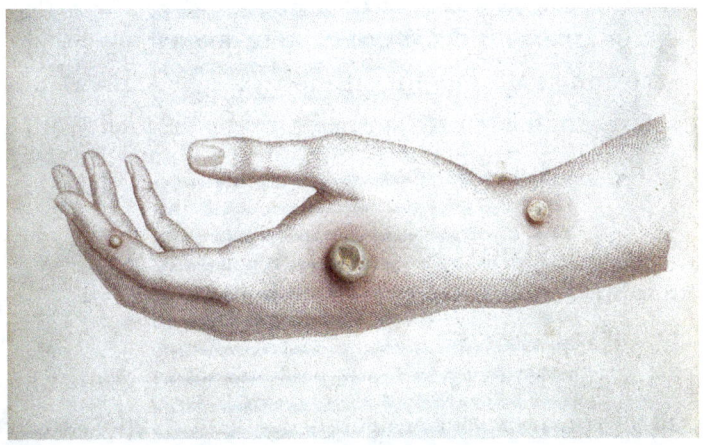

Figure 9.2 William Skelton, "The hand of Sarah Nelmes infected with the cowpox" (1798), Courtesy of the Wellcome Collection, CC BY 4.0.

Less than two decades later, Edward Jenner, an English physician, made a historic breakthrough in 1796, when he determined that inoculation with a far less risky virus could provide protection against smallpox. A CDC webpage succinctly explains:

> The basis for vaccination began in 1796 when the English doctor Edward Jenner noticed that milkmaids who had gotten cowpox were protected from smallpox. Jenner also knew about variolation and guessed that exposure to cowpox could be used to protect against smallpox. To test his theory, Dr. Jenner took material from a cowpox sore on milkmaid Sarah Nelmes's hand and inoculated it into the arm of James Phipps, the 9-year-old son of Jenner's gardener. Months later, Jenner exposed Phipps several times to variola virus, but

Phipps never developed smallpox. More experiments followed, and in 1801 Jenner published his treatise "On the Origin of the Vaccine Inoculation." In this work, he summarized his discoveries and expressed hope that "the annihilation of the smallpox, the most dreadful scourge of the human species, must be the final result of this practice."[12]

Jenner's treatise and his observation that the cowpox virus of his day could offer protection against smallpox led over time to widespread acceptance of vaccination.

After thousands of years of prayers for a remedy, humanity at last possessed a ready means of protection against smallpox. To stem the immense death toll that smallpox inflicted, governments around the world began to mandate that all citizens undergo vaccination using cowpox. The small Italian Principality of Lucca and Piombino made smallpox vaccination mandatory in 1806.[13] Bavaria did the same in 1807, and Prussia followed in 1815. Great Britain made the move in 1853, eventually introducing fines as punishment for those who refused vaccination and imprisonment for those who failed to pay those fines.[14] In the United States, compulsory vaccination was handled state by state. Massachusetts introduced mandatory vaccination in 1809, and 10 further states followed.[15] Some states and cities even imposed fines on the unvaccinated.

But along with an answer to myriad prayers lifted over centuries for relief from a scourge came concerted resistance to the means at hand. Vaccination became a point of immense contention. Feeling as if their civil liberties had been infringed upon by the government, vaccine opponents mounted fierce resistance to vaccine mandates, and perhaps for an understandable reason — this early vaccine, while it did far, far more good than harm, was not 100% safe. Risk was and is always relative — the risk posed by vaccination versus risk posed by unmitigated disease. Behavioral psychologists tell us that human beings are not especially good at assessing relative risk and readily reel off the biases that tend to cloud our judgment.

Under immense political pressure from opponents of vaccination, some U.S. states (California, Illinois, Indiana, Minnesota, Utah, West Virginia, and Wisconsin), reversed their earlier vaccination requirements and forbade mandatory vaccination instead.[16] But in 1905, when anti-vaxxer Henning Jacobson challenged the state of Massachusetts in court over its statute granting local public health boards the authority to require smallpox vaccination, the U.S. Supreme Court ruled in *Jacobson v Massachusetts* that an individual's personal preference is not more important than public health, especially when that individual's choice risks the lives of others:

> There is, of course, a sphere within which the individual may assert the supremacy of his own will and rightfully dispute the authority of any human government, especially of any free government existing under a written constitution. But it is equally true that in every well-ordered society charged with the duty of conserving the safety of its members the rights of the individual in respect of his liberty may at times, under the pressure of great dangers, be subjected to such restraint, to be enforced by reasonable regulations, as the safety of the general public may demand.[17]

The court upheld the Massachusetts law and local vaccine mandates (and thereby laid the foundation for vaccine requirements nationwide that would, in conjunction with a worldwide effort launched in the 1960s, eradicate smallpox by 1977).[18]

The smallpox vaccine, which contained cowpox, was seen by anti-vaxxers as tiny pieces of diseased cow being injected into their bodies, and they envisioned dire results. Cartoonist James Gillray's 1802 satirical sketch caricatured the outlandish nonsense that proliferated, along with the genuine anxiety that the new practice of vaccination could inspire.

Figure 9.3 James Gillray, satirical cartoon, "The cow-pock, or, The wonderful effects of the new inoculation! : vide - the publications of ye Anti-Vaccine Society" (1802), courtesy of the library of Gordon N. Ray, The Morgan Library and Museum.

Playwright and polemicist George Bernard Shaw called the vaccine a "filthy piece of witchcraft" after he contracted smallpox despite having been vaccinated, as occasionally happened.[19] While Shaw deployed emotive language for rhetorical effect, others believed that the inoculation was indeed actual witchcraft with the potential to introduce "demons" and "ghouls" into the body.[20]

The vaccination would leave, for life, a red pock mark. This scar was seized upon by anti-vaxxers. Prophecies in the Book of Revelation had foretold that when the angel poured out the first of seven bowls of the apocalypse upon the earth, "there fell noisome and grievous sores upon the men who had the mark of the beast and upon them that worshipped his image."[21] The red pox mark left by the vaccine came to be seen by some as the mark of the beast and thus a mark of the devil.

Unfounded fears aside, a small measure of risk remained. There was a small chance that a vaccination could go awry and lead to death or severe disease. An Englishman named Ira Connell reported that he was infected by vaccination with an incurable form of pox that would continually erupt to plague him. His feet and legs became unusable, and he spent at least the next 22 years consumed by unending pox and forced by the condition of his feet to walk on his knees.[22] Disastrous outcomes such as Connell's understandably reinforced fears of the vaccine.

Some viewed vaccination as an attempt to interfere with the will of God, apparently believing that God chose to smite people with smallpox and would be minus a key tool for meting out his divine will should smallpox be prevented by vaccination. Some, even among the religious, believed that smallpox was useful because it tended to kill the children of the poor and thus kept society from being overrun by the lower classes.[23]

Many doctors who had made their livelihood on ineffective cures thoroughly denounced the vaccine. Several would spread a popular theory that the vaccine would mutate people into human-cow hybrids. This disinformation held that horns would sprout from the forehead and that children would run around on all fours.[24] Gillray's 1802 cartoon plays on such beliefs that made their way into pamphlets disseminated in great quantities to spread disinformation against the vaccine. The ludicrousness of the vaccine's creating a race of minotaurs was laughable to the educated but catnip to the masses.

Jenner, the creator of the cowpox vaccine, commented on the spread of this disinformation.

> It is computed that not less than 6,000 persons in
> the metropolis (London), and the adjacent villages,

have fallen victims to the Smallpox since April last. One would scarcely conceive it possible, but these murders are, for the most part, to be attributed to the absurd productions of Moseley, Rowley, and that pert little Squirrel, to say nothing of Goldson. It is about London that the venom of these deadly serpents chiefly flows.[25]

Beyond the narrow time frame and geographic area Jenner referenced, it is probable that many more than 6000 died due to the disinformation. For the majority of the vaccinated, on the other hand, the vaccine made the difference between a full-blown case of smallpox and a far less consequential encounter with the virus. A photo of two boys taken in 1901 depicts the difference. Both boys were infected with smallpox, while only the boy on the right had been vaccinated.

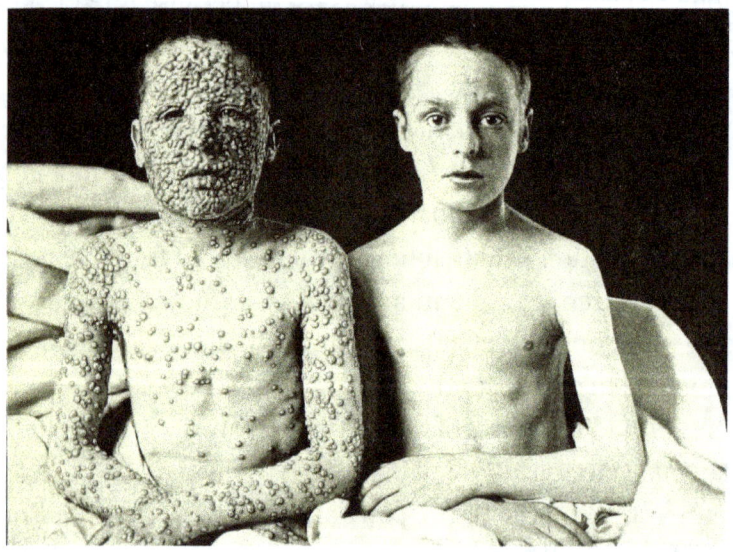

Figure 9.4 Two thirteen-year-old boys with smallpox. The one on the right was vaccinated; the one on the left was unfortunately not. Photographed by Dr. Allan Warner of the Isolation Hospital at Leicester, England (1901), via Wikimedia Commons, public domain.

Following Edward Jenner's world-changing smallpox vaccine, Louis Pasteur developed a vaccine for fowl cholera in chickens in 1872, followed with a vaccine for anthrax in cattle in the 1870s, and in 1885 used a series of rabies vaccinations to successfully protect a patient who had been exposed to that fatal disease.[26]

Germ Theory Prevails

As the modern era dawned, various breakthroughs in the fight against disease, including Pasteur's, would not have occurred without the broadening acceptance of germ theory. Across the world, there have been those who grasped at one time or another that diseases are transmitted from one person to another. Fact is, medical understanding has made no steady march of progress through history. In antiquity, the Greek physician Galen theorized that there might be "seeds" of plague or fever present in the body and in the air, but it was his miasma theory of bad air that persisted for many centuries.[27] The Roman scholar Marcus Terentius Varro in 36 BCE theorized about the existence of germs.[28] In a book on farming he suggested avoiding swamps because "certain minute creatures [animalia minuta] grow there which cannot be seen by the eye, which float in the air and enter the body through the mouth and nose and there cause serious diseases."[29] But he had no proof.

Using a powerful handheld lens he had ground and polished, Antonie van Leeuwenhoek was the first to observe single-celled organisms in a drop of water, in 1675. He called these "wee little beasties" "animalcules."[30] The problem for Varro and others was that their insights did not catch on. Fortunately, beginning in the 1860s, French chemist Louis Pasteur and German doctor Robert Koch conducted research that would convince the world, over a span of years, that germs were in fact real. Pasteur showed that microorganisms were responsible for fermentation and that heat could kill them (pasteurization). Koch discovered the connection between specific bacteria and anthrax, cholera, and tuberculosis.[31] British surgeon Joseph Lister promoted the idea that an antiseptic (carbolic acid) could be used to kill germs that caused infections, such that wounds could be disinfected and surgery became far less dangerous than it had been before.[32]

A New Mindset

Medical science had finally begun to forge understanding that could be used to fight infectious diseases. By the early 20th century, humanity had moved past an age when epidemics and pandemics seemed to almost everyone inexplicable acts of God. Many people began to understand that infections and their spread could be suppressed or eliminated. A functional sewer system and resulting clean water could prevent cholera outbreaks. Vaccination could prevent deaths. In her masterful historical work *Pale Rider: The Spanish Flu of 1918 and How It Changed the World,* Laura Spinney wrote: "In the nineteenth century, epidemics were still regarded — like earthquakes — as acts of God. Germ theory forced people to consider the possibility that they could control them...."[33]

Armed with a modicum of accurate actionable information, people possessed a measure of agency that they had not had before, and the brightest scientific and medical minds among them acted with immense dedication and determination on the hope that rigorous scientific experimentation and discovery could transform the practice of medicine and enable victory in humanity's long war against infectious disease. The "Age of Bacteriology" had dawned, as Kyle Harper observed in *Plagues upon the Earth: Disease and the Course of Human History.* Germ theory had, at long last, won the day, such that "By 1900, for a scientist or medical professional to believe anything else was becoming ignorant or downright mulish."[34]

Harper described how the "hygiene revolution" — a declared war against germs — altered life:

> The home was transformed into the aseptic ecological niche that we recognize today. White china toilets came into widespread popularity. Cold, easily scrubbed tile surfaces came to dominate bathrooms. Bodily hygiene became more punctilious and reliant on chemicals. Beards went out of fashion, and ladies turned away from skirts with hems touching the ground. Spitting was forcefully driven out of style, turned into an act of uncouth barbarity. The twentieth century also witnessed radical changes in food safety, particularly in the processing of meat and milk, and soon saw the spread of refrigeration.[35]

Public health and public works projects in cities, sanitation, and hygiene had transformed the infectious disease risk landscape by the end of the century, dialing back risks posed by bacterial infections.[36] Soon after, and widely by the 1910s, chlorine deployed in municipal water systems made water safe for drinking. Cholera, typhoid, and dysentery no longer plagued cities.[37]

That said, no one yet knew what a virus was, and it would be 1928 before Alexander Fleming, a professor of bacteriology at St. Mary's Hospital in London, discovered that mold growing in one of his petri dishes inhibited the growth of Staphylococcus bacteria, an observation that led to the development of penicillin, the first antibiotic.[38]

Research-driven medical science was young, but an enormous transformation was well underway by the time the first of the 20th century pandemics erupted in 1918. No biography captures the arc of this transformation in the United States better than that of renowned pathologist William Henry Welch, whose story John M. Barry told in chapter two of his 2004 bestseller *The Great Influenza,* a work perfectly timed, as fate would have it, to help inform thinking and planning in the latter half of the 2000s, for a possible H5N1 pandemic.[39] The son of a country doctor, Welch was unimpressed with what his father set out to teach him, and he chose first to study chemistry at Yale's Sheffield Scientific School before completing his early training at a leading medical school in New York, the College of Physicians and Surgeons. Welch's teachers there lectured in ungraded courses; there were no labs; there was no chemistry; there were no residencies and thus no patients; the only hands-on experience was the dissection of cadavers in anatomy class. There was no licensing board in the State of New York. The final exam that made him a doctor he judged to be "the easiest examination I ever entered since leaving boarding school." When he won a microscope as a prize for his performance in a course, he had no clue as to how to use it.[40] Such was the state of medical education in the U.S. in the 1870s.

Medical education in Europe was far ahead of that in America, as Welch knew from his professors who had sought their training in Europe; and he sailed for Germany in 1876 to learn what there was to know of laboratory science, including how to use his microscope.[41] He studied under Robert Koch, deemed a "father of microbiology," among other luminaries of medical science.[42] With a whole new world of understanding and methodology opened to him, he would return to the United States to teach pathology at Bellevue Hospital Medical College, where he was given three rooms to use for his courses, equipped only with bare tables. Both his living and his equipment would have to come from student fees — the traditional model.[43] It was a humble and uncertain beginning, but Welch purposed to do what he could do.

Figure 9.5 William Henry Welch, Johns Hopkins University Medical School, via Wikimedia Commons, public domain.

What Welch did, by dint of his vision, his determination, and his personality, was to help transform medical education in the United States. He created the first pathology lab in the U.S. in those rooms he was given at Bellevue, and his courses were in high demand. At the Johns Hopkins School of Medicine, he overhauled the template for medical education. A student of Welch's and his biographer, Simon Flexner, detailed Welch's plan for the requirements and curriculum at the new Johns Hopkins Medical School, which aimed to be the best in the nation. It began with entrance requirements: "preliminary training in biology, chemistry, and physics, and a reading knowledge of French and German." Once Welch was made dean of the school, laboratories were set up so that students could train and do research in anatomy, physiology, pharmacology, and chemistry.[44] His biographical sketch at the Johns Hopkins Bloomberg School of Public Health website summarizes highlights of his long career beyond Johns Hopkins, where he also served as the first director of the School of Hygiene and Public Health and the Institute of the History of Medicine:

> Welch also took an active role in national and international medical affairs. In 1896 Welch founded the Journal of Experimental Medicine. He was elected president of the Congress of American Physicians and Surgeons in 1897 and president of the Maryland State Board of Health from 1898 to 1922, serving on its board until 1929. He was also president of the American Association for the Advancement of Sciences in 1907 and of the American Medical Association in 1910. From 1913 to 1916, Welch served as president of the National Academy of Sciences. Welch's influence also extended to the military, where he became one of the chief advisors to the U.S. Army's medical department. He served as president of the board of directors of the Rockefeller Institute for Medical Research from 1901 to 1932. During this time, he was an advisor to John D. Rockefeller, who funded the establishment of the Peking Union Medical College. Welch helped set the goals for this western-style medical school which was devoted to research, premedical teaching, and clinical training. He hoped it would become the "Johns Hopkins in China."[45]

The son of a country doctor who did not always measure amounts in the concoctions he mixed to treat people grew up to profoundly shape the practice of medicine in the United States. It is telling of the era and its attitude toward science and medicine that Welch's 80th birthday was celebrated around the world in 1930. John Barry described the occasion, which spanned the globe from Tokyo and Peking to London and Geneva and across the U.S.:

> Telegraph and radio linked the celebrations, and their starting times were staggered to allow as much overlap as time zones made possible. The many halls were thick with scientists in many fields, including Nobel laureates, and President Herbert Hoover's tribute to Welch at the Washington event was broadcast live over American radio networks.[46]

That a celebration such as this could happen is not just a testament to one man's career and impact; it speaks also of a widely felt appreciation of and faith in the victories that medical science had begun to win over humanity's oldest foes: microbes that cause disease. Looking back on his education and career in 1932, Welch himself reflected, voicing that faith:

> Among the thoughts that occur to one who has lived through the last 60 years of progress in medicine, one that comes to me forcibly in this moment is that while the general direction of advancement can be foretold, the particular lines opened by new discoveries are quite unpredictable, as may be illustrated by the discoveries in biophysics, biochemistry, immunity, and the virus diseases. I should love to return after half a century and see what is disclosed when the curtain is lifted from mysteries in these fields. It is safe to predict the

prospect will surpass all that we can now conceive and imagine, and that the power of man over disease will be greatly increased.[47]

It is hard to imagine a similar birthday celebration for a giant in the field of medicine happening today, with anti-science sentiment and disinformation gaining momentum and decades of progress in public health now in jeopardy. The contrast is stark and sobering, even as it has become clear that the long war between humanity and pathogens will never really be over and is, in fact, intensifying.

The first pandemic of the 20th century, the H1N1 influenza pandemic that spanned the world in 1918, would pose a sobering test of the limits of the progress medical science had made, and it would be the new U.S. Federal Reserve's first experience of a pandemic and its economic impacts.

---

1. Stefan Riedel, "Edward Jenner and the history of smallpox and vaccination," *Baylor University Medical Center Proceedings*, 18:1, 21, https://www.ncbi.nlm.nih.gov/pmc/articles/PMC1200696/.

2. "Ramses V, King of Egypt," *Britannica,* last updated March 16, 2015, https://www.britannica.com/biography/Ramses-V.

3. Mathew W. Lively, "Abraham Lincoln, Smallpox, and the Gettysburg Address," Civil War Profiles, November 15, 2013, https://www.civilwarprofiles.com/abraham-lincoln-smallpox-and-the-gettysburg-address/.

4. Greig Watson, "The anti-vaccination movement that gripped Victorian England," BBC News, December 28, 2019, https://www.bbc.com/news/uk-england-leicestershire-50713991.

5. Stavros Grimanis, "Read in TravelTrails: The First Inoculation against Smallpox," *American School of Classical Studies at Athens* (October 12, 2022): 1. https://www.ascsa.edu.gr/news/newsDetails/traveltrails-tells-us-about-the-first-inoculation-against-smallpox.

6. Arthur Boylston, "The Origins of Inoculation," *Journal of the Royal Society of Medicine* 105, no. 7 (July 2012): 310. https://www.ncbi.nlm.nih.gov/pmc/articles/PMC3407399/.

7. A. De La Motraye, Travel Through Europe, Asia, and into Part of Africa 2 (London: 1723), 75. Google Books.

8. Stefan Riedel, "Edward Jenner and the history of smallpox and vaccination," *Baylor University Medical Center Proceedings* 18, no. 1, 23.

9. Arthur Boylston, "The Origins of Inoculation," 312.

10. Ann M. Becker, "Smallpox in Washington's Army: Strategic Implications of the Disease during the American Revolutionary War," *The Journal of Military History*, 68, no. 2 (April 2004): 389, https://www.sjsu.edu/people/ruma.chopra/courses/h174_MW_F11/s3/smallpox_GWarmy.pdf.

11. Becker, "Smallpox in Washington's Army,"422; Phillip J. Smith, David Wood, and Paul M. Darden, "Highlights of Historical Events Leading to National Surveillance of Vaccination Coverage in the United States," *Public Health Reports* no. 126 (2011), https://www.ncbi.nlm.nih.gov/pmc/articles/PMC3113425/.

12. "History of Smallpox," Centers for Disease Control and Prevention (CDC), last reviewed February 20, 2021, https://www.cdc.gov/smallpox/history/history.html.

13. Alexander Grab, "Smallpox vaccination in Napoleonic Italy," *Napoleonica La Revu*, no. 30, (March 2017): 42, https://www.cairn.info/revue-napoleonica-la-revue-2017-3-page-38.htm.

14. Stanley Williamson. *The Vaccination Controversy: The Rise, Reign and Decline of Compulsory Vaccination.* (Liverpool: Liverpool University Press, 2007), 254, https://www.jstor.org/stable/j.ctt5vjnhh.

15. Phillip J. Smith, David Wood, and Paul M. Darden, "Highlights of Historical Events Leading to National Surveillance of Vaccination Coverage in the United States," *Public Health Reports* no. 126 (2011): 4. https://www.ncbi.nlm.nih.gov/pmc/articles/PMC3113425/.

16. Smith, Wood, and Darden, "Highlights of Historical Events Leading to National Surveillance of Vaccination Coverage in the United States."

17. Jacobson v Massachusetts, 197 U.S. 11 (1905).

18. Wendy K. Mariner, George J. Annas, and Leonard H. Glantz, "Jacobson v Massachusetts: It's Not Your Great-Great-Grandfather's Public Health Law," *American Journal of Public Health*, 95, no. 4 (2005): 581–90. Republished at the NIH National Library of Medicine, https://www.ncbi.nlm.nih.gov/pmc/articles/PMC1449224/.

19. Gareth Williams, "1843 Magazine: The Original Anti-vaxxers," *The Economist*, August 30, 2019, https://www.economist.com/1843/2019/08/30/the-original-anti-vaxxers.

20. Nadja Durbach, *Bodily Matters: The Anti-Vaccination Movement in England, 1853–1907* (Durham: Duke University Press, 2004), 116–117.

21. Book of Revelation 16:12, King James Version.

22. Ira Connell, "My Experience of Vaccination," cited in Nadja Durbach, *Bodily Matters: The Anti-Vaccination Movement in England, 1853–1907*, 118.

23. Gareth Williams, "The Original Anti-vaxxers."

24. Gareth Williams, "The Original Anti-vaxxers."

25. William White, *The Story of a Great Delusion in a Series of Matter-of-fact Chapters* (London: E.W. Allen, 1885), 361. Internet Archive.

26. "A Brief History of Vaccines," World Health Organization, accessed Nov. 29, 2023, https://www.who.int/news-room/spotlight/history-of-vaccination/a-brief-history-of-vaccination.

27. Vivian Nutton, "The Seeds of Disease: An explanation of contagion and infection from the Greeks to the Renaissance," *Medical History*, January 1983, https://www.ncbi.nlm.nih.gov/pmc/articles/PMC1139262/.

28. Marcus Terentius Varro, *M. Terenti Varronis Rerum Rusticarum Libri Tres*, 12.2, Internet Archive.

29. OpenStax, "What Our Ancestors Knew," Chapter 1.1, *Allied Health Microbiology,* 2019, https://open.oregonstate.education/microbiology/chapter/1-1-what-our-ancestors-knew/.

30. OpenStax, "What Our Ancestors Knew, Chapter 1.1, *Allied Health Microbiology.*

31. OpenStax, "What Our Ancestors Knew, Chapter 1.1, *Allied Health Microbiology.*

32. Spyros N Michaleas, Konstantinos Laios, Alexandros Charalabopoulos, George Samonis, and Marianna Karamanou, "Joseph Lister (1827-1912): A Pioneer of Antiseptic Surgery," *Cureus,* December 2022, republished at the NIH National Library of Medicine, https://www. ncbi.nlm.nih.gov/pmc/articles/PMC9854334/.

33. Laura Spinney, *Pale Rider: The Spanish Flu of 1918 and How It Changed the World* (New York: PublicAffairs, 2017), 28.

34. Kyle Harper, *Plagues upon the Earth,* The Princeton Economic History of the Western World (Princeton: Princeton University Press, 2021), 474.

35. Harper, *Plagues upon the Earth,* 476–477.

36. Harper, *Plagues upon the Earth,* 475–76.

37. Harper, *Plagues upon the Earth,* 479.

38. American Chemical Society International Historic Chemical Landmarks, "Discovery and Development of Penicillin," https://www.acs.org/education/whatischemistry/landmarks/ flemingpenicillin.html, accessed October 11, 2023; adapted for the internet from Susan Aldridge, John Parascandola, and Jeffrey Louis Sturchio, *The Discovery and Development of Penicillin 1928–1945,* (Washington, DC: American Chemical Society and the Royal Society of Chemistry, 1999).

39. John M. Barry, *The Great Influenza: The Epic Story of the Deadliest Plague in History* (Penguin Books, 2005, 2021), Kindle Edition.

40. Barry, *The Great Influenza,* 41–42.

41. Barry, *The Great Influenza,* 42.

42. William H. Welch, "Reminiscences of the Early Days of the Medical School," Films of Commerce, 1932, https://www.youtube.com/watch?v=emGPMVfad1M.

43. Barry, *The Great Influenza,* 46.

44. Simon Flexner, "Biographical Memoir of William Henry Welch: 1850–1934, National Academy of Sciences, Biographical Memoirs, Volume XXII, 1942, 220, https://www.nasonline. org/publications/biographical-memoirs/memoir-pdfs/welch-william.pdf.

45. "Heroes of Public Health: William Henry Welch, MD," Johns Hopkins, Bloomberg School of Public Health, accessed October 1, 2023, https://publichealth.jhu.edu/about/history/ heroes-of-public-health/william-henry-welch-md.

46. Barry, *The Great Influenza,* 36.

47. William H. Welch, "Reminiscences of the Early Days of the Medical School," Films of Commerce, 1932, https://www.youtube.com/watch?v=emGPMVfad1M.

Chapter 10

The New Fed's First Flu:
The 1918 H1N1 Influenza Pandemic

*"Go as far as you can see; when you get there,
you'll be able to see farther."*

— John Pierpont Morgan, who died in 1913 and never got
to see the final creation of the Federal Reserve

The U.S. Gains a Central Bank

Figure 10.1 Federal Reserve Board: P. Warburg, J.S. Williams, W.H.G. Harding,
A.C. Miller, C.S. Hamlin, W.G. McAdoo, Fred. Delano (1915), courtesy of
Bain News Service / Library of Congress, public domain.

I n order to contextualize the Federal Reserve's priorities and policies during the 1918 pandemic shock, we must look first at the early history of the Fed. Students of the history of the Federal Reserve know that the Fed came into existence in response to the banking panic of 1907. From the creation of the concept by J.P. Morgan, to the meeting at Jekyll Island, Georgia, where details were hammered out, to the eventual legislation implemented in 1913 and taking effect in 1914, the formation of the Federal Reserve centered on the banking system and the banking crisis of 1907. At its creation, the Federal Reserve was not thinking about inflation. It was not thinking about unemployment. It did not consider things like the Phillips curve trade-off between inflation and unemployment. The Fed at the time was focused most intently on one thing: ensuring financial stability and the avoidance of another banking panic, with runs on banks and a banking system shock to the economy.

In the 19th century, the banking system of the United States reflected the nation's federal system of government. Most banks were chartered by the states and did not have branches in other states. Thousands of small banks, each with one location, dotted the country — too small to muster efficiencies or diverse loan portfolios and without recourse to assistance or lending from larger reserve banks.[1] Banking panics happened again and again: Depositors sought to withdraw their funds; payments to depositors were halted; interest rates rose; and recessions sometimes followed. With bank reserves concentrated in a limited number of major cities, stock market speculators took advantage of short-term loans; and sometimes the house of cards, which was based on a single inelastic currency — the dollar — collapsed into chaos.[2]

And that was what happened in the Banking Panic of 1907. In the years before the panic, the Treasury had expanded the supply of money by purchasing government bonds on a large scale, and banks were no longer required to keep reserves against government deposits.

Credit was easy, and stock market speculators were having a heyday. Meanwhile, though national banks averaged a 25% cash-to-deposit ratio, New York City's state-chartered trust companies averaged a meager 5% ratio, making them especially vulnerable.[3] The trust companies made loans, without requiring collateral, that were due each day by the close of business. Jon R. Moen and Ellis W. Tallman have explained the crucial role the trust companies played:

> Brokers used these loans to purchase securities for themselves or their clients and then used these securities as collateral for a call loan — an overnight loan that facilitated stock purchases — from a nationally chartered bank. The proceeds of the call loan were used to pay back the initial loan from the trust company. Trusts were a necessary part of this process, because the law prohibited nationally chartered commercial banks from making uncollateralized loans or guaranteeing the payment of checks written by brokers on accounts without sufficient funds. The extra liquidity provided by trusts supported new daily transactions on the floor of the exchange. Runs on trust company deposits, however, short-circuited their role as the initial liquidity provider to the stock market.[4]

As Moen and Tallman have detailed in their Federal Reserve history essay, the panic began when two speculators — Augustus Heinze and Charles Morse — tried to corner the stock of United Copper and failed. They incurred large losses and failed to repay their call loan, imperiling the banks from which they had borrowed. The New York Clearing House stepped in to offer loans to impacted banks and was able to stop the runs on them, calming depositors. But there was contagion;

and the runs spread to the trust companies, spurring a tightening of credit that drove the annualized rate of interest for overnight loans on stock collateral to 100% within days. The credit market locked up.[5]

There was no central bank to save the situation. The dramatic crisis, which knocked industrial output back by 17% and real GNP back by 12%, was short-lived only because wealthy investors and financiers — J.P. Morgan and John D. Rockefeller among them — stepped up with personal funds and guarantees to restore stability. They had every reason to support the creation of a banking system designed to ensure that there would never be a repeat of the 1907 crisis, which bears many resemblances to the Great Financial Crisis of 2008, except that in 2008 the Federal Reserve stepped in to save the financial system of the United States.[6]

In the years that followed the Panic of 1907, Senate Finance Committee Chairman Nelson Aldrich cosponsored a bill creating the National Monetary Commission, whose advisers met with central bankers in Europe and studied banking systems with the goal of creating a central bank that could provide stability and prevent another banking crisis. When the commission's information-gathering process was complete, in November of 1910, six men, including Aldrich, gathered at the Jekyll Island Club to come up with a plan to build a better banking system for the United States.

Those who attended — Senator Aldrich, A. Piatt Andrew, Henry Davison, Arthur Shelton, Frank Vanderlip, and Paul Warburg — kept that meeting at the exclusive Georgia resort a secret until the 1930s. Why? Their ties to Wall Street could have proven an insurmountable political liability for the passage of the bill that they would help to craft. So, they stuck to a cover story: They had traveled to Jekyll Island (probably at J.P. Morgan's invitation) for a duck-hunting trip. For the duration, they used only first names and thus became members of the "First Name Club." Another member of the First Name Club, though many scholars believe he did not attend the Jekyll Island meeting, was Benjamin Strong, who would become the first governor of the Federal Reserve.[7]

Liaquat Ahamed, author of the 2010 Pulitzer-winning history *Lords of Finance: The Bankers Who Broke the World*, has disagreed, however, and concluded instead that Benjamin Strong was there. Ahamed described the lengths to which the giants of finance went in order to maintain secrecy as they made their way from New York to an idyllic and exclusive Georgia Island resort:

> The preparations were elaborate. Each guest was told to go to Hoboken Station in New Jersey on November 22 and board Senator Aldrich's private railroad car, which they could find hitched with its blinds drawn to the Florida train. They were not to dine together, nor meet up beforehand, but to come aboard singly and as unobtrusively as possible, all using only their first names. Strong was to be Mr. Benjamin, Warburg Mr. Paul. Davison and Vanderlip went a step further and adopted the ringingly obvious pseudonyms Wilbur and Orville.[8]

Gary Richardson and Jessie Romero of the Federal Reserve Bank of Richmond have explained the challenge these men actually convened to grapple with, one far harder than taking out a duck rising off the water at 50 yards:

> The problem facing the framers of the Aldrich Plan was how to create a central bank that could effectively function in a country such as the United States, with its diverse geographic, political, and economic interests. The resulting plan for a "decentralized central bank" was incorporated, with some modification, into the

legislation that brought the Federal Reserve into being
— the Federal Reserve Act of 1913.[9]

Figure 10.2 The old clubhouse at the Jekyll Island Club,
via Wikimedia Commons, public domain.

In 1913, in legislation reflecting the work of that meeting, the
Federal Reserve System was created by an act of Congress. Its raison
d'être was to provide stability to the banking system, thereby preventing panics and runs on banks along with the economic shocks that
accompanied them. The Federal Reserve Act created the 12 regional
Federal Reserve Banks we know today. National banks had to purchase
capital in their regional Reserve Bank, though state-chartered banks
did not have to do so, and many did not at that time. Member banks
had access to loans at the "discount window," which was, then, an
actual window, while nonmember banks could not access loans from
the Federal Reserve or any other services that the new Fed offered.
The United States had a "lender of last resort" at last, but only for
member banks.[10] Under the Federal Reserve Act, national banks could
open foreign branches and issue bankers' acceptances. After World
War I began and Europe's financial markets were disrupted, U.S.
banks quickly took on a growing share of the financing for interna-

tional trade, setting the stage for the U.S. dollar to become the world's leading reserve currency in the 1920s.[11]

With figures such as J.P. Morgan behind them, Benjamin Strong and his First Name Club colleagues were responsible for the creation of the central bank of United States. All of them were people with a global world view. Their banking relationships included Europeans and the central bankers of European countries. They were skilled in international money flows and especially the movement of gold reserves. They saw the world through the lens of global commerce and finance as it was visible to them at the time.

The Federal Reserve was envisioned and founded in the period before the 1918 "Spanish flu" and before the First World War. This was also the period following the Russian Flu pandemic (pandemic number 7 of the of 19 studied by economists Òscar Jordà, Sanjay Singh, and Alan Taylor), which killed a million people worldwide, with more than 100,000 dead in England. It was also the period immediately following the banking crisis of 1907 in the United States.

Much history is recorded about how these First Name Club members and others agreed with J. P. Morgan and wanted to create the American central bank as a preventive measure against a future banking crisis. We know the group had a forward-looking crisis-prevention mentality. There are many books about the banking crisis in 1907, about J. P. Morgan's bailing out banks and convening a meeting of other bankers to avoid future bank failures, and about preventing runs on banks. Morgan was the driving force behind the creation of the Federal Reserve even if he did not live to see it become a formal American institution.

So, what was the motivating factor behind the creation of the Federal Reserve? It was not an economic lesson from Knut Wicksell, even though he was a contemporary of these Fed founders. And it was not a reaction to the Russian Flu pandemic economic shock that preceded the 1907 banking crisis. No, the Fed's creation was driven by a handful of the leading bankers in New York who had money and desired to preserve their wealth. Never again did they want to serve as the U.S. banking system's lender of last resort. They knew that, without financial stability, wealth is imperiled — for the poor, for the rich, and for everyone in between.

We will leave the rest of the history lesson about the founding of the Federal Reserve to those readers who seek more details. Here is what is missing.

Nowhere in this history lesson is there any reference to pandemic risks and how they flow to finance. Nothing in the literature or records suggests that Jordà, Singh, and Taylor's depiction of a pandemic-induced decline in the natural rate of interest was understood to have been a factor in causing the banking crisis of 1907. The notion was simply not in the minds of the bankers at that time. They could see risks from gold outflows, but they could not see risks from pandemic-induced behavioral finance outcomes. They could understand fear from a bank run but not conceive of how fear of disease and death alters behaviors and changes the savings rate or impacts the wage rates or changes the allocation of capital.

The 12 Federal Reserve banks that composed the system opened for business on November 16, 1914. Treasury Secretary William McAdoo's press announcement stressed the import of the occasion:

> The opening of these banks marks a new era in the history of business and finance in this country. It is believed that they will put an end to the annual anxiety from which the country has suffered for the past generation about insufficient money and credit to move the crops each year, and will give such stability to the banking business that the extreme fluctuations

in interest rates and available credits which have characterized banking in the past will be destroyed permanently.[12]

McAdoo guided the new Federal Reserve banks with this advice:

Buy a few chairs and pine-top tables. Hire some clerks and stenographers, paint "Federal Reserve Bank" on your office door and open up. The way to begin is to begin. When you make a start, everything will be smoothed out by practice.[13]

The Fed's opening was both timely and urgent in November of 1914, as World War I had erupted in the first week of August, and global economic impacts were already underway.[14] The start of the war in Europe led swiftly to a financial crisis, which soon eased. But with Europe's pouring resources into the war and demand for U.S. exports high, gold poured into the U.S., and inflation resulted. When America entered the Great War on April 6, 1917, the Federal Reserve had a new task at hand — helping the nation finance the enormous costs of that war. The Treasury sold "Liberty Bonds," and the 12 Federal Reserve banks organized to facilitate bond sales and provided lower interest rates on loans to local banks if the money was to be used to purchase Liberty Bonds. The Fed also gave banks low rates for purchasing Treasury certificates. With low interest rates on loans easing credit conditions, growing the money supply, and stimulating economic growth, inflation continued to jag upward. At the time, though, the war effort took precedence over managing inflation. That would remain true until the war was over.[15]

A New Flu Strikes

During World War I, the war took precedence over everything, including the comprehensive reporting of news. In many countries, in the late spring of 1918, censors suppressed news of a deadly sickness sweeping the globe in hopes of maintaining morale and of curbing fear that might detract from the war effort. However, in Spain, a country that remained neutral in the war, a new flu made the news when it hit hard in May and especially when King Alfonso XIII fell ill. As a result, the world began to call the new affliction the "Spanish flu" everywhere except in Spain, where the Spanish called it the "French flu," thinking it had originated in France.[16] The naming of pandemics has never been an exact science.

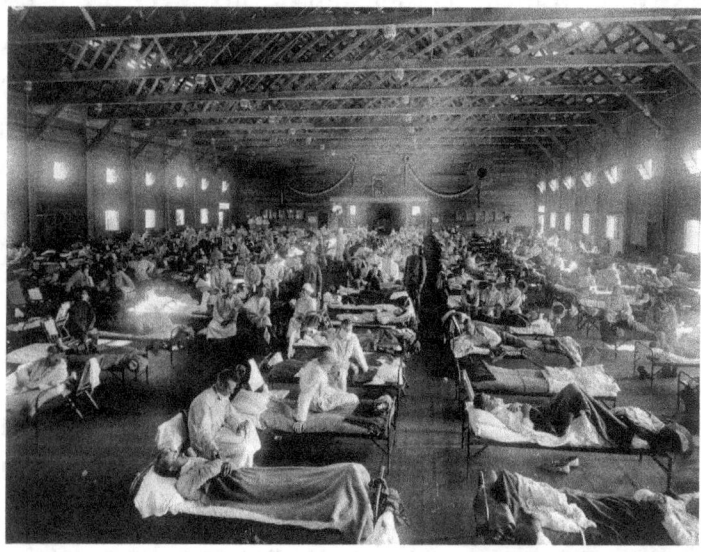

Figure 10.3 Emergency hospital during influenza epidemic, Camp Funston, Kansas, circa 1918, courtesy of Otis Historical Archives, National Museum of Health and Medicine, public domain.

The H1N1 influenza pandemic of 1918–1922 might more properly have been named the "Funston Flu," because it ignited not in Spain but in an overcrowded training camp at Camp Funston in

Kansas. Camp Funston was one of 16 U.S. training camps chocked overfull with troops training for deployment at the Western Front. Overcrowding made the camps the perfect petri dish for the incubation of pandemic disease. One U.S. Army doctor at the time, I.W. Brewer, gathered data on crowding in the barracks and other factors that affected the spread and severity of illness. It turned out that the most crowded barracks translated to a 10-fold higher risk of infection and a 5-fold increase in pneumonia as a complication of the flu.[17]

In *Pale Rider*, Laura Spinney recounted the spread of the new flu that erupted at Camp Funston on March 4, 1918. A hundred men fell sick by lunchtime. So many fell ill that they had to be hospitalized in a repurposed hangar.

By April, flu had spread across the Midwest; and it traveled with troops to the trenches in Europe and spread from there, reaching Africa in May and shortly afterward, China. By July it found Australia. After subsiding for a while in summer in the places where it had first burned through the population, the virus surged again in August, commencing the deadliest wave of the pandemic.[18]

Remarkably, one tank-training center, Camp Colt in Gettysburg, Virginia, managed to stem the tide of infection and proved to be an example later studied by the War Department. The camp commander was none other than 28-year-old Captain Dwight D. Eisenhower, who was then just a few years out of West Point. In the fall of 1918, the flu spread through Camp Colt, just as it was spreading elsewhere. Eisenhower followed the advice of his chief surgeon, Lt. Colonel Thomas Scott, and empowered his medical team to implement every measure they deemed likely to help stop the virus. Troops were inoculated against smallpox and typhoid. They moved out of the barracks and set up tents on the field where the Battle of Gettysburg had been fought, with no more than four men per tent and the tent flaps open. Tent floors were sterilized daily, and Colonel Scott had everyone endure burning nose sprays twice a day. Everyone had a daily health check. Those who fell ill or had been exposed were separated from everyone else, insofar as possible; and the camp remained under quarantine for a time, with no one allowed to leave.[19]

The flu would infect about one third of the camp and 150 men would die; but Colonel Scott's measures, authorized by Captain Eisenhower, would result in far fewer deaths than other camps experienced.[20] Ohio's Camp Sherman, by contrast, would lose 1,777 men to influenza in 1918.[21] Flu ultimately killed 45,000 U.S. soldiers during WWI, whereas 53,402 were killed in combat.[22]

When the U.S. entered the First World War, the country appointed a key advisor to the Defense Department and the Surgeon General's office — none other than Lieutenant Colonel William Henry Welch, the renowned Johns Hopkins pathologist, who had by that time served as president of the National Academy of Sciences, chairman of the Executive Committee of the Carnegie Institution, and president of the Board of Scientific Directors for the Rockefeller Institute for Medical Research.[23] Having volunteered to serve his country at the age of 67, Welch helped to organize the medical service for the armed forces, ensuring that the camps were well organized and supplied. When he had completed that task, he expected to resign from the army and return to the project of opening the Johns Hopkins School of Hygiene and Public Health, which had been funded by a grant from the Rockefeller Institute. Instead, on September 22, he was ordered, along with other members of his scientific team, to investigate a deadly new outbreak of flu at Camp Devens, in Massachusetts.

Historian John Barry recounted the team's visit to the camp. When they arrived, they had to step around sick men in the base hospital hallways — the hospital, designed to handle 1,500 patients, was now bursting with 6,000. Many sick soldiers were turning blue from cyanosis, and some were spitting up blood as the disease took its deadly course. The nurses who cared for them were falling ill, too, and there were not enough medical personnel to care for all who were ill.[24] In the morgue, where the team had to step over corpses, autopsies of some of the dead shocked them. Physician and Colonel Rufus Cole, who would become the director of the Rockefeller University Hospital, later recalled, in a letter to Simon Flexner, Dr. Welch's reaction to what they saw when an autopsy was performed on one of the deceased soldiers:

> When the chest was opened and the blue swollen lungs were removed and opened, and Dr. Welch saw the wet, foamy surfaces with real consolidation, he turned and said, "This must be some new kind of infection or plague," and he was quite excited and obviously very nervous.... It was not surprising that the rest of us were disturbed, but it shocked me to find that the situation, momentarily at least, was too much even for Dr. Welch.[25]

The alarm that the situation at Camp Devens evoked in William Henry Welch, Rufus Cole, and the rest of the scientific team was by no means an overreaction. H1N1 flu produced an enormous pandemic shock in the United States in 1918 and 1919, killing an estimated 675,000 Americans, according to the CDC. Around the world, perhaps 500 million were infected, and as many as 50 million died. The "Spanish flu," rather than claiming lives mostly among the very young and the very old, hit hardest young adults in the prime of their lives. The average age of its victims was 28. Nurses were in such short supply that the Red Cross called for volunteers to nurse the sick.[26] While most people think of the pandemic as spanning only a couple of years, there was a smaller but significant wave as late as 1922.[27] Furthermore, it behooves us to keep in mind a point made by NIH influenza expert Jeffery Taubenberger in an interview for the *Washington Post* in 2020: "All those pandemics that have happened since — 1957, 1968, 2009 — all those pandemics are derivatives of the 1918 flu.... The flu viruses that people get this year, or last year, are all still directly related to the 1918 ancestor."[28]

Neither the media nor the government opted to be frank with the public about how dire the situation was, given that the war was still going on that fall (until November 11), which made matters worse. No country wanted its enemies to know that its forces were afflicted, and governments were intent on keeping morale high.

Figure 10.4 William H. Welch (center), Simon Flexner (left), John D. Rockefeller, Jr. (right) (ca. 1931), courtesy of the Alan Mason Chesney Medical Archives.

Nonetheless, people did know about the flu. There were news reports. And the titans of industry and finance who were instrumental in the creation of the Fed, along with members of the Fed itself, certainly knew about the spreading plague. Medical progress reflected not only the interests of physicians and scientists but also of those who funded the transformation they envisioned. John D. Rockefeller and Andrew Carnegie were vitally important in funding advances in medical research capacity and medical training. Welch collaborated directly with the Rockefeller family, Andrew Carnegie, and others who worked to advance medical science. These philanthropists were part of a small circle of the elite in America. Educator Abraham Flexner, a contemporary fellow architect of medical training reform in the United States and the younger brother of Dr. Welch's student and biographer Simon Flexner, would persuade others — Julius Rosenwald, Nicholas Eastman, and Cornelius Vanderbilt — to provide large donations, with matching funds from the Rockefeller Foundation, to help found medical schools at Chicago, Rochester, and Vanderbilt.[29]

By 1918, the titans of finance and industry who funded the effort to make U.S. medical schools and research institutions the best in the world knew about the risks of epidemic disease. Many of them had lived through the Russian Flu pandemic of 1889. Why was it, then, we might ask, that the Fed's founders and the Fed itself seemed so oblivious to the linkage between banking and economics on one hand and the impacts of epidemics on the other hand? We do not know. But we do know that the early Fed never made the connection.

John Barry's famous 2005 account of the 1918 pandemic, *The Great Influenza*, defined the Spanish flu for the general public and contributed a great deal to thinking about how to prepare for the next pandemic. Yet nowhere in his book did Barry mention the Federal Reserve, the newly formed central bank of the United States. He did list various economic shocks and the rise of fear of the Spanish flu; these factors increase the savings rate and thereby lower the natural rate of interest, as Jordà, Singh, and Taylor found in their study of 19 pandemics. Barry's landmark book addressed the disease, resulting deaths, the first serious engagement between medical science and a pandemic pathogen, and the virus's political impact on the course of history.

When the H1N1 pandemic struck, "a dominant force in U.S. monetary and banking affairs" was the president of the Federal Reserve Bank of New York, Benjamin Strong, Jr., who served in that position from 1914 until his death in 1928 at age 55. Strong was, like many other prominent figures of the day, deeply invested in supporting U.S.

allies in the war and in enhancing the international role of the U.S. financial system. Historian Priscilla Roberts has explained the broader goals of the Fed's founders:

> The prominence of international considerations in Strong's policymaking should also be perceived as part of the broad outlook of the New York financial community, and as one aspect of the development since the late nineteenth century of a sense that the United States was a world power, which should both behave and be treated as one. One important goal of the Federal Reserve System's founders, particularly those New York bankers who were among its most prominent architects, was to provide the United States with a central banking system which would enable their country to fulfill its potential as an international financial power. Throughout the First World War and the 1920s, Strong and other leading New York bankers perceived the System primarily in this light, as part of America's mechanisms for dealing with the outside world.[30]

Roberts describes the period surrounding the end of the war, which was concurrent with the ongoing pandemic. The U.S. economy, with the war as its engine, boomed. The U.S. financial system became key not only to the war effort but also to Europe's recovery and rebuilding after the war. Inflation resulted, and when the Federal Reserve raised interest rates to curb that inflation after the war ended (sharply downshifting the economic engine that had supplied the Allies), a "short but intense recession" followed in 1920–21.[31]

What Roberts does not mention in her portrait of Strong, who devoted himself single-mindedly to his work for the Federal Reserve, is the flu — the Blue Death — that, worldwide, claimed more lives than World War I did. That immense human toll and the economic shock it delivered are absent from the Federal Reserve's annals of this period. Disease and its impacts did not register. Perhaps infectious disease had been so deeply woven into the tapestry of human existence that its threads of blue, red, and black did not stand out when war and money were the primary concerns.

As it happened, Strong himself suffered from a different all-too-common respiratory disease, tuberculosis, diagnosed in 1916, around the time of his separation from his second wife. Liaquat Ahamed detailed Benjamin Strong's confrontation with the disease in *Lords of Finance*:

> That same summer, as his marriage was falling apart, he also fell ill, developing a nagging cough that became progressively worse. He was soon bringing up blood and experiencing terrible chest pains. That June he was diagnosed with tuberculosis. Then commonly known as consumption, the highly contagious disease, caused by airborne bacteria that attack the membranes of the lungs, was then the most common cause of civilian deaths in both Europe and America, affecting people of all classes, often in the prime of life.[32]

The 1918 flu pandemic is not mentioned in any of the Benjamin Strong papers now archived at the St. Louis Fed. Benjamin Strong's personal letters describe his health struggles and challenges; he repeats that personal description in many communications. So here we have the most dominant person in the new American central bank, who was personally confronting a respiratory disease, and yet he was silent as this newly institutionalized central bank of the United States faced a virulent new influenza virus. The Fed's leaders failed to connect the dots when it came to monetary policy and the banking system policy in the midst of a worldwide pandemic that was killing hundreds of thousands of people in the United States and millions around the world.

The economic impacts of the 1918 H1N1 pandemic were slow to be studied and recognized. Indeed, they were ferreted out later as other pandemic threats emerged. Allan Meltzer's masterful work, *A History of the Federal Reserve, Volume 1, 1913–1951,* does not mention the pandemic.[33] Neither does the 1963 masterwork by Milton Friedman and Anna Schwartz, *A Monetary History of the United States, 1867–1960.*[34] In all the literature about the Fed and its activities during this formative period, a recognition of the economic impact of the millions of deaths from the pandemic is curiously absent. There is discussion about the war loans, the setting of interest rates, gold reserves, devaluation of foreign currencies, and international gold flows. But there is no mention of the economic impacts of so many deaths attributable to intense waves of a deadly flu.

In their 1933 treatise, *Prices,* George Warren and Frank Pearson detailed the history of prices in the United States. They cite many references to the peaking of inflation in 1919–1920 and the subsequent decline in prices.[35] In his work first published in 1963, *A History of Interest Rates,* Sidney Homer described the peaking of interest rates in 1920 and the subsequent decline.[36] Causes of those interest-rate changes and economic shocks are explained, but nowhere do we see the discovery that Jordà, Singh, and Taylor have articulated in their paper published by the Federal Reserve Bank of San Francisco. The natural rate of interest declined after the 1918 H1N1 flu pandemic. Surely there were employees in the Federal Reserve regional banks that succumbed to the Spanish flu. Their managers failed to connect the dots.

In a 2007 report, "Economic Effects of the 1918 Influenza Pandemic: Implications for a Modern-day Pandemic," Thomas A. Garrett, who served as assistant vice president and an economist at the Federal Reserve Bank of St. Louis, examined evidence of the economic impacts of the 1918 pandemic, particularly in the Eighth Federal Reserve District. Noting a dearth of available data, he turned to newspaper reports from the time, particularly those of the *Arkansas Gazette* in Little Rock and the *Commercial Appeal* in Memphis. While drugstores and makers and sellers of mattresses and beds saw an increase in demand, most types of businesses reported significant losses and a decline in business of 40% or more. Industrial plants struggled to keep up production, given illnesses on top of the labor shortage created by the draft; and the Memphis Street Railway had to cut service when nearly one third of its operators were ill. Tennessee coal production dipped by 50% during the fall 1918 wave, and many mines struggled to remain open at all.[37]

Garrett also discussed research on the connection between pandemic mortality and manufacturing wage groups. He concluded, "Cities and states having greater influenza mortalities experienced a greater increase in manufacturing wage growth over the period 1914 to 1919." Another study, Garrett noted, found that state per capita income growth over the decade following the pandemic also correlated with mortality rates in each state.[38]

Note the date of the Garrett paper — 2007. The economic impacts of the 1918 pandemic were not studied in 1920 or 1930. They were studied as subsequent influenza pandemics occurred and in 2007 as the world braced for a possible H5N1 influenza pandemic, which looked then (and still looks) like a dire prospect given the fatality rate among those who have been infected with the virus. The story of what the Fed ultimately did in response to the COVID pandemic is, in fact, the story of what the Fed learned from the 1918 flu pandemic and from other shocks since the Federal Reserve System was formed.

In April of 2020 (another year when the lessons that could be gleaned from the 1918 pandemic were deemed essential), François Velde, a senior economist and research advisor at the Federal Reserve

Bank of Chicago, published a working paper examining the short-term economic impacts of the 1918 flu pandemic, using what high-frequency data is available from that time.[39] Velde notes that government agencies were only beginning to systematically collect data, with many series starting in January of 1919. Still, *Commercial and Financial Chronicle* and *Bradstreet's* weeklies, along with the BLS's *Monthly Labor Review* and the Fed's *Bulletin*, number among the public and private sources of data from the H1N1 pandemic flu period.[40]

The economic impact of the disruptive and deadly fall 1918 wave of flu was cushioned in part by the robust war-time economy and already loose monetary policy, in the form of low interest rates, that facilitated war bond sales through four Liberty Loan drives. Velde observed that a short recession was triggered that fall (as was first noted by Burns and Mitchell in 1946), with a trough in April of 1919, precipitated not by the pandemic alone but also by uncertainty surrounding the end of the war in November and a transition back to a peacetime economy. The recession of 1920–1922 was longer and deeper, reflecting the impact of sharply higher interest rates imposed to curb spiking inflation.[41]

Velde found a short-lived dip in industrial production, evident in the fledgling automotive industry. In the retail sector, mail order chains and pharmacies saw an increase in demand, while dry goods stores and grocery stores saw weaker sales. October was a hard month, but as flu cases dropped, sales and demand increased once again. The BLS recorded a 12% decline in its Employment Index during the height of the fall wave, but by December that dip was over. The disruption and associated nonpharmaceutical interventions did not last long enough to occasion a rise in business failures.[42] Much depended on both the disease (which came in succinct waves) and on the economic, financial, and geopolitical context in which the pandemic unfolded.

Change those variables, and a pandemic's economic impacts can be significantly greater. Velde concluded,

> The 1918 recession was mild and brief, particularly when compared to that of 1920–21. This seems surprising given the size of the demographic shock, on the order of 0.5% of the labor force and the population. The coal industry data confirms that labor supply was indeed an important channel affecting industrial output, but the impact was very brief. If anything, the recession might have been even briefer (or unnoticed) without the uncertainty brought by the Armistice. The need to shift from wartime to peacetime economy became more probable as rumors of peace talks floated in October 1918 and a certainty on November 11. The government had been heavily involved in the economy in various ways, first of all by running a deficit of 20% of GDP and using it for government purchases. Non-essential economic activities like construction and consumer durables were curtailed. Prices were controlled, in some cases by floors and others by ceilings. All this was presumably coming to an end, but contemporaries were uncertain about the timing. By March 1919 the uncertainty had dissipated, the economy had worked through various internal imbalances, and expansion resumed.[43]

In June of 2020, a Federal Reserve Bank of New York staff working paper by Haelim Anderson, Jin-Wook Chang, and Adam Copeland examined the impact of liquidity support that the Federal Reserve provided to its member banks through the discount window during the 1918 pandemic. Comparing lending data from member banks to lending data in nonmember banks in the State of New York, the authors aimed to investigate "the relationship between pandemics and financial stability," during a time when "the economy's ability to survive the impact of a pandemic depends in part on the availability of credit, which banks may or may not be able to extend given their ability to handle the economic fallout from the pandemic."[44]

The authors compared banks' balance sheet data with flu death rates in the county in which they operated. They compared data for Federal Reserve member banks and nonmember banks. While member banks increased their borrowing at the Fed's discount window to respond to lending needs exacerbated by the pandemic, they did not or could not borrow enough to make up for outflows, such that they had to curtail lending to some degree. Nonmember banks, meanwhile, could not borrow against collateral from the Federal Reserve at all, and money did not pass through member banks to them, so they had to reduce lending even further. Anderson, Chang, and Copeland concluded that pandemic shocks jeopardize financial stability, such that a central bank has an essential role to play in providing sufficient liquidity, especially to "localities, industries, or markets" hardest hit.[45] The pandemic's impact on banking, however, though significant, was also short-lived. "By the end of 1919, banks were able to restore the balance sheet portfolio they had before the pandemic," the authors found.[46]

The Flu and a Peace That Led to War

Around the time that the short 1918–1919 recession was bottoming out in April of 1919, H1N1 flu debuted as an uninvited participant at the Paris peace negotiations, perhaps with fateful results, though we can never know the alternate history that might have been.

In Chapter 32 of *The Great Influenza,* Barry described the 1919 post-war peace negotiations in Paris, where the virus effectively sidelined U.S. President Woodrow Wilson at a crucial juncture. Influenza was afoot in Paris that spring — 1,517 Parisians had died in March. Barry wrote:

> That month Wilson's wife, his wife's secretary, Chief White House Usher Irwin Hoover, and Cary Grayson, Wilson's personal White House physician and perhaps the single man Wilson trusted the most, were all ill. Clemenceau and Lloyd George both seemed to have mild cases of influenza.[47]

During this time, Woodrow Wilson was fighting hard for a peace agreement that would incorporate the principles that he had laid out before Congress the year before — his Fourteen Points — including open diplomacy, free trade and equal trade conditions, government by the consent of the governed, "political independence and territorial integrity" for nations, and the creation of the League of Nations.[48]

But on April 3, the flu caught up with Wilson, who was, according to one witness, "seized with violent paroxysms of coughing, which were so severe and frequent that it interfered with his breathing."[49] Not only did the virus make him very ill, but it changed his behavior, too. He barked out strange orders that evidenced mental disorientation and believed that French spies had infiltrated his home.[50] He suffered for weeks afterward from a lethargy and evidenced personality changes that have suggested to some medical experts a case of encephalitis and to others the possibility of a minor stroke that might have been a consequence of Wilson's history of hypertension and vascular disease, as his biographer A. Scott Berg observed.[51] According to Irwin Hoover, who had known Wilson for years, Wilson was never the same after the flu and the apparent neurological damage the president seemed to suffer.[52] Needless to say, Woodrow Wilson's role in the peace negotiations was affected by his illness, even when he could rejoin the talks.

Figure 10.5 President Woodrow Wilson, seated at his desk at the White House with his wife, Edith Bolling Galt Wilson, standing at his side. This was the first posed picture taken after Wilson's illness, Harris & Ewing (June 1920), via Wikimedia Commons, public domain.

So how did Wilson succumb to the arguments of Georges Clemenceau and Lloyd George? There has been much speculation about Woodrow Wilson, including the common story about his stroke. John Barry did not find the stroke explanation convincing. He observed,

> Only one historian, Alfred Crosby, seems to have paid any attention to Wilson's actual symptoms — including high fever, severe coughing, and total prostration, all symptoms that perfectly fit influenza and have no

association whatsoever with stroke — and the on-site diagnosis of Grayson, an excellent physician highly respected by such men as Welch, Gorgas, Flexner, and Vaughan.[53]

In the end, the Treaty of Versailles did not resemble the policy Wilson had proposed and fought for, and its harsh terms with regard to Germany would later fuel the rise of Adolph Hitler. H1N1 influenza, the ancestor of all influenza pandemics since, had at least something to do with that.

Responses and Results

As soon as the new flu struck, medical science attempted to create a vaccine to protect against the disease. But all the assiduous, well-funded efforts were doomed from the start. Back in 1918, pathologists still believed that influenza was another bacterial infection. Despite all the advancements in medical science to date, the best medical minds of the time were engaged in a proverbial wild goose chase. It would be 1933 before a British research team at London's National Institute for Medical Research discovered the influenza virus. Thomas Francis and Jonas Salk would develop the first flu vaccine, using inactivated virus, for use with the military and, in 1945, for the broader population.[54]

As in 2020, without a vaccine, the world in 1918 had to face a pandemic armed only with nonpharmaceutical interventions (NPIs). In the United States, as elsewhere, the list of interventions attempted is familiar. Laura Spinney recounts them in *Pale Rider*. Schools were closed for a time, along with theaters and churches. Public gatherings were suspended, including funerals, and quarantine measures were put into place for newly arrived travelers. Public health education messages recommended using handkerchiefs to contain sneezes and coughs, washing hands often, and keeping windows open whenever possible. Social distancing was required on public transportation. Hospitals treated flu victims in isolation wards in an attempt to contain the spread of infection. Some localities required people to wear masks made of layers of gauze in public.[55] Historical photographs capture widespread compliance with mask requirements, but compliance was not universal. The Spanish flu period had its anti-maskers, too.

There was considerable variation in what interventions were used where and at what stage in the pandemic. In an influential 2007 paper, three of the "Wolverines" whose riveting story Michael Lewis told in *The Premonition: A Pandemic Story* — Richard Hatchett, Carter Mecher, and Marc Lipsitch — studied the correlations between what 17 U.S. cities did and the intensity of pandemic waves in those cities — specifically the peak weekly excess death rate from influenza and pneumonia and the cumulative excess death rate from influenza and pneumonia. What they found was that cities that moved quickly to control the spread of disease very early in an outbreak succeeded in lowering excess deaths by around 50% in comparison to cities that either chose not to implement mitigations or waited until an epidemic outbreak was already widespread. Two cities the authors chose to contrast in their analysis were Philadelphia and St. Louis.[56]

George Petras and Karl Gelles, writing for *USA Today* in May of 2020, building on the earlier, highly technical paper, told the story of the two cities' responses to the deadly wave that spread across the country in the fall of 1918. The fall wave arrived in Philadelphia first, after 300 sailors arrived from Boston, where there were already cases, on September 8. Three days later, the flu was spreading in the shipyard and soon beyond. Health officials underreacted early on: Though they issued flu warnings, they did not expect widespread cases among Philadelphians, so they did not impose measures to forestall transmission of the disease. It was the war that remained foremost in people's minds, and some dismissed the flu threat as hype concocted by the Germans to undermine the war effort. (Conspiracy theories are, of course, nothing new.)[57]

With the City Hospital already brimming with flu cases, what Philadelphia opted to do, rather than implementing NPIs to slow the spread of disease, was to hold on September 28 a parade attended by 200,000 people — the city's fourth Liberty Loans Parade. Liberty Bond sales, conducted and promoted by the 12 Federal Reserve banks, were vital to the war effort and equated with patriotism. Parades and contests among cities were a part of the government's massive advertising campaign. To the city's leaders and even to the public health director, canceling the parade seemed unthinkable. A surge in cases ripped through the city, inundating hospitals. An estimated 13,936 Philadelphians died of influenza and pneumonia between September and December.[58]

St. Louis, in contrast, fared far better during the same time period, with an estimated 2,883 deaths. What did St. Louis do differently? In fact, both cities ordered the closures of schools, churches, and theaters in early October. St. Louis limited gatherings to 20 people and limited ridership on streetcars. But the closures and limits on gatherings were more extensive in St. Louis and lasted longer. Whereas schools, churches, and businesses reopened in Philadelphia in late October, nonessential businesses remained closed in St. Louis until mid-November despite protests from businesses, when a gradual reopening commenced. School reopenings happened more gradually, too, in November, with junior and senior high schools resuming classes first. It would be January 2, 1919, before all St. Louis schools were open again. Finally, St. Louis's city health commissioner, Dr. Max Starkloff, with the support of the mayor, canceled St. Louis's Liberty Loans parade, prioritizing public health over war bond sales. Under Starkloff's leadership, St. Louis managed to halve the city's death rate per 100,000 people as compared with Philadelphia's.[59]

Philadelphia and St. Louis are two well-known case studies that are usefully juxtaposed, but others also reflect a wide range of outcomes based on measures taken. In Summit County, Colorado, for example, a local historical guide, Phyl Rubenstein, has pieced together a history of how the 1918 pandemic played out in that more rural area, dotted in those days by small towns. Early on, residents were advised to wash their hands, avoid crowds, and isolate themselves if they were sick. In the town of Breckenridge, businesses and entertainment venues were shut down in early October, but schools remained open. Still, by November, half the town of Breckenridge was sick. Local leaders divided the town into quadrants and appointed a person for each quadrant to report cases and coordinate assistance to families who had fallen ill and were in quarantine. That way, the community ensured that the sick had food, fuel to heat their homes, and medical care.[60] (Their concept of community-organized mutual assistance has its analog today in the form of neighborhood emergency teams [NETs].[61])

By January of 1919, the situation was better in Breckinridge, and the town was taking measures to keep it that way. Visitors from the nearby town of Dillon, where an outbreak was underway, were turned back or sent to a hospital where they would be quarantined. As cases dropped across the county, people were soon ready to forget about the flu and to believe that the epidemic was finally over. A year after that, in January of 1920, a number of Summit County residents made the 83-mile trip to take in the Western National Stock Show at the stockyards in Denver.

The Denver stock show had been a tradition since 1906, and people came from far and near to attend it. Cattle and horses were exhibited and shown, bought and sold. Stockmen who attended learned about best practices for breeding and feeding their livestock.[62] The public enjoyed the show. The show had been canceled only once, in 1915, when an outbreak of hoof and mouth disease ensured that no one wanted to expose their animals to anyone else's.[63] But in January of 1920, the

City of Denver was keeping quiet about yet another uptick in flu cases. The stock show that had been canceled for hoof and mouth disease was not canceled for flu. As a result, nearby Summit County, including the town of Breckenridge, saw an unexpected and unwelcome new wave of flu cases as residents exposed to the flu at the show returned home again. Eleven people died within three weeks across the county. Breckenridge closed schools and theaters and banned public gatherings all over again, ordering that the sick be quarantined once more.[64]

Leaders in Denver had made the same fateful choice before. William Sharpley, the city's manager of health and charity, had instituted numerous measures to control the spread of flu after the first case arrived from Chicago (and died); but as soon as the number of cases had begun to decrease, the pressure to lift onerous mitigation measures had won out.[65]

Under pressure from business owners in the fall of 1918, the city had reopened into the teeth of what was destined to become the pandemic's deadly second wave. In early October, the city's Liberty Loan Parade drew 10,000 people, resulting in 1,200 new cases. Restrictions on indoor gatherings were reintroduced but then lifted in time for Armistice Day on November 11, when people filled the streets and the city auditorium to celebrate. Two weeks later the city saw hundreds of cases of flu. Twenty-two people died of H1N1 influenza in a single day. Restrictions were imposed once more until cases trended downward again.[66]

Communities across the country, large and small, faced the same difficult decisions about when to implement measures to curb the spread of illness and death and when to roll them back so that business and economic activity could get back on its feet and children could go back to school. The instruments used were similar — the closing of schools, churches, and businesses; the banning of public gatherings; mask ordinances (which the majority of people ignored in Denver, so Sharpley relented and resorted to merely recommending masking);

the imposition of quarantines — but their orchestration varied from place to place, as did public health outcomes and economic outcomes in the years that followed.

One city that fared better than most was densely populated Chicago. According to the National Academy of Sciences, the estimated death rate per 100,000 in the city was 390, lower than 422 in St. Louis and far lower than Philadelphia's 817.[67] This outcome is an interesting one, because the city did not act decisively when the first local cases occurred at Great Lakes Naval Training Center or even as cases emerged in the northern suburbs of the city two weeks later.[68]

The usual measures were in place, with some exceptions and additions, and the timeline of their implementation was included in a contemporaneous report on the epidemic by John Robertson and Gottfried Koehler, Chicago's commissioner and assistant commissioner of health. Entertainment venues and restaurants were closed so that children could more safely remain in school, and schools did not close. In the fall of 1918, the city included improving ventilation among the measures that it took (as did Denver). With children warmly dressed, classroom windows remained open. Children were screened daily, and students with symptoms of illness were sent home.

Churches were not closed but were instructed to improve ventilation by opening windows. Street cars kept their windows open. The city did away with "rush hour": Workers' hours were staggered to limit the number of people riding a streetcar at any given time. Vigorous social distancing restrictions were enforced otherwise. Public funerals were banned, and private funerals could have only 10 attendees. Quarantines for the sick were strictly enforced — police were on the lookout for people who coughed in the streets or in public spaces without using handkerchiefs, and they arrested them if they did not promise to do better after being lectured and warned. Masking was required in hospitals, which were closed to visitors. Public gatherings were canceled unless they were deemed essential to the war effort.

There was also an effort to aid Chicagoans. Health officers — 150 of them employed and paid $200 a month by the United States Public Health Service — were charged with treating those who could not afford a doctor or find one. To address the shortage of care that the city saw during the pandemic, Robertson would in 1919 advocate for the training of a new type of nurse, a "practical nurse" who could be trained in a matter of months, an idea later endorsed by the Journal of the American Medical Association.[69]

Six weeks into the outbreak, by early November, however, Chicago began to reopen — and, remarkably, without driving a new surge of deaths. Orla Hegarty, who teaches architecture at University College Dublin, has shared, in an extensive thread on X, her historical research regarding Chicago's response to the 1918 pandemic. She highlighted the city's efforts to improve ventilation in buildings. Chicago had begun implementing improved ventilation standards for buildings years earlier, in 1911, guided by the understanding that tuberculosis was an airborne disease. Hegarty cited a report for 1911–1918 from the Chicago Bureau of Sanitation, detailing the rationale for improved ventilation, ventilation standards for new and existing buildings, and rigorous procedures for measuring air quality in buildings, including testing air samples for concentrations of carbon dioxide. For several years, Chicago had been insisting on air quality improvements in its 1,700 streetcars, enforcing standards for new buildings, and requiring improvements in older ones.[70] In November of 1918, theaters, lodge halls, dance halls, and skating rinks were permitted to reopen once they passed a rigorous ventilation inspection.[71]

If Denver's and Philadelphia's experiences demonstrated in 1918 that crowded outdoor events could be superspreaders, Hegarty reasoned that Chicago's relative success in limiting infections and deaths constituted evidence that improved indoor ventilation had played a role in lowering the burden of illness and death.[72] Robertson and Koehler, however, noted in their report that the Windy City had seen an intense flu season in the winter of 1917, especially for children, and questioned in their report whether the new flu might have been among the influenza strains circulating that winter, too.[73] No evidence we have encountered suggests that this was the case. Whether Chicago's winter flu season in 1917–18 might have blunted the severity of the H1N1 flu wave in the fall 1918 is not a question we have seen addressed elsewhere. The 1918 pandemic histories of communities large and small comprise a labyrinth of details about decisions and consequences, from the individual to the societal.

Economic Effects of NPIs

But what are the economic implications of varying approaches and varying results over the short and medium term? In 2022, economists Sergio Correia (Federal Reserve Board of Governors), Stephan Luck (Federal Reserve Bank of New York), and Emil Verner, (MIT's Sloan School of Management) delved into the evidence we have from the 1918 pandemic. They studied U.S. cities that mandated stringent infection control measures and cities that did not. They found that the pandemic itself disrupted economic activity, whether or not NPIs were in place, such that stricter NPIs did not intensify the pandemic's economic shock. Instead, illnesses, deaths, and behavioral responses were a primary driver of economic impacts with or without NPIs in play.[74]

In the short term, cities that implemented high levels of NPIs and cities that were comparatively lax in their mitigations both saw similar declines in a "combined business disruptions index" that Correia, Luck, and Verner developed from the characterizations of business conditions in *Bradstreet's* weekly trade journal.[75] In the medium term, the Fed economists used data from the Census of Manufacturers to draw conclusions about the economic trajectories of the cities they studied, beginning in 1919, when that census went from being published every two years rather than every five. Cities that had imposed more thoroughgoing NPIs had managed to halve their deaths relative to cities that had not. Not surprisingly, in the years that followed the pandemic, these cities, having lost fewer workers, "had a higher level of employment from 1919 onward than those with more lenient NPIs."[76]

One variable that Correia, Luck, and Verner concluded that they needed to control for, however, was growth patterns prior to the pandemic. Since the pandemic had moved from east to west, cities in the Midwest and the West had time to learn from the experience of cities in the East. St. Louis is an example. They eliminated from their calculations some cities in the far West, such as Los Angeles and Seattle, that were growing quickly before the pandemic and controlled for pre-pandemic city growth rates. But even when they had controlled for these factors, the lower mortality associated with stricter NPIs, implemented early, appeared to have improved a city's prospects during the post-pandemic recovery period. They wrote,

> The estimates for both employment and output are generally positive across all three NPI measures. The estimates are not always significant, but the point estimates suggest moderate positive effects. Our preferred specification suggests High NPI cities see around 17 percent higher manufacturing employment and 12 percent higher manufacturing output after the pandemic.... The confidence intervals reject a large negative effect of NPIs on both measures of economic activity.[77]

Absent a deadly pandemic that sickens, kills, creates worker shortages, and inspires changes in behavior, the measures that stricter cities implemented earlier and often for longer would have caused considerable economic disruption. But during the 1918 pandemic, attendance at entertainment and hospitality venues plummeted even in the absence of closures and other measures. Absenteeism in Chicago schools reached 50% as children fell ill and many worried parents kept their children home.[78] Philadelphia asked residents to limit phone calls, as more than a quarter of its workers were home because of illness.[79] On October 24, the *Wall Street Journal* sized up the flu's impact on production this way:

> Widespread epidemic of influenza has caused serious inroads on the retail merchandise trade during the current month. Heads of large organizations report that not only has sickness cut down the shopping crowds, but in many cities the health authorities have shut down the stores. The chain store companies have felt the effect of the sickness not a little, for in addition to the smaller business done a number of their employees are sick.[80]

On the one hand, measures taken to lower the burden of illness took a toll on business in the short term; on the other hand, without optimally orchestrated nonpharmaceutical interventions, the disease itself doubled its toll. The difference was that where NPIs were most successful in blunting worst outcomes, recovery post-pandemic was made at least somewhat easier because the labor supply was less impacted.[81]

Correia, Luck, and Verner published their analysis of the economic impacts of the 1918 pandemic and of selected U.S. cities' varying responses to it in 2022. The Federal Reserve on the job in 1918, which focused narrowly on its original mission, did not yet have the perspective that the Spanish flu experience would offer the Federal Reserve a century later, when the Fed acted decisively in 2020 to mitigate a pandemic economic shock dealt by a different virus.

1.   David C. Wheelock, "Overview: The History of the Federal Reserve: 1913 to Today," *Federal Reserve History*, September 13, 2021, https://www.federalreservehistory.org/essays/federal-reserve-history.

2.   David C. Wheelock, "The Fed's Formative Years: 1913–1929," *Federal Reserve History*, November 22, 2013, https://www.federalreservehistory.org/essays/feds-formative-years.

3.   The Investopedia Team, "Bank Panic of 1907: Causes, Effects, and Importance," *Investopedia*, updated September 21, 2023, https://www.investopedia.com/terms/b/bank-panic-of-1907.asp#.

4.   Jon R. Moen and Ellis W. Tallman, "The Panic of 1907," *Federal Reserve History*, December 4, 2015, https://www.federalreservehistory.org/essays/panic-of-1907.

5.   Moen and Tallman, "Bank Panic of 1907."

6.   Moen and Tallman, "Bank Panic of 1907."

7.   Gary Richardson and Jessie Romero, "The Meeting at Jekyll Island," *Federal Reserve History*, December 4, 2015, https://www.federalreservehistory.org/essays/jekyll-island-conference.

8.   Liaquat Ahamed, *Lords of Finance: The Bankers Who Broke the World* (New York: Penguin Press, 2009), 55. Kindle edition.

9.   Richardson and Romero, "The Meeting at Jekyll Island."

10.   Wheelock, "Overview: The History of the Federal Reserve."

11.   Wheelock, "The Fed's Formative Years."

12.   News release, Federal Reserve Board, Department of the Treasury, November 15, 1914, (https://fraser.stlouisfed.org/files/docs/meltzer/bogsub111514.pdf), cited in Sandra Ghizoni, "Reserve Banks Open for Business," *Federal Reserve History*, November 22, 2013, https://www.federalreservehistory.org/essays/reserve-banks-open.

13.   Ghizoni, "Reserve Banks Open for Business."

14.   Ghizoni, "Reserve Banks Open for Business."

15.   Phil Davies, "The Federal Reserve's Role During WWI: August 1914–November 1918," *Federal Reserve History*, November 22, 2013, https://www.federalreservehistory.org/essays/feds-role-during-wwi.

16.   Evan Andrews, "Why Was It Called the 'Spanish Flu'?" History.com, January 12, 2016, updated July 12, 2023, https://www.history.com/news/why-was-it-called-the-spanish-flu.

17.   C Andrew Aligne, "Overcrowding and Mortality During the Influenza Pandemic of 1918," *American Journal of Public Health* 106, no. 4 (April 2016): 642–644, reprinted by the NIH National Library of Medicine, https://www.ncbi.nlm.nih.gov/pmc/articles/PMC4816079/.

18.   Laura Spinney, *Pale Rider: The Spanish Flu of 1918 and How It Changed the World* (New York: Public Affairs, 2017), 37.

19.   Jack M. Holl, "The Second Battle of Gettysburg: Eisenhower's Fight with the 1918 Flu Pandemic," in *Dwight D. Eisenhower's Religious Journey: Duty, God and Country* (Grand Rapids: Eerdmans, 2021), reprinted in Michael J. Halvorson, "PLU Alum Discusses Eisenhower's Work During 1918 Pandemic," *Pacific Lutheran University Department of History News*, May 29, 2020, https://www.plu.edu/history/news/plu-alum-discusses-eisenhowers-work-during-1918-pandemic/.

20. "The Army's First Tank School: Camp Colt at Gettysburg," National Park Service, December 7, 2022, https://www.nps.gov/articles/the-armys-first-tank-school-camp-colt-at-gettysburg.htm.
21. "The Influenza Pandemic of 1918 at Camp Sherman," National Park Service, April 8, 2020, https://www.nps.gov/articles/influenza-at-camp-sherman.htm.
22. Eric Durr, "Flu Outbreak Killed 45,000 U.S. Soldiers During World War," National Guard, August 30, 2018, https://www.nationalguard.mil/News/Article/1616713/flu-outbreak-killed-45000-us-soldiers-during-world-war-i/.
23. Simon Flexner, "Biographical Memoir of William Henry Welch: 1850–1934,"*Biographical Memoirs, Volume XXII*, National Academy of Sciences, 1942, 220–2022, https://www.nasonline.org/publications/biographical-memoirs/memoir-pdfs/welch-william.pdf.
24. John Barry, *The Great Influenza: The Story of the Deadliest Pandemic in History* (London: Penguin Books, 2005), 188–189.
25. Rufus Cole, letter to Simon Flexner, May 26, 1936, https://quod.lib.umich.edu/f/flu/1570flu.0015.751/3/--letter-to-dr-simon-flexner-from-dr-rufus-cole, 3.
26. "The 1918 Flu Pandemic: Why It Matters 100 Years Later," *Public Health Matters Blog*, CDC Centers for Disease Control and Prevention, May 14, 2018, https://blogs.cdc.gov/publichealthmatters/2018/05/1918-flu/.
27. Emily Martin, "The Lessons Learned from 1918 Flu Fatigue, according to Historians," *National Geographic*, March 4, 2022, https://www.nationalgeographic.com/history/article/the-lessons-learned-from-1918-flu-fatigue-according-to-historians.
28. Jeffery Taubenberger, "'The 1918 flu is still with us': The deadliest pandemic ever is still causing problems today," *Washington Post*, September 3, 2020, quoted in Teddy Amenabar, https://www.washingtonpost.com/history/2020/09/01/1918-flu-pandemic-end/.
29. Edward D. Frohlich, "Leadership in American Medicine as I See it: A Background in the Beginning," *Ochsner Journal* 12, no. 4 (Winter 2012): 302–307, https://www.ncbi.nlm.nih.gov/pmc/articles/PMC3527854/.
30. Priscilla Roberts, "Benjamin Strong, the Federal Reserve, and the Limits to Interwar American Nationalism, Part I: Intellectual Profile of a Central Banker," *Federal Reserve Bank of Richmond Economic Quarterly* 82, no. 2 (Spring 2000): 64–65.
31. Roberts, "Benjamin Strong, the Federal Reserve, and the Limits to Interwar American Nationalism," 62.
32. Ahamed, *Lords of Finance*, 93.
33. Allan Meltzer, *A History of the Federal Reserve, Volume 1: 1913–1951* (Chicago: University of Chicago Press, 2004).
34. Milton Friedman and Anna Schwartz, *A Monetary History of the United States 1867–1960* (Princeton: Princeton University Press, 1963).
35. George Warren and Frank Pearson, *Prices* (Hoboken: Wiley, 1933), 183–195.
36. Sidney Homer, *A History of Interest Rates* (New Brunswick: Rutgers, 1963). See Chart 50 on page 633.
37. Thomas A. Garrett, "Economic Effects of the 1918 Influenza Pandemic: Implications for a Modern-day Pandemic," Federal Reserve Bank of St. Louis, November 2007, 19–20, https://

www.stlouisfed.org/-/media/project/frbstl/stlouisfed/files/pdfs/community-development/research-reports/pandemic_flu_report.pdf.

38. Thomas Garrett, "Economic Effects of the 1918 Influenza Pandemic," 20.

39. Francois Velde, April 2020. "What Happened to the U.S. Economy During the 1918 Influenza Pandemic? A View Through High-Frequency Data," Working Paper No. 2020-11, Federal Reserve Bank of Chicago, https://www.chicagofed.org/publications/working-papers/2020/2020-11.

40. Velde, "What Happened to the U.S. Economy During the 1918 Influenza Pandemic?" 6.

41. Velde, "What Happened to the U.S. Economy During the 1918 Influenza Pandemic?" 10, 19.

42. Velde, "What Happened to the U.S. Economy During the 1918 Influenza Pandemic?" 7–14.

43. Velde, "What Happened to the U.S. Economy During the 1918 Influenza Pandemic?" 40–41.

44. Haelim Anderson, Jin-Wook Chang, and Adam Copeland, "The Effect of the Central Bank Liquidity Support during Pandemics: Evidence from the 1918 Spanish Influenza Pandemic," *Finance and Economics Discussion Series 2020-050*, Federal Reserve Board, 1, https://www.federalreserve.gov/econres/feds/files/2020050pap.pdf.

45. Anderson, et al., "The Effect of the Central Bank Liquidity Support during Pandemics," 20.

46. Anderson, et al., "The Effect of the Central Bank Liquidity Support during Pandemics," 2–4.

47. Barry, *The Great Influenza,* 382.

48. Wilson, Woodrow, "The Fourteen Points," speech to Congress, January 8, 1918, archived by The National WWI Museum and Memorial, https://www.theworldwar.org/learn/peace/fourteen-points.

49. Barry, *The Great Influenza,* 383.

50. Barry, *The Great Influenza,* 385.

51. A. Scott Berg, *Wilson* (New York: Berkley, 2013), 568. Kindle Edition.

52. Barry, *The Great Influenza,* 385.

53. Barry, *The Great Influenza,* 387.

54. "History of the Influenza Vaccine," World Health Organization, last accessed June 15, 2024, https://www.who.int/news-room/spotlight/history-of-vaccination/history-of-influenza-vaccination.

55. Spinney, *Pale Rider,* 96.

56. Richard J. Hatchett, Carter E. Mecher, and Marc Lipsitch, "Public health interventions and epidemic intensity during the 1918 influenza pandemic," *PNAS* 104, no. 18 (May 2007): 7583, https://pubmed.ncbi.nlm.nih.gov/17416679/.

57. George Petras and Karl Gelles, "100 Years Ago, Philadelphia Chose a Parade over Social Distancing during the 1918 Spanish Flu – and Paid a Heavy Price," *USA Today,* May 25, 2020, https://www.usatoday.com/in-depth/news/2020/05/22/second-wave-coronavirus-spanish-flu-1918-philadelphia-st-louis-influenza-deaths-COVID-19/3085405001/.

58. Petras and Gelles, "100 Years Ago, Philadelphia Chose a Parade over Social Distancing."

59. Petras and Gelles, "100 Years Ago, Philadelphia Chose a Parade over Social Distancing."

60. Taylor Sienkiewicz, "Historians draw parallels between Spanish flu and coronavirus outbreaks in Summit County," *Summit Daily,* March 31, 2020, https://www.summitdaily.com/news/historians-draw-parallels-between-spanish-flu-and-coronavirus-outbreaks-in-summit-county/.

61. For examples of neighborhood emergency teams, see "Neighorhood Emergency Teams Guidelines" Lewiston-Nez Perce County Emergency Management, http://www.catastrophicresponse.org/Portals/40/PDF/NETGuidebook.pdf and "Neighborhood Emergency Teams (NETs)," Portland City Government, https://www.portlandoregon.gov/pbem/index.cfm?c=31667.

62. Leigh Jeremias, "Topics in History: National Western Stock Show," Colorado Virtual Library, January 13, 2017, https://www.coloradovirtuallibrary.org/digital-colorado/colorado-historic-newspapers-collection/topics-in-history-national-western-stock-show/.

63. Jeremias, "National Western Stock Show."

64. Sienkiewicz, "Historians draw parallels between Spanish flu and coronavirus outbreaks in Summit County."

65. "Denver and the 1918 Influenza Pandemic," Influenza Encyclopedia: The American Influenza Epidemic of 1918–1919, University of Michigan Center for the History of Medicine and Michigan Publishing, University of Michigan Library, last accessed June 15, 2024, https://www.influenzaarchive.org/cities/city-denver.html#.

66. John Aguilar, "Not Colorado's first pandemic: What we can learn from the Spanish flu," *Denver Post,* March 29, 2020, https://www.denverpost.com/2020/03/29/pandemic-1918-spanish-flu-colorado-coronavirus/.

67. Petras and Gelles, "100 Years Ago, Philadelphia Chose a Parade over Social Distancing."

68. Edward McClelland, "How Chicago Dealt with the 1918 Spanish Flu," *Chicago Magazine,* March 17, 2020, https://www.chicagomag.com/city-life/march-2020/how-chicago-dealt-with-the-1918-spanish-flu/.

69. "Chicago, Illinois," Influenza Encyclopedia: The American Influenza Epidemic of 1918–1919, University of Michigan Center for the History of Medicine and Michigan Publishing, University of Michigan Library, last accessed June 15, 2024, https://www.influenzaarchive.org/cities/city-chicago.html#.

70. Orla Hegarty (@Orla_Hegarty), "Chicago didn't have a second wave of Spanish Flu… so what did they do, & how did the city re-open when there was no vaccine?" X, Mar 20, 2021, 5:57 AM, https://x.com/Orla_Hegarty/status/1373212120171610120?s=20. (See entire thread. The discussion on ventilation begins at https://x.com/Orla_Hegarty/status/1373220541763612674?s=20.)

71. John Robertson and Gottfried Koehler, "Preliminary Report on the Influenza Epidemic in Chicago," *American Journal of Public Health* 8, no. 11 (November 1918): 849–56, https://www.ncbi.nlm.nih.gov/pmc/articles/PMC1362263/.

72. Orla Hegarty, "Opening Statement to Joint Oireachtas Committee on Health," Speech to the Joint Oireachtas Committee on Health, May 17, 2021, 2, https://data.oireachtas.ie/ie/oireachtas/committee/dail/33/joint_committee_on_health/submissions/2021/2021-05-19_

opening-statement-orla-hegarty-associate-professor-school-of-architecture-ucd-member-of-the-expert-advisory-group-on-ventilation-and-COVID-19_en.pdf.

73. Robertson and Koehler, "Preliminary Report on the Influenza Epidemic in Chicago," 854.

74. Sergio Correia, Stephan Luck, and Emil Verner, "Pandemics Depress the Economy, Public Health Interventions Do Not: Evidence from the 1918 Flu," *The Journal of Economic History* 82, no. 4 (December 2022): 917–957, https://ssrn.com/abstract=3561560.

75. Correia, et al., "Pandemics Depress the Economy, Public Health Interventions Do Not," 944.

76. Correia, et al., "Pandemics Depress the Economy, Public Health Interventions Do Not," 946.

77. Correia, et al., "Pandemics Depress the Economy, Public Health Interventions Do Not," 946.

78. Correia, et al., "Pandemics Depress the Economy, Public Health Interventions Do Not," 952.

79. Correia, et al., "Pandemics Depress the Economy, Public Health Interventions Do Not," 951.

80. *Wall Street Journal,* October 24, 1918, cited in Correia, et al., "Pandemics Depress the Economy, Public Health Interventions Do Not," 950.

81. Correia, et al., "Pandemics Depress the Economy, Public Health Interventions Do Not," 953–954.

Chapter 11

The 1957 H2N2 Influenza Pandemic
(Asian Flu)

Eight Sentences and an Opportunity

The 1957 Asian flu pandemic would be the second pandemic to occur during the history of the Federal Reserve. It would mark a historic first, but not where the Fed was concerned.

On April 17, 1957, microbiologist Maurice Hilleman was perusing the *New York Times*. On page three, his eye was likely drawn first to the photo of Marines landing on a beach in Turkey, but he must have also been interested to read the article at the top left, about a possible link between radiation exposure from hydrogen bomb tests and bone cancer. The slim article titled "Hong Kong Battling Influenza Epidemic," though, was just four inches of copy — a mere eight sentences — sandwiched just above the ads for Brooks Brothers worsted suits, Macy's shoes, men's ties, a lacy nylon blouse, and a beauty treatment for blackheads. The article reported "thousands of cases" of influenza in Hong Kong and mothers standing in long lines seeking treatment for their "glassy-eyed children, tied to their backs."[1] Maurice Hilleman immediately recognized a possible flu pandemic in the making.

At the time, Hilleman was working at the Walter Reed Institute of Army Research, where he had identified changes that could happen when a virus mutated. The next day, he sent a message to the Army Medical General Laboratory in Japan, asking them to investigate the outbreak. They were able to send him a saliva sample from a U.S. servicemember who had caught the virus. Studying the new influenza virus in the sample, he quickly identified two key changes that rendered most people susceptible to the new strain. He verified that U.S. soldiers had no antibodies to fight the new flu. Only elderly survivors of the Russian Flu pandemic of 1889–1890 would have any immunity. (That epidemic infected 4 million people in Britain and killed at least 125,000 of them.) Once other labs confirmed his findings, Dr. Hilleman announced that an influenza epidemic was coming, and he set out to ensure that a vaccine would be available by the time schools reopened in September.[2] Because of his timely realization and quick action, 40 million doses of vaccine were produced in the United States by fall.[3]

Since the U.S. population by the end of 1957 was just shy of 172 million people, 40 million doses of vaccine were not nearly enough for everyone who wanted protection to have it, but the vaccine assuredly saved lives. The Asian flu pandemic marked the first time in history that a vaccine had been developed to blunt the impacts of an influenza pandemic. Such a vaccine might not have existed in 1957 either had it not been for Hilleman and an eight-sentence report in the *New York Times*. The 1957 experience — when the World Health Organization had missed foreseeing the outbreak and matters came down to a physician scientist reading a newspaper — underlines the never-ending importance of global surveillance that enables early detection of new infectious diseases in time to prepare and react.

The key observation that Dr. Hilleman made about influenza viruses — that genetic drift caused the flu to mutate regularly — would presage the need for annual flu shots. The epidemic in 1957 might have been even worse if not for Dr. Hilleman.[4] The vaccine would limit the death toll among Americans, but the toll might have been even lower if the vaccine had been made available to everyone sooner.

Maurice Hilleman developed more than 40 vaccines in his long career, a record that remains unmatched today. He created vaccines for the measles, mumps, hepatitis A and B, rubella, pneumonia, and meningitis, among others. At least a million lives were saved by his measles vaccine alone.[5]

Though the Hong Kong epidemic finally made the news in April of 1957, it actually began in February in East Asia, when a subtype of influenza A underwent genetic modifications after an animal host was infected with both that strain and an avian influenza strain. The two viruses combined, reassorting their genes and producing a new influenza A strain that would be named H2N2. Such mutations are common occurrences. Genetic drift and more reassortment would combine to eradicate H2N2 and replace it with another virus, H3N2, in just over a decade. H3N2, in turn, would cause the influenza pandemic of 1968.[6]

The winter and spring of 1957 saw the new flu virus spread slowly throughout China and its nearest Asian neighbors. It reached the United States by midsummer but infected few people at first. The situation changed when 53,000 Boy Scouts from around the country gathered for their Jamboree at Valley Forge, Pennsylvania, in mid-July. Their 25,000 tents were arrayed across the green fields where Washington's continental army had spent the difficult winter of 1777–1778. The annual Jamboree that summer, however, turned into a superspreader event. Three hundred fifty boys fell ill, and the Asian Flu traveled home with the scouts to every corner of the country (see Figure 11.1 on the next page).[7]

As historian Niall Ferguson recounted in Chapter 7 of *Doom: The Politics of Catastrophe,* July brought a massive outbreak in Tangipahoa Parish, Louisiana, that sickened many and left two dead. More outbreaks followed throughout Louisiana and across the river into Mississippi. More would follow in Ohio, Kentucky, Utah, and California. The epidemic surged further when schools opened. The CDC estimated that 60% of all U.S. students fell ill with flu that fall, and absenteeism in one study was 20–30% higher than average. Absences in Manhattan peaked on October 7 with 43% of students absent at once. By March of 1958, nearly 70,000 Americans had died from the flu.[8] By 1960, H2N2 influenza had claimed an estimated 116,000 American lives.[9]

Figure 11.1 The 1957 National Boy Scout Jamboree at Valley Forge, PA, National Park Service (1957), public domain. (Eagle Scout David Kotok, who missed this event, explains, "I had committed to a job as a camp counselor at a Boy Scout camp in NJ and therefore did not attend the Jamboree.")

As with most strains of flu, the 1957 pandemic varied in its course and its symptoms from one individual to another. Some people had few symptoms at all. Others had cough, fever, malaise, nausea, and vomiting. Still others would develop complications such as pneumonia.

Some would die. The Asian flu killed between one and two million people worldwide during the period 1957–1960.[10] The death toll could have been significantly worse had Hilleman not read his morning paper on a fateful Wednesday morning in April.

Pandemic Governance

Though medical science at Walter Reed made historic strides in connection with the 1957 Asian flu pandemic, the U.S. government's pandemic response as a whole was otherwise constrained by the politics of the time, as government responses to all sorts of things are inclined to be. As we noted in the previous chapter, President Dwight D. Eisenhower had firsthand experience in dealing with a pandemic as a young commander at Camp Colt in Gettysburg, Pennsylvania, during the 1918 flu pandemic.[11] Knowing that disease is the worst enemy of the soldier, Eisenhower was concerned about the military and the soldiers who would face the flu. Predictably, he ordered the vaccination of all U.S. forces. But he declined to spearhead a mass vaccination program for the public at large. He left the public health aspect to the private sector — the pharmaceutical companies — and to state and local governments. The strategy fell short of fully meeting the nation's needs for a vaccine.

Why did the Eisenhower administration choose not to spearhead an effort to protect the American people as a whole even as it protected the troops? After all, the president had already demonstrated a pro-vaccine stance with an initiative to make the polio vaccine widely available both quickly and at no cost in 1955.[12] A closer look at the history of the polio vaccine rollout and the politics of the period, however, suggests likely answers to that question.

The fight against polio enjoyed broad public support. In 1952, the country had weathered its worst polio outbreak to date, leaving 21,000 Americans paralyzed and more than 3000 dead. The prospect of seeing their children in iron lungs or struggling to walk with braces had fearful parents keeping their children at home.[13] A single first-grade class in Dewitt, New York, lost three students in a single outbreak. Pools closed; bowling alleys closed; camps were canceled; theaters shut their doors; the start of school in some areas was delayed.[14]

When Jonas Salk announced, on April 12, 1955, that a polio vaccine was ready, there was widespread rejoicing; but there were no actual doses to administer in the United States; and there was no plan yet in place for vaccine distribution. Indeed, the nation's first Secretary of Health, Education, and Welfare, Oveta Culp Hobby, was opposed to the federal government's getting involved in coordinating the distribution of the vaccine or making polio vaccination compulsory for children. She wanted other entities to handle distribution — the states or charities or corporations rather than the federal government. A conservative Republican from Texas, Hobby was opposed to what she viewed as "socialized medicine."

Eisenhower, on the other hand, wanted a free vaccine distributed with the help of the federal government; and when Hobby, whom Eisenhower had appointed, dragged her feet, he had to find another way.[15] It would be the National Foundation for Infantile Paralysis (later renamed the March of Dimes) that first distributed the vaccine instead, in the beginning only enough to vaccinate those most vulnerable to poliomyelitis — young children in first and second grade.

Eisenhower then tasked his Secretary of Health, Education and Welfare to allocate the vaccine to the states as it became available, apportioning doses according to the population of children ages five through nine. He asked Congress to allot funding to the states to pay for the vaccine.[16] The Polio Vaccine Assistance Act of 1957 was signed into law on August 12, twelve days after Hobby left the administration, having resigned in July.[17]

As popular as the battle against polio was, the Polio Vaccine Assistance Act was destined to pass; but trust in the vaccine nosedived for a time when a bad batch of vaccine went into schoolchildren's arms in late April of 1955, transmitting rather than preventing polio and resulting in hundreds of polio cases, some causing paralysis and, in 11 cases, death. Faith in the Salk vaccine was shaken, and vaccinations ceased until the bad batch could be traced to its source, Cutter Laboratories in California. The "Cutter Incident" was a stumble from which the initiative to protect people against polio had to recover. It also seeded a measure of distrust in vaccines, at least for some.

The 1950s saw concerted, coordinated resistance to anything that smacked of what critics termed *socialized medicine*. In 1945, Eisenhower's predecessor, Harry Truman, had proposed a national health insurance program to rectify what he saw as a problem that needed to be solved: "Millions of our citizens do not now have a full measure of opportunity to achieve and enjoy good health. Millions do not now have protection or security against the economic effects of sickness."[18] But the American Medical Association would launch a $5 million, three-year campaign in 1949 to fight the idea that government might be involved in medicine in any way — whether in funding research or supporting care. Such activities were painted as instances of "creeping socialism" by AMA lobbyists and others who opposed them — and in their eyes opposition to such initiatives amounted to a struggle for freedom, while national healthcare amounted to communism.[19] Truman's plan did not pass, and the AMA pressed for private insurance plans instead.

So, when Eisenhower purposed to protect schoolchildren from the possibility of paralysis or a life spent in an iron lung, he had powerful forces to contend with who opposed the federal government's playing a role in healthcare. Oveta Hobby was not alone in her views.

The same political environment, of course, prevailed in 1957 when H2N2 influenza surged across the United States. Eisenhower was a

Republican, not a Democrat as Truman had been, and what he could do as commander in chief of the military was not what he felt he could do on behalf of all Americans as president.

The Eisenhower administration left the manufacture and distribution of the Asian flu vaccine to the private sector. In August, a Bronx attorney named Robert Himmelfarb wrote to Eisenhower, expressing concern that only six companies would be producing the vaccine and that this strategy would be inadequate to vaccinate the population in time to prevent mortality. The response from the White House simply said that everything possible was being done to make the vaccine available to everyone as soon as possible. In reality, the Public Health Service was letting the vaccine manufacturers distribute the vaccine on a "voluntary" basis in proportion to state populations, with priorities guided by state and local authorities.[20] Science journalist Jen Pinkowski, writing for *Yale Insights,* explained:

> They developed a "voluntary allocation" plan with vaccine manufacturers that would distribute the shots through the free market. There would be no central federal management. In theory, it was to be an equitable distribution. But as historian George Dehner writes in *Influenza: A Century of Science and Public Health Response,* pharmaceutical companies had already taken vaccine preorders from corporate clients such as Ford and AT&T. One pharma executive said the companies "would need to be considered in any allocation plan."

> The military had claimed the first 2.6 million doses; sailors and soldiers began to receive inoculations in August. Vulnerable populations, healthcare workers, and essential transportation, communications, and utility employees were next on the list; they needed 12

million doses. Officials then launched a promotional campaign to encourage all Americans to get the vaccine once it became more widely available.[21]

As political scientist Max Skidmore has noted, some public health experts had appealed to the Eisenhower administration for a mass vaccination program but were rebuffed, though they did get funding for surveillance. The free market failed at providing the vaccine in a timely fashion because, as Skidmore observed, "without government coordination classical supply-and-demand relationships work mischievously" during an epidemic. Proper timing of a vaccination campaign should have had the vaccine available in large quantities at least a month before the peak of the epidemic.[22]

In many places, the spread of the virus simply outpaced the arrival of the vaccine, which, once administered, took two weeks to provide maximum protection. Vaccinating the military and a fraction of the population with a modestly effective vaccine did blunt the Asian flu's impact after a peak in infections in October, but results fell short of what they might have been had a vaccine been widely available earlier. President Eisenhower himself was at first reluctant to be vaccinated because he did not want to jump ahead of ordinary Americans, but the Public Health Service finally persuaded him to do so in late August, after putting out a news release recommending that older people with heart conditions should be prioritized. Ike himself was a member of the primary target audience.[23] In taking the shot, he exercised leadership as a role model.

There were lessons yet to be learned about optimizing the manufacture and distribution of a vaccine designed to curb the impact of a rapidly evolving pandemic. The 1957 Asian flu became an object lesson in the importance of public/private partnerships with key leadership and coordination from the federal government.

The 1950s Fed, a Recession, and the Flu

What did the Fed do during the pandemic of 1957–1958? Nothing at all. The Fed had not yet learned that a pandemic can cause an economic shock as well as a public health shock. Even as the pandemic raged in December of 1957, both in the United States and globally, the Federal Reserve took no notice of it. The minutes of the meeting from December 3rd do not mention the pandemic. Neither FOMC Chairman William McChesney Martin, Jr., nor Vice Chair Alfred Hayes, Jr., seem to have considered the possibility of the pandemic's having been a cause of the shock.

Figure 11.2 FOMC Chairman William Martin (left) courtesy of the U.S. Federal Reserve and Vice Chair Alfred Hayes (right) courtesy of the Federal Reserve Bank of New York.

Hayes, reporting to the Federal Reserve Board of Governors, described business conditions in the third quarter of 1957 this way. (Keep in mind that a pandemic wave had recently crested across the country, infecting millions.)

Since our last meeting the System has surprised the

country and the rest of the world with a sudden overt signal that our posture with respect to monetary policy has undergone a substantial change. Time will tell whether the timing and form of this action were the best we could have chosen. It had seemed to most of us at the last meeting that some preparation in the form of diminished restraint through open market operations would be advisable before any change was made in discount rates. However, the move has been made, and it may well turn out to have been useful on purely monetary grounds — at least it is now even clearer than it was three weeks ago that the economy is experiencing a rather broad and general decline, so far very moderate in degree, but carrying with it some risk of a cumulative recession.

Confirmation of the business decline is to be found in a wide variety of statistical measures of current trends, including figures on employment, average hours worked, personal income, retail sales, and industrial production. Other statistical data foreshadowing future levels of activity, such as reports of new orders, point to a continuation of the decline. Besides the expected drop in private plant and equipment expenditures, which may of course be accentuated by future adverse psychological factors, I have in mind also the likelihood that business expectations, the ready availability of goods and the current level of inventories may lead to some inventory liquidation in the next few months. Uncertainties and depleted monetary reserves in a number of countries point to a decline in exports. Among the few remaining strong spots in the economy are non-Federal Government expenditures and construction in general.

The greatest uncertainties with respect to the future level of activity concern consumer spending and Federal Government spending. As for the first, the Christmas season will provide a significant test. Over the next few months, the crucial factor, apart from the course of personal income, may be the degree of willingness of consumers to defend their level of living by means of reduced savings or increased borrowing. By and large, consumers are in a strong financial position and may be ready to reduce their liquid assets and/or to incur further debts, if their confidence is not shaken. As for Federal spending, the short-run outlook is for only a mild expansion, but it is quite possible that over the longer-term heavier defense outlays may involve substantial Government deficits and may give new impetus to inflationary influences in the economy.[24]

As he articulated factors impacting the economic outlook, Hayes was conscious of health matters — at least with regard to President Eisenhower — though he appears oblivious to the pandemic. He continued: "It is evident that intangible elements such as the Russian satellite development, political uncertainties abroad, and now the grave question as to the President's health, will play a major and unpredictable role in shaping the future course of business activity."[25]

In fact, the Fed appears not to have considered the Asian flu even once during the two-year pandemic. At least, such a discussion, if it occurred, did not make Fed minutes or reports. Discussions at meetings addressed issues as far-ranging as Sputnik and the health of President Eisenhower but never mentioned the influenza outbreak.

The Fed did discuss the possibility of a recession and eventually eased interest rates to help avoid one but never tied the decline to the flu.[26] The 1958 Annual Report of the Federal Reserve was likewise silent on the pandemic.[27]

This period saw the Fed operating as a newly independent central bank under the Fed-Treasury Accord of 1951. That working agreement marked a compromise born of a policy rift between the Fed and the Truman White House during the Korean War, when war bonds were once again important but CPI inflation had risen to an annualized rate of 21%.[28] Former Philadelphia Fed President Charles Plosser, writing as a visiting fellow for the Hoover Institution in 2022, has characterized the importance of the 1951 agreement:

> In March 1951, after a long, and at times acrimonious, debate, the U.S. Treasury and the Federal Reserve reached an agreement that allowed the central bank to end nearly a decade of pegging the interest rate on government debt. The country was facing uncomfortably high inflation following World War II and the Fed was frustrated by the fiscal demands of the Treasury that, in its view, rendered it unable to ensure price stability. The Treasury-Fed Accord of 1951 was an institutional arrangement, not a legal agreement, that established an understanding of how both parties would conduct policy, and it was an important milestone in the transformation of the Fed into an independent central bank. As described by Allan Meltzer (2003, p. 738), it "prevented an administration from deciding unilaterally to use monetary expansion to gain temporary political advantage or to finance too much of the budget at the central bank." Its goal was to permit the Fed to control its own balance sheet

rather than have it be controlled by the Treasury for the purpose of debt management.[29]

Having won a measure of monetary policy independence, the Fed was, once again, operating under a new construct, as had been the case when the 1918 pandemic struck. Independent or not, however, when an influenza pandemic erupted a half dozen years later, the Federal Reserve was loath to do anything that would overstep the narrow bounds of what it saw as its scope. Further, it does not appear that the Fed contemplated any actions regarding the flu or viewed the pandemic as a factor in the economic decline that commenced in the final quarter of 1957.

To better understand why the Fed did not consider the pandemic as it mapped the economic landscape or its monetary policy, we must look at what the Fed was focused on instead. William Martin, who served as chairman of the Federal Reserve from 1951 to 1970, had in 1956 and the first half of 1957 purposed, above all, to rein in inflation, which had reached 3% by the end of 1956 as the economy had recovered from the 1953–54 recession. As his biographer Robert Bremner observed, Martin believed that the Federal Reserve's role and key goal was to keep prices stable and thus to stamp out inflation that would devalue the U.S. dollar. In those years, long before Fed economists embraced 2% inflation as a desirable target, Bill Martin viewed 3% inflation as being 3% above a target of zero. Under Martin, the Fed had been tightening monetary policy by raising interest rates for two years in an effort to stop inflation, even as the recovery slowed and the Council of Economic Advisors predicted a recession ahead for the second quarter of 1957.[30]

Bremner described Chairman Martin's thinking:

For his part, Martin described full-blown inflation as carrying within it the seeds of its own destruction.

The speculative influences unleashed by inflation generate investment in inventory and physical plant at a rate that cannot be profitably sustained and, inevitably, economic activity begins to decline. Unchecked, the decline leads to collapse. The person most likely to be injured in the inflationary cycle was the "hardworking and thrifty . . . little man" on fixed income who could protect neither his income nor the value of his savings. Often, he was also the unemployed victim of the collapse.[31]

Martin saw the various repercussions of higher rates — slower capital spending, restrained economic activity, higher unemployment, and negative impacts on some sectors — as acceptable consequences in the battle against inflation, and he felt that the economy would adjust.

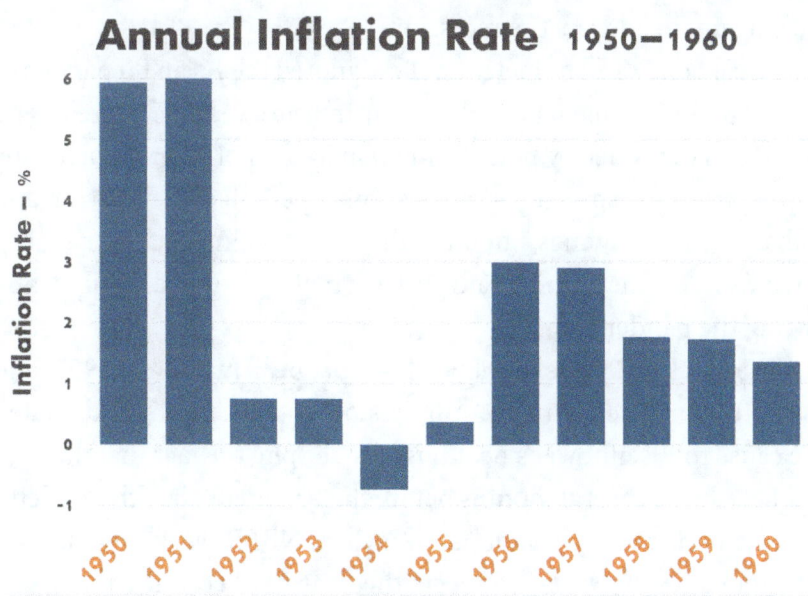

Figure 11.3 Annual U.S. Inflation Rate 1950–1960 (Data source: MacroTrends).

Meanwhile, the Treasury Department was deeply concerned about the prospect of its own rising costs, fearing widespread redemptions of lower-yielding Treasury certificates. Sales of longer-term bond issues in 1957 languished, and the Fed provided $400 million in extra reserves to incentivize banks to buy those bonds.[32] It also shrank its holdings of government securities by $1.8 billion. Its purposes were "to offset the effect on reserves of seasonal factors and the sale of $600 million of gold to the United States Treasury by the International Monetary fund, and to exert pressure on bank reserve positions by bringing about a higher level of member bank borrowings."[33] In August, Chairman Martin, hewing to his goal to reduce inflation that had risen well above 3%, wrangled from a split FOMC a half percent increase in the discount rate, from 3% to 3.5% (see Figure 11.3).

By September the economy was in recession, and by October the Fed increased its holdings of government securities by $1 billion. In the fourth quarter, the Fed reduced its discount rate from 3.5% back to 3.0% again, to address the recession.

Fiscal policy and monetary policy ignored the Asian flu pandemic even as Maurice Hilleman worked to formulate a vaccine. There was no expansion of monetary policy and no incremental federal borrowing as the pandemic spread and the nation experienced a recession and a change in the savings rate in addition to the impact on the labor force from sickness and death. Inflation also dropped significantly during the pandemic.

The stock market experienced a short bear market in 1957, and the Fed mentioned it in the minutes of its meetings but attributed the cause to Eisenhower's health issues, despite the fact that the bear market started several months before the President's health problems became public. Jordà, Singh, and Taylor's NBER working paper on 19 pandemics, however, connects the bear market to the pandemic (see Figure 11.4).[34]

The authors concluded that "Capital is destroyed in wars, but not in pandemics; pandemics instead may induce relative labor scarcity and or a shift to greater precautionary savings.[35] This is exactly what occurred during the Asian flu pandemic. The savings rate went up. Labor absenteeism increased dramatically. Federal borrowing did not expand since no offsetting additional fiscal stimulus occurred. Jordà, Singh, and Taylor found that the natural interest rate under these conditions should fall by 1.5%, such that a natural tightening would occur if the Fed missed the effect of a pandemic and did not adjust the interest rate down. The result would be a recession. History shows that is exactly what happened in 1957.

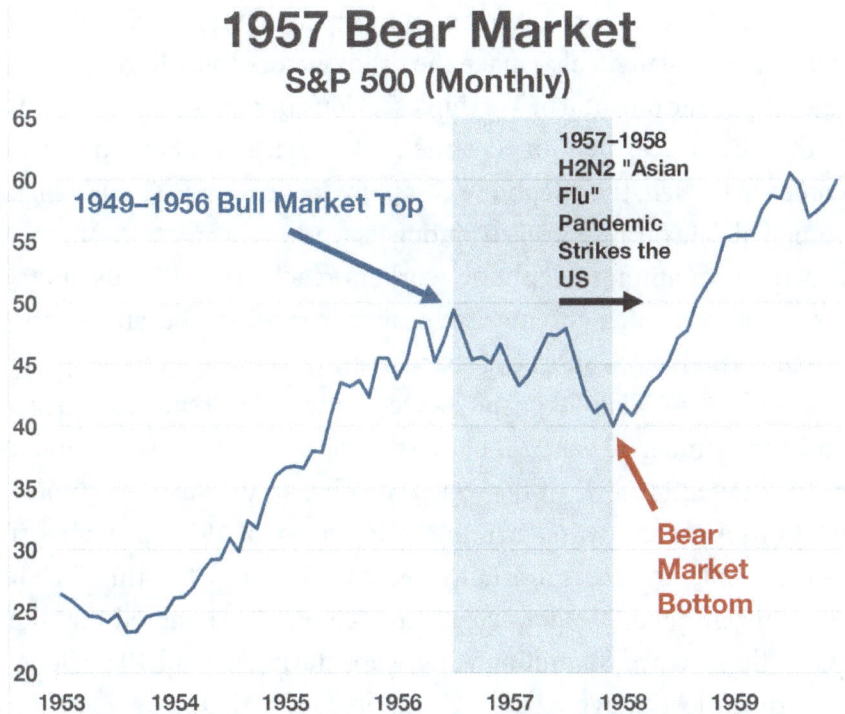

Figure 11.4 S&P 500 Index: The 1957 Bear Market (Data source: MacroTrends).

If we look at economic literature generally to ascertain the causes of the recession in the second half of 1957, the flu is generally not mentioned. Tight monetary policy, especially the 0.5% boost in the discount rate, is an obvious factor. Other factors cited are a dip in consumer confidence attributed to such events as the Suez Canal Crisis in 1956 and the successful launch of Sputnik 1, which did not happen until October of 1957. That was around the time that half the counties in America had flu outbreaks, college football games were being cancelled, some schools were experiencing absentee rates of 30–60%, and the automobile and housing markets were weakening.[36] (Automobile sales had peaked at almost 8 million in 1955, following the 1953–1954 recession, but fell by 1958 to 4.3 million.[37]) All of this was going on, but so was the pandemic.

Recessions often result from an interplay of factors. Should the fall wave of Asian flu also make the list of factors contributing to the intensity of the downturn? We think so. Consider rates of absenteeism in the labor force, mentioned earlier. A key piece of data we do have, comes from Bell, the telephone company that became AT&T, which compiled data on absenteeism among its workers in 36 cities. At peak, absenteeism among telephone workers reached 8–10%, usually a couple of weeks after absenteeism peaked in schools. The labor-force-absenteeism hit was short but sharp in any given place, lasting just a few weeks.[38] As Niall Ferguson has recounted, children, adolescents, and adults under 40 were hit hardest in the fall of 1957. Those under 65 accounted for 40% of flu-related deaths, an unusually high pro-portion. A second wave, striking in February of 1958 "saw almost as big a spike in excess mortality," Ferguson wrote, "but this time it was concentrated in older age groups (45–74)."[39] He noted that the Asian flu sickened 82 million Americans during the fall 1957 alone. Americans lost an aggregate 282 million days to illness.[40]

Consider recent data from the Omicron surge of December 2021 and January 2022. The Household Pulse Survey found that U.S. workplace absenteeism for health-related reasons reached 3.5% partway through January of 2022.[41] Statista shows a peak at 5.37% for the entire month.[42] During this period still fresh in our memories, staff shortages impacted schools, businesses, and services such as garbage collection, hospitals, and airlines, which were forced to cut back on flights.[43] HIS Markit found that, because of Omicron-driven absences, manufacturing output plunged to a 19-month low as workplace absenteeism peaked in January.[44] The flash U.S. Composite PMI Output Index dipped to 50.8 in January from 57 in December. Demand slipped only slightly, but production faltered more.[45]

Given what we saw during Omicron (when there were, as in 1957, no lockdowns in place), high workplace absenteeism during the 1957 Asian flu pandemic could not have magically had zero effect on businesses, services, or production. The Fed and many later economists missed the 1957 Asian flu as a contributing factor to the recession of 1957–1958, but the pandemic was assuredly part of the mix, intensifying a contraction that began in the summer of 1957. The following chart showing ISM Manufacturing's PMI Composite Index from 1948 to 2012 puts the 1957 downturn into historical perspective.

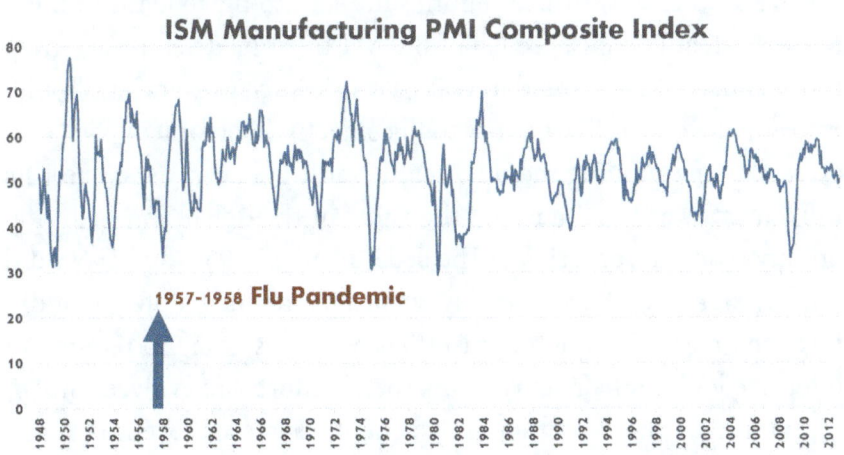

Figure 11.5 PMI Composite Index, 1948–2012 (Data source: the Financial Forecast Center).

Though economists were not yet thinking about a flu pandemic in terms of its economic impacts or what the Fed might do to mitigate them, the Fed's original lending facility had evolved in the wake of the Great Depression. Tim Sablik, a senior economic writer in the Research Department at the Richmond Fed, has traced this history. Congress amended the Federal Reserve Act in 1932, when it empowered the Fed to make commercial loans to businesses and individuals — but with all sorts of strings attached that limited their use — and in 1934, when it reduced restrictions on those loans and how they had to be approved. Use of this new Fed lending facility picked up, then, to some degree.

Loans were available on better terms, however, from the Reconstruction Finance Corporation (RFC), which was created in 1932 and functioned until Congress voted in 1953 to abolish it. The year that the RFC was to begin winding up its business, the Small Business Administration was created to "aid, counsel, assist and protect, insofar as is possible, the interests of small business concerns." The SBA was able to help coordinate loans for small businesses, while the Commodity Credit Corporation, established in 1933, provided loans to farmers.

With other government entities in place to make loans to businesses and individuals, Fed Chair Bill Martin argued before Congress in 1957 that the Fed should not play a role in such matters but should, instead, "devote itself primarily to the objectives set for it by the Congress, namely, guiding monetary and credit policy so as to exert its influence toward maintaining the value of the dollar and fostering orderly economic progress."[46] The Fed during the 1950s and 1960s did not envision having a role to play when a pandemic erupted. Nor did it see the need. Coming to grasp that need was going to require an intensive look in the rear-view mirror, an effort that evolved only in recent decades in response to subsequent threats and events.

In the interim, an examination of the 1968–1969 Hong Kong flu, the eighth largest in terms of deaths among the 19 pandemics that Jordà, Singh, and Taylor studied, would look much the same in terms of the Fed's nonresponse to a new influenza pandemic. Martin still served as Fed chair and would until 1970, when Arthur Burns succeeded him. Though an analysis would require an effort to disentangle the effects of the Vietnam War, it would still show that the arguments remain true and that the results were similar to those of the pandemic shock of 1957–1958, despite the Vietnam War's altering the fiscal response and the labor scarcity element because of the military draft during that period.

Note, however, that there was a bear market in stocks. Here is what that looked like.

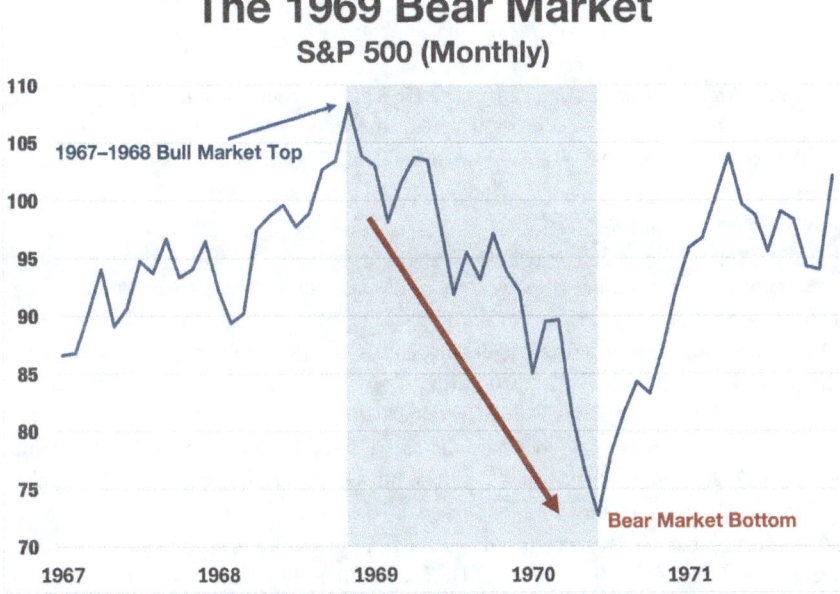

Figure 11.6. S&P Large Cap Index: The 1969 Bear Market (Data source: MacroTrends).

In the next chapter we turn to the ongoing COVID pandemic and a very different Fed response.

---

1. "Hong Kong Battling Influenza Pandemic," *New York Times*, April 17, 1957, https://timesmachine.nytimes.com/timesmachine/1957/04/17/96951365.html?pageNumber=3.

2.   Becky Little, "How the 1957 Flu Pandemic Was Stopped Early in Its Path," *History Stories*, March 18, 2020, https://www.history.com/news/1957-flu-pandemic-vaccine-hilleman.

3.   Sydney Combs, "This Virologist Saved Millions of Children — and Stopped a Pandemic," *National Geographic*, May 29, 2000, https://www.nationalgeographic.com/history/article/virologist-maurice-hilleman-saved-millions-children-stopped-pandemic.

4.   Mark Honigsbaum and Lakshmi Krishnan, "Taking Pandemic Sequelae Seriously: From the Russian Influenza to COVID-19 Long-Haulers," *Lancet* 396, no. 10260 (October 2020): 2489–1391, https://www.thelancet.com/article/S0140-6736(20)32134-6/fulltext.

5.   Combs, "Virologist Saved Millions of Children."

6.   "1968 Flu Pandemic," Brittanica, accessed June 10, 2024, https://www.britannica.com/event/1968-flu-pandemic#ref1119852.

7.   David Brown, "Lessons to Be Learned from 1957 Pandemic," *Seattle Times,* August 26, 2009, https://www.seattletimes.com/seattle-news/health/lessons-to-be-learned-from-1957-pandemic/.

8.   Niall Ferguson, *Doom: The Politics of Catastrophe* (New York: Penguin Books, 2021, 2022), 217–219.

9.   Emily Moon, "How the U.S. Fought the 1957 Flu Pandemic," *Smithsonian,* June 2020, https://www.smithsonianmag.com/smithsonian-institution/united-states-vaccine-1957-flu-pandemic-180974906/; "1957–1958 Influenza Pandemic," Wikipedia, accessed June 10, 2024, https://en.wikipedia.org/wiki/1957–1958_influenza_pandemic. (Note: the data sources cited at the CDC are no longer posted there.)

10.   Kara Rogers, "1957 Flu Pandemic," *Brittanica,* February 25, 2010, updated March 25, 2020, https://www.britannica.com/event/1957-flu-pandemic/additional-info#history.

11.   Ferguson, *Doom: The Politics of Catastrophe,* 220–21.

12.   Mark A. Abramson, "History Does Repeat Itself: Lessons from the Polio Vaccine," *Government Executive,* July 21, 2020, https://www.govexec.com/management/2020/07/history-does-repeat-itself-lessons-polio-vaccine/167068/.

13.   Dave Roos, "How a New Polio Vaccine Faced Shortages and Setbacks," History.com, August 4, 2020, updated September 27, 2023, https://www.history.com/news/salk-polio-vaccine-shortages-problems.

14.   Francine Uenuma, "Parents Are Facing Tough Choices About School in the COVID-19 Era. Here's How People Made the Same Decisions When It Came to Polio," *TIME,* August 25, 2020, https://time.com/5882286/coronavirus-school-reopening-polio/.

15.   Abramson, "History Does Repeat Itself: Lessons from the Polio Vaccine."

16.   Dwight D. Eisenhower, "Statement by the President on the Polio Vaccine Situation," The American Presidency Project, May 31, 1955, https://www.presidency.ucsb.edu/documents/statement-the-president-the-polio-vaccine-situation.

17.   Dwight D. Eisenhower, "Letter Accepting the Resignation of Mrs. Oveta Culp Hobby, Secretary of Health, Education, and Welfare," The American Presidency Project, July 13, 1955, https://www.presidency.ucsb.edu/documents/letter-accepting-the-resignation-mrs-oveta-culp-hobby-secretary-health-education-and.

18.   Harry S. Truman, "Special Message to the Congress Recommending a Comprehensive Health Program," National Archives, Harry S. Truman Library, November 19, 1945, https://

www.trumanlibrary.gov/library/public-papers/192/special-message-congress-recommending-comprehensive-health-program.

19. Whet Moser, "How the AMA Scared Us Away from 'Socialized Medicine' and Prepared Us for Obamacare," *Chicago*, October 19, 2012, https://www.chicagomag.com/city-life/october-2012/how-the-ama-scared-us-away-from-socialized-medicine-and-prepared-us-for-obamacare/.

20. Max J. Skidmore, "Misguided Responses to Public Health Emergencies," PMC (October 2016): 25–41, reprinted in the NIH National Library of Medicine, https://www.ncbi.nlm.nih.gov/pmc/articles/PMC7123304/.

21. Jen Pinkowski, "The History of the Forgotten Pandemic," Yale Insights, January 7, 2021, https://insights.som.yale.edu/insights/the-history-of-the-forgotten-pandemic.

22. Davis, quoted in Skidmore, "Misguided Responses to Public Health Emergencies."

23. John Kelly, "In 1957, a New Flu Appeared in Asia. The World Watched and Waited for It to Spread," *Washington Post,* March 17, 2020, https://www.washingtonpost.com/local/in-1957-a-new-flu-appeared-in-asia-the-world-watched-and-waited-for-it-to-spread/2020/03/17/9f5205b4-685f-11ea-b313-df458622c2cc_story.html.

24. "Historical Minutes, Meeting of the Federal Open Market Committee, December 3, 1957," digitized at FRASER, Federal Reserve Bank of St. Louis, December 1957, 22–23, https://fraser.stlouisfed.org/title/federal-open-market-committee-meeting-minutes-transcripts-documents-677/meeting-december-3-1957-22778.

25. "Historical Minutes, Meeting of the Federal Open Market Committee, December 3, 1957," 23.

26. Ferguson, *Doom: The Politics of Catastrophe,* 226.

27. "Forty-Fifth Annual Report of the Board of Governors of the Federal Reserve System Covering Operations for the Year 1958," Board of Governors, Federal Reserve System, 1959, https://fraser.stlouisfed.org/title/annual-report-board-governors-federal-reserve-system-117/1958-2414.

28. Jesse Romero, "The Treasury-Fed Accord," Federal Reserve History, November 22, 2013, https://www.federalreservehistory.org/essays/treasury-fed-accord.

29. Charles Plosser, "Federal Reserve Independence: Is It Time for a New Treasury-Fed Accord?" Economics Working Paper 22104 (2022), *Essays in Honor of Marvin Goodfriend: Economist and Central Banker,* eds. Robert G. King and Alexander L. Wolman (Richmond: Federal Reserve Bank of Richmond, 2022), https://www.richmondfed.org/publications/research/goodfriend/plosser.

30. Robert P. Bremner, *Chairman of the Fed: William McChesney Martin Jr. and the Creation of the American Financial System* I (New Haven: Yale University Press, 2004), 120–121. Kindle edition.

31. Bremner, *Chairman of the Fed: William McChesney Martin Jr.,* 123.

32. Bremner, *Chairman of the Fed: William McChesney Martin Jr.,* 123–125.

33. "Forty-Fourth Annual Report of the Board of Governors of the Federal Reserve System Covering Operations for the Year 1957," Board of Governors, Federal Reserve System, 1958, https://www.federalreserve.gov/monetarypolicy/files/fomcropa19570618.pdf.

34. Oscar Jordà, Sanjay R. Singh, and Alan M. Taylor (2020). "Longer-Run Economic

Consequences of Pandemics," Working Paper 2020-09, Federal Reserve Bank of San Francisco, https://www.nber.org/system/files/working_papers/w26934/w26934.pdf.

35. Jordà, et. al, "Longer-Run Economic Consequences of Pandemics," abstract, 2.

36. "The Eisenhower Recession (1957–1958)," TrendSpider Learning Center, accessed June 10, 2024, https://trendspider.com/learning-center/the-eisenhower-recession-1957-1958/; Jen Pinkowski, "The History of the Forgotten Pandemic," Yale Insights, January 07, 2021, https://insights.som.yale.edu/insights/the-history-of-the-forgotten-pandemic.

37. William M. McClenahan, Jr., and William H. Becker, *Eisenhower and the Cold War Economy* (Baltimore: John Hopkins University Press, 2011), 85–86. Cited in "American Automobile Industry in the 1950s," Wikipedia, accessed June 10, 2024, https://en.wikipedia.org/wiki/American_automobile_industry_in_the_1950s.

38. David Brown, "Lessons to Be Learned from 1957 Pandemic," *Seattle Times,* August 26, 2009, https://www.seattletimes.com/seattle-news/health/lessons-to-be-learned-from-1957-pandemic/.

39. Ferguson, *Doom: The Politics of Catastrophe,* 218, 220.

40. Ferguson, *Doom: The Politics of Catastrophe,* 225.

41. Matt Egan, "Worker Absences Triple because of Omicron," CNN Business, January 21, 2022, https://www.cnn.com/2022/01/21/economy/workers-omicron-absent/index.html.

42. "Percentage of Full-Time Workers in the U.S. Absent from Work for Health-Related Reasons from 2015–2022, by Month," Statista, last accessed June 11, 2024, https://www.statista.com/statistics/1259414/health-related-workplace-absenteeism-full-time-us-workers/.

43. Theresa Waldrop and Julia Jones, "Omicron Devastates Services, Schools, Travel as Workers are Sick or in Quarantine," CNN, January 11, 2022, https://www.cnn.com/2022/01/10/us/omicron-impact-on-economy-workers-shortage/index.html.

44. Justin Ho, "Manufacturing Growth Slows as Workers Get Omicron," Marketplace, January 24, 2022, https://www.marketplace.org/2022/01/24/manufacturing-growth-slows-as-workers-get-omicron/.

45. "U.S. Business Activity Slows in January amid Omicron Wave -IHS Markit Survey," Reuters, January 24, 2022, https://www.reuters.com/world/us/us-business-activity-slows-january-amid-omicron-wave-ihs-markit-survey-2022-01-24/.

46. Tim Sablik, "The Fed's Emergency Lending Evolves," *Econ Focus,* (Second/Third Quarter 2020), reprinted online by the Federal Reserve Bank at Richmond, https://www.richmondfed.org/publications/research/econ_focus/2020/q2-3/federal_reserve.

Chapter 12

2020 COVID-19 Pandemic: The Fed Steps In

The Fed Evolves

Things started to change at the Fed as the institution matured. One key foundational change was the 1977 amendment to the Federal Reserve Act, which broadened the Federal Reserve's mission in ways that were key to its response to COVID. Going forward, the Fed would have the responsibility to manage monetary policy with three goals in mind: "maximum employment, stable prices, and moderate long-term interest rates." The narrower focus of the William McChesney Martin Fed had segued to a broader one. The Fed would now be responsible for representing the interests of services, labor, and consumers in addition to agriculture, commerce, and industry as specified in the original Federal Reserve Act signed by Woodrow Wilson in 1913.

In recent decades, the financial and economic impacts posed by disease outbreaks have made their way into the Fed's thinking. Pandemic shocks and responses to them may not be part of the official language of the Federal Reserve Act, but the modern Fed has certainly grasped what they mean and why it is important for Fed policy to deal with them, given its mission.

The Fed has been studying the notion of pandemic shock risk for the last 30 years or so, as relevant literature has emerged in tandem with studies and books from academics in public health policy, medicine, economics, and history. Beniamino Callegari and Christophe Feder's review of the evolution of the literature on the economic impacts of pandemics, completed in October of 2021, is not exhaustive (it missed the paper that inspired this book), but it is fascinating and indicative.[1] While Callegari and Feder cited a single paper from the 1970s and another single paper in the 1980s, they found 9 in the 1990s, 29 in the 2000s, 35 in the 2010s, and 18 by the time of publication in the 2020s. Societal awareness of epidemics and pandemics grew in general terms, economics aside. Laurie Garrett published *The Coming Plague: Newly Emerging Diseases in a World Out of Balance* in 1994. Her book would remain a *New York Times* bestseller for two years. John Barry focused the world's attention on the 1918 influenza pandemic when he published another *New York Times* bestseller, *The Great Influenza: The Story of the Deadliest Pandemic in History,* in 2004. (Interestingly, Charles Graves' book *Invasion by Virus,* now long out of print, was ready to go to press in 1957, but its publication was delayed by the publisher until 1968 because back in 1957 the publisher did not want to scare the public when the Asian flu struck.[2])

Such studies, whether book-length historical bestsellers or articles in academic journals or publications by researchers associated with the Federal Reserve, were made possible by the gathering of data, both in the public health sphere (starting in Britain during the Victorian period) and the economic sphere. Data makes fully visible what was not fully visible before. The opposite is also true, of course. If data is suppressed or sufficient data cannot be gathered, what should be visible is hidden or partly hidden, no matter how important it may be to human health and to societies and their economies. The ready accessibility of data is another factor. As a practical matter, research and information sharing has become immensely easier since the advent of the internet and the World Wide Web. Historians, virologists, epidemiologists, and economists can more swiftly build upon the work of others and more effectively share their findings in the age of information than in the past.

Pandemic disease threats in recent decades have likewise focused the Fed's attention on the economic implications of pandemics. The SARS scare in 2003 occasioned a number of studies globally on potential economic fallout should the outbreak in China and Hong Kong become a pandemic.[3] In 2006, acting as program chair for the Global Interdependence Center, I (David Kotok) helped to organize a conference held in Philadelphia on "Avian Flu, Pandemic Diseases, and Their Economic and Social Consequences: A Template for Preparedness." The keynote, "Pandemics, Financial Markets, and the Federal Reserve's Preparations," was delivered by Thomas J. Cunningham, Vice President and Associate Director of Research at the Federal Reserve Bank of Atlanta.[4] (Tom Cunningham would later serve on the Economic Impact Committee of Georgia's Coronavirus Task Force convened by Georgia Governor Brian Kemp in March of 2020.[5]) The Federal Reserve was, by the 2000s, sizing up the economic shock that a pandemic could deliver, and actively preparing. Gone were the days when the Fed compartmentalized infectious disease threats as a public health sideshow irrelevant to the business of maintaining a stable economy and formulating monetary policy.

We see evidence of the U.S. central bank's increasing sensitivity to pandemic risk in a paper published by the Fed's Board of Governors in its International Finance Discussion Papers series in August 2020: Chang Ma, John Rogers, and Sili Zhou's "Modern Pandemics: Recession and Recovery."[6] Dates become important. The paper covers six epidemic periods, starting with number eight on the list of Jordà et al (2013).

Here is the abstract of that paper, from page two:

We examine the immediate effects and bounce-back from six modern health crises: 1968 Flu, SARS (2003), H1N1 (2009), MERS (2012), Ebola (2014), and Zika (2016). Time-series models for a large cross-section of countries indicate that real GDP growth falls by around three percentage points in affected countries relative to unaffected countries in the year of the outbreak. Bounce-back in GDP growth is rapid, but output is still below pre-shock level five years later. Unemployment for less educated workers is higher and exhibits more persistence, and there is significantly greater persistence in female unemployment than male. The negative effects on GDP and unemployment are felt less in countries with larger first-year responses in government spending, especially on healthcare. Affected countries' consumption declines, investment drops sharply, and international trade plummets. Bounce-back in these expenditure categories is also rapid but not by enough to restore pre-shock trends. Furthermore, indirect effects on own-country GDP from affected trading partners are significant for both the initial GDP decline and the positive bounce-back. We discuss why our estimates are a lower bound for the global economic effects of COVID-19 and compare contours of the current pandemic to the historical episodes.

In their introduction, the authors noted that "Although economists have documented that many financial and political crises are associated with severe recessions ..., until very recently little attention was paid to global health crises. This changed dramatically with the outbreak of COVID-19...."[7] The Fed has greatly expanded its view of the world since its founding over 100 years ago. After the prior two major pandemics in America in the last century, Fed researchers and Fed leaders started to understand that this major type of shock threatened the United States' economy and that pandemics could dramatically interfere with the Fed's mandate of "full employment and price stability." Specifically, the Fed observed that it was not possible to maintain stable employment metrics when a large number of people die in a short period of time, so that the death rate far exceeds what is normal and predictable. Likewise, the Fed realized that a labor force shortage would create a wage price shock. Simultaneously, a pandemic would impact the collective savings rate as individuals and agent members raised their savings in response to pandemic fears.[8]

This recognition led to the pioneering work done by Jordà, Singh, and Taylor. They converted the concepts outlined above into a forecast metric by using the concept of the natural rate of interest. The authors purposefully ignored the panic-induced short-term trading swings that occur during pandemic shock periods. They developed a medium-term forecast for the post-COVID period, based on all 19 of the observations in the 700 years of history that they studied. They stated that a pandemic causes the medium-term natural rate to decline by about 1.5 percentage points.

In the decades that intervened between the Fed chairmanship of William Martin and that of Jerome Powell, the Federal Reserve's thinking about liquidity crises and the Fed's role in them had also evolved. As Tim Sablik of the Richmond Fed recounts, the S&L crisis and the "Black Monday" stock market crash of October 19, 1987, taught the Fed that bank crises were not the only source of risk to the financial system. Its emergency lending powers, broadened to enable the Fed to accept any securities it approved as collateral, would need to be used in all types of liquidity crises to ensure that the financial system could continue to function. The Great Financial Crisis of 2007–2008 would mark the first time since the 1930s that the Fed, as lender of last resort, made emergency loans under section 13(3) of the Federal Reserve Act, to both financial and nonfinancial institutions including those deemed "too big to fail." In 2010, the Dodd-Frank Act stipulated that the purpose of loans had to be ensuring the stability of the financial system rather than merely the survival of particular financial companies and that such loans needed to be secured so that American taxpayers would not be left on the hook. As Fed Chair, Ben Bernanke urged Congress to avoid further restricting Fed responses to financial crises, lest the Fed not be in a position to shield the American people and businesses from the fallout from those crises. In short, since the days of William Martin, the Fed has gained considerable additional experience in reckoning with crises.[9]

In the COVID pandemic period, the Fed moved quickly to respond, in keeping with its mandate as outlined in the 1977 amendment to the Federal Reserve Act. And while the Fed did not explicitly say that it was acting to offset the prospective medium-term decline in the natural rate, that is what the Fed was doing. The Fed speakers did refer at times to the natural rate or to "r^*" (pronounced "r-star"), which is defined as the real short-term interest rate expected to prevail when an economy is at full strength and inflation is stable.[10] Detractors of the Fed might phrase things differently by saying that is what the Fed was *trying* to do. Detractors tend to be Monday morning quarterbacks. They are quick to criticize after the event has passed but slow to admit the need for the Fed to make decisions in real time without complete information.

Richard H. Clarida, who was Vice Chairman of the Board of Governors as the pandemic hit, had this to say about the Fed's aggressive response to the crisis:

> The COVID-19 pandemic and the mitigation efforts
> put in place to contain it delivered the most severe

blow to the U.S. economy since the Great Depression. In this paper, we argue that the Federal Reserve acted decisively and with dispatch to deploy all the tools in its conventional kit and to design, develop, and launch within weeks a series of innovative facilities to support the flow of credit to households and businesses. These measures, taken together, provided crucial support to the economy in 2020 and are continuing to contribute to what is expected to be a robust economic recovery in 2021.[11]

We could spend a lot of time and space recounting each of the emergency programs instituted by the Fed during the COVID period. Most readers know some, if not all, of them; but we will summarize them and touch on some of the most significant ones. Milstein and Wessel (2021) have grouped the Fed's actions into six categories and corresponding subcategories[12]:

Easing Monetary Policy
  Federal funds rate
  Forward guidance
  Quantitative easing (QE)
Supporting Financial Markets
  Lending to securities firms
  Backstopping money market mutual funds
  Repo operations
  Foreign and International Monetary Authorities (FIMA)
    Repo Facility
  International swap lines
Encouraging Banks to Lend
  Direct lending to banks
  Temporarily relaxing regulatory requirements

Supporting Corporations and Businesses
    Direct lending to major corporate employers
    Commercial Paper Funding Facility (CPFF)
    Supporting loans to small and mid-sized businesses
    Supporting loans to nonprofit institutions
Supporting Households and Consumers
    Term Asset-Backed Securities Loan Facility (TALF)
Supporting State and Municipal Borrowing
    Direct lending to state and municipal governments
    Supporting municipal bond liquidity

As COVID-19 escaped China and spread like wildfire in spring 2020, the global economy contracted sharply. Equities markets plunged, and volatility was historically high. The Fed moved quickly. At unscheduled meetings on March 3 and March 15, 2020, the FOMC reduced the target range for the federal funds rate by a total of 1.5 percentage points, taking it to near zero. Along with these rate moves, the FOMC provided strong forward guidance, stating that it expected to keep the policy rate at that level until the economy was on track to meet the Fed's dual mandate.

At the same time, by mid-March, spreads on corporate bonds over comparable-maturity Treasury securities had widened to the highest levels since the Great Financial Crisis, and the Treasury market was becoming severely dislocated. At the March 15 meeting, the FOMC said it would buy at least $500 billion in Treasury securities and $200 billion in government-guaranteed mortgage-backed securities in the coming months. On March 23, it made the purchases open-ended, stating that it would purchase securities "in the amounts needed to support smooth market functioning and effective transmission of monetary policy to broader financial conditions."[13] The Fed also provided direct support to households, businesses, governments, and financial markets, as outlined in Table 12.1.

COVID-Era Federal Reserve Emergency Lending Programs				
Facility	Funding Source	Duration	Capacity (billions)	Peak Assets (billions)
Commercial Paper Funding Facility	Fed, Treasury Exchange Stabilization Fund (ESF)	4/14/2020–3/31/2021	Unlimited	4.2
Money Market Mutual Fund Liquidity Facility	Fed, Treasury (ESF)	3/23/2020–3/31/2021	Unlimited	53.2
Paycheck Protection Program Liquidity Facility (serving small businesses)	Fed	4/16/2020–7/30/2021	953.0 (allocated by Congress)	90.6
Primary Dealer Credit Facility	Fed	3/20/2020–3/31/2021	Unlimited	33.4
Main Street Lending Program (serving small to mid-sized businesses and nonprofits)	Fed, Treasury (CARES Act)	7/6/2020–1/8/2021	600.0	16.6
Municipal Liquidity Facility (serving state and local governments)	Fed, Treasury (CARES Act)	5/26/2020–12/31/2020	500.0	6.4
Primary Market Corporate Credit Facility (serving large businesses)	Fed, Treasury (CARES Act)	6/29/2020–12/31/2020	750.0 for Primary Market and Secondary Market Corporate Credit Facilities combined	0
Secondary Market Corporate Credit Facility (serving large businesses and ETFs)	Fed, Treasury (CARES Act)	5/12/2020–12/31/2020		14.3
Term Asset-Backed Securities Loan Facility (serving securities markets to support loans to consumers and businesses)	Fed, Treasury (CARES Act)	6/17/2020–12/31/2020	100.0	4.1
Data Source: Federal Reserve				

Table 12.1 COVID-Era Federal Reserve Emergency Lending Programs.

Note that each of these programs had support limits of hundreds of billions of dollars, and that three of them — the Commercial Paper Funding Facility (CPFF), the Money Market Mutual Fund Liquidity Facility (MMLF), and the Primary Dealer Credit Facility (PDCF) — had no limits.

Regarding Federal Reserve balance sheet expansion, the St. Louis Fed provides us with an initial estimate. The chart below shows the Fed's first-year response to COVID.

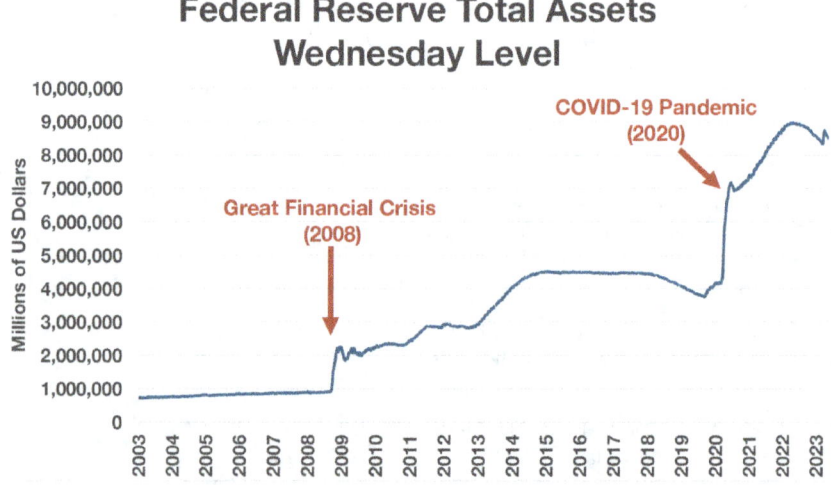

Figure 12.1 Total Assets, Federal Reserve: Wednesday Level
(Data source: FRED at the Federal Reserve Bank of St. Louis).

The actions that the Fed took were critically important, as Eric Milstein and David Wessel of the Hutchins Center on Fiscal and Monetary Policy at Brookings have explained. The Fed provided credit to households and businesses when measures taken to slow the spread of COVID-19 in March of 2020 contracted economic activity sharply, sending the economy off a pandemic shock precipice into deep recession. Thanks to Fed intervention, financial markets did not seize up, making bad matters worse. Instead, credit continued to be accessible through the banking system, and capital markets continued to function.[14]

Don Kohn, former Federal Reserve Vice Chair, characterized the situation back in March 2020 as nonessential businesses closed their doors:

> The Treasury market in particular is the foundation for trading in many other securities markets in the U.S. and around the world; if it's disrupted, the functioning of every market will be impaired. The Fed's purchase of securities is explicitly aimed at improving the functioning of the Treasury and MBS markets, where market liquidity had been well below par in recent days.[15]

But, Kohn pointed out, "targeting the Treasury market proved insufficient" — the recession was too deep for that to be enough — so the Fed acted to make sure that corporations and municipalities could pay their workers and not go bankrupt. Their weathering the storm was critical to preserving the economic capacity to mount a recovery as the COVID threat subsided.

Banks, too, needed help in order to serve businesses and households, as Kohn explained:

> When financial markets are clogged, firms tend to draw on bank lines of credit, which can lead banks to pull back on lending or selling Treasury and other securities. The Fed supplied unlimited liquidity to financial institutions so they could meet credit drawdowns and make new loans to businesses and households feeling financial strains.[16]

What about the rest of the world? The Federal Reserve led, but most other central banks in the world joined the Fed, and we saw a coordinated global response to the pandemic, which has been usefully cataloged by the IMF and the UN.[17]

So, what impact will these COVID responses ultimately have with regard to the natural rate decline of about 1.5 percentage points in the medium term, as Oscar Jordà, Sanjay Singh, and Alan Taylor forecast in June of 2020, based on their study of pandemic shocks in the past?

The short answer is simple: It is too soon to know. The COVID threat has only recently ebbed (though the virus remains a leading cause of death and disability), and the natural rate forecast is for the medium term — that is, still several years in the future. But there are some indicators to help us now.

The easiest reference that Jordà, Taylor, and Singh had for a Wicksellian natural rate change induced by a pandemic was to observe the savings rate. Here is a graph of the savings rate in the United States.

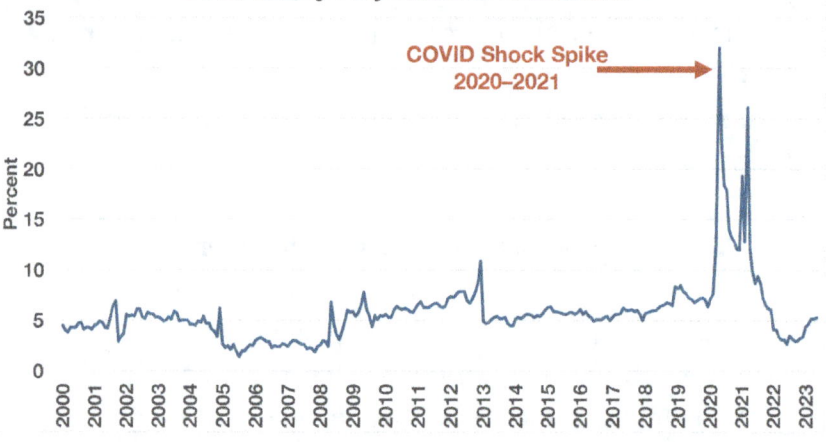

Figure 12.2 Personal Saving Rate (Data source: FRED at the Federal Reserve Bank of St. Louis).

Savings shot up during the pandemic, as expected, and then returned over time to close to their historical trend. That would suggest that COVID mitigation through vaccines and treatments helped to reduce fear for many (whereas efforts to minimize public concern about the virus reduced fear for others). It also suggested that payouts to American citizens gave many Americans more money than they had seen in a long time, and they saved it or used it to pay down debt. Since the COVID emergency was declared over, however, the personal savings rate has dipped. In September of 2023, a Lending-Club report found that 62% of Americans were living from paycheck to paycheck. A CNBC survey found that 61% of Americans were living from paycheck to paycheck as of August 2023, up from 58% in December 2022.[18] Inflation driven by COVID supply chain shocks and compounded by supply chain shocks imposed by two wars and even shipping accidents has taken a toll on many Americans' budgets.

That initial savings rate decline from the COVID spike, however, suggests in part that the Fed's actions alleviated individuals' and business agents' worries over a COVID-induced economic collapse or depression. In the United States, we can reasonably conclude that the Fed blunted a protracted period of a savings rate rise reflecting fear of an economic collapse. At a minimum, we can claim that the Fed was successful in doing so in response to the initial COVID shock.

If the Fed was successful in blunting the rise in the savings rate, we would see the reallocation of those shock-induced excess savings into other assets. The prices of those assets would rise because of the inflows of money redirected from savings. We have seen that happen in real estate prices, and we have witnessed it in speculative ventures and new types of trading like cryptocurrencies and nonfungible tokens (NFTs). We have also observed it in stock prices, as shown in Figure 12.3. On the left axis is the enlargement of the size of the Fed's balance sheet; on the right axis is the level of the S&P 500 Index.

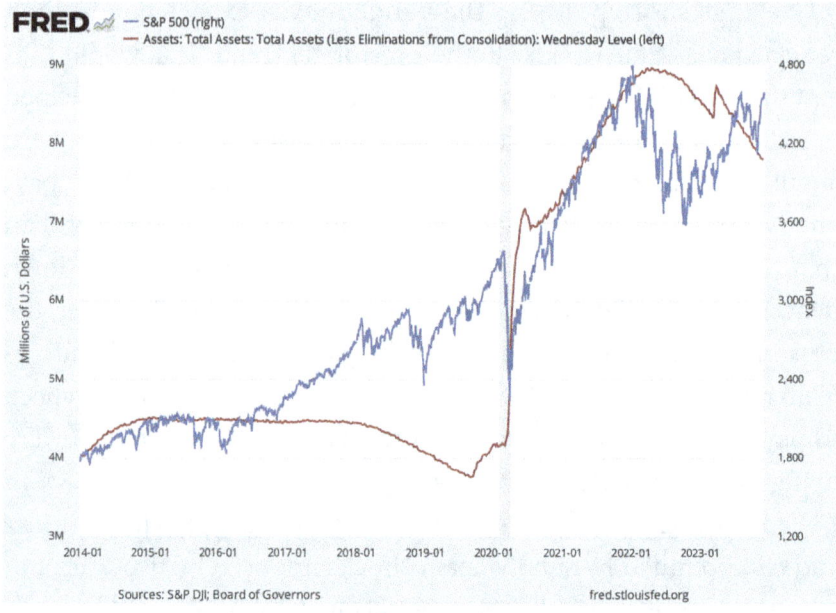

Figure 12.3 S&P 500 and Total Assets
(Data sources: S&P 500, FRED at Federal Reserve Bank of St. Louis).

During the COVID shock period, there were essentially no bank failures. And there were no major defaults. The failure of Silicon Valley Bank (driven by imprudent banking practices that left the bank vulnerable to rising interest rates designed to curb inflation), followed by that of Signature Bank and First Republic Bank, would not happen until 2023. The various interventions by the Fed kept the entire U.S. dollar funding system liquid and stable worldwide when COVID hit. Readers may recall the days of the Great Financial Crisis. Bank failures happened every weekend. The weekend news was the dreaded media alert period. Why? Because it took the weekends for the Fed and the FDIC teams to go into banks and reorganize them after they failed. During the business weekday, the transaction rate was so fierce that a failure in the middle of a day was deemed impossible. The Fed learned from the Great Financial Crisis. During the COVID emergency period and then during the SVB banking crisis, it was not about to permit a sharp contraction of economic activity to spiral into a depression and spill over into the capital markets and the banking system. The Fed under Chair Powell was quite different from the Fed during the Spanish flu period when Benjamin Strong was the dominant personality. The Fed brought what it had learned to bear not only during the COVID shock period but later during the critical time when the failure of Silicon Valley Bank threatened the financial system.

In the post-COVID period, a labor shortage developed and has since been resolved. This pandemic effect has been witnessed after every pandemic in history. In this book we have cited early examples of labor shortages dating back as far as we have historical records.

A chart of job openings according to the monthly Job Openings and Labor Turnover Survey (JOLTS) depicts this trend:

Figure 12.4 Job Openings: Total Nonfarm
(Data source: FRED, Federal Reserve Bank of St. Louis, U.S. Bureau of Labor Statistics).

In the post-pandemic-shock period, there were more job openings than people to fill them. We have seen that development in every pandemic shock throughout history, and this one is no different from all the others referenced in this book. This economic phenomenon is part of the calculations performed by Jordà, Singh, and Taylor. The U.S. unemployment rate is depicted below.

All Employees, Total Nonfarm

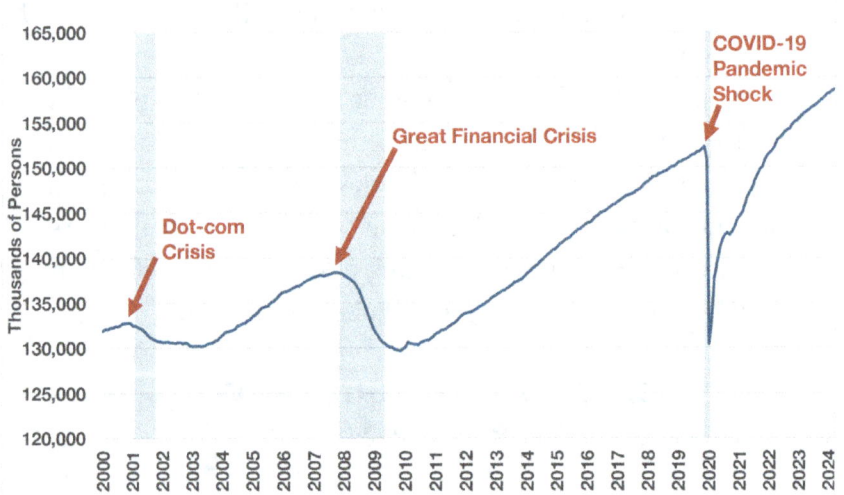

Figure 12.5 All Employees, Total nonfarm. Shaded areas indicate U.S. Recessions. (Data source: FRED, Federal Reserve Bank of St. Louis, U.S. Bureau of Labor Statistics).

But the unemployment rate does not tell the whole story. It is important to observe the shrinkage of the available labor force. We do that by observing the employment-population ratio. It tells us the percentage of the labor force that is either employed or looking to be employed. There are people missing because of death or disability, and some who are working cannot do the jobs they once did because of long COVID (see Figure 12.6).

To sum up, the unemployment rate surged to its highest level since the Great Depression; the employment-population ratio plummeted to its worst level since the Great Depression; and, after nosediving to a low of 133 million in April of 2020, the total of U.S. employed persons did not recover its pre-COVID level of almost 159 million until September of 2022. Is it any wonder that there was a rise in wages as a result of the pandemic shock? The Fed cannot create workers; no central bank in the world has that ability. As of the summer of 2024, the total employed number was 161 million, and it was immigration that made up the labor force deficit.[19]

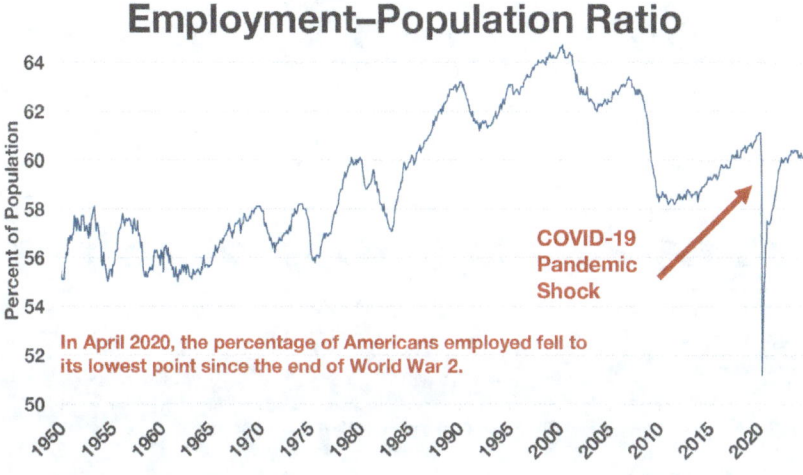

Figure 12.6 Employment-Population Ratio
(Data source: FRED, Federal Reserve Bank of St. Louis).

The Fed did, however, have the ability to rescue the capital markets and to avoid a Great Depression scenario, and it did so. Capital markets were temporarily impaired and threatened to seize. We can see that when credit spreads spiked and quickly retreated to pre-COVID levels or lower as the Fed unfolded various programs to alleviate the fear and panic in those markets. Figure 12.7 compares the interest rate on the highest-grade corporate bonds versus U.S. Treasury securities. Note that the spread between the AAA Corporate Bond and the 10-year U.S. Treasury had narrowed to normal levels by the end of 2020.

Figure 12.8 depicts the BBB corporate bond versus the 10-year U.S. Treasury.

Figure 12.7 AAA Corporate Bonds vs 10-yr U.S. Treasury (Data source: Bloomberg).

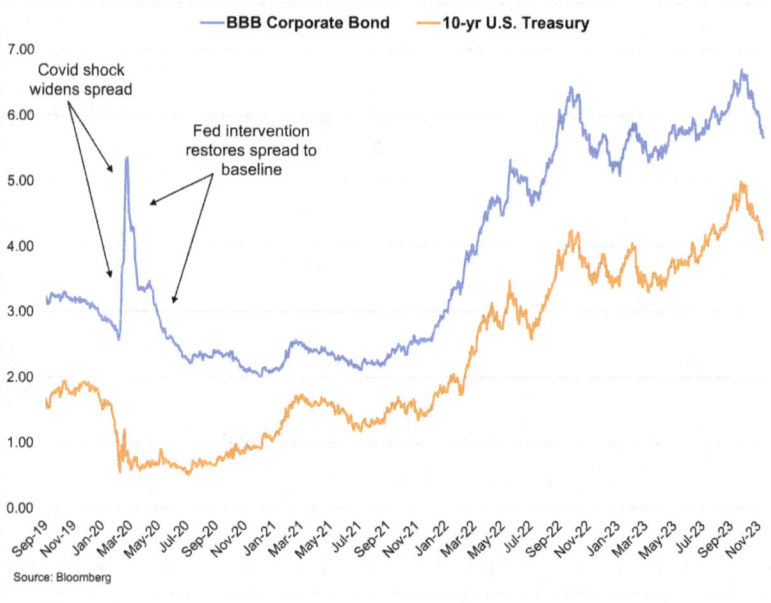

Figure 12.8 BBB Corporate Bond vs 10-yr U.S. Treasury (Data source: Bloomberg).

In its 110-year history, the Federal Reserve has traveled a long way since the Jekyll Island meeting and the Federal Reserve Act of 1913. The Fed has witnessed several pandemics and several major wars, where its role was to enable the United States to finance military action. It has seen a Great Depression. And it has dealt with periods of high inflation, an oil price shock, a stock market crash, a banking panic, and a mortgage crisis. Now we can add the COVID pandemic shock to that list.

We are reminded of William McAdoo's advice for a fledgling Fed more than a century ago, as the 12 Federal Reserve banks first opened their doors for business: "The way to begin is to begin. When you make a start, everything will be smoothed out by practice."[20]

There will be more practice — and more learning. Pandemics intermittently but inevitably open new battle fronts in the age-old war between pathogens and people, with economic and labor market shocks as a result. The Federal Reserve anticipated beginning a review, in late 2024, that will involve an assessment of its pandemic-era policy in light of its dual mandate to foster maximum employment while managing inflation to bend it to its target rate. There will be much to discuss.

In August of 2020, Fed policy shifted to "average inflation targeting," meaning that the Fed was comfortable allowing inflation to run a little above its target of 2% for a time, given that inflation had sagged below the target for some time before the pandemic struck. In early 2021, when inflation was still low, former Fed Governor Lael Brainard reflected on the employment aspect of the Fed's mission during the COVID pandemic period, in a speech titled "How Should We Think about Full Employment in the Federal Reserve's Dual Mandate?":

> So, what conclusions can we draw from this high-level overview of a variety of labor market indicators, their current readings, and their performance in the previous expansion? First, the headline unemployment

rate by itself can obscure important dimensions of labor market slack, so it is important to heed Dr. Palmer's dictum and consult a broad set of aggregated and disaggregated measures. Second, groups that have faced the greatest challenges often make important labor market gains late in an expansion, consistent with Augustus Hawkins's emphasis on the importance of full employment for all Americans.

So where does this leave us today? Jobs are still down by 10 million relative to pre-COVID levels, and COVID has disproportionately harmed certain sectors, groups of workers, businesses, and states and localities, leading to a K-shaped recovery. The fiscal support that is enacted and expected will provide assistance to vulnerable households, small businesses, and localities and a significant boost to activity when vaccinations are sufficiently widespread to support a reopening of in-person services. Monetary policy will continue to provide support by keeping borrowing costs for households and businesses low.

The assessment of shortfalls from broad-based and inclusive maximum employment will be a critical guidepost for monetary policy, alongside indicators of realized and expected inflation. The Federal Open Market Committee has said it expects the policy rate to remain in the current target range until labor market conditions have reached levels consistent with the Committee's assessments of maximum employment and inflation has risen to 2 percent and is on track to moderately exceed 2 percent for some time. It has noted that asset purchases will continue at least at the current pace until substantial further progress has been made toward the maximum-employment and inflation goals.

In assessing substantial further progress, I will be looking for sustained improvements in realized and expected inflation and examining a range of indicators to assess shortfalls from maximum employment. I will be looking for indicators that show the healing in the labor market is broad based, rather than focusing on the narrow aggregate U-3 unemployment rate, in light of the significant decline in labor force participation since the spread of COVID and the extremely elevated unemployment rate for workers in the lowest wage quartile.

For nearly four decades, monetary policy was guided by a strong presumption that accommodation should be reduced preemptively when the unemployment rate nears its normal rate in anticipation that high inflation would otherwise soon follow. But changes in economic relationships over the past decade have led trend inflation to run persistently somewhat below target and inflation to be relatively insensitive to resource utilization. With these changes, our new monetary policy framework recognizes that removing accommodation preemptively as headline unemployment reaches low levels in anticipation of inflationary pressures that may not materialize may result in an unwarranted loss of opportunity for many Americans. It may curtail progress for racial and ethnic groups that have faced systemic challenges in the labor force, which is particularly salient in light of recent research indicating that additional labor market tightening is especially beneficial for these groups when it occurs in already tight labor markets, compared with earlier in the labor market cycle. Instead, the shortfalls approach means that the labor market will be able to continue to improve absent high inflationary pressures or an unmooring of inflation expectations to the upside.[21]

Governor Brainard's remarks highlighted the Fed's concerns about fostering inclusive and full employment during a period when it had not yet become clear that inflation would rear its head and prove not to be as "transitory" as the Fed predicted that it might.

Two years into the pandemic, as Chair Jay Powell has noted, the Fed had learned something new about the longevity of pandemic supply chain shocks and their protracted rather than transitory impacts on inflation. Some argued, as Don Kohn has done, for beginning tightening sooner to forestall the kind of inflation that followed pandemic supply chain snarls and spiked further when Vladimir Putin went to war against Ukraine. Chicago Fed President Austan Goolsbee has suggested that the inflation target should be a range rather than a single figure. The Fed has had to reckon with how to balance or prioritize pandemic-era challenges of (1) supporting the labor market and the economy as a whole and (2) acting to curb inflation that may result in the short term (though still years rather than a few months) from a pandemic shock and from disrupted supply chains that require considerable time to recover.[22]

The question is still open as to whether the medium-term outcome of a 1.5 percentage point decline in the natural rate of interest predicted by Jordà, Singh, and Taylor will play out in the aftermath of the COVID crisis, in the medium term, one to four decades from now. Will history predict the medium term post-COVID? Or is this time different? Has the remarkable list of COVID shock response initiatives by the Fed lowered the likelihood that history will repeat itself? We may find out in another 10 or 20 years.

According to one 2023 analysis, the economic cost of that shock in the U.S. was predicted to reach $14 trillion by the end of 2023. In an article about the study, published in *The Conversation,* team members Jakub Hlavka and Adam Rose offered perspective:

> The COVID-19 pandemic's economic consequences are unprecedented for the U.S. by any measure. The toll we estimate that it took on the nation's gross domestic product is twice the size of that of the Great Recession of 2007–2009. It's 20 times greater than the economic costs of the 9/11 terrorist attacks and 40 times greater than the toll of any other disaster to befall the U.S. in the 21st century to date.[23]

It is not a pleasant exercise to estimate the damage that might have been done had the Fed not acted decisively in 2020, based on what it had learned from history about pandemics' economic impacts.

One thing is a certainty: The COVID pandemic's effects will flow into others generated by a complex swirl of events in years to come — the AI revolution with all its remarkable potential and its capacity for creative destruction, regional conflicts with enormous global geopolitical implications, accelerating climate change with its enormous costs and its demands for human adaptation among them, and even other pandemics that the future may have in store within that time frame.

In Part 4, we turn away from the Fed to another factor driving the economic toll that pandemics take: people. Pandemic economic outcomes, as well as human health outcomes, depend not only on the characteristics of the pathogen involved but also on the response of societies, governments, municipalities, institutions, and individuals. In short, pandemic outcomes are a function of pathogens x people. The COVID-19 pandemic has not only been a nightmare people fervently wish to put behind them (even if the virus has not and will not disappear as a threat); it has also offered insights and lessons to glean for the future. There are ways to respond to pandemics that drive higher human and economic costs and, on the other hand, ways to respond to pandemics and to remain vigilantly prepared for them in order to limit the damage they do. There is also a factor that does not disappear: Medical science may advance; technology may advance; but people are still people; and typical human responses to pandemics have remained consistent over centuries and millennia. We might have expected that this time might be different (and some of us did), but it was not. It was more of the same, but in spades, with tendencies amplified by connectivity. The Fed has no role in such matters, but societal responses to pandemics do shape pandemic outcomes and the economic landscape that the Fed must navigate as it develops policy to fulfill its mission.

---

1. Beniamino Callegari and Christophe Feder, "A Literature Review of Pandemics and Development: the Long-Term Perspective," *Economics of Disasters and Climate Change* 6 (2022): 183–212.

2. Mark Honigsbaum, "Revisiting the 1967 and 1968 Influenza Pandemics," *The Lancet* 395, no. 10240(2020): 1824–1826, https://www.ncbi.nlm.nih.gov/pmc/articles/PMC7247790/.

3. See Jong-Wha Lee and Warwick J. McKibben, "Globalization and Disease: The Case of SARS," *Brookings Discussion Papers in International Economics*, No. 156, February 2004, https://www.brookings.edu/wp-content/uploads/2016/06/20040203-1.pdf.

4. "Avian Flu, Pandemic Diseases, and Their Economic and Social Consequences: A Template for Preparedness," Conference Agenda, Conference of the College of Physicians of Philadelphia and the Global Interdependence Center, Philadelphia, September 28, 2006.

5. "Gov. Kemp Taps Center for Economic Development Research Director for Corona-virus Task Force," *Georgia Tech News Center*, March 22, 2020, https://news.gatech.edu/news/2020/03/22/gov-kemp-taps-center-economic-development-research-director-coronavirus-task-force.

6.   Chang Ma, John Rogers, and Sili Zhou, "Modern Pandemics: Recession and Recovery." *Board of Governors of the Federal Reserve System, International Finance Discussion Papers,* Number 1295 (2020), https://www.federalreserve.gov/econres/ifdp/files/ifdp1295.pdf.

7.   Chang Ma, John Rogers, and Sili Zhou, "Modern Pandemics: Recession and Recovery," 3.

8.   By way of explanation, the term *agent members* refers to the securities brokers and dealers, banks and trust companies, clearing organizations, and certain other organizations that are participants in the Depository Trust Company, founded in 1973, a New York corporation that performs the functions of a central securities depository as part of the U.S. National Market System.

9.   Tim Sablik, "The Fed's Emergency Lending Evolves," *Econ Focus,* Second/Third Quarter 2020, 16, published online at the Federal Reserve Bank of Richmond, https://www.richmondfed.org/-/media/RichmondFedOrg/publications/research/econ_focus/2020/q2-3/federal_reserve.pdf.

10.   "Measuring the Natural Rate of Interest." Federal Reserve Board of New York, accessed June 15, 2024, https://www.newyorkfed.org/research/policy/rstar.

11.   Richard H. Clarida, Burcu Duygan-Bump, and Chiara Scotti, "The COVID-19 Crisis and the Federal Reserve's Policy Response," *Finance and Economics Discussion Series 2021–035,* June 2021, https://doi.org/10.17016/FEDS.2021.035.

12.   Eric Milstein and David Wessel, "What Did the Fed Do in Response to the COVID-19 Crisis?" Series: The Hutchins Center Explains, Brookings, 2021, https://www.brookings.edu/articles/fed-response-to-covid19/.

13.   Milstein and Wessel, "What Did the Fed Do in Response to the COVID-19 Crisis?"

14.   Donald Kohn, "The Fed's Actions Sunday: All in on Monetary Policy; Partly in on Liquidity Support," Brookings, March 16, 2020, https://www.brookings.edu/articles/the-feds-actions-sunday-all-in-on-monetary-policy-partly-in-on-liquidity-support/.

15.   Kohn, "The Fed's Actions Sunday: All in on Monetary Policy; Partly in on Liquidity Support."

16.   Kohn, "The Fed's Actions Sunday: All in on Monetary Policy; Partly in on Liquidity Support."

17.   For those details see "Policy Responses to COVID-19," International Monetary Fund, accessed June 15, 2024, https://www.imf.org/en/Topics/imf-and-COVID19/Policy-Responses-to-COVID-19, and "UN DESA Policy Brief No. 129: The Monetary Policy Response to COVID-19: The Role of Asset Purchase Programmes," *United Nations Department of Economic and Social Affairs Economic Analysis,* February 9, 2022, https://www.un.org/development/desa/dpad/publication/un-desa-policy-brief-no-129-the-monetary-policy-response-to-COVID-19-the-role-of-asset-purchase-programmes/.

18.   Jessica Dickler, "62% of Americans are Still Living Paycheck to Paycheck, Making It 'the Main Financial Lifestyle,' Report Finds" *CNBC,* October 31, 2023, https://www.cnbc.com/2023/10/31/62percent-of-americans-still-live-paycheck-to-paycheck-amid-inflation.html.

19.   For total employed persons, see "U.S. Employed Persons (I:U.S.ESM)," YCharts, https://ycharts.com/indicators/us_employed_persons; re immigration and the labor shortage, see Greg Iacurci, "Immigration is 'taking pressure off' the job market and U.S. economy, expert

says," March 2, 2024, https://www.cnbc.com/2024/03/02/immigration-taking-pressure-off-the-job-market-us-economy-expert.html.

20.   Sandra Ghizoni, "Reserve Banks Open for Business," Federal Reserve History, November 22, 2013, https://www.federalreservehistory.org/essays/reserve-banks-open.

21.   Brainard, Lael. "How Should We Think about Full Employment in the Federal Reserve's Dual Mandate?" Lecture at the Ec10, Principles of Economics, Faculty of Arts and Sciences, Harvard University Cambridge Massachussetts (via webcast), February 24, 2021, https://www.federalreserve.gov/newsevents/speech/brainard20210224a.htm.

22.   Howard Schneider, "Did pandemic central banking work? Fed review to eye inflation, jobs tradeoffs," Reuters, December 1, 2023, https://www.reuters.com/business/finance/did-pandemic-central-banking-work-fed-review-eye-inflation-jobs-tradeoffs-2023-12-01/.

23.   Jakub Hlavka and Adam Rose, "COVID-19's total cost to the economy in U.S. will reach $14 trillion by end of 2023 – new research," *The Conversation*, May 16, 2023, https://theconversation.com/COVID-19s-total-cost-to-the-economy-in-us-will-reach-14-trillion-by-end-of-2023-new-research-205379.

PART 4

Pandemic Lessons

Introduction

In the 21st century, the COVID-19 pandemic has afforded us an opportunity to examine in unprecedented detail the economic impacts of a pandemic shock and the factors that play into them, from a pathogen and its evolving variants to politics to human behavior. Much more has been made visible and shareable, for those who care to delve, the Fed included, than we have ever had to work with before.

The COVID experience has taught us much about pandemics, how we as human beings respond to foes we cannot see as opposed to foes we can, and how we calculate our priorities as we adjust to new risks and disruptions. Human psychology and behavior prove a key factor in driving pandemic outcomes. In fundamental ways, history demonstrates, people have not changed across millennia in terms of how they tend to respond to pandemics, and we are left to reckon with that reality and its implications for pandemic planning and response going forward.

We have also seen that old battle plans may not work with new enemies (a coronavirus pandemic is different from a flu pandemic or a plague pandemic or a smallpox pandemic, for instance, in terms of how it plays out). Further, problematically, what we think we know can blind us to what we need to learn on the fly and thereby seduce us into making strategic mistakes.

In Part 4 we look at lessons we have gleaned from the COVID experience over the last four years, paying close attention to what data can tell us and fully recognizing that the learning is not over; and in Part 5 we depict the COVID pandemic shock in Mike Englund's U.S. Pandemic Chart Book.

Chapter 13

Pandemic Lesson 1:
Pandemics Drive Societal Shifts

The COVID pandemic has driven a number of societal shifts, including the rise of remote work and geographic relocations that remote work made possible, with implications for real estate markets. Social distancing drove online collaborations (we all remember the Zoom choruses as well as innumerable meetings) while social media carved out perceptual worlds where misinformation and disinformation thrived, to the detriment of those who believed it and to the bonds of civil society.

In 2021, the Pew Research Center surveyed "innovators, developers, business and policy leaders, researchers, and activists," who were asked to envision how the world would change by 2025 because of the COVID pandemic. While some foresaw worsening economic inequality, the rise of big tech, the widening and tightening grip of authoritarianism, and a world torn by misinformation peddled by rival political forces, others foresaw new reforms aimed at equity and lives enhanced by flexible work arrangements and empowered by technology and AI. The survey was conducted, of course, before ChatGPT made the scene. A universal theme was the expanding, accelerating role of technology.[1]

The pandemic realigned social connections and changed people's patterns of interacting with their world. People reevaluated their lives, rethought career paths, took less for granted. Some seized upon their personal freedoms, while others lost a significant measure of faith in their peers' capacities for reasoning and for caring. The medically vulnerable found their lives transformed. The vivacious, medically vulnerable teacher, for instance, retired to create artwork in the company of her dog, her interactions with family and friends curtailed as others dropped COVID precautions.

Sharing of data and medical research, even before it could be peer-reviewed, surged as the world scrambled to assess a new coronavirus and its impacts and possible treatments — though those who thought that economic recovery required carrying on as if it were still 2019 sometimes found case and death data to be a pesky reminder that COVID has changed the risk landscape.

Businesses reconsidered where and how to do business. Supply chain issues made a case for producing vital products such as computer chips, medical supplies (including PPE), and medications closer to home.

Divisions in society deepened. To one person a mask was a prudent means of reducing risk; to another it was a symbol of oppression, and the compliant were "sheep" or "snowflakes." Some states maintained public health measures for longer periods than others did, adjusting policy to levels of infection and levels of vaccination, while others outlawed public health mandates for both the present and the future, tying their own hands.

The pandemic has changed us. In a study published in PLOS ONE in September of 2022, researchers found that, in the second year of the pandemic, "extroversion, openness, agreeableness and conscientiousness all declined across the population, but especially for younger adults, who also showed an increase in neuroticism." Young people in particular had become significantly less hopeful about their economic prospects for the future, though the pandemic hardly stands alone as a potential driver for that shift. Professor Angelina Sutin, one of the authors of the study, observed, "The first year [of the pandemic] there was this real coming together. But in the second year, with all of that support falling away and then the open hostility and social upheaval around restrictions ... all the collective good will that we had, we lost, and that might have been very significant for personality."[2] To what degree the personality changes that the pandemic experience wrought turn out to be lasting ones remains to be seen.

Public health pandemic response plans hit a reality check as COVID "burned like a forest fire" rather than following the pattern of the 1918 H1N1 pandemic that had informed pandemic planning. Yes, there were surges and lulls; but rather than the number of infections hitting bottom between those surges, as waves of influenza infections did, the SARS-CoV-2 virus kept right on infecting people. While peaks lessened in height as vaccines and prior infections conferred a measure of immunity, a line drawn from trough to trough to trough sloped upward, not down toward zero.

Tolerance and stamina for mitigations waned, and resistance to them gathered momentum. Moreover, even the most stringent zero-COVID measures could not stamp out a virus whose variants became ever more contagious; nor could vaccines forestall infection, given new variants. Populations grew tired of COVID and tired of measures taken to prevent its spread. We learned lessons from all this about human behavior and limits to our collective patience and capacity for rational response. Pandemic planning for the future will need to include huge helpings of research on human behavior and on effective communication around mitigations, vaccines, and risks, as well as on the thorny question of how to combat the misinformation and disinformation that is sure to arise.

We also learned that what we thought we knew could get in the way of what we needed to learn on the fly, given a new pandemic pathogen. History has taught us this lesson over and over again — if we have paid attention. The miasma theory persisted not for mere centuries but for millennia before germ theory finally displaced it. Influenza was not caused by a bacterium, as it was believed to be in 1918 as an influenza outbreak ignited at Camp Funston in Kansas, but by a virus. And, in the case of the H1N1 "Spanish flu," influenza was not the relatively mild illness most doctors of the time had assumed it to be until young adults began dying. COVID was transmitted not only by means of large droplets — the prevailing assumption in 2020 — but also by aerosols.

In each instance, what people did not understand cost lives. And in each case, vital new knowledge was slow to displace old understandings; instead, it was hard-won by experience and took time and often a tipping point to catch on. With COVID, we found we could stop washing our groceries, but we needed to breathe uninfected air if we wanted to remain healthy rather than being infected and reinfected. COVID was not "just a cold" as some assumed it to be, and we could not reach a level of "herd immunity" that would render the virus harmless rather than damaging and potentially disabling. Instead, we have found that COVID infections cause cumulative multisystem organ damage; and we would do best to avoid repeat infections, insofar as we can, while we carry on with our lives.

Our assumptions were stumbling blocks in the case of COVID, and one of the most significant of these misbegotten assumptions is that we had to make a stark choice between allowing rampant infection and maintaining the economic activity that provides our needs, our wants, and our means. Resorting to either stark choice entailed enormous costs in a world where it became increasingly clear that zero COVID was not achievable.

As this book was written, most countries and most jurisdictions within them had yet to navigate optimally between those extremes, neither of which has served us well, though there are exceptions, such as Taiwan. It took humanity most of its history to understand the value of personal hygiene and clean water and infection control in the operating theater. It turns out that it is also taking humanity time to grasp the value of ensuring, by various means, that the air we breathe in indoor spaces is not laden with heavy inoculation doses of airborne viruses (not limited to SARS-CoV-2) that can deal us lasting harm. COVID has taught us once again that old models may not serve in novel circumstances.

We will never be able to entirely separate the impacts of a pandemic from the complex forces and events that shape a particular place and time. And we cannot predict just how the future will break, given a pandemic with a long tail of impacts on human health, regional conflicts and global tensions, and an era of accelerating change encompassing everything from climate to technology.

We can, however, be sure of three things:

1. There will be future pandemics, and they will once again require us to respond even as we are learning the enemy.

2. People will continue to see pandemics through whatever lenses they see the rest of the world and will be inclined to believe whatever best fits the narratives they believe about the way things are.

3. All the old human foibles and predilections will operate alongside humanity's most valiant, well-informed, and scientifically advanced efforts to forestall disease, death, and damage.

---

1. Janna Anderson, Lee Rainie, and Emily A. Vogels, "Experts Say the 'New Normal' in 2025 Will Be Far More Tech-Driven, Presenting More Big Challenges," *Pew Research Center*, February 18, 2021, https://www.pewresearch.org/internet/2021/02/18/experts-say-the-new-normal-in-2025-will-be-far-more-tech-driven-presenting-more-big-challenges/.
2. Maggie Mertens, "Personalities don't usually change quickly but they may have during the pandemic," *NPR*, October 5, 2022, https://www.npr.org/sections/health-shots/2022/10/05/1126825073/pandemic-stress-impact-personalities; and Angelina R.

Sutin , Yannick Stephan, Martina Luchetti, Damaris Aschwanden, Ji Hyun Lee, Amanda A. Sesker, and Antonio Terracciano, "Differential personality change earlier and later in the coronavirus pandemic in a longitudinal sample of adults in the United States," *PLOS ONE* 17, no. 9 (September 28, 2022), https://journals.plos.org/plosone/article?id=10.1371/journal.pone.0274542.

Chapter 14

Pandemic Lesson 2:
Pandemics Erode the Labor Force and Drive Innovation

Pandemics that result in significant mortality erode the labor force and thus productivity, with effects in keeping with the mortality rates among people of working age. Over human history, this effect has been dramatic when an emperor could not muster armies sufficient to maintain an empire or when fields lay fallow for lack of farmers.

The Johns Hopkins Coronavirus Resource Center, a key resource, stopped collecting data on COVID deaths on March 10, 2023, as data had become harder and harder to collect. That caveat aside, the Johns Hopkins' global total confirmed deaths stood at 6,881,055. Of that total, U.S. confirmed deaths totaled 1,123,836, an outsized share relative to most other countries.[1] Our World in Data reported 6.89 million deaths globally as of March 29, 2023, while its central estimate of excess deaths during the pandemic was 21.21 million. The U.S. central excess death estimate was 1.36 million.[2] Case fatality rates varied from 4.9% in Peru to 0.1% in South Korea, with the U.S. mortality rate — the same as Canada's and higher than Europe's — at 1.1%.[3]

Countries around the world saw a dip in life expectancy with the spread of COVID-19, though the decline was reversed in many countries as vaccines were deployed. The United States has been a glaring exception.[4]

Life expectancy at birth in years, 1980-2021

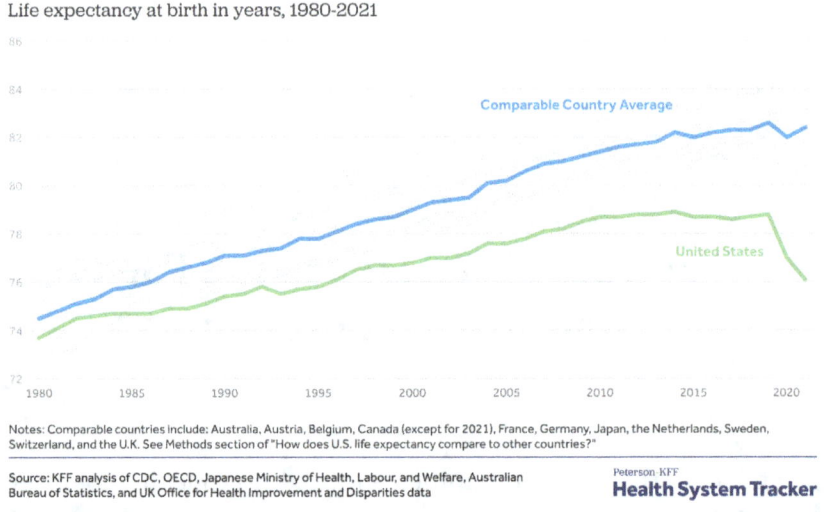

Notes: Comparable countries include: Australia, Austria, Belgium, Canada (except for 2021), France, Germany, Japan, the Netherlands, Sweden, Switzerland, and the U.K. See Methods section of "How does U.S. life expectancy compare to other countries?"

Source: KFF analysis of CDC, OECD, Japanese Ministry of Health, Labour, and Welfare, Australian Bureau of Statistics, and UK Office for Health Improvement and Disparities data

Peterson KFF
Health System Tracker

Figure 14.1 Life expectancy at birth in years, 1980–2021, Peterson KFF Health System Tracker.

The life expectancy story in the U.S. is complex; and COVID is but one element, as the Peterson-KFF Health System Tracker chart makes clear. The life expectancy gap between the U.S. and comparable countries long preceded 2020. The ready availability of guns, the opioid epidemic, a frayed safety net, adverse macroeconomic conditions, personal financial challenges, and a lack of affordable healthcare have also played significant roles.[5]

Just as important, the green line in the life expectancy chart above fails to capture the vast disparities within the U.S. As of 2019, for example, life expectancy in Summit County, Colorado, at 91.72 years, was 27 years longer than life expectancy in Oglala Lakota County, South Dakota, at 64.5 years.[6]

Since 2020, an uptick in already high levels of U.S. gun violence is, in part, a reflection of the multifaceted stresses that a pandemic inflicts, such that gun-related deaths among children (along with gun violence in general) have risen by 50% since 2020; but we cannot forget, either, that the risk of a new mental illness rises after COVID infection.[7] Whether prior COVID infection correlates to an increase in the risk that a person will resort to gun violence, we cannot currently say. One measure of the impact of gun violence is this startling fact: The number one killer of children in the U.S. is not COVID or even automobile crashes. Since 2020, gun violence has killed more American children than automobile crashes have, and more than all diseases put together have.[8]

COVID has been an add-on to all those other factors that were already impacting U.S. life expectancy in 2019 and before. The pandemic drove a further 2% decrease in U.S. life expectancy. Where COVID hit hardest, however, the impact was more dramatic. The death rate in New York City spiked by 50% in 2020, with 172,000 deaths in New York elder care facilities alone; and life expectancy in the city plunged by 4.6 years that year. New York had not seen such a heavy death toll and loss of life expectancy since the cholera epidemic of 1834.[9] (Other American cities, such as Philadelphia and Boston, were hit harder by the H1N1 influenza pandemic sparked in 1918.)

It was the rapid development and deployment of vaccines that forestalled the worst that COVID might have done in terms of demographic damage. The authors of a 2022 modeling study drew the following conclusions:

> From December 2020 through November 2022, we estimate that the COVID-19 vaccination program in the U.S. prevented more than 18.5 million additional hospitalizations and 3.2 million additional deaths. Without vaccination, there would have been nearly 120 million more COVID-19 infections. The vaccination program also saved the U.S. $1.15 trillion (Credible

Interval: $1.10 trillion–$1.19 trillion) in medical costs that would otherwise have been incurred.[10]

To the extent that Americans refused vaccination, whether out of fear because the vaccine was new or out of faith in misinformation about the relative risks of vaccination versus infection, more of them died. In a speech delivered on November 30, 2022, Fed Chair Jerome Powell noted that the United States had seen about 400,000 excess deaths among people of working age since the pandemic began, including those who had died of COVID.[11] Back-of-the-envelope math based on the percentage of unvaccinated working-age Americans who died suggests that, had many Americans not stepped up to be vaccinated, the United States would have lost between 1.1 and 1.2 million *more* people of working age, further exacerbating the labor shortage.

However, because of the lives COVID vaccines did save, the largest factor in the U.S. labor shortfall, accounting for about one million fewer workers, was not COVID mortality but the slowing of immigration during the pandemic shock. March 2020 shutdowns at U.S. embassy consulates suspended most visa services except for the H-2A visas for migrant farmworkers, who are essential to producing the nation's food supply. In June 2020, as unemployment spiked, President Trump suspended most temporary work visas (visas for migrant farmworkers excepted) with the intention of protecting American jobs.[12] The number of green cards issued fell from 240,000 in the first quarter of 2020 to 79,000 in April of 2020, climbing to only 130,000 by the close of the year.[13] But as the nation reopened and job openings picked up again, a labor shortfall quickly resulted.

As employers struggled to find workers in 2021, the Biden administration restored the flow of visas that had been halted during the first year of the pandemic and has subsequently raised the cap on nonimmigrant H-2B visas. Since then, in 2022 and 2023, the number of immigrants working in the United States has more than doubled from 2020 and 2021 and now exceeds 2015 and 2016 highs. Immigration more than made up for the shortfall created by pandemic deaths and helped to fuel the U.S. economic recovery.[14] Foreign-born U.S. workers now account for 18.6% of the U.S. workforce, up from 14% before the pandemic.[15] These workers have done the most to mitigate staffing shortages in leisure and hospitality, followed by professional and business services, construction, manufacturing, and mining.[16] Deutsche Bank Research U.S. Economist Justin Weidner estimates that by mitigating the pandemic labor force shock, the influx of foreign-born workers also slowed wage growth post pandemic and trimmed core PCE inflation by 25–50 bps as of mid 2024.[17] The chart below, courtesy of Apollo Chief Economist Torsten Sløk and the team at Apollo Academy, captures the reality: U.S. labor force growth post-pandemic has been enabled by immigration.[18]

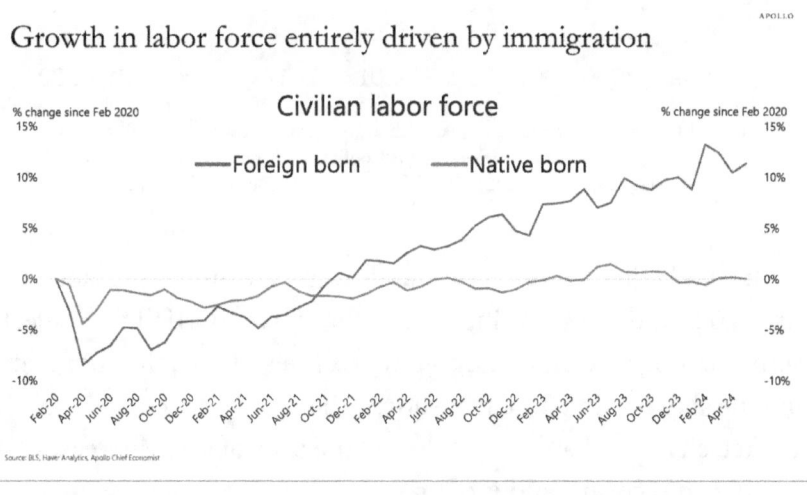

Figure 14.2 Growth in labor force entirely driven by immigration, courtesy of Torsten Sløk and Apollo Academy (Data sources: BLS, Haver Analytics, Apollo Chief Economist).

On its own, population growth among U.S. native-born citizens, which cratered during the pandemic to 0.1% in 2021, remains insufficient to grow the labor force, as Philippa Dunne and Doug Henwood have pointed out in their subscription letter *TLRWire*. (The number of native-born workers was not sufficient on its own to keep the U.S. economy humming before the pandemic, either.) In the chart below, Dunne and Henwood depict the immigration-related labor force shock that accompanied the pandemic shock.[19]

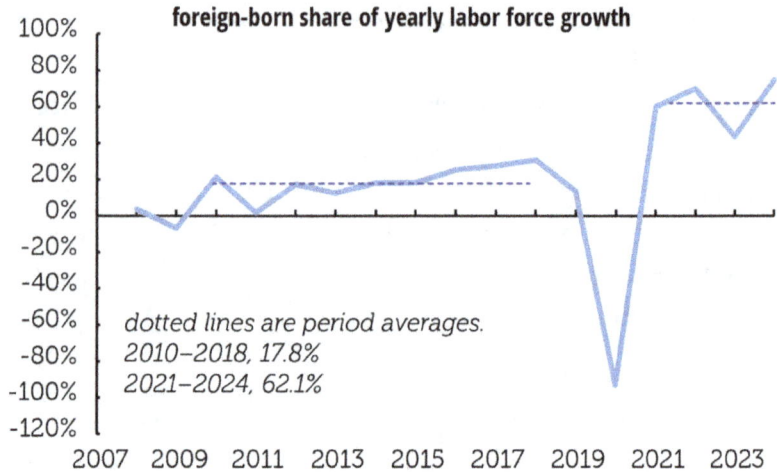

Figure 14.3 Foreign-born share of yearly labor force growth, courtesy of Philippa Dunne and Doug Henwood, "Immigration Is Cooling the Labor Market," TLRwire, TLR Analytics, June 19, 2024 (Data source: U.S. Bureau of Labor Statistics).

In the United States, a renewed influx of immigrant labor went far in 2022 and 2023 to mitigate the labor force shortfall that reflected both the longer-term demographic realities of an aging population and the short-term pandemic shock. That influx has cooled the labor market, shaved inflation, and slowed the pace of wage increases even as it fueled recovery and growth.

Acknowledging that immigration is currently a politically fraught issue, Jim Reid of Deutsche Bank Research points out the implications of rejecting the contributions of immigrants:

> To the extent that immigration flows are curtailed, this would act as a negative supply shock, dampening growth while providing a tailwind for inflation.[20]

Jim Reid's point cannot be dismissed. Foreign-born workers make vital economic contributions, as outlined in a recent article from CNBC:

> In simple terms, more workers generate more goods and services. A larger number of people earning paychecks means more consumer spending, the lifeblood of the U.S. economy. More people paying income tax on earnings boosts tax revenues at a time of growing U.S. budget deficits and helps prop up social programs such as Social Security and Medicare, which are funded by payroll taxes and facing a shortfall.[21]

As of mid 2024, the post-pandemic-shock influx of foreign-born workers had not impinged upon the employment opportunities of native-born U.S. citizens. The unemployment rate for both groups as of May 2024 sat at a low 3.6%.[22]

The labor shortage caused by COVID deaths paled in comparison to the labor shortages created by higher mortality epidemics and pandemics of the past, such as the Black Death or the Plague of Justinian; but it exerted pressure on wages and negatively impacted businesses, healthcare, and education. Shoring up the labor force following a deadly pandemic is not a new problem in human history, and bringing in workers from someplace else is a pandemic shock recovery solution that cities and nations have resorted to at least as far back as classical Athens and ancient Rome. To the degree that adaptations, innovations, and immigration can make up for workers missing because of a pandemic, economies recover more quickly. At the same time, pressure driving increases in real wages is countered to one degree or another. Real wages rise in the medium term when there is no ready way to expeditiously augment a depleted labor force to meet demand.

The labor force shortfall in the wake of the COVID pandemic was not driven only by deaths, illness, and a temporary reduction in immigration; in some fields it was also worsened by an uptick in early retirements and career transitions. In 2022, teachers and other education workers surveyed were more likely to retire earlier than originally planned (4.3%), along with hospitality workers (3.6%).[23] While some 3,600 U.S. healthcare workers died in the first year of the pandemic (the World Health Organization estimates that between 80,000 and 180,000 healthcare workers died worldwide between January 2020 and May 2021),[24] the exodus of many more healthcare workers in a time of intensified demand for services left the healthcare system in a crisis from which it has not recovered. Extraordinarily difficult working conditions during the pandemic led to burnout among workers in some professions, especially healthcare, and drove many to seek new jobs in better circumstances. The exhausted and traumatized hospital nurse switched jobs to work in a doctor's office. The beleaguered public schoolteacher decided to work in the private sector instead. The hospitality or retail worker, tired of the risk and/or the verbal abuse from some customers, opted out. The labor shortage that resulted from these factors and others spurred wage growth that began to reverse only as the Fed acted to cool the economy in order to curb persistent inflation driven first by pandemic-related supply chain issues and then further by other events.

The implications of COVID deaths are not limited to actual lives lost or to the number of unfilled jobs. Around the world, 10.4 million children lost a parent or another primary caregiver. In the United States, that number is estimated to be 214,000.[25] (In one instance we know of personally, children lost both parents, one after the other.) Children who lost primary caregivers, whether those caregivers were parents or grandparents, face futures laced with challenges. The CDC lists the added risks: "Orphanhood increases the likelihood of poverty, abuse, delayed development, mental health challenges, reduced access to education, and institutionalization."[26] Mental health challenges include depression, anxiety, and suicidality. Losing a parent raises the likelihood that a person will resort to substance abuse and increases the likelihood that a child will drop out of school, impacting later employment opportunities. Adverse childhood events such as the loss of a parent also handicap a person's ability to successfully navigate relationships.[27]

Pandemic deaths erode workplaces and, for a time, economies, and devastate families, with long-term implications for the lives of survivors. Effects are both large and immediate and more subtle and lasting. Some can be measured, and some cannot. Because COVID claimed more lives among the elderly than it did among adults of working age and because vaccines were available in record time, the impact of COVID deaths on the labor supply has been noticeable but far more limited than it would have been had the virus more severely impacted the young, its virulence unchecked by vaccinations.

Pandemic-driven labor shortages, however, are not caused by deaths alone. Long COVID had sidelined, as of late 2022, perhaps 280,000 to 680,000 additional individuals aged 16 to 64 from the U.S. labor force.[28] Some will recover, but others never will, and still others who enjoy good health today will develop long COVID after repeated infections. Officially declaring an end to the pandemic emergency cannot stop COVID from infecting people or damaging their health a little or a lot, for a shorter time or for a lifetime. To the extent that infections are not or cannot be deterred, an erosion of health, productivity, and even lifespans will continue. Data from the National

Health Interview Survey indicates that 0.5% of U.S. children suffered from long COVID as of 2022, with a higher incidence among girls (1.6%) than boys (0.9%).[29]

The United States is hardly alone in facing the costs of long COVID. A 2024 study, "The Impacts of long COVID across OECD Countries" estimates that long COVID may be sidelining 3 million workers across OECD countries. That's $141 billion USD in wages lost. The authors of the study estimate that reduced labor force participation and the loss of perhaps as many as 7 million quality-adjusted life years annually is probably eroding OECD economies by $864 billion–$1.04 trillion USD each year.[30]

Deaths and disability and resulting worker shortages, as has always been the case, drive changes designed to replace lost labor and to rein in higher labor costs. In the U.S., H-1B visas for 2023 and 2024 remained capped at 85,000 (including 20,000 for those specifically for workers with advanced degrees), and firms worked around those caps to find the skilled workers they needed. Britta Glennon, an assistant professor at the Wharton School of Business at the University of Pennsylvania, noted in 2023 that globalized multinational firms "hire 0.9 employees abroad for every visa rejection."[31] An opportunity to strengthen U.S. competitiveness, Glennon notes, is lost.

In response to the labor shortage, lawmakers in 11 U.S. states have sought to relax child labor laws to one degree or another as some industries, from the hospitality industry to homebuilders, pushed for changes that would allow younger teens to work (in some instances as young as fourteen).[32] Many of these jobs are billed as opportunities for young people to learn job skills, though many of the jobs offered do not entail learning many transferrable skills beyond those essential for employability, such as showing up on time. Instead, if the hours worked are too many and extend too late into the evening, they impact adolescents' performance in school and thus the trajectory of their futures.[33]

A stronger case can be made for keeping older workers in the workforce by lifting the financial penalty that younger retirees who draw Social Security benefits face if they choose to return to work. The penalty phases out at full retirement age.[34]

Technological advances, including AI, continue their transformative march through workplaces, extending what workers can do or replacing their roles altogether. In healthcare, AI's roles include crunching research data to provide results more quickly, automating administrative tasks, assisting in diagnoses, and helping patients and doctors track patients' health.[35] Worker shortages in both healthcare and education, for instance, will accelerate the adoption of technological solutions. *The Future of Jobs Report 2023* from the World Economic Forum anticipated a "structural labor market churn of jobs" between 2023 and 2028. While 69 million jobs will be created, some 83 million jobs will disappear.[36] Much of that structural change will be driven by the implementation of AI, which has already begun radically altering our lives and the world of work.

Some labor market shifts will also be driven by climate change and climate change response, which will open new jobs as humanity adapts. The number of net new jobs will, of course, depend on the policy path chosen.

COVID — the deaths it has caused and the disability and damage and worker absenteeism that infections continue to inflict — is but one of the factors in play in the complex labor market picture going forward. Teasing the pandemic's impacts apart from all the rest will become ever more difficult. That said, it is clear that the tightened labor market caused by the pandemic has recalibrated the demand for foreign-born workers, accelerated interest in and acceptance of artificial intelligence, precipitated a regression in child labor laws in some states, and lent momentum to other innovations that will change our lives and our work in profound ways, leveraging greater productivity with fewer people.

1.   "COVID-19 Dashboard," Johns Hopkins University of Medicine Coronavirus Resource Center, https://coronavirus.jhu.edu/map.html, last accessed June 11, 2024.

2.   "Estimated cumulative excess deaths during COVID, World," Our World in Data, Global Change Data Lab, https://ourworldindata.org/grapher/excess-deaths-cumulative-economist-single-entity?country=~OWID_WRL, last accessed June 11, 2024.

3.   "Mortality Analyses," Johns Hopkins University of Medicine Coronavirus Resource Center, last accessed June 11, 2024, https://coronavirus.jhu.edu/data/mortality.

4.   Shameek Rakshit, Matthew McGough, Krutika Amin Twitter, and Cynthia Cox, "How does U.S. life expectancy compare to other countries?" *Peterson-KFF Health System Tracker,* December 6, 2022, https://www.healthsystemtracker.org/chart-collection/u-s-life-expectancy-compare-countries/#Life%20expectancy%20at%20birth%20in%20years,%201980-2021.

5.   Selena Simmons-Duffin, "'Live free and die?' The sad state of U.S. life expectancy," *Morning Edition,* NPR, March 25, 2023, https://www.npr.org/sections/health-shots/2023/03/25/1164819944/live-free-and-die-the-sad-state-of-u-s-life-expectancy; Jeremy Ney, "Life Expectancy and Inequality," *American Inequality*, February 2, 2021, https://americaninequality.substack.com/p/life-expectancy-and-inequality.

6.   "Life Expectancy at Birth; Both Sexes; All racial and ethnic groups; 2019," U.S. Health Map, IHME, University of Washington, last accessed June 11, 2024, https://vizhub.healthdata.org/subnational/usa; GBD U.S. Health Disparities Collaborators, "Life expectancy by county, race, and ethnicity in the USA, 2000–19: a systematic analysis of health disparities," *The Lancet* 400, no. 10345 (June 2022): 25-38, https://www.thelancet.com/journals/lancet/article/PIIS0140-6736(22)00876-5/fulltext.

7.   Nirmita Panchal, Heather Saunders, Robin Rudowitz, and Cynthia Cox Follow, "The Implications of COVID-19 for Mental Health and Substance Use," *KFF*, March 20, 2023, https://www.kff.org/coronavirus-COVID-19/issue-brief/the-implications-of-COVID-19-for-mental-health-and-substance-use/; Kristina Sauerwein, "COVID-19 survivors face increased mental health risks up to a year later," News Hub, Washington University School of Medicine in St. Louis, February 16, 2022, https://medicine.wustl.edu/news/COVID-19-survivors-face-increased-mental-health-risks-up-to-a-year-later/.

8.   John Gramlich, "Gun deaths among U.S. children and teens rose 50% in two years," *Pew Research Center,* April 6, 2023, https://www.pewresearch.org/fact-tank/2023/04/06/gun-deaths-among-us-kids-rose-50-percent-in-two-years/; Paige Sutherland and Meghna Chakrabarti, "Why Black children bear the brunt of gun deaths, and what can be done to stop it," *On Point,* WBUR, April 3, 2023, https://www.wbur.org/onpoint/2023/04/03/why-black-children-bear-the-brunt-of-gun-deaths-and-what-can-be-done-to-stop-it.

9.   Joseph Goldstein, "N.Y.C. Life Expectancy Dropped 4.6 Years in 2020, Officials Say," *New York Times,* April 7, 2023, https://www.nytimes.com/2023/04/07/nyregion/nyc-COVID-deaths.html; Michael Gold and Ed Shanahan, " What We Know About Cuomo's Nursing Home Scandal," *New York Times,* August 4, 2021, https://www.nytimes.com/article/andrew-cuomo-nursing-home-deaths.html.

10.   Meagan C. Fitzpatrick, Seyed M. Moghadas, Abhishek Pandey, and Alison P. Galvani, "Two

Years of U.S. COVID-19 Vaccines Have Prevented Millions of Hospitalizations and Deaths," The Commonwealth Fund, December 13, 2022, https://www.commonwealthfund.org/blog/2022/two-years-COVID-vaccines-prevented-millions-deaths-hospitalizations.

11. Jerome H. Powell, "Inflation and the Labor Market," speech at the Hutchins Center on fiscal and monetary policy, November 30, 2022, https://www.federalreserve.gov/newsevents/speech/powell20221130a.htm.

12. Claire Klobucista and Diana Roy, "U.S. Temporary Foreign Worker Visa Programs," Council on Foreign Relations, as updated June 8, 2023, https://www.cfr.org/backgrounder/us-temporary-foreign-worker-visa-programs.

13. Jens Manuel Krogstad and Ana Gonzalez-Barrera, "Key Facts about U.S. Immigration Policies and Biden's Proposed Changes," Pew Research Center," January 11, 2022, https://www.pewresearch.org/short-reads/2022/01/11/key-facts-about-u-s-immigration-policies-and-bidens-proposed-changes/.

14. Elior Cohen, "Rising Immigration Has Helped Cool an Overheated Labor Market," Economic Bulletin, Federal Reserve Bank of Kansas City, May 22, 2024, https://www.kansascityfed.org/research/economic-bulletin/rising-immigration-has-helped-cool-an-overheated-labor-market/.

15. "Economic News Release: Labor Force Characteristics of Foreign-born Workers Summary," U.S. Bureau of Labor Statistics, May 21, 2024, https://www.bls.gov/news.release/forbrn.nr0.htm.

16. Elior Cohen, "Rising Immigration Has Helped Cool an Overheated Labor Market."

17. Jim Reid of Deutsche Bank Research noted this estimate from DBR's U.S. economist Justin Weidner in a June 29, 2024, email to subscribers, "DB CoTD: Immigration Song."

18. Torsten Sløk, "Growth in the Labor Force Coming Entirely From Immigration," Apollo Academy, June 17, 2024, https://www.apolloacademy.com/growth-in-the-labor-force-coming-entirely-from-immigration/.

19. Philippa Dunne and Doug Henwood, "Immigration Is Cooling the Labor Market," TLRwire, TLR Analytics, June 19, 2024.

20. Jim Reid, "DB CoTD: Immigration Song," Deutsche Bank Research, email, June 29, 2024.

21. Greg Iacurci, "Immigration Is 'Taking Pressure Off' the Job Market and U.S. Economy, Expert Says," CNBC, March 2, 2024, https://www.cnbc.com/2024/03/02/immigration-taking-pressure-off-the-job-market-us-economy-expert.html.

22. "Economic News Release: Labor Force Characteristics of Foreign-born Workers Summary," May 21, 2024.

23. Daniel Thompson, "Pandemic Disrupted Labor Markets But Had Modest Impact on Retirement Timing," America Counts: Stories, U.S. Census Bureau, https://www.census.gov/library/stories/2022/09/did-COVID-19-change-retirement-timing.html.

24. Jane Spencer and Christina Jewett, "12 Months of Trauma: More Than 3,600 U.S. Health Workers Died in COVID's First Year," KFF Health News, April 8, 2021, https://khn.org/news/article/us-health-workers-deaths-COVID-lost-on-the-frontline/; "Health and Care Worker Deaths during COVID-19," World Health Organization, October 20, 2021, https://www.who.int/news/item/20-10-2021-health-and-care-worker-deaths-during-COVID-19.

25. Amy McKeever, "COVID-19's hidden, heartbreaking toll: millions of orphaned children,"

National Geographic, May 6, 2022, https://www.nationalgeographic.com/science/article/COVID-19-hidden-heartbreaking-toll-millions-of-orphaned-children.

26. "COVID Children: The Hidden Pandemic 2021," *Centers for Disease Control,* July 20, 2021.

27. David Cox, "What will happen to the orphans of COVID-19?" *BMJ* 379, no. 02838 (December 2022), https://www.bmj.com/content/379/bmj.o2838.

28. Powell, "Inflation and the Labor Market."

29. Anjel Vahratian, Dzifa Adjaye-Gbewonyo, Jin-Mann S. Lin, and Sharon Saydah, "Long COVID in Children: United States, 2022," NCHS Data Brief No. 479, September 2023, https://www.cdc.gov/nchs/products/databriefs/db479.htm.

30. Ana Espinosa Gonzalez and Elina Suzuki, "The Impacts of Long COVID across OECD Countries," OECD Health Working Paper No 167, OECD, https://doi.org/10.1787/8bd08383-en.

31. Stuart Anderson, "U.S. Companies Denied H-1B Visas Hire Talent Abroad," *Forbes,* April 4, 2023, https://www.forbes.com/sites/stuartanderson/2023/04/04/us-companies-denied-h-1b-visas-hire-talent-abroad/?sh=274a967956cc.

32. Stephen Elliott, "Republicans push for teenagers as young as 14 to work in restaurants, industrial jobs," *USA Today,* April 18, 2023, https://www.usatoday.com/story/news/nation/2023/04/18/child-labor-laws-targeted-lawmakers-11-states-seek-weaken/11682548002/.

33. Jeremy Staff, John E. Schulenberg, and Jerald G. Bachman, "Adolescent Work Intensity, School Performance, and Academic Engagement," *Sociology of Education 83, no. 3*(July 2010): 183–200, accessed at PMC PubMed Central, NIH National Library of Medicine, https://www.ncbi.nlm.nih.gov/pmc/articles/PMC2926992/.

34. "2023 Social Security Changes," Fact Sheet, Social Security Administration, last accessed June 11, 2024, https://www.ssa.gov/news/press/factsheets/colafacts2023.pdf.

35. Raj Leventhal, "Use of AI in healthcare & medicine is booming – here's how the medical field is benefiting from AI in 2023 and beyond," eMarketer, Insider Intelligence, January 11, 2023, https://www.insiderintelligence.com/insights/artificial-intelligence-healthcare/.

36. "The Future of Jobs Report 2023," *World Economic Forum*, Report Summary, April 30, 2023, https://www.weforum.org/reports/the-future-of-jobs-report-2023/digest.

Chapter 15

Pandemic Lesson 3:
Disability Derails Lives, Drives Costs

Pandemic pathogens have long resulted in lasting health impairments of one kind or another. Polio famously paralyzed about 0.5% of those it infected, and 20% or more of those who contracted the disease saw a relapse later in life, a condition called *post-polio syndrome*. Influenza viruses can have neurological impacts, infecting the brain itself; and influenza pandemics are associated with increases in cases of encephalitis.[1] People born in early 1919, when the 1918 H1N1 influenza pandemic was raging, suffered higher rates of diabetes in later life and, by the time they reached their 60s, 25% more heart disease than people born in other years. Data suggests the possibility that they were at least somewhat developmentally impaired, as they did not grow as tall as people born in surrounding years did; neither did they achieve the education and economic productivity that near agemates did.[2]

SARS-CoV-2 has proven to be a particularly insidious pandemic virus. According to the Household Pulse Survey, as of January 2023, 11% of those who had been infected with COVID were reporting long COVID symptoms. That figure does not include those who believe that COVID is "just a cold" and who thus do not connect their new

337

health issues with that run-in they had with COVID six months before. Fortunately, more than half of those who have suffered long COVID symptoms have seen those symptoms abate over the course of the following year, but about 5% of all U.S. adults are currently grappling with long COVID symptoms that restrict their activities, and 27% of those report that their activities are significantly restricted.[3]

An analysis of Household Pulse Survey data by the Center for Economic and Policy Research (CEPR) in December of 2022 concluded that 6% of working-age adults (ages 25–54) found that long COVID limited their activities, while 1.7% reported that their activities were limited "a lot."

Estimates vary with regard to the impact of long COVID on the workforce. In September of 2022, Gopi Shah Goda (Stanford) and Evan J. Soltas (MIT) estimated in an NBER working paper that long COVID had reduced the U.S. labor force by about 500,000 workers,[4] whereas Katie Bach (Brookings) estimated in August of 2022 that long COVID had sidelined between 2 million and 4 million workers.[5] A study by the New York State Insurance Fund found that 18% of workers affected by long COVID had not returned to work a year after their initial illness. Of those, fewer than one in four were over 60 years of age. Many who returned to work earlier, while still receiving treatment, required workplace accommodations such as reduced hours.[6]

Given deaths and rising levels of disability paired with a period of sharply restricted legal immigration during the pandemic, the number of unemployed persons available to fill each job opening dipped to the point that, from December of 2021 through early 2023, there were approximately two openings for each unemployed person. The number of unemployed workers available to fill open positions remained low as of the fall of 2023 but continued to rise through the summer of 2024, as depicted in Figure 15.1.

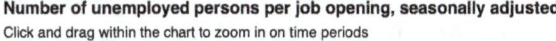

Number of unemployed persons per job opening, seasonally adjusted
Click and drag within the chart to zoom in on time periods

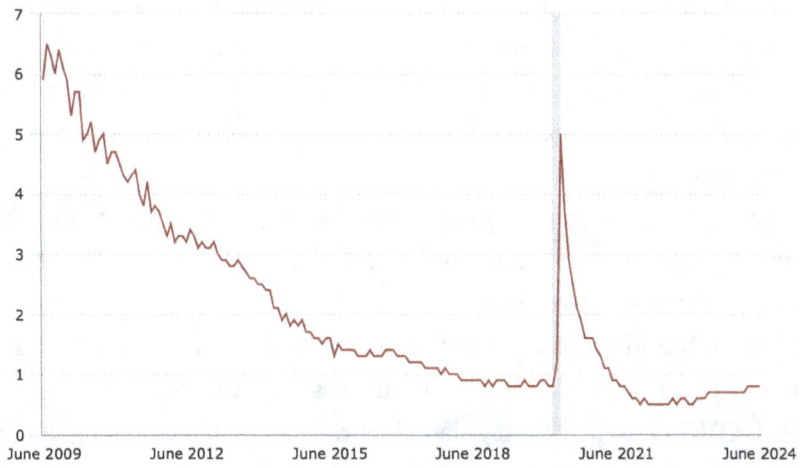

Source: U.S. Bureau of Labor Statistics.

Figure 15.1 Number of unemployed persons per job opening, seasonally adjusted
(Data source: U.S. Bureau of Labor Statistics)

Long COVID symptoms aside, COVID infections are associated with higher risk for a number of conditions. COVID raises the risk of cardiovascular disease such that a person who has had a COVID infection has a five times greater risk of dying during the ensuing 18 months than does a person who has not been infected.[7]

COVID speeds the progression of preexisting dementia and raises the risk of a new dementia diagnosis.[8] COVID infections and reinfections will drive a higher incidence of dementia worldwide, but it is too early to say by how much. We will need to compare the course of whole lives in the time of COVID to the course of whole lives prior to determine that.

COVID raises the risk of a new diabetes diagnosis by 66%, introducing a whole new world of health concerns for those who are newly diagnosed.[9] A Canadian cohort study based on the health records of more than 600,000 people found that 3–5% of new type 1 or type 2 diabetes diagnoses are linked to COVID.[10] That's on top of the increase in type 2 diabetes already driven by lifestyle factors in years prior to the pandemic.

A COVID infection also raises the risk for hypertension and hyperlipidemia (excess fats, cholesterol, and triglycerides in the blood, contributing to heart disease). Post-COVID, people may find themselves on blood pressure and cholesterol medications for the first time, battling their increased risk of cardiovascular disease.[11]

COVID can also dysregulate the immune system, causing damage akin to that caused by Hepatitis C or HIV, by dampening the immune response that CD8+ T cells mount against subsequent infections.[12] Immunologists Nu Zhang and Michael J. Bevan characterize CD8+ T cells as "the foot soldiers of the immune system." They explain that these cells have "an astounding capacity to react to pathogens by massive expansion and differentiation into cytotoxic effector cells that migrate to all corners of the body to clear the infection."[13] But when this army of foot soldiers is partly incapacitated as a result of COVID or HIV, people are more susceptible to illnesses, and their bodies are less able to fight them.

Reinfections, which are hard to avoid given the high transmissibility of newer variants and the lifting of mitigations, compound risk of death, hospitalization, long COVID symptoms such as fatigue, along with cardiovascular damage, kidney damage, pulmonary damage, blood clots, diabetes, cognitive impairment, and more.[14] The implications are clear: We are not "beating" COVID with lasting "herd immunity." Coronaviruses do not work that way, unfortunately.

Among long COVID patients, organ damage is common. CIDRAP reported the findings of British researchers studying organ damage in long COVID patients, published in the *Journal of the Royal Society of Medicine*:

> Sixty-two percent of participants had organ damage 6 months after their initial diagnosis, as did 59% of those who underwent a 40-minute multi-organ magnetic resonance imaging (MRI) scan at 1 year — even those with non-severe infections.
>
> Among all patients, 29% had multi-organ impairment, with lingering symptoms and impaired function at 6 and 12 months, while 59% of long-COVID patients had single-organ damage at 1 year.
>
> Long-COVID symptoms declined from 6 to 12 months, with extreme shortness of breath dropping from 38% to 30% of patients, brain fog from 48% to 38%, and poor HRQoL from 57% to 45%.[15]

What economic impact can we expect from long COVID? The final tally will be the work of future historians and economists, but we can anticipate that the costs will be very high. While in 2020 Larry Summers and David Cutler anticipated that the economic cost of long COVID might be $2.6 trillion, David Cutler revised his estimate in July of 2022 to $3.7 trillion.[16] The total included almost $2.2 trillion in reduced quality of life (priced at $100,000 per year of good health lost); $997 billion in reduced earnings; and $528 billion in increased medical spending.

Years of lost health and lost income equate, of course, to trips not taken, hobbies and sports not pursued, and purchases not made, such that the impact of the spending that long COVID sufferers are not doing impacts the overall economy. Impacts are not limited to an individual long COVID sufferer's finances. Reduced means, for those who can no longer work full time or at all, are refocused on medical issues and cost of care. In cases where long COVID is debilitating, family members who act as caregivers may also see reduced productivity and income.

Compounding the significance of long COVID and its overt symptoms is the fact that COVID infection causes damage that may remain undetected for some time. COVID is associated, for example, with an elevated risk of heart disease and stroke one year out not only for those reporting long COVID symptoms but even for those who experienced only mild symptoms or none at all. In specific terms, risks among those studied were elevated for "cerebrovascular disorders, dysrhythmias, ischemic and non-ischemic heart disease, pericarditis, myocarditis, heart failure, and thromboembolic disease."[17] A study published in *Nature Medicine* in May of 2024 found that people who had weathered mild Covid infections had elevated risks for developing GI, neurological, and pulmonary issues over a three-year period following infection. Those who were hospitalized with COVID in 2020 saw increased risk of these problems developing within three years — they had a 52% higher risk of GI problems, a 21% higher risk for new neurological issues, and a 57% greater risk of lung-related problems.[18]

The mental health issues that COVID infections can precipitate include "anxiety, depression, and suicidal ideation, as well as opioid use disorder, illicit drug and alcohol use disorders, and disturbances in sleep and cognition."[19] COVID "brain fog," or cognitive damage, impairs productivity even among those who are still working, and it affects about half of long COVID sufferers.[20] A COVID infection shaves people's IQs — a mild infection results in a loss of about three points; those with lingering symptoms lose, on average, six points; a COVID infection serious enough to land a person in intensive care results in a nine-point drop.[21] "Brain fog" is brain damage.

Evidence now suggests a link between COVID infection and an elevated risk of Parkinson's Disease in the future. Brain cells called *microglia,* when infected with the SARS-CoV-2 virus, exhibited the same inflammatory response that is linked to cases of Parkinson's or Alzheimer's.[22] COVID infections have also been found to worsen Parkinson's symptoms, both motor and non-motor.[23]

Contracting COVID during pregnancy is another concern, not just for the pregnant parent, who is at increased risk of more severe illness or death, but also for the baby, especially if the baby is male. A maternal infection during pregnancy raises the risk that a male child, in particular, will be diagnosed with neurodevelopmental delays before he is two years old. Conditions more common among boys whose mothers caught COVID during pregnancy include intellectual disabilities and developmental delays in speech, language, psychological development, and motor function. How significant is the risk? Dr. Andrea Edlow, the lead author of a study comparing outcomes for 18,000 babies explains: "If a mom had a SARS-CoV-2 infection in pregnancy and had a male child, her 12-month-old was 94% more likely to have any neurodevelopmental diagnosis."[24]

COVID is, of course, not the only viral infection associated with altered fetal development. Edlow, a maternal-fetal medicine specialist on the faculty of Harvard Medical School, explains that the impacts of maternal infections, COVID and influenza among them, occur because of the immune response that a mother's body mounts to infection. An exception to that is, of course, Zika, which "directly attacks a developing brain."[25]

The preceding discussion is in no way intended to be a complete accounting of what we are learning (and will learn) about the longer-term health implications of COVID infections. Instead, it is an early indication that COVID is changing the health trajectories of human lives, with significant economic implications.

As this book is written, vaccines and certain COVID treatments reduce the risk of long COVID, but they do not eliminate that risk. The number of long COVID sufferers seems likely to rise as people are infected and reinfected, sans mitigations to curb transmission, along with the economic, personal, and societal costs of long COVID. Some long COVID sufferers will substantially recover within a year or so; others will not. In the meantime, the search for effective treatments has progressed only very slowly. The NIH's $1.15 billion initiative to pursue research on long COVID and its treatments had not yet enrolled patients in any clinical trials as of April 2023.[26] Thus far, we have learned far more about the problems long COVID encompasses — some 200 conditions (as reported in an in-depth 2024 report from the National Academy of Sciences, Engineering, and Medicine) — than we have learned about how to treat it.[27]

Long COVID health impairments leave some unable to go to school and some adults unable to work for six months to two years or longer.[28] The healthcare costs precipitated by a COVID infection are noted in a study published in *BMC Medicine* in February of 2024 and based on a study of the de-identified health records of U.S. adults in Optum's Clinformatics® Data Mart Database. The database captured healthcare costs in the year preceding a COVID infection and the 13 months that followed:

> Cost increases varied in magnitude but were observed for every healthcare outcome across all categories of the acute COVID-19 level of care. Even among those who were not hospitalized during the acute phase of COVID-19, inpatient visit costs during the post-acute phase increased by 578%, outpatient visit costs increased by 139%, and total medical costs increased by 138%.[29]

Given a virus that reinfects us and serves with each new infection a dollop of additional long COVID risk, we can expect that the demand for care from our beleaguered U.S. healthcare system will remain elevated for the foreseeable future, though the affordability of that care and access to care will be limiting factors.

---

1. Laura Spinney, "Pandemics disable people — the history lesson that policymakers ignore," *Nature*, February 16, 2022, https://www.nature.com/articles/d41586-022-00414-x.
2. Beth Newcomb, "A century of COVID-19: what history tells us about the long-term effects of a pandemic," USC Leonard Davis School of Gerontology, December 8, 2020, https://gero.usc.edu/2020/12/08/century-COVID-pandemic-risk/.
3. Alice Burns, "Long COVID: What Do the Latest Data Show?" KFF, January 26, 2023, https://www.kff.org/policy-watch/long-COVID-what-do-latest-data-show/.
4. Gopi Shah Goda and Evan J. Soltas, 2022. "The Impacts of COVID-19 Illnesses on Workers." Working Paper 30435, National Bureau of Economic Research, https://www.nber.org/system/files/working_papers/w30435/w30435.pdf.
5. Katie Bach, "New data shows long COVID is keeping as many as 4 million people out of work," *Brookings*, August 24, 2022, https://www.brookings.edu/research/new-data-shows-long-COVID-is-keeping-as-many-as-4-million-people-out-of-work/.
6. Greg Iacurci, "Long COVID has an 'underappreciated' role in labor shortage, study finds," *CNBC*, Jan. 30, 2023,
https://www.cnbc.com/2023/01/30/long-COVID-has-underappreciated-role-in-labor-gap-study.html.
7. Sophia Antipolis, "COVID-19 patients retain elevated risk of death for at least 18 months after infection," European Society of Cardiology, January 19, 2023, https://www.escardio.org/The-ESC/Press-Office/Press-releases/COVID-19-patients-retain-elevated-risk-of-death-for-at-least-18-months-after-inf.
8. "COVID-19 Infection Accelerates the Progression of Dementia," *Neuroscience News*, April 4, 2023, https://neurosciencenews.com/COVID-19-dementia-22938/.
See also Yu-Hui Liu, Yang Chen, Qing-Hua Wang, Ling-Ru Wang, Li Jiang, Ying Yang, Xian Chen, Ying Li, Yuan Cen, Cheng Xu, Jie Zhu, Wei Li, Ye-Ran Wang, Li-Li Zhang, Juan Liu, Zhi-Qiang Xu, and Yan-Jiang Wang, "One-Year Trajectory of Cognitive Changes in Older Survivors of COVID-19 in Wuhan, China: A Longitudinal Cohort Study," *JAMA Neurology* 79, no. 5 (March 2022): 509–51, https://jamanetwork.com/journals/jamaneurology/fullarticle/2789919.
9. Mary Van Beusekom, "COVID-19 Omicron infection linked to new-onset diabetes," *CIDRAP*, February 14, 2023, https://www.cidrap.umn.edu/COVID-19/COVID-19-omicron-infection-linked-new-onset-diabetes.

10. Zaeema Naveed, Héctor A. Velásquez García, Stanley Wong, James Wilton, Geoffrey McKee, Bushra Mahmood, Mawuena Binka, Drona Rasali, and Naveed Z. Janjua, "Association of COVID-19 Infection With Incident Diabetes," *JAMA Network Open* 6, no. 4 (April 2023), https://jamanetwork.com/journals/jamanetworkopen/fullarticle/2803938.

11. Alan C. Kwan, Joseph E. Ebinger, Patrick Botting, Jesse Navarrette, Brian Claggett, and Susan Cheng, "Association of COVID-19 Vaccination with Risk for Incident Diabetes After COVID-19 Infection," *JAMA Network Open Access* 6, no. 2 (February 2023), https://jamanetwork.com/journals/jamanetworkopen/fullarticle/2801415.

12. Kevin Kavanaugh, "COVID-19: Study Suggests Long-term Damage to Immune System," *Infection Control Today,* March 21, 2023, https://www.infectioncontroltoday.com/view/COVID-19-study-suggests-long-term-damage-immune-system.

13. Nu Zhang and Michael J. Bevan, "CD8+ T Cells: Foot Soldiers of the Immune System," *Immunity* 35, no. 2 (August 2011): 161–168. Reprinted at NIH National Library of Medicine, National Center for Biotechnology Information, PubMed Central, https://www.ncbi.nlm.nih.gov/pmc/articles/PMC3303224/.

14. Benjamin Bowe, Yan Xie, and Ziyad Al-Aly, "Acute and postacute sequelae associated with SARS-CoV-2 reinfection," *Nature Medicine* 28 (November 2022): 2398–2405, https://www.nature.com/articles/s41591-022-02051-3.

15. Mary Van Beusekom, "COVID's aftermath: Persistent organ damage at 1 year, lung abnormalities at 2," CIDRAP, February 15, 2023, https://www.cidrap.umn.edu/COVID-19/COVIDs-aftermath-persistent-organ-damage-1-year-lung-abnormalities-2.

16. David M. Cutler, "The Economic Cost of Long COVID: An Update," Harvard University, July 2022, https://scholar.harvard.edu/files/cutler/files/long_COVID_update_7-22.pdf.

17. Yan Xie, Evan Xu, Benjamin Bowe, and Ziyad Al-Aly, "Long-term cardiovascular outcomes of COVID-19," *Nature Medicine* 28 (February 2022): 583–590, https://www.nature.com/articles/s41591-022-01689-3.

18. Sumathi Reddy, "Mini-Strokes, Gut Problems: Scientists See Links to an Old Bout of COVID," *Wall Street Journal,* July 2, 2024, https://www.wsj.com/health/wellness/covid-new-health-problems-old-infections-06cb84be. See also Miao Cai, Yan Xie, Eric J. Topol, and Ziyad Al-Aly, "Three-year outcomes of post-acute sequelae of COVID-19," *Nature Medicine* 30, 1564–1573, May 30, 2024, https://www.nature.com/articles/s41591-024-02987-8.

19. Kristina Sauerwein, "COVID-19 survivors face increased mental health risks up to a year later," *Washington University School of Medicine in St. Louis,* February 16, 2022, https://medicine.wustl.edu/news/COVID-19-survivors-face-increased-mental-health-risks-up-to-a-year-later/.

20. Sara Berg, "What doctors wish patients knew about long COVID-19 brain fog," *American Medical Association,* February 17, 2023, https://www.ama-assn.org/delivering-care/public-health/what-doctors-wish-patients-knew-about-long-COVID-19-brain-fog.

21. Ziyad Al-Aly, "Mounting research shows that COVID-19 leaves its mark on the brain, including significant drops in IQ scores," The Conversation, February 28, 2024, https://theconversation.com/mounting-research-shows-that-covid-19-leaves-its-mark-on-the-brain-including-significant-drops-in-iq-scores-224216.

22. Morgan Liotta, "Study identifies link between COVID-19 and Parkinson's," NewsGP, November 2, 2022, https://www1.racgp.org.au/newsgp/clinical/study-identifies-link-between-COVID-19-and-parkins.

23. "Latest Research on COVID-19 & Parkinson's Disease," American Parkinson Disease Association, October 27, 2020, https://www.apdaparkinson.org/article/newly-published-studies-on-COVID-and-pd/.

24. Jon Hamilton, "COVID during pregnancy may alter brain development in boys," NPR, April 18, 2023, https://www.npr.org/sections/health-shots/2023/04/18/1170087779/COVID-pregnancy-fetus-brain-delays.

25. Hamilton, "COVID during pregnancy may alter brain development in boys."

26. Liz Highleyman, "Where Are the Treatments for Long COVID?" *Slate*, May 8, 2023, https://slate.com/technology/2023/05/long-COVID-treatments-where-research-recover.html.

27. For a comprehensive study see National Academies of Sciences, Engineering, and Medicine, *Long-Term Health Effects of COVID-19: Disability and Function Following SARS-CoV-2 Infection,* eds. Paul A. Volberding, Bernice X Chu, and Carol Mason Spicer (Washington, DC: The National Academies Press, 2024), https://doi.org/10.17226/27756.

28. National Academies of Sciences, Engineering, and Medicine, *Long-Term Health Effects of COVID-19,* 218.

29. Amie Scott, Wajeeha Ansari, Richard Chambers, Maya Reimbaeva, Tomasz Mikolajczyk, Michael Benigno, Florin Draica, and Joanna Atkinson, "Substantial health and economic burden of COVID-19 during the year after acute illness among U.S. adults not at high risk of severe COVID-19," *BMC Medicine* 22, no. 47, February 2, 2024, https://doi.org/10.1186/s12916-023-03235-5.

Chapter 16

Pandemic Lesson 4: Disinformation, Misinformation, and Distrust Worsen Pandemic Impacts

When we look back at the Antonine Plague and the episode of Glycon the puppet, we may laugh and ask how people were so foolish as to place faith in a ventriloquist's act. But in the 21st century, when medical disinformation and misinformation continue to compete effectively against conclusions based on sound, rigorously collected data, the faith that people put in misinformation and disinformation is less amusing. We confront the reality that many of us are not any less vulnerable to misinformation and disinformation than our ancestors were. The human race has come far; but in many ways that make us human, we are unchanged.

The truth can at times seem difficult to believe, while the lie can at times seem more plausible than the truth, especially if it aligns with narratives that we are already invested in. Further, what we know about a new, rapidly mutating pathogen or treatments or vaccines emerges over time, so we must continually update our understandings to stay abreast of emerging research. That ongoing project requires an open mind, time, energy, and sheer stamina, while most people are caught up in the business of "stayin' alive," as the old Bee Gees song goes, and rely, as a matter of efficiency, on trusted sources, whether those are entirely trustworthy or not. The only means we humans have to decipher what is true from what is false — or current best understandings and best practices from yesterday's working assumptions now debunked — is our ability to systematically collect and analyze evidence.

False information comes in two forms. Misinformation and disinformation are both "messages that contradict the best expert evidence available at the time." Misinformation is messaging that contradicts the facts, but the factual error is not an intentional one, with ulterior motives involved. Disinformation, on the other hand, is intentional. A disinformer is aware of the facts and spreads inaccurate information anyway.

In the case of disinformation, where falsehoods are intentional and a tool for gaining influence and power or for pursuing profit, the story of the modern model for disseminating and utilizing disinformation cannot be told without a succinct discussion of the Third Reich. The Nazis provided a blueprint for weaponizing a lie. The lie could be used to cause chaos that would undermine the political establishment; it would then be used to gain and maintain power. To the typical person, the Nazis and Hitler left a tragic legacy of death and sorrow. Some, however, see not tragedy but a blueprint for causing chaos and, by that means, gaining power.

In order for people to accept a would-be cult leader's anti-reality, reality itself must first be undermined. The leader must convince people to mistrust the government, history, science, religion, and even at times medicine. Every authority on every subject must be undermined so that the disinformer can present himself as the real authority on the subject. When pillars of civilization have collapsed, chaos ensues, and a cult leader can gain power. This was the Nazis' path to power and remains the primary technique used by cults around the world to brainwash their victims.

In the 21st century, the internet has given a podium to everyone and provided a recruiting platform for every peddler of disinformation and every cult and conspiracy theory on the planet. The internet and especially social media have turned the so-called age of information into an age of disinformation. We must navigate an information landscape cloaked in the fog and fury of competing claims.

The War on Medicine

Much of the disinformation surrounding the COVID pandemic can be traced to just 12 influencers. These individuals have been primarily focused on anti-vaccination propaganda but also on anti-masking, anti-modern-medicine, and anti-public-health messaging. A study by the Center for Countering Digital Hate (CCDH) found that 65% of anti-vaccine content on social media is attributable to these 12 disinformers. From February 1, 2021, to March 16, 2021 — a mere six weeks — the disinformation they spread was shared a total of 812,000 times on social media.[1]

Disinformation about COVID vaccines came at a heavy cost of life. As of May of 2022, according to a Brown University analysis, 319,000 Americans had died because they refused vaccination.[2] Undoubtedly, many of these individuals chose not to get vaccinated based on something they read or saw or heard that originated with this "Disinformation Dozen."

Disinformation that distorted the relative risks of vaccination (extremely small) with the risks of COVID infection (much greater) impacted the choices and beliefs of some groups more than others. Distrust of government and of pharmaceutical companies aligned with distrust of the vaccines. Unfortunately, disinformation surrounding COVID vaccinations would disproportionately influence conservatives in the United States. A study done by the National Bureau of Economic Research on mortality during the pandemic in Florida and Ohio, found that, from March 2020 to December 2021,

76% more Republicans than Democrats died of COVID in those two states during that timeframe. From March 2020 to March 2021, the death rate among Republicans was 95% higher than among Democrats. From the March 2021 to April 2021, that number climbed to 153% more Republicans dying than Democrats.[3]

What was happening was straightforward: Once the vaccine became widely available, Democrats were choosing to be vaccinated against COVID at far higher rates than Republicans were. People's choices depended on which voices they believed. Watchers of FOX News, for example, saw Tucker Carlson sow doubt and resistance about the vaccines, while other FOX News personalities initially reported getting their vaccines or posted photos of themselves getting the shot.[4] On the whole, viewers of that network were found to be less likely to be vaccinated.[5]

The higher death rate among conservatives in the country correlates squarely with vaccination rates — there is no mystery regarding the cause that drove the outcomes. As of December 2022, 37% of Republicans were still unvaccinated compared to 9% of Democrats.[6]

The anti-vaccination movement in general displays egregious historical ignorance. In 1860, life expectancy in the United States was 39.4 years. Since the advent of germ theory in 1861 and the development of vaccines and antibiotics, U.S. life expectancy has risen dramatically.[7] Vaccines and modern medicine have drastically curbed (and in the case of smallpox eliminated) the worst diseases in human history and have contributed to the life expectancy of Americans nearly doubling.

Misinformation about the safety of COVID vaccines administered during pregnancy proved especially unfortunate, as pregnant women are more vulnerable to serious illness or death from a COVID infection. In the spring of 2022, 16% of pregnant people believed that the vaccine could make them infertile, while 44% weren't sure. Only 40% felt confident about the safety of the vaccine.[8] Many avoided the shots, believing that the vaccines were not safe for themselves or their babies. In 2021, deaths among pregnant women rose by 40%: 400 of the 1,205 deaths of pregnant women reported in the U.S. were attributed to COVID.[9]

Snake Oil Cures

Amid the scramble to find treatments that worked against COVID and with disinformation driving doubt in vaccines and modern medicine, misinformation about various possible cures was sure to follow. As the coronavirus pandemic spread in 2020, a massive research effort began to determine what treatments might work against SARS-CoV-2. Hundreds of existing medications were tested in the hope that some relatively inexpensive and common drugs might turn out to be effective treatments. Some, including doctors, latched onto early hopeful observations about treatments by doctors on the front lines, along with hopeful results from initial studies that were not adequately well designed to afford definitive answers. But when results of rigorously designed and executed research studies did not confirm early hopes, what people wanted to believe tended to blind them to what turned out to be true, and they did not get the update.

The malaria drug hydroxychloroquine (HCQ), which is also used to treat rheumatoid arthritis and lupus, was an early hopeful; but it did not pan out as an effective treatment for COVID, and neither did a subsequent favorite hopeful, ivermectin, an antiparasitic. One licensed physician who, in the spring of 2020, made claims for hydroxychloroquine as a cure for COVID was Stella Emmanuel, whose videos on the subject caught the attention of then-President Donald Trump. As pastor of Fire Power Ministries in Houston, Texas, Emmanuel also made a number of other medical claims in her sermons. COVID was spread via sex or rape by demonic forces, she preached, the sperm of demons being the virus itself. She also warned that treatments for COVID were tainted with alien DNA and therefore should not be taken.[10]

The cure she offered instead was hydroxychloroquine. Her assertion that she had cured hundreds of patients using HCQ won the drug support from then-President Donald Trump, who was eager to have something to offer to counter a pandemic in an election year. The president, along with others, would tout hydroxychloroquine as a cure for COVID. The drug gained a broad following. It took months and many studies to sort out the facts: Hydroxychloroquine as a treatment for COVID was a dud.

Ivermectin, another among the hundreds of drugs tested for efficacy against COVID-19, likewise became the darling of those who wanted an alternative to an mRNA vaccine. Ivermectin hype began when an Australian study, published in April 2020, found that ivermectin could kill the SARS-CoV-2 virus in a laboratory setting. (Much of the world had yet to learn that what kills a virus in a lab may not do the same thing in a human body.) In the months that followed, ivermectin flew off the shelves of veterinary supply vendors and farm stores.[11] Republican Senator Ron Johnson would announce the miracle cure and line up panelists to offer testimony on behalf of hydroxychloroquine and ivermectin before a Senate committee,[12] and this would be followed by celebrities such as Joe Rogan and Aaron Rodgers touting the effectiveness of ivermectin and hydroxychloroquine (along with monoclonal antibodies) in treating their own cases of COVID.

Some who placed their faith in ivermectin as a treatment for COVID landed in the hospital or lost their lives.[13] While the drug can be used safely to eliminate certain human parasitic infestations, it is not intended to be used over the longer term in either people or animals; and people dosing themselves, especially with concentrated animal meds, sometimes used far more than was safe.

Misinformation and disinformation resulted when many people, including doctors, failed to update their perspectives and practice given the results of randomized, double-blind, placebo-controlled trials that ultimately confirmed that these drugs did not, in fact, show benefit in the treatment of COVID-19, and could harm instead. A CDC Health Advisory published in August of 2021 noted that ivermectin use had increased 24-fold from its pre-pandemic baseline, while ivermectin-related calls to poison control centers had increased five-fold.[14] A year earlier, the number of hydroxychloroquine prescriptions spiked to 890,000, creating a shortage of the drug for those who actually needed it for conditions that it effectively treats. Prescribing HCQ became increasingly problematic when people opted for the imagined powers of HCQ over the verifiable benefits of vaccination, sometimes demanding the drug for themselves or their loved ones despite the fact that it was ineffective against COVID-19.[15]

There were other individuals who sought to make money off the demand for COVID cures. Snake oil salesmen would make a prodigious return during the pandemic, with fake cures aplenty. In the vein of the useless counsel offered by Glycon, the false puppet god of the Antonine Plague, one of the most detrimental scams was created by a man who claimed to be a one-billion-year-old god from the Andromeda galaxy. According to Jim Humble, he was given permission by the "space navy" to come to earth and share with us all the knowledge of the aliens. Humble reports that he discovered the healing power of his Miracle Mineral Solution (MMS), also known as Master Mineral Solution, in 1996. MMS, which is essentially bleach, would be his gift to the masses. The ex-scientologist founded a cult called the Genesis II Church of Health and Healing, centered around his purported cure-all. He would go on to peddle MMS as a cure for cancer, autism, HIV, and malaria, and to make millions of dollars before appointing his successor, Mark Grenon, to take over the "Church of Bleach."[16]

Humble's retirement and subsequent flight from the United States would not be the end of MMS. With the arrival of the COVID pandemic, Mark Grenon claimed that the MMS bleach cocktail was also a cure for COVID and that vomiting and diarrhea were signs that the product was working to cure the illness.[17] The church sold a million dollars' worth of MMS before sales were shut down. At least seven people died from consuming the so-called cure.[18]

In February of 2023, journalists Kristen Brown and Kate Mishkin, reporting for Bloomberg, found that Americans could still search for "Miracle Mineral Solution" or "Master Mineral Solution" and find it or an equivalent for sale at Amazon and on Etsy, Poshmark, and eBay, platforms that have since taken action to remove the product.[19] As this book was written, it was possible to find the formulation at Amazon under a different name, and searching for information on Jim Humble and MMS results in advertising pitches for the product. Toxic snake oil cures are difficult to eradicate as long as there is demand from the gullible.

Alex Jones offered his own cure on his Infowars website, a toothpaste made with colloidal silver, as well as a topical ointment containing colloidal silver. It was almost inevitable that advocates of colloidal silver as an antiviral and general cure-all would seize upon it as a treatment for the new coronavirus, too. The FDA quickly noticed and shut down Jones and other vendors pushing colloidal silver as a COVID-19 preventative or cure.[20] For the record, the NIH's National Center for Complementary and Integrative Health reports that taking colloidal silver can tint the skin permanently blue (a ghastly, undead blue, not a perky Smurf blue or an enchanted Avatar blue), can interfere with the absorption of some medications, and can cause damage to the kidneys, liver, and nervous system.[21]

In his book *We Want Them Infected: How the failed quest for herd immunity led doctors to embrace the anti-vaccine movement and blinded Americans to the threat of COVID*, Jonathan Howard, associate professor of neurology and psychiatry at NYU Langone Health and chief of neurology at Bellevue Hospital in New York City, has traced in painstaking detail how much misinformation and disinformation about COVID actually originated with doctors themselves. Among them were self-assured doctors with pet theories that they clung to despite emerging science regarding COVID; doctors who made specious arguments based on flawed studies; doctors vying for notoriety and attention; doctors who underestimated and minimized the COVID threat; doctors who fell for conspiracy theories; and doctors out to make a buck with an alternative cure or protocol. Most dangerous were those who believed that the answer — the goal — was herd immunity to be achieved through infection rather than vaccination, despite the fact that infection was dangerous and damaging.[22] It turned out that truly lasting herd immunity, whether achieved by infection or vaccination (which, though not risk-free, is far less risky), simply was not to be had, given a rapidly mutating, increasingly contagious coronavirus.

Howard, who worked in America's oldest public hospital through COVID's early onslaught in NYC, as morgue trucks filled with the dead, had every reason to question and counter the medical messaging of those who minimized, misinformed, and disinformed the public about COVID, the risks it posed, treatments, and the vaccines that offered a time-limited measure of protection. He undertook the work of compiling the messaging of medical professionals who, whatever their intentions, swayed many to underestimate the COVID threat, to eschew vaccination, to embrace ineffective treatments, and to bend public policy toward the normalization of COVID infections as inevitable, with any mitigation of risk becoming, to an ever-greater extent, the responsibility of the individual rather than society as a whole.

Some politicians would seize upon such messaging, amplify it, and strive to base policy upon it because they trusted or found advantageous or appealing what certain doctors said. Since viruses, utterly indifferent to human views or sentiments, simply infect wherever there is an opportunity to do so, more infections result where policy does not align with realities surrounding a virus and what works to make transmission less likely.

Misinformation and Scams from around the World

While the United States was heavily affected by disinformation and misinformation, the rest of the world fell victim as well. Many of the healing tonics recommended around the globe bear similarity to ancient medical and magical healing formulas. Early in the pandemic, people the world over fell back on plant-based remedies traditionally used for colds and flu — from garlic to ginger, to honey, to teas, to elderberry, to apple cider vinegar.[23]

While some traditional remedies do have legitimate medical uses confirmed by research, they proved no match for COVID-19, though at least they were generally not likely to cause harm. In the Middle East, however, one self-proclaimed prophetic healer promoted camel urine, consumed "fresh and warm" to be a miracle cure (though his suggestion was widely rejected).[24] U.S. anti-vaxxer Christopher Key, leader of the "Vaccine Police," advocated for "urine therapy" in addition to his daily dose of bleach, prompting Reuters to publish a fact check regarding his false claims.[25]

In India, where Hindus regard cattle as holy, all that cows produce is deemed a purifying agent, whether milk or urine or dung, and has been traditionally used for wellness. During COVID, believers covered themselves with manure and washed that manure, when it dried, off with milk or buttermilk. That practice is, of course, a public health concern.[26]

People turned to accessible treatments of all kinds in hope of a cure and prayed for divine intervention. Faith healing was also attempted worldwide. In Sri Lanka a well-known shaman claimed to be able to cure COVID with holy water, though he ultimately perished from the disease.[27] Many, of course, turned to the power of prayer, much as Mursili II, the Hittite king, did millennia ago. Innumerable prayer requests were made online or in churches or through phone prayer hotlines.[28] Some of the faithful survived or saw their loved ones survive; others did not.

Many of the ineffective cures peddled during the coronavirus pandemic are not dissimilar from ineffective cures attempted in the ancient world. Of course, people have always tried what they thought could work. They always will. But the remarkable difference in the 21st century is that many have clung to unproven measures even once there were ready alternatives (vaccines, treatments) proven by meticulously gathered data to significantly improve COVID outcomes.

That people would do this boils down to a matter of trust — trust in alternative voices that is sometimes far stronger than trust in messaging and data offered by scientists and through authoritative channels. During COVID, setting aside the active work of disinformers to erode public trust for political, social, or financial purposes, trust in messaging that should have represented our best knowledge at any given time was eroded in a number of ways.

First, because there was everything to learn about a new pathogen, its modes of transmission, its impacts on the human body, and effective treatment, working understandings about a new coronavirus were always bound to change on the fly, with experience and research. Messaging did not go far enough to forge that expectation. Thus, when best available understandings and practices shifted with new information, many people saw inconsistencies and unreliability rather than an inevitable learning process.

In the United States, a second blow to trust came with avoidable missteps. The CDC's faulty COVID tests proved an early setback for the U.S. response. The CDC was also maddeningly slow to acknowledge the reality and the substantial risk of long COVID or the fact that the virus was, in fact, airborne rather than dependent solely on transmission via the virus's hitching a ride on large droplets. Further, touting the mRNA vaccine's early success in preventing infection proved to be a mistake when new variants proved capable of infecting the vaccinated, though the vaccinated had far better odds for survival than the unvaccinated did.

Finally, public health messaging in the U.S. ultimately yielded to expediency. The public's use of masks was discouraged at the beginning of the pandemic, when there were not enough masks and other PPE even for healthcare workers on the front lines. Then, when the supply chain permitted, masks were mandated. Over time, public backlash against masking, often along political lines, resulted in masking's becoming optional in most places. And as SARS-CoV-2 evolved, the variants that beat out other contenders did so because they became ever more contagious, such that only the best masks — N95s or KN95 respirators or better — provided meaningful, though not invincible, protection.[29]

A call that seemed to have been made in spite of data and experience rather than guided by it was the CDC's determination that people could return to work five days after becoming infected, with the stated assumption that most would no longer be contagious by then. At that point, economic and business concerns had trumped public health realities entirely, as *many* people who catch COVID continue to test positive (and thus to be contagious) well more than five days.

Once highly regarded around the world as a leader in public health and pandemic response planning, the U.S. CDC saw trust in its guidance erode, whether among people hoodwinked by misinformation and disinformation or among people who closely followed the emerging science concerning COVID and its evolution. Regaining that trust will be difficult.

Faye Flam, writing for Bloomberg, sized up the problem, reporting the results of a survey released in March of 2023:

> A survey of over 4,000 Americans led by Harvard
> researchers and published in the journal *Health Affairs*

showed that only 37% said they still had a great deal
of trust in CDC. The rest answered that they either
trusted CDC somewhat, not very much, or not at all,
and among those, 74% cited political influence on the
agency's recommendations and policies.[30]

Political influence over public health messaging and decisions
during the COVID-19 pandemic emergency was evident in both the
Trump and the Biden administrations and never more so than when
an election was at stake. President Trump prioritized limiting public
concern about the viral threat in order to fuel the economy before the
2020 election, and President Biden's COVID strategy succumbed to
the population's pandemic fatigue ahead of the 2022 midterms (mitigation measures having become, by then, political kryptonite for the
Democrats) and to the refusal of Congress to invest in another round
of funding for COVID mitigation.

The U.S. Vaccine Adverse Event Reporting System, or VAERS,
proved to be widely misunderstood and misused and thus became
another source of mistrust. VAERS is used to collect information
from the public about adverse events that people experience after
taking a vaccine. Since not all things that happen after a vaccination
are caused by a vaccine, and since there is no mechanism for verifying
each report, VAERS is not useful for drawing conclusions about what
effects a vaccine may or may not have. It is, instead, a kind of radar
system. Managed by the FDA and CDC, VAERS alerts those agencies
to adverse events that should be investigated to determine whether
they are associated with a vaccine and what the level of risk might
be if they are. VAERS reports suggest what next questions should be
studied regarding a vaccine, but they do not supply the answers —
that is a different step.[31] Regardless, many, and especially anti-vaxxers,
pointed to the reports submitted to VAERS as if conclusions could be
drawn directly from them.

In some quarters, disinformation regarding the pandemic was wielded like a weapon by racist hate groups. In Britain, the UK's Commission for Countering Extremism warned about extremist groups advancing conspiracy theories and even encouraging their adherents to deliberately infect members of certain racial, religious, or ethnic groups.[32]

In the United States 2024 presidential candidate and anti-vaxxer Robert F. Kennedy, Jr., targeted a free online film to Black audiences, replete with vaccine-related disinformation connecting instances of medical racism in the past (which were both horrific and all too real) to vaccines today. The intent was to render Black Americans suspicious of vaccines.[33] Kennedy's efforts to promote the anti-vaccine agenda have hardly been limited to one community, however.

Further, past horrors like the Tuskegee Syphilis Study have not been a primary factor that accounted for a lag in COVID vaccinations among Black Americans in 2021. According to a UCLA study published in 2022, history was not the issue. Present-day inequities are, instead. Black Americans' more negative experiences with today's U.S. medical system correlated with their greater distrust, their feeling less cared for by their physicians, and their being less inclined to seek a COVID vaccination.[34]

In significant segments of the broader U.S. population, distrust of government, of pharmaceutical companies and other corporations, and of the U.S. medical system in general runs deep and strong, like a river at flood stage that can sweep away potential trust in proven vaccines, proven medicines, etc. Second-guessing authorities or science itself becomes habitual and self-reinforcing and renders people more susceptible to misinformation and disinformation peddled by sources they prefer to trust. When public health communication falls short of being both clear and fully representative of latest understandings and data, the trust problem worsens.

Is There a Cure?

The only possible remedy for curtailing the assault of disinformation and misinformation is to act. Instruction in logic, data analysis, and critical thinking should be a part of every child's education. An educated populace that is more difficult to fool is a powerful defense against misinformation or disinformation. A second measure is to take legal action against those who would willfully use their freedom of speech to disinform and thereby harm others. In the U.S., the criminal element has discovered how to exploit the First Amendment to cause harm to others without repercussions. Closing those loopholes would be a powerful step toward ending disinformation. This is an area where the U.S. government, because of First Amendment protections for free speech, must walk a fine line.

A United Nations treaty, the International Covenant on Civil and Political Rights (ICCPR), provides in Article 19 the exceptions to allow the limitation of free speech in the event that that speech is a danger to national security, to public order, or to public health or morals, as follows:

Article 19

1. Everyone shall have the right to hold opinions without interference.

2. Everyone shall have the right to freedom of expression; this right shall include freedom to seek, receive and impart information and ideas of all kinds, regardless of frontiers, either orally, in writing or in print, in the form of art, or through any other media of his choice.

3. The exercise of the rights provided for in paragraph 2 of this article carries with it special duties and responsibilities. It may therefore be subject to certain restrictions, but these shall only be such as are provided by law and are necessary:

(a) For respect of the rights or reputations of others;

(b) For the protection of national security or of public order (ordre public), or of public health or morals.[35]

The United States, however, has fewer limits on free speech than many other countries do. This fact has not been lost on the peddlers of disinformation and is one reason the United States has found itself a primary target of disinformation and hostile speech. The only types of disinformation that are currently illegal fall under defamation/slander and fraud. Even then when it comes to disinformation, these crimes are rarely prosecuted by the government itself but rather in civil suits brought by the victims of the lies. It would have been possible, for instance, for Pfizer, Moderna, or Johnson & Johnson to have filed civil suits for defamation against individuals who made false claims about their vaccines. Such suits remain the only legal tool Americans currently have to stop disinformation.

A 2021 report from the Johns Hopkins Center for Health Security extends a call for a multi-pronged strategy for combatting misinformation and disinformation that imperils public health, as a matter of national security.[36] Tara Kirk Sell, a senior scholar at the Johns Hopkins Center for Health Security and one of the authors of the report, outlines the four pillars of the proposal:

- Intervene against false and damaging content as well as the sources propagating it

- Promote and ensure the abundant presence and dissemination of factual information
- Increase the public's resilience to misinformation and disinformation
- Coordination of a national strategy that includes input from social and news media, government, national security officials, public health officials, scientists, and the public[37]

Though the implementation of a national strategy to counter health-related misinformation and disinformation seems unlikely in the current political climate, such a strategy is sorely needed. There is nothing easy about the work to be done, but the cost of not doing it has already proved too high. Many thousands of lives were lost that might have been saved.

Disinformation and misinformation play a deadly part in any chaotic event, and a pandemic is no exception. They are a plague in their own right — a coinfection, if you will, that makes a pandemic more deadly and more damaging economically. As of November of 2021, a KFF survey found that fully 78% of Americans believed or were unsure about at least one out of eight common misconceptions about COVID and COVID vaccines. Many Americans tended to rely on television news and social media for COVID information, and how well informed they were correlated with the media outlets they trusted.[38]

Estimates regarding the costs of pandemic-related disinformation and misinformation are staggering. In October of 2021, following the surge of infections and deaths caused by the Delta variant, the Johns Hopkins Bloomberg School of Public Health's Center for Health Security estimated that misinformation and disinformation that had deterred people from getting vaccinated against COVID had cost a total of between $50 million and $300 million per day from May of 2021, when most American adults became eligible to be vaccinated, to

October of that year. The total included costs to the healthcare system, along with economic costs such as those incurred when workers were absent due to illness.[39] Disinformation and misinformation exact high costs in terms of disease, death, disability, and dollars.

---

1.   Shannon Bond, "Just 12 People Are Behind Most Vaccine Hoaxes On Social Media, Research Shows," *All Things Considered,* NPR, May 14, 2021, https://www.npr.org/2021/05/13/996570855/disinformation-dozen-test-facebooks-twitters-ability-to-curb-vaccine-hoaxes; and "The Disinformation Dozen: Why Platforms Must Act on Twelve Leading Online Anti-Vaxxers," *Center for Countering Digital Hate,* March 24, 2021, https://counterhate.com/research/the-disinformation-dozen/.

2.   A. Martinez and Allison Aubrey, "How vaccine misinformation made the COVID-19 death toll worse," NPR, May 16, 2022, https://www.npr.org/2022/05/16/1099070400/how-vaccine-misinformation-made-the-COVID-19-death-toll-worse.

3.   Wallace, Jacob, Goldsmith-Pinkham, Paul, and Schwartz, Jason L. 2022. "Excess Death Rates for Republicans and Democrats During the COVID-19 Pandemic," Working Paper 30512, National Bureau of Economic Research, https://www.nber.org/papers/w30512.

4.   Jeremy Barr, "Fox News viewers are getting mixed messages about whether to take the coronavirus vaccine," *Washington Post,* May 14, 2021, https://www.washingtonpost.com/media/2021/05/14/fox-vaccine-mixed-message/.

5.   Matteo Pinna, Léo Picard, and Christoph Goessmann, "Cable news and COVID-19 vaccine uptake," *Nature,* Scientific Reports 12, no. 16804 (October 2022), https://www.nature.com/articles/s41598-022-20350-0.

6.   Yasmin Tayag, "How Many Republicans Died Because the GOP Turned Against Vaccines?" *The Atlantic,* December 23, 2022, https://www.theatlantic.com/health/archive/2022/12/COVID-deaths-anti-vaccine-republican-voters/672575/.

7.   Aaron O'Neill, "Life expectancy in the United States, 1860–2020," Statista, June 21, 2022, https://www.statista.com/statistics/1040079/life-expectancy-united-states-all-time/.

8.   "Misinformation About COVID-19 Vaccines and Pregnancy is Widespread, Including Among Women Who are Pregnant or Planning to Get Pregnant," KFF News, May 22, 2022, https://www.kff.org/coronavirus-COVID-19/press-release/misinformation-about-COVID-19-vaccines-and-pregnancy-is-widespread-including-among-women-who-are-pregnant-or-planning-to-get-pregnant/.

9.   Roni Caryn Rabin, "COVID Worsened a Health Crisis Among Pregnant Women," *New York Times,* March 16, 2023, https://www.nytimes.com/2023/03/16/health/COVID-pregnancy-death.html.

10. Dickens Olewe, "Stella Immanuel — the doctor behind unproven coronavirus cure claim," BBC, July 29, 2020, https://www.bbc.com/news/world-africa-53579773.

11. Sophia Andrade, "Farm Supply Stores Are Running Short on a Horse Dewormer/

Pseudoscience COVID Cure," *Slate,* August 10, 2021, https://slate.com/technology/2021/08/ivermectin-COVID-cure-farm-supply-stores.html.

12. Paul McLeod, "A Vaccine Critic Told Congress To Focus On Toilets Instead Of Masks To Stop COVID," Buzzfeed News, December 8, 2020, https://www.buzzfeednews.com/article/paulmcleod/senate-johnson-COVID-misinformation; Courtney Degen and Cristobella Durrette, "Fact Check: Johnson's "COVID-19: A Second Opinion" Panel Criticized as a Vehicle for Misinformation," *Medill News Service,* January 26, 2022, https://dc.medill.northwestern.edu/blog/2022/01/26/fact-check-johnsons-COVID-19-a-second-opinion-panel-criticized-as-vehicle-for-misinformation/#sthash.5qo13Q4T.dpbs.

13. Maia Anderson, "New Mexico links 2 deaths to ivermectin misuse," *Becker's Hospital Review,* September 27, 2021, https://www.beckershospitalreview.com/pharmacy/new-mexico-links-2-deaths-to-ivermectin-misuse.html.

14. "Rapid Increase in Ivermectin Prescriptions and Reports of Severe Illness Associated with Use of Products Containing Ivermectin to Prevent or Treat COVID-19," CDC Health Alert Network, CDCHAN-00449, August 26, 2021, https://emergency.cdc.gov/han/2021/pdf/CDC_HAN_449.pdf.

15. Marie Rosenthal, "Stop Prescribing Hydroxychloroquine, Ivermectin for COVID-19; No Proof That They Work," *Infectious Disease Special Edition (ISDE),* August 30, 2021, https://www.idse.net/COVID-19/Article/08-21/Stop-Prescribing-Hydroxychloroquine-Ivermectin-for-COVID-19-No-Proof-That-They-Work-/64533.

16. David Ono and Lisa Bartley, "'Church of Bleach': ABC News confronts founder of Genesis II Church," ABC News, October 29, 2016, https://abc7.com/church-of-bleach-genesis-ii-2-health-and-healing/1578279/.

17. "Product Warning: Miracle Mineral Solution," Montserrat: Ministry of Health, archived from the original on June 6, 2013.

18. Tom Porter, "Taking toxic bleach MMS has killed 7 people in the U.S., Colombian prosecutors say — far more than previously known," Business Insider, August 12, 2020, https://www.businessinsider.com/mms-bleach-killed-7-americans-new-from-colombia-arrest-2020-8.

19. Kristen V. Brown and Kate Mishkin, "Plenty of Americans Are Drinking Bleach, Still for Sale on Amazon," Bloomberg News, February 1, 2023, https://www.bloomberg.com/news/articles/2023-02-01/drinking-bleach-is-deadly-why-are-some-americans-still-consuming-mms.

20. Andrew Marantz, "Alex Jones's Bogus Coronavirus Cures," *The New Yorker,* March 30, 2020, https://www.newyorker.com/magazine/2020/04/06/alex-jones-bogus-coronavirus-cures.

21. "Colloidal Silver: What You Need to Know," National Center for Complementary and Integrative Health (NCCIH), accessed June 11, 2024, https://www.nccih.nih.gov/health/colloidal-silver-what-you-need-to-know.

22. Jonathan Howard, *We Want Them Infected: How the failed quest for herd immunity led doctors to embrace the anti-vaccine movement and blinded Americans to the threat of COVID* (Hickory, NC: Redhawk Publications, 2023).

23. Andrea Pieroni, Ina Vandebroek, Julia Prakofjewa, Rainer W. Bussmann, Narel Y.

Paniagua-Zambrana, Alfred Maroyi, Luisa Torri, Dauro M. Zocchi, Ashley T. K. Dam, Shujaul M. Khan, Habib Ahmad, Yeter Yeşil, Ryan Huish, Manuel Pardo-de-Santayana, Andrei Mocan, Xuebo Hu, Odara Boscolo, and Renata Sõukand, "Taming the pandemic? The importance of homemade plant-based foods and beverages as community responses to COVID-19," *Journal of Ethnobiology and Ethnomedicine* 16, no. 75 (December 2020), https://www.ncbi.nlm.nih.gov/pmc/articles/PMC7724619/.

24. "Drink Camel Urine To Cure Coronavirus, Prophetic Medicine Man Says ," Radio Farda, April 20, 2020, https://en.radiofarda.com/a/drink-camel-urine-to-cure-coronavirus-prophetic-medicine-man-says/30565663.html.

25. Reuters Fact Check, "Fact Check — No evidence that 'urine therapy' cures COVID-19," *Reuters*, January 12, 2022, https://www.reuters.com/article/factcheck-urine-COVID/fact-check-no-evidence-that-urine-therapy-cures-COVID-19-idU.S.L1N2TS215.

26. Sohel Daria and Md Rabiul Islam, "The use of cow dung and urine to cure COVID-19 in India: A public health concern," *The International Journal of Health planning and Management* 36, no. 5 (September 2021): 1950–1952, https://www.ncbi.nlm.nih.gov/pmc/articles/PMC8239506/.

27. John Yoon and Aanya Wipulasena, "A Sri Lankan shaman who touted a cure for COVID died after contracting the disease," *New York Times,* September 28, 2021, https://www.nytimes.com/2021/09/28/world/asia/COVID-sri-lanka-shaman-holy-water.html.

28. Michelle Boorstein, "Can faith healing work by phone? Charismatic Christians try prayer to combat the coronavirus," *Washington Post*, April 3, 2020, https://www.washingtonpost.com/religion/2020/04/03/supernatural-healing-christian-faith-coronavirus-pandemic/.

29. Trisha Greenhalgh, C. Raina MacIntyre, Michael G. Baker, Shovon Bhattacharjee, Abrar A. Chughtai, David Fisman, Mohana Kunasekaran, Amanda Kvalsvig, Deborah Lupton, Matt Oliver, Essa Tawfiq, Mark Ungrin, and Joe Vipond, "Masks and Respirators for Prevention of Respiratory Infections: a State of the Science Review," *Clinical Microbiology Reviews,* Vol. 37, Issue 2:e00124-23, May 2024, https://journals.asm.org/doi/10.1128/cmr.00124-23.

30. Faye Flam, "CDC's Top Priority Has to Be Rebuilding Public Trust," *Bloomberg*, March 29, 2023, https://www.bloomberg.com/opinion/articles/2023-03-29/cdc-s-top-post-COVID-priority-has-to-be-rebuilding-public-trust.

31. "About VAERS," Department of Health and Human Services, U.S. Federal Government, last accessed June 11, 2024, https://vaers.hhs.gov/about.html.

32. Amy Woodyatt, "Neo-Nazis encouraging followers to 'deliberately infect' Jews and Muslims with coronavirus," CNN, July 9, 2020, https://www.cnn.com/2020/07/09/uk/extremism-deliberately-COVID-19-intl-scli-gbr/index.html.

33. Will Stone, "An Anti-Vaccine Film Targeted To Black Americans Spreads False Information," NPR, June 8, 2021, https://www.npr.org/sections/health-shots/2021/06/08/1004214189/anti-vaccine-film-targeted-to-black-americans-spreads-false-information.

34. Holly Ober, "Black Americans' COVID vaccine hesitancy stems more from today's inequities than historical ones," UCLA Newsroom, October 22, 2022, https://newsroom.ucla.edu/releases/causes-of-COVID-vaccine-hesitancy-among-black-americans.

35. "International Covenant on Civil and Political Rights," Office of the United Nations High Commissioner for Human Rights; adopted December 16,1966, entry into force March

23, 1976, https://www.ohchr.org/en/instruments-mechanisms/instruments/international-covenant-civil-and-political-rights.

36. Tara Kirk Sell, Divya Hosangadi, Elizabeth Smith, Marc Trotochaud, Prarthana Vasudevan, Gigi Kwik Gronvall, Yonaira Rivera, Jeannette Sutton, Alex Ruiz, Anita Cicero. "National Priorities to Combat Misinformation and Disinformation for COVID-19 and Future Public Health Threats: A Call for a National Strategy," Center for Health Security, Johns Hopkins Bloomberg School of Public Health, March 2021, https://centerforhealthsecurity.org/sites/default/files/2023-02/210322-misinformation.pdf.

37. Tara Kirk Sell, "Meeting COVID-19 Misinformation and Disinformation Head-On," Johns Hopkins Bloomberg School of Public Health, https://publichealth.jhu.edu/meeting-COVID-19-misinformation-and-disinformation-head-on.

38. Liz Hamel, Lunna Lopes, Ashley Kirzinger, Grace Sparks, Mellisha Stokes, and Mollyann Brodie, "KFF COVID-19 Vaccine Monitor: Media and Misinformation," KFF Polling, November 8, 2021, https://www.kff.org/coronavirus-COVID-19/poll-finding/kff-COVID-19-vaccine-monitor-media-and-misinformation.

39. Richard Bruns, Divya Hosangadi, Marc Trotochaud, and Tara Kirk Sell, "COVID-19 Vaccine Misinformation and Disinformation Costs an Estimated $50 to $300 Million Each Day," Center for Health Security, Johns Hopkins Bloomberg School of Public Health, 2021, https://publichealth.jhu.edu/sites/default/files/2023-02/20211020-misinformation-disinformation-cost.pdf.

Chapter 17

Pandemic Lesson 5:
Crime Undermines Mitigation

The chaos that epidemics and pandemics bring is seized upon not only by those who would spread disinformation but also by opportunistic criminals. In accounts from the ancient world, we saw evidence of looting and similar criminal behavior. The plague of Athens brought such chaos that law and order completely broke down, and people did as they liked. The Justinian Plague saw such death that the desperate of society engaged in mass looting of abandoned and plague-ridden properties. Merchants engaged in price-gouging.

Unlike some highly pathogenic ancient plagues that we have examined, however, the coronavirus pandemic did not have the mortality rate required to drive people to mass looting, though opportunists managed to plunder through fraud billions intended for COVID relief. The pandemic led to a wide array of crimes that undermined efforts to mitigate economic disruption, suffering, the inundation of the healthcare system, and death.

Historic Levels of Fraud

Signed into law by President Donald J. Trump on March 27, 2020, the CARES Act provided $2.2 billion in economic stimulus — the largest stimulus package in U.S. history — designed to minimize economic suffering precipitated by the COVID pandemic emergency. It provided cash payments to American taxpayers and created the Paycheck Protection Program (PPP) to provide forgivable loans to small businesses, corporations, and state and local governments. A second $900 billion stimulus bill provided further relief in December of 2020.

The $1.9 trillion American Rescue Plan Act of 2021, signed into law by President Joe Biden on March 11, 2021, supplemented unemployment payments with an additional $300 weekly; increased food stamp benefits; and provided emergency paid leave; grants to small businesses; aid for education and for state, local, and tribal governments; funding for rental assistance; and funding for COVID testing and surveillance, among other measures.

With the massive push to provide economic assistance quickly at the height of the COVID shock came ample opportunities for the unscrupulous, including ordinary Americans from all walks of life, to fraudulently obtain benefits, especially from the PPP program. Dan Fruchter, chief of the fraud and white-collar crime unit at the U.S. Attorney's office in the Eastern District of Washington, explained to AP News, "Here was this sort of endless pot of money that anyone could access. Folks kind of fooled themselves into thinking that it was a socially acceptable thing to do, even though it wasn't legal."[1]

In March of 2022, NBC News tallied estimates of the cost of COVID relief fraud: $80 billion from the $800 billion PayCheck Protection Program (PPP), $90–$400 billion from the $900 billion COVID unemployment relief program, plus almost $80 billion from the Small Business Administration's Economic Injury Disaster Loans. Twenty-one million PPP loans were issued with little in the way of verification in hopes of acting in time to stem the worst of the economic damage COVID would otherwise have done to businesses and households. Individuals intent on fraud used stolen identities to procure unemployment benefits. Some employers who sought PPP loans exaggerated the number of workers they employed or conjured companies out of thin air for the purposes of applying for low-interest loans that could be forgiven and thus turned into grants. Those who fraudulently applied for Economic Injury Disaster Loans registered fake businesses or simply applied in the names of real businesses owned by others.[2]

The CARES Act Fraud Tracker, maintained by the law firm of Arnold & Porter, ran 117 pages long as of mid 2024 and summarizes cases to date. One individual continued to request and receive benefits after returning to work at a dental office. She was paid more than $18,000 in benefits for which she did not qualify. Another individual requested and received $6 million in benefits on behalf of restaurants that were no longer in business. A third participated in an extensive fraud scheme involving 90 faked applications for a total of $24 million in fraudulently obtained funds.[3] The Fraud Tracker is a fascinating and disturbing parade of schemes small and large, all designed to tap the giant pool of money that the U.S. government made available as an economic lifeline. The IRS Criminal Investigation (IRS-CI) division reported on March 23, 2023, that it had "investigated 975 tax and money laundering cases related to COVID fraud with alleged fraud in these cases totaling $3.2 billion."[4]

Of the stimulus checks sent out by the IRS, 1%, it turns out, went to people who were ineligible to receive them — in this instance, not a crime but a mistake. That 1% amounts to another $8 billion.[5] Among those who received checks in error were non-Americans who receive Social Security and other federal benefits and foreign guest workers who filed the wrong kind of tax return, an error that made them appear eligible. Efforts to recover those funds have not gone smoothly; and sometimes money has been withdrawn, with the assistance of foreign banks, from the accounts of U.S. citizens living overseas who were actually eligible to receive stimulus checks.[6]

The search for fraud has continued. Much of the money, which is ultimately stolen from American taxpayers, of course, is not recoverable; but some of it is, and not all of it had been paid out as this book was written. It is estimated that every dollar spent in the effort to track down fraud returns $10 that would otherwise never be recovered.[7] As of April 2024, the Justice Department had recovered more than $3 billion.[8]

A Backlash against Public Health Mitigations and Healthcare Workers

A predominant element of crime during the COVID emergency reflected the resistance that emerged against public health mitigations. Such resistance is not new. For example, though historical photos taken during the 1918 H1N1 influenza pandemic depict people dutifully wearing six-ply white cotton masks, looking as if compliance was the order of the day, the reality was patchier.

Masking was strongly recommended in October of 1918 by the United States Public Health Service. Though newspaper ads and posters promoted the practice as patriotic at a time when patriotic messaging helped to fuel the war effort, it was masking, rather than business and school closures or isolating the ill, that some chose not to comply with. Where masking was mandated (mostly in western states), fines and/ or short jail sentences were imposed for "mask slackers" who violated local ordinances. Still, enforcement proved difficult. Businesses did not want to turn away unmasked shoppers, and streetcar conductors declined to turn away passengers. Facing widespread resistance, the City of Denver finally just gave up its mandate. Then, as now, many viewed mask mandates as a violation of civil liberties.[9]

Individual liberty has long been treasured in the United States (though sometimes most vociferously by those who wish to roll back the individual liberties of others). There are times and situations, of course, when an expression of individual liberty might usefully be weighed in the balance with collective good that includes our own. Some Americans exercised their personal liberty to wear masks to protect others as well as themselves; others believed that masks were not effective in reducing risk of infection (not true) or that masks trapped CO_2 (not true) or that rights were being stepped on when masks were required.[10] For some, forgoing masks became an aspect of identity politics — Team Freedom. The catch was that it was not possible to play on Team Freedom without also playing on Team Virus.

In August of 2020, the Brookings Institution reported the results of a survey regarding masking choices:

> 40% of Americans who do not wear a mask say this is because it is "their right as an American to not wear a mask." This modal response was followed by Americans who say they do not wear a mask "because it is uncomfortable" at 24%. The data reveals that a combined 64% of Americans believe that their right to not have to be inconvenienced by wearing a mask or scarf over their face is more important than reducing the probability of getting sick or infecting others.[11]

Notably, 11% of Americans who eschewed masks did so because they believed that there was no sense in masking because COVID was a conspiracy as opposed to an actual pandemic. Given beliefs in misinformation and disinformation, given the fact that many began to see masks as a symbol of oppression rather than a tool for saving lives, and given the fact that many found wearing them unpleasant, clashes were bound to occur over mask mandates.[12]

Those clashes over masks became common. They happened in stores. They happened in schools and at school board meetings. They happened on planes. Sometimes they turned violent, and we watched them play out on videos captured by onlookers. Arrests were made. We remember the headlines:

"The Fight over Mask Mandates in Schools Turns Violent"[13]

"Five Men Arrested After Refusing to Wear Masks on Spirit Airlines Flight"[14]

"Man Gets 10-Year Sentence for Attacking and Coughing on Person Who Asked Him to Pull Up Mask"[15]

"Video Shows 2 Men Allegedly Assaulting Target Security Guard Over Face Mask Rule"[16]

In scores of separate attacks at least 25 workers were shot, and 8 people were killed over confrontations that played out after customers were asked to wear a mask and refused to do so.[17] When resentment regarding masking requirements did not play out violently, it often took the form of verbal abuse. Being a store employee or a teacher or a school board member or a flight attendant became far harder and more dangerous and seemed to many less and less worth the risk. Conflicts over masks ultimately would ease only as the mandates did.

Societal responses to masking vary, of course. In the United States only a small minority of people continued to mask in public settings in 2023 and 2024. But when Japan relaxed masking requirements in April of 2023, 86% of Japanese still opted to mask.[18] As of June 2023, 30% of Japanese were still masking.[19] In Asian societies wearing a mask to prevent the spread of respiratory infections or to protect against pollution has long been a widely accepted practice.[20] The COVID pandemic has demonstrated that some societies are more willing than others to utilize masks to curb the spread of diseases capable of respiratory transmission.

Over the course of the pandemic, healthcare workers came to bear the brunt of considerable verbal abuse and even violence. Veneration and appreciation of "healthcare heroes" early in the pandemic over time segued to threats and violence against them, fueled mainly by disinformation and misinformation.[21] There were those who continued to believe that COVID was not real even as they died of it, railing against the nurses and doctors who tried to save them.[22] There were those who became angry when a loved one was not given a touted treatment that research found not to have a benefit — hydroxychloroquine or ivermectin, for example.[23] With the anger came an uptick in violence in general. Several factors were in play: a society stressed, a country intentionally divided along partisan lines, and perhaps even the increase in mental illnesses seen post COVID infection.[24] The falsehoods spread about COVID ("It's a hoax!" "It's just a cold!" "The number of deaths is inflated!") would create a fierce resistance against unforgiving pandemic realities.

Individuals sorely frustrated by pandemic mitigation measures from temporary business closures to masking requirements to vaccination mandates directed their ire against public health officials from the county level all the way up to Anthony Fauci, long-time director of the National Institute of Allergy and Infectious Diseases, who served on President Donald Trump's White House COVID-19 Response Team and later as chief medical advisor to President Joe Biden until the end of 2022. Public health officials were subject to harassment and death threats, leading some to quit. A survey conducted by researchers at Johns Hopkins University found that about 10% of the 583 members of the National Association of County and City Health Officials who responded to the survey had experienced threats to their safety and/or the safety of their families between March of 2020 and January of

2021. Forty-four percent of state and local officials experienced some form of harassment.[25]

Once vaccines became widely available to U.S. adults in the spring of 2021 and then required for travel and work, vaccinations and those who gave them became targets for ardent anti-vaxxers who firmly believed misinformation about the vaccine. In early 2022, 43-year-old Thomas Apollo attacked healthcare workers at a mobile vaccination clinic in Tustin, California, showering them with invectives and calling them murderers for administering COVID vaccinations.[26] In Kitchener, Ontario, a pharmacist was beaten to the point of internal injury by a man who accused him of "giving that vaccine to everyone."[27] In July of 2021, anti-vaxxers in France vandalized two vaccination centers, flooding one and setting the other on fire.[28] In Georgia (U.S.) in the fall of 2021, a mobile vaccination clinic had to shut down after the team was subjected to "harassment, bullying, and threats."[29] In Australia, a doctor whom anti-vaxxers and conspiracy theorists targeted with death threats resorted to suicide out of despair.[30]

Violence was, of course, an extreme response. Other forms of COVID vaccination sabotage included tampering with the vaccine doses themselves. A hospital pharmacist in Grafton, Wisconsin, for example, removed Moderna doses from the hospital freezer to render them ineffective, such that 57 people received compromised doses of the vaccine.[31] While not an act of violence, the pharmacist's actions cheated people of the protection they sought against possible severe disease and death.

Fake Everything

Resistance to public health mandates surrounding masking, testing, and COVID vaccination often took the form of faking compliance. Fake vaccination records, fake vaccine exemption cards, fake vaccines, fake face mask exemptions, and fake COVID test results proliferated. As of September of 2021, there were more than 10,000 sellers of fake vaccine cards, which cost an average of $100 apiece.[32] Many cards were faked; some people who sold them or attempted to use them were caught, while many others, no doubt, got away with this COVID crime. For a while, harsh federal penalties were on the books — $5000 and/or 5 years in jail.[33] In August of 2021, a Miami Beach couple presented fake vaccination cards to an airport screener in Hawaii, including cards for their children who were too young to be vaccinated — an obvious tipoff that the cards were fake. They were fined $8000 by the State of Hawaii.[34] Sellers of the cards included all sorts of people, from a California doctor to a Texas soldier to a Northern California bar owner to an anti-vax mom on Instagram.[35]

As the pandemic ground on and intense months on the frontlines at COVID-besieged hospitals became years, as some healthcare workers lost their lives or their health and others fled jobs that had left them traumatized, a worsening shortage of nurses ramped up the number of fake nursing degrees issued to those who had money to pay for them. Fake nursing diplomas were issued, sometimes to people who thought they were legitimately becoming nurses.[36] In one scheme, a Florida nursing school, now closed, issued 7600 of them to aspiring nurses who were then able to take national nursing board exams. Nearly 3000 passed the exams, but without the experience and accredited training they needed to be fully prepared for the jobs they would fill. States — Georgia, Texas, Florida, Delaware, and Washington State among them — have been clawing back the nursing licenses issued to those either knowingly or unwittingly involved in the scheme.[37]

Redefining COVID Crime

While in broad terms a crime can be defined as a shameful offense against morality, in legal terms crime is defined by the state. The battle against COVID mitigation measures was waged first by influencers in the media and on social media, in stores, on planes, and at school board meetings; but it was finally and more successfully waged in courts and in state legislatures. In states where anti-COVID-mitigation sentiments ran strong and political advantage could be gained by opposing public health measures, new laws and policies began to emerge early, pulling the plug on COVID public health measures and even tying states' hands should future coronavirus variants or pandemics driven by other pathogens emerge to inundate humanity with further surges of disease and death and disruption.

As new policies were enacted, the definition of behaviors that qualified as crimes changed. In a growing number of states, businesses and school districts and cities found themselves in violation of state laws for requiring masks or proof of vaccination. For example, in September of 2022, the State of Florida fined the Orlando's WESH 2 News $10,000 for requiring either proof of vaccination or proof of prior COVID infection and recovery for entry.[38] In 2021, the state fined Leon County $3.5 million for requiring that its employees be vaccinated against COVID and firing those who refused the shot, though the fine was ultimately withdrawn when the county agreed to allow fired employees to reapply for their jobs.[39] In short, what constitutes a pandemic-related crime varies according to place, its governance, and laws in place at the time. We will leave further discussion of governance to our next chapter.

Reactance

The counterproductive backlash against public health mitigations and vaccines is not the stuff of evidence and logic. And whether it takes the form of defiance at the entrance to a store or aboard a plane or in the form of legislation designed to end public health mitigations, it does not constitute anything new under the sun. Instead, at the root of it all, it has to do with a very human tendency to resist change, a psychological response that Loran Nordgren and David Schonthal, authors of *The Human Element: Overcoming the Resistance That Awaits New Ideas,* term *reactance.*

Nordgren and Schonthal note the parallels between resistance against seatbelts in the 1980s, despite the evidence that they saved lives, and resistance against masks during the pandemic. The reaction against seatbelts evidenced the same human impulse: human beings resist being told what to do. They do not wish to be pressured to change, so they respond to the pressure with resistance. Trotting out the evidence over and over again or implementing mandates can and does intensify that resistance, or *reactance,* because there is more perceived pressure. Distrust of science, medicine, and government only intensifies the resistance.[40]

Yet what is there to do when behavioral change is a primary tool for managing risks posed by a new, deadly, and damaging pathogen that has adapted to readily infect humanity? Pandemic response going forward will assuredly have to be informed by large helpings of behavioral science as surely as it is by epidemiology. Unwillingness to adapt when new challenges arise sometimes comes with high costs for humanity, and it certainly drove certain types of crimes during the COVID pandemic emergency.

One key for overcoming resistance to change, according to Nordgren and Schonthal, is to open opportunities for people to persuade themselves to change, using questions, especially "yes" questions or questions that uncover common ground. Behavior changes when people find their own reasons for making the changes. Nordgren and Schonthal use the example of the smoker who quits only when she finds compelling reasons to quit. The problem when a pandemic bursts on the global scene, of course, is that the need for society-wide behavioral change is so urgent if suffering is to be mitigated.

Scapegoating — Harassment and Violence

The ancient trend of blaming a minority group for a plague continued in the COVID era. In the Plague of Cyprian, it was the Christians who were blamed and killed; in the Black Death of the late Middle Ages, Jews were blamed and killed in pogroms by the angry populace and were occasionally suspected of disseminating the plague through magic.

Since SARS-CoV-2 was identified first in China (though evidence establishes that the virus was already present elsewhere), Asians were blamed for the pandemic and experienced hate crimes, with 9,000 incidents reported by mid 2021 and 11,000 reported by May 2023, the majority being verbal harassment or shunning; but about one third of those incidents that were reported proved to be violent.[41] Xenophobic language from some public officials correlated with the increase of anti-Asian sentiments and resulting hate crimes.[42] President Donald Trump, who was mightily inconvenienced by a pandemic in an election year, would by late March of 2020 shift away from calling the world's newest coronavirus "the China virus," and by April he was actively attempting to deter racial attacks against Asians and Asian Americans by saying that the Chinese should not be blamed for the pandemic. But early damage had been done and, for some, minds made up.[43] Violent attacks against people of Asian descent averaged 8.1 per year before the pandemic, but in 2020 and 2021, they increased 11-fold — there were 163 attacks over two years for an average of 81.5 a year.[44] About one third of those were attacks against property, while 60% were (often spontaneous rather than premeditated) attacks against individuals. Forty-nine people were injured.[45] In April of 2021, a Chinese-American man named Yao Pan Ma was attacked from behind while he was collecting cans in East Harlem and beaten so badly over the head that he never recovered but died eight months later. His attacker, Jarrod Powell, admitted that the attack was racially motivated. Powell ultimately pled guilty for the crime and was sentenced to 22 years in prison.[46]

Scapegoating during the COVID pandemic took different forms the world over. Mark Schaller, professor of psychology and author of *The Psychology of Prejudice* suggests that the human aversion to outsiders appears to be knit into our evolutionary psychology, though it no longer serves a constructive purpose — quite the opposite. In many places anti-immigrant sentiment quickly intertwined with COVID fears.[47]

As the pandemic ground on, Jewish people were again scapegoated, this time by neo-Nazis and others with antisemitic leanings. An anti-science/anti-vaccine stance in some cases converged with antisemitism, targeting Jewish biomedical scientists.[48] Death threats targeting Peter Hotez, a 2022 Nobel Prize nominee and co-creator of the patent-free COVID vaccine Corbevax, serve as a prominent example.[49]

Prizing Individual Rights, Eschewing Responsibility for Others

Four years into the pandemic, an immunocompromised person navigates a grocery store amid a sea of unmasked faces, knowing full well that one-way masking can be insufficient against highly contagious variants. A cancer patient faces an appointment at a medical facility where masking is no longer required. A medically vulnerable family member forgoes yet another family gathering because no one else is willing to take COVID precautions anymore. A child at high risk of COVID complications sits in a poorly ventilated classroom where almost no one else masks and classmates are sent to school with a cough, untested, because "It's just a cold" or "It's over." (A recent study, for example, found that fully 24% of parents have hidden the fact that their children were COVID positive from others.[50])

We can set aside, for the moment, the inconvenient fact that no one knows who may turn out to be vulnerable to significant and last-ing health damage as a result of a COVID infection, regardless of age, gender, or prior health. Those who know themselves to be at higher risk of serious illness or death from a COVID infection face a difficult reality: A society eager to "get back to normal" has brushed off the fact that not everyone can do the same without incurring significant risk.

Few laws on the books in 2023 (unless we consider those found, say, in the world's major religions) require that we regard another person's wellbeing as we do our own. In any legal sense, disregard for the medically vulnerable in the time of COVID is not a prosecutable offense — a crime. It has become, instead, a moral matter many currently prefer to ignore in policy and in practice and even in medical settings, even as patients in hospitals incur COVID infections. How history will judge such choices remains to be seen and will likely depend on who is writing the history.

The various types of crimes committed during the time of COVID invite reflection and study, especially with an eye toward determining what we can do to mitigate our most counterproductive pandemic responses the next time a pandemic unfolds.

---

1. Richard Lardner, Jennifer McDermott, and Aaron Kessler, "The Great Grift: How billions in COVID-19 relief aid was stolen or wasted," AP News, June 13, 2023, https://apnews.com/article/pandemic-fraud-waste-billions-small-business-labor-fb1d9a9eb24857efbe46113443 11ae78.
2. Ken Dilanian and Laura Strickler, "'Biggest fraud in a generation': The looting of the COVID relief plan known as PPP," NBC News, March 28, 2022, https://www.nbcnews.com/politics/justice-department/biggest-fraud-generation-looting-COVID-relief-program-known-ppp-n1279664.
3. "CARES Act Fraud Tracker," Arnold & Porter, last updated June 2024, https://www.arnoldporter.com/en/general/cares-act-fraud-tracker.
4. "IRS-CI releases COVID fraud statistics ahead of the 3rd anniversary of the CARES Act," Internal Revenue Service, U.S. Federal Government, March 23, 2023, https://www.irs.gov/compliance/criminal-investigation/irs-ci-releases-COVID-fraud-statistics-ahead-of-the-3rd-anniversary-of-the-cares-act.
5. Lardner, et al., "The Great Grift: How billions in COVID-19 relief aid was stolen or wasted."
6. Sacha Pfeiffer, "Overseas Bank Helped Recover IRS Stimulus Checks to Non-Americans.

It Didn't Go Well," NPR, June 5, 2021, https://www.npr.org/2021/06/05/1003256306/a-foreign-bank-helped-recover-irs-stimulus-checks-to-non-americans-it-didnt-go-w.

7.   "White House pushing Congress to pass funding to combat pandemic-related fraud," *CBS News,* March 2, 2023, https://www.cbsnews.com/news/COVID-19-pandemic-fraud-white-house-efforts-to-combat/.

8.   Peter Musurlian, "COVID-Fraud Crackdown Has Netted over $3B since 2021," Federal News Network, April 12, 2024, https://federalnewsnetwork.com/federal-newscast/2024/04/covid-fraud-crackdown-has-netted-over-3b-since-2021/.

9.   J. Alexander Navarro, "Mask resistance during a pandemic isn't new – in 1918 many Americans were 'slackers,'" The Conversation, July 13, 2020, https://theconversation.com/mask-resistance-during-a-pandemic-isnt-new-in-1918-many-americans-were-slackers-141687; Knut Berger, "The mask wars of the 1918 flu pandemic," Crosscut, July 17, 2020, https://crosscut.com/2020/07/mask-wars-1918-flu-pandemic.

10.   Yanying Dong, Zezhi Peng, Hao Fan, Xinyi Niu, Jian Sun, Liu Yang, Hongmei Xu, Junji Cao, and Zhenxing Shen, 2024, "Effect of Wearing N95 Facemasks on the Mode of Transmission of SARS-CoV-2 in the Indoor Environment of a Hospital," *Aerosol Science and Technology* 58, no. 8: 865–73, https://www.tandfonline.com/doi/full/10.1080/02786826.2024.2359561. See also Trisha Greenhalgh, C. Raina MacIntyre, Michael G. Baker, Shovon Bhattacharjee, Abrar A. Chughtai, David Fisman, Mohana Kunasekaran, Amanda Kvalsvig, Deborah Lupton, Matt Oliver, Essa Tawfiq, Mark Ungrin, and Joe Vipond, "Masks and Respirators for Prevention of Respiratory Infections: a State of the Science Review," *Clinical Microbiology Reviews,* 37, no. 2, May 2024, https://journals.asm.org/doi/10.1128/cmr.00124-23.

11.   Edward D. Vargas and Gabriel R. Sanchez, "American individualism is an obstacle to wider mask wearing in the U.S.," Brookings, August 31, 2020, https://www.brookings.edu/blog/up-front/2020/08/31/american-individualism-is-an-obstacle-to-wider-mask-wearing-in-the-us/.

12.   Vargas and Sanchez, ""American individualism is an obstacle to wider mask wearing in the U.S."

13.   Ivana Saric, "The Fight Over Mask Mandates in Schools Turns Violent," Axios, August 26, 2021, https://www.axios.com/2021/08/23/mask-school-mandate-violence-COVID.

14.   Brendan Cole, "Five Men Arrested After Refusing to Wear Masks on Spirit Airlines Flight," *Newsweek,* July 30, 2021, https://www.newsweek.com/face-mask-plane-florida-arrest-airport-1614698.

15.   Timothy Bella, "Man gets 10-year sentence for attacking and coughing on person who asked him to pull up mask," *Washington Post,* June 12, 2021, https://www.washingtonpost.com/nation/2021/06/12/shane-michael-mask-assault-iowa/.

16.   Minyvonne Burke, "Video shows 2 men allegedly assaulting Target security guard over face mask rule," *NBC News,* May 12, 2020, https://www.nbcnews.com/news/us-news/two-men-arrested-attack-target-security-guard-over-face-mask-n1205321.

17.   Jemima McEvoy, "Killing of Georgia Cashier Is Latest in a String of Fatal Shootings over Mask-Wearing, Here Are the Rest," *Forbes,* June 15, 2021, https://www.forbes.com/sites/jemimamcevoy/2021/06/15/killing-of-georgia-cashier-is-latest-in-a-string-of-fatal-shootings-over-mask-wearing-here-are-the-rest/.

18. Karin Kaneko, "Mask use in Japan at 86% despite eased guidelines, AI analysis finds," *Japan Times*, April 11, 2023, https://www.japantimes.co.jp/news/2023/04/11/national/japan-masks-ai-analysis/.

19. "Many in Japan Still Wearing Masks to Avoid Infection," *Nippon.com*, June 19, 2023, https://www.nippon.com/en/japan-data/h01701/many-in-japan-still-wearing-masks-to-avoid-infection.html.

20. Ralph Jennings, "Not Just Coronavirus: Asians Have Worn Face Masks for Decades," VOA News, March 11, 2020, https://www.voanews.com/a/science-health_coronavirus-outbreak_not-just-coronavirus-asians-have-worn-face-masks-decades/6185597.html.

21. Heather Hollingsworth and Grant Shulte, "From heroes to the harassed: Health workers being threatened, attacked," 13News Now, September 29, 2021, https://www.13newsnow.com/article/news/health/coronavirus/virus-outbreak-threatened-health-workers/507-a5b1b5c1-18cc-4e6a-a09a-0321dc6f3c6c.

22. Paulina Villegas, "South Dakota nurse says many patients deny the coronavirus exists — right up until death," *Washington Post*, November 16, 2020, https://www.washingtonpost.com/health/2020/11/16/south-dakota-nurse-coronavirus-deniers/.

23. Matt Volz, "Hospitals Refused to Give Patients Ivermectin. Lockdowns and Political Pressure Followed," *KFF Health News*, Dec. 2, 2021, https://kffhealthnews.org/news/article/ivermectin-COVID-treatment-hospital-threats-political-pressure/.

24. Kristina Sauerwein, "COVID-19 survivors face increased mental health risks up to a year later," *Washington University School of Medicine in St. Louis*, February 16, 2022, https://medicine.wustl.edu/news/COVID-19-survivors-face-increased-mental-health-risks-up-to-a-year-later/.

25. Mary Van Beusekom, "Harassment of public health officials all too common in pandemic," CIDRAP, March 18, 2020, https://www.cidrap.umn.edu/harassment-public-health-officials-all-too-common-pandemic.

26. Jessica De Nova, "Video shows man violently attack workers at COVID vaccine clinic in Tustin," *Eyewitness News*, ABC 7, January 8, 2022, https://abc7.com/orange-county-attack-vaccine-clinic-video/11439108/.

27. Stephanie Vellella and Chris Thomson, "'I'm very scared': Kitchener, Ont. pharmacist believes he was attacked for administering COVID-19 vaccines," *CTV News*, September 3, 2022, https://kitchener.ctvnews.ca/i-m-very-scared-kitchener-ont-pharmacist-believes-he-was-attacked-for-administering-COVID-19-vaccines-1.6054642.

28. "COVID vaccination centres vandalised in France," *BBC News*, July 19, 2021, https://www.bbc.com/news/world-europe-57883397.

29. Andrea Salcedo, "A Georgia vaccine site had to close after protesters bullied health-care workers: 'This is absolutely wrong,'" *Washington Post*, September 1, 2021, https://www.washingtonpost.com/nation/2021/09/01/georgia-vaccination-site-shuts-down/.

30. Michael Shields, "Austria mourns suicide of doctor targeted by anti-COVID vaccine campaigners," Reuters, July 30, 2022, https://www.reuters.com/world/europe/austria-mourns-suicide-doctor-targetted-by-anti-vaccine-campaigners-2022-07-30/.

31. "Hospital Pharmacist Sentenced for Attempt to Spoil Hundreds of COVID Vaccine Doses," Justice News, U.S. Department of Justice, June 8, 2021, https://www.justice.gov/opa/

pr/hospital-pharmacist-sentenced-attempt-spoil-hundreds-COVID-vaccine-doses.

32. Jenni Bergal, "Fake Vaccine Card Sales Have Skyrocketed Since Biden Mandate," *Stateline,* Pew Trusts, September 16, 2021, https://www.pewtrusts.org/en/research-and-analysis/blogs/ stateline/2021/09/16/fake-vaccine-card-sales-have-skyrocketed-since-biden-mandate.

33. Deedee Sun, "FBI warns of harsh penalty that comes with faking COVID vaccination cards," *Kiro 7 News,* May 7, 2021, https://www.kiro7.com/news/local/fbi-warns-harsh-penalty-that-comes-with-faking-COVID-vaccination-cards/SGBUBY5OK5GKZMIWU5QDBPEV2A/.

34. "Miami Beach Couple Arrested in Hawaii for Using Fake Vaccination Cards," NBC 6, August 19, 2021, https://www.nbcmiami.com/news/local/miami-beach-couple-arrested-in-hawaii-for-using-fake-vaccination-cards/2531905/.

35. Liz Kreutz, Amanda del Castillo, and Kayla Galloway, "California Doctor Arrested for Fake Vaccine and Immunization Card Scheme," *ABC 7 News,* July 15, 2021, https://abc7news. com/fake-COVID-19-vaccine-vaccination-cards-scheme-fraud/10887317/; Chacour Coup, "Texas soldier sold fake COVID vaccine cards on Instagram, feds say. 'How many u need!'," *Fort Worth Star Telegram,* August 20, 2021, https://www.star-telegram.com/news/nation-world/national/article253637703.html; Don Thompson, "Authorities: Fake Vaccination Cards Sold at California Bar," *NBC Bay Area,* July 14, 2021, https://www.nbcbayarea.com/ coronavirus-2/authorities-fake-vaccination-cards-sold-at-california-bar/2539297/; Jonah E. Bromwich, "Instagram User @AntiVaxMomma Charged With Selling Fake Vaccine Cards," *New York Times,* Aug. 31, 2021, https://www.nytimes.com/2021/08/31/nyregion/fake-vaccine-cards-woman-charged.html.

36. Paige Twenter, "Texas board charges 23 nurses in fake degree scheme as other students speak out," *Beckers Hospital Review,* February 20, 2023, https://www.beckershospitalreview. com/nursing/texas-board-charges-23-nurses-in-fake-degree-scheme-as-other-students-speak-out.html.

37. Emma Whitford and Janet Novack, "How Thousands Of Nurses Got Licensed With Fake Degrees," *Forbes,* Feb. 21, 2023, https://www.forbes.com/sites/emmawhitford/2023/02/21/ how-thousands-of-nurses-got-licensed-with-fake-degrees/?sh=654a38fe5c6d.

38. Eric Daugherty, "DeSantis administration fines WESH over vaccine mandate for political debate," Florida's Voice, Feb. 8, 2023, https://flvoicenews.com/desantis-administration-fines-wesh-over-vaccine-mandate-for-political-debate/.

39. Allison Prang, "Florida Fines County More Than $3 Million Over Vaccine Mandate (Leon County)," *Wall Street Journal,* October 13, 2021, https://www.wsj.com/articles/ florida-fines-county-more-than-3-million-over-vaccine-mandate-11634131437; William L. Hatfield, "Florida pulls $3.5M fine over vaccine mandate as Leon County agrees to consider rehiring fired employees," *Tallahassee Democrat,* December 21, 2021, https://www. tallahassee.com/story/news/2021/12/21/leon-county-settles-state-florida-over-vaccine-mandate-fine/8988982002/.

40. Loran Nordgren and David Schonthal, *The Human Element: Overcoming the Resistance That Awaits New Ideas* (Hoboken: John Wiley & Sons, 2022), 155–156. Kindle edition.

41. Terry Tang, "More Than 9,000 Anti-Asian Incidents Have Been Reported Since The Pandemic Began," AP News, August 12, 2021, https://apnews.com/article/lifestyle-joe-biden-health-coronavirus-pandemic-race-and-ethnicity-d3a63408021a247ba764d40355ecbe2a;

"Righting Wrongs: How Civil Rights Can Protect Asian Americans & Pacific Islanders Against Racism," Stop AAPI Hate, May 2023, https://stopaapihate.org/wp-content/uploads/2023/05/23-SAH-CivilRightsReport.pdf.

42. Angela R. Gover, Shannon B. Harper, and Lynn Langton, "Anti-Asian Hate Crime During the COVID-19 Pandemic: Exploring the Reproduction of Inequality," *American Journal of Criminal Justice* 45, no. 4 (July 2020): 647-667, reprinted by the NIH National Library of Medicine, https://www.ncbi.nlm.nih.gov/pmc/articles/PMC7364747/.

43. Gover, et al., "Anti-Asian Hate Crime During the COVID-19 Pandemic."

44. Arie Perliger, "Anti-Asian violence spiked in the U.S. during the pandemic, especially in blue-state cities," The Conversation, February 17, 2022, https://theconversation.com/anti-asian-violence-spiked-in-the-us-during-the-pandemic-especially-in-blue-state-cities-176501.

45. Perliger, "Anti-Asian violence spiked in the U.S. during the pandemic."

46. Rob Frehse and Alaa Elassar, "New York City man pleads guilty to hate crime in death of Asian man, district attorney says," CNN, January 12, 2023, https://www.cnn.com/2023/01/12/us/new-york-man-attack-asian-death-pleads-guilty/index.html.

47. Diane Cole, "Why Scapegoating Is a Typical Human Response to a Pandemic," NPR, August 29, 2020, https://www.npr.org/sections/goatsandsoda/2020/08/29/906225199/why-scapegoating-is-a-typical-human-response-to-a-pandemic.

48. Judy Siegel-ItzKovich, "Anti-vaccine activism melded with U.S. antisemitism – study," *Jerusalem Post*, January 30, 2023, https://www.jpost.com/diaspora/antisemitism/article-729992.

49. Sarah Goudarzi, "Viral spread: Peter Hotez on the increase of anti-science aggression on social media," January 20, 2023, https://thebulletin.org/2023/01/viral-spread-peter-hotez-on-the-increase-of-anti-science-aggression-on-social-media/.

50. Bruce Y. Lee, "Study: 24% Of Parents Hid That Their Children Were COVID-19 Positive," *Forbes*, March 25, 2023, https://www.forbes.com/sites/brucelee/2023/03/25/study-24-of-parents-hid-that-their-children-were-COVID-19-positive/?sh=29570ca63d89.

Chapter 18

Pandemic Lesson 6:
Governance Impacts Pandemic Outcomes

When reports about a pneumonia outbreak in Wuhan, China, circulated at the end of December 2019 and Chinese doctor Li Wenliang raised the alarm, the world was not ready for the pandemic that would claim Dr. Li's life and sweep the world.[1] Just months earlier, in October 2019, the Global Health Security Index found no nation fully prepared for a pandemic but concluded that the United States was most prepared among nations.[2] The results of that written survey of 140 questions, however, were quite different from the road test of an actual pandemic. A year in, Ian Bremmer, writing for *TIME*, catalogued what the world already knew. The U.S. had stumbled badly in its pandemic response relative to other countries in the developed world. As of February of 2021, Taiwan had recorded only 9 deaths, Singapore 29, South Korea 1544, and New Zealand 26, whereas the United States was still playing catchup, losing 2,400 lives to COVID every day.[3]

When the Johns Hopkins COVID-19 Dashboard ceased gathering data on March 10, 2023, Taiwan had seen 17,672 deaths, Singapore 1,722, South Korea 34,093, New Zealand 2,550, and the United States 1,123,836.[4] These are absolute numbers among populations of vastly different sizes, but a different figure — deaths per 100,000 people — also affirms dramatically different outcomes. For each 100,000 people, Taiwan lost 74; Singapore lost 29; South Korea lost 67; New Zealand lost 53; and the United States lost 341. U.S. losses also exceeded those in European countries, including the United Kingdom, Italy, and Spain.[5]

For the United States, several factors proved significant. One was the challenge posed by characteristics of the U.S. healthcare system and the limits of its affordability and accessibility. U.S. healthcare is an expensive, fragmented layering of healthcare providers, insurers, and programs. *Patchwork* may arguably be too generous a word to describe it, because the word implies that the pieces are coordinated and stitched together according to a design in some sort of continuous pattern. We think, perhaps, of a patchwork quilt that covers us from head to toe and keeps us warm. But the patchwork of American healthcare is full of holes where many Americans are concerned. *System* is another overly generous word. Because of all the holes, many Americans on the eve of the pandemic lacked critical access to affordable medical care. They still do.

In 2019, according to the Kaiser Family Foundation, 28.9 million Americans were not covered by health insurance. (By 2021, that number was 27.5 million.)[6] In 2019, some 33% of Americans put off seeking medical care, often because of cost. That figure dropped to its lowest level since 2004 during 2020 and 2021 — 26% — and then rose in 2022 to a record high of 38%.[7]

As the pandemic spread, access to care, to tests, and to vaccines for all posed a massive problem to be solved in short order. It was, in fact, not possible to protect anyone — or a society as a whole or an economy — without better protecting people everywhere. That is an abiding but often forgotten principle. The HRSA COVID-19 Uninsured Program covered COVID-19 vaccines and treatments until funding ran out in March 2022. Medicaid programs were required to keep people continuously enrolled, and usage of the system increased until the COVID public health emergency was permitted to expire on May 11, 2023. About 3.7 million Americans have been disenrolled since, NPR reported in August of 2023, including more than a half million of them in the State of Texas alone.[8] For a time, the U.S. federal government demonstrated a bipartisan willingness to meet the moment and address the need — after all, many Americans who were most exposed both physically and financially to the worst that COVID could do were also those most essential to the functioning of society.

There was not, however, a bipartisan willingness to extend COVID funding. Further, under debt ceiling deals that prevented a U.S. default, much unspent COVID funding was clawed back. Surges of COVID infections may come and go, but Americans will be on their own going forward, and the country will make do with less for surveillance and preparedness. That is a governance choice that leaves the nation more exposed to risks posed by a rapidly mutating virus that is not going to disappear and to other pandemic threats.

A further challenge for the U.S. was the layered and overlapping, yet loosely connected nature of public health authority and functions at the federal, state, and local levels. While the federal government provides legislation and funding for public health, setting standards, conducting research, gathering data, and issuing guidance, states have considerable autonomy in terms of the way they structure public health and utilize federal funding, so the U.S. COVID response looked, at some points during the pandemic, quite different from state to state.

State governance and local governance sometimes came into conflict, such as when Georgia Governor Brian Kemp sued Atlanta Mayor Keisha Lance Bottoms and the Atlanta City Council in 2020 because Kemp wanted masking to be optional statewide (though still recommended in public), while Bottoms and the City Council had imposed a citywide masking ordinance, concerned about Atlantans' safety in a densely populated urban environment.[9] (Kemp would later drop the suit.) Federal policies met resistance from states, as happened in 2021 when Republican governors sued the Biden administration to overturn its policy mandating vaccines or weekly negative COVID tests for the employees of businesses who employed 100 or more workers. The majority-conservative Supreme Court would ultimately overturn the Biden administration's policy.[10] In short, U.S. COVID response was not a unified defense against a common enemy, and competing visions of both the pandemic and appropriate response came into conflict at all levels of governance.

The decentralized structure of U.S. public health posed from the beginning (and continues to pose today) a formidable challenge for the critical task of data gathering. To implement public health interventions, public health officials need to know where the virus is spreading and what variants are circulating. Testing, reporting, and genomic surveillance are essential. In their book *Lessons from the COVID War: An Investigative Report,* the COVID Crisis Group has explained the problem:

> The United States has twenty-eight hundred local public health departments, but these authorities are not organized into any coherent system. Half report to a centralized board of health; half do not. Some have carve-outs and carve-ins, where animal health is excluded but environmental health is included, and vice versa. No two are the same. Add to that antiquated information technology systems and it is no wonder that these departments cannot collect complete, reliable data on public health threats.[11]

The clearest picture regarding disease transmission, the early clues as to modes of transmission, and, in time, the best data on the incidence of long COVID came from countries that tested widely, did genomic sequencing to establish who transmitted the virus to whom and in what settings, and had access to anonymized healthcare data that yielded evidence as to the prevalence of long COVID symptoms.

National leadership proved another fateful factor. The Trump administration lost weeks in marshaling a response beyond attempted containment, apparently slow to realize that the U.S. would inevitably be fighting a war, though one against a microscopic pathogen rather than another nation. As Ed Pilkington and Tom McCarthy noted, writing for the *Guardian,* the U.S. and South Korea saw their first cases on the very same day — January 20, 2020. While South Korea had a diagnostic test within two weeks, having marshaled 20 private companies to develop the tests, the U.S. was slower to act. Private companies in America were not immediately enlisted to help develop the tests.[12] Instead, the Trump administration touted travel bans as the way to keep the virus at bay, though that strategy was doomed from the start. The CDC, for its part, would not look to tests developed by the World Health Organization or other countries or the 10 or so U.S. companies that could have helped.[13]

Instead, the CDC's first tests, sent to the states in early February, turned out to be flawed; and when tests that worked came at the end of that month, there were not nearly enough of them. Worse yet, receiving results took five days to a week or more because lab capacity was inadequate. By the time the results came, they were too late to be of much help. Diagnostic testing was far too large an enterprise for the CDC alone, but it would be February 29 before anyone beyond the CDC was authorized by the FDA to conduct diagnostic testing for the new virus.[14]

Testing labs had to be cobbled together, sometimes even staffed by volunteers. There were no national-level solutions for the testing challenge or for the nation's unmet need for medical supplies such as personal protective equipment. In the absence of coordination at the federal level, states had to compete with each other for scarce supplies sourced mainly from China or wherever they could get what they needed. In his riveting book *The Premonition: A Pandemic Story*, Michael Lewis recounts the experience of biochemist Joe DeRisi, who transformed an empty lab space at the University of California San Francisco into a COVID testing facility. The quest for testing supplies when the supply chains broke was a daunting one. One coveted box of essential "nasal swabs," acquired on a tip, turned out to be eyelash brushes instead.[15]

There is no more thoroughgoing and incisive account and analysis of the U.S. COVID response under both the Trump and Biden administrations than that produced by the 34-member COVID Crisis Group, which formed in 2021 and published *Lessons from the COVID War: An Investigative Report* in April of 2023. As the COVID Crisis Group noted, the U.S. had focused its preparations and 2019 drill on an influenza pandemic scenario. Several aspects of the COVID pandemic were not anticipated in that drill — the scope of the need for testing, for example, or the fact that we would face a virus for which we had zero effective antivirals and zero effective treatments. (For influenza viruses, even novel ones, on the other hand, we have four FDA-approved antivirals.)[16]

The national stockpile lacked critical supplies, and the nation lacked the ready capacity to produce enough of them at a time when global supply chains were drained dry by extraordinary demand globally. Some healthcare workers wore garbage bags for gowns, and many cared for the ill wearing disposable one-use masks over and over again or even cloth masks made by volunteers from patterns found online. Where were adequate N95 respirators and other PPE, nasal swabs for testing, or an adequate supply of working ventilators?

In managing the Strategic National Stockpile, Robert Kadlec, as the Assistant Secretary for Preparedness and Response (ASPR) at HHS, had placed a greater focus on mustering defenses against bioterror attacks waged by human enemies than on fortifying defenses against new infectious diseases. ASPR invested in smallpox vaccines and anthrax vaccines, but Obama-era plans to create a machine that could make 1.5 million N95 masks per day were scrapped in 2018, citing limited resources.[17] When COVID hit, Kadlec's policy-oriented office would not have resources to supply the nation with N95s or to launch a race to develop a vaccine.[18] In 2011, in a hearing on U.S. bioterrorism threats, Kadlec had explained his thinking:

> The first obstacle we have to overcome is understanding of the difference between bioterrorism, biowarfare and natural disease pandemics. Quite frankly, mother nature is not a thinking enemy intent on inflicting grievous harm to our country, killing our citizens, undermining our government or destroying our way of life. Mother nature doesn't develop highly virulent organisms that are resistant to our current stockpiles of antibiotics or disseminate them in high doses to result in more rapid onset and more virulent clinical course than we've seen in nature.[19]

Unfortunately, what has been made clear over and over again through human history is that organisms simply doing what they do — infecting, reproducing, mutating — can deal immense harm, upending our way of life. There are several erroneous assumptions evident in Robert Kadlec's 2011 testimony — first, that natural processes of evolution are unlikely to churn out highly virulent organisms; second, that human beings are somehow unlikely to encounter these organisms, some of which may be capable of triggering a pandemic; and third, that intent is any sort of prerequisite for infectious disease impacts that we, the infected, deem insidious.

As the COVID Crisis Group points out, in 2018 the White House National Security Council Directorate for Global Health Security and Biodefense created during the Obama administration had been disbanded, though the NSC retained some of the expertise from that team. The concerted focus on pandemic risk enabled by the team, however, became another issue on a national security "radar screen" tracking all risks. That same year, the CDC scaled back its global work in the area of detecting and preventing pandemics by 80% when funding from a 2014 initiative launched in response to Ebola was not renewed. Consequently, the CDC narrowed its surveillance focus to 10 countries. Fatefully, China was not among them.[20]

Where pandemics are concerned, scares or crises drive funding and preparedness, but complacency sets in again when other funding needs seem more pressing, and then funding for preparedness dries up.[21] This pattern flies in the face of an ongoing risk. A 2021 study published in *PNAS*, found that, judging from the last 400 years, the likelihood of a pandemic in any given year is about 2% and may double in coming years. Further, we know from our study of ancient epidemics and pandemics, that the last 400 years are not exceptional.[22]

When the COVID pandemic began, less than 10% of the world's supply of N95 respirators was manufactured in the U.S. (by 3M).[23] Global supply chains for medical N95s and their equivalents were tapped out well before the end of January. Some Americans pulled out their sewing machines and, following patterns published on the internet, sewed cloth masks for healthcare workers, hoping to offer them some measure of protection. Doctors and nurses wore these or scarce N95s day after day, or they turned to surgical masks ("baggy blues") that were never designed to seal to their faces. More than 3,600 U.S. healthcare workers died of COVID in a year.[24]

The U.S., along with the rest of the world, also faced by March a shortage of working ventilators. During the first wave of the pandemic, hospitals had to develop triage guidelines to determine who would have first priority access to ventilators that could potentially save lives, knowing that once a patient was on a ventilator, that patient might continue to need it for some time. The elderly and those with chronic conditions that worsened their odds of surviving COVID often found themselves at the end of the line.[25]

Meanwhile, believing that the spread of the virus could somehow be contained with border closures (always porous), the Trump administration waited until March 18 to invoke the Defense Production Act, which could be used to enlist companies to produce supplies critical in the fight against COVID. Even then, President Trump preferred that businesses step up on their own.[26] By March 24, GE Healthcare had partnered with Ford to manufacture 80,000 ventilators, 30,000 of them for the National Stockpile.[27] More domestic producers of N95 respirators also emerged in 2020, among them Aidway (California) and Armbrust American (Austin, Texas).

The lack of supplies, equipment, and manufacturing capacity was a readily observable deficit to be addressed, but there were other problems. The U.S. failed to mount a seamlessly orchestrated "whole of government" response to the COVID pandemic. While the Trump administration took the approach of intentionally downplaying the pandemic in order to get the country back to work and the economy back on its feet ahead of the election, other agencies and departments with varied and not always well-defined roles had to stretch beyond their usual capacities and competencies. New working partnerships had to be forged, and deficiencies remained.

Alongside inadequate preparation and resources, the CDC's response proved fatefully inadequate. In "Building the CDC the Country Needs," a report from the CSIS Commission on Strengthening America's Health Security at the Center for Strategic and International Studies, authors J. Stephen Morrison and Tom Inglesby have laid out the problems that plagued the CDC's COVID response in particular and made recommendations for the future. First, the CDC was underfunded to fulfill its global surveillance mission. It lacked the budgetary flexibility to muster adequate funds quickly as the crisis unfolded (as did the ASPR), as well as the flexibility to hire needed additional expertise efficiently. Flexibility on both those fronts under-pins rapid response on an adequate scale. Further, its mission with regard to the pandemic needed clarification. Its working relationships on every front needed to be strengthened and maintained — with the rest of the federal government up in DC, with other countries, with the American people, and with states and local public health depart-ments. The CDC needed its staff to be a part of many conversations at many levels, with partnerships in place and relationships maintained. "Whole-of-government" drills needed to take place to ensure that agencies and departments from the federal level to the local level were primed to work together— and with private-sector partners — without surprises or power struggles.[28]

Speed was another issue, as was timely, clear messaging. Outside of an emergency, a research institution has the luxury of time and the opportunity to gather extensive data before drawing rock-solid conclu-sions. But the same institution leading a country through a pandemic needs to be able to access and analyze critical data quickly, including data coming out of other countries, and to provide timely guidance amid the fog of war against an infectious disease. The CDC did not, in a pandemic emergency, have the luxury of muddling through months of research before it issued clear, readily understandable guidance reflecting the best currently available information. Just as important was imparting the clear message to the American people that, as the virus changed and as what was known about it changed, guidance would need to change, too. Communicating in a timely, effective manner to optimize a public health response requires more than just expertise in the area of infectious disease: It requires input and feedback from stakeholders and from behavioral scientists and communications specialists.

For the CDC and for the nation, given a series of missteps and public impatience with changing guidance, trust became and remains a significant, indeed a formidable problem. Confidence in the CDC's leadership nosedived during the pandemic, declining by 50% among Republicans and less dramatically among Democrats and independents.[29] While plummeting trust can seem to politicians like a justification to cut an agency's scope and funding, that approach can only further undermine America's level of preparedness. The COVID pandemic cost the lives of more than 1.2 million Americans, including almost half a million people of working age.[30] If the U.S. is caught flat-footed and less prepared than ever when the race to respond to the next pandemic begins, the damage may be far greater, depending on the pathogen and its transmissibility and virulence.

Morrison and Inglesby close the CSIS report by envisioning the CDC that the U.S. actually needs:

> CDC needs a strong and clearly understood mission that bridges domestic and global needs. It needs a major shift in incentives and culture that elevates speed, capability, and closer engagements with policymakers and frontline responders. The agency needs a guaranteed future talent base and essential capabilities that ensure the access and quality of data, that allow it to surge to meet rapidly scaling outbreaks, that ensure its ability to hire and deploy in emergencies, and that tap the innovating power of the private sector. It needs a far greater presence and integration in Washington decisionmaking that will more effectively represent its perspective in executive chambers and on Capitol Hill, as well as build national security process at CDC and among its staff. The agency also needs to become less centralized and distant from its state and local partners by intensifying frontline engagement and by embedding young CDC talent routinely into state and local public health structures on a much larger scale.[31]

The COVID pandemic taught the governments of the U.S. and every other country that paper plans, where those existed, were not enough. Instead, operational readiness will always be critical, drawing on the strengths of all responsible departments and agencies and orchestrated in a coherent and coordinated response that taps the expertise and production capacities of the private sector. The early response must be enabled by funding that can be immediately and flexibly marshaled to meet needs, and the response needs to be quickly scaled up through public/private partnerships that stand at the ready. These lessons, of course, have yet to sink in with a broad swath of the U.S. Congress. The July 2023 debt ceiling deal cut CDC funding by $1.3 billion, undermining both infectious disease response and vaccination programs.[32]

The COVID experience has also amply demonstrated that pandemics have immense political repercussions, and politics at every level of governance from the presidency to the governor's office to the local school board can powerfully shape pandemic responses and outcomes. As any sitting president would be, President Trump himself was mightily inconvenienced by the intractable reality of a pandemic in an election year. He could not make COVID go away — not by ignoring it, not by claiming that it was under control when it was not, not by wishing it away and encouraging the rest of the country to do the same, not by minimizing its severity. Cases and deaths mounted. Once the CDC finally reversed its previous guidance and recommended masks, Trump himself was not keen on wearing them — they were reminders of the pandemic and of vulnerability, when what he wanted most was to get the economy wide open and booming again, and well before November. Masks became politicized, leaving those who eschewed them unprotected.

Both the CDC and the WHO would be extremely, unconscionably slow to acknowledge that SARS-CoV-2 was spread readily by means of aerosols and not just via large droplets, despite convincing evidence, even early on, that the virus was airborne. Given President Trump's personal choices, the political battles that followed over mask mandates, mask-related misinformation, and institutional groupthink at CDC and WHO about how the virus is transmitted, masking as a common practice fell by the wayside in the U.S.[33]

President Trump did look for some form of medical magic to offer the American people, but not always from best sources. As noted in Chapter 16, he stirred great demand and enthusiasm for hydroxychloroquine, based on anecdotal reports, before the verdict was in as to whether that drug worked against COVID, and wondered aloud about outlandish and assuredly toxic treatments such as bleach. He tended to listen to what he wanted most to hear, such as radiologist Scott Atlas's argument that allowing younger people to become infected would enable the population to develop herd immunity, in keeping with the Great Barrington Declaration of October 4, 2020.[34] The herd immunity theory made everything easier for the administration, because it favored a return to normal economic activity for all except those deemed most vulnerable.

The herd immunity theory, however, was and is deeply flawed on multiple counts where COVID is concerned: First, there was no sufficiently protective lasting immunity to be had, it turned out; instead, there was a substantial long COVID risk with each new infection; and a percentage of those younger, previously healthy Americans deemed not to be vulnerable saw their lives upended by long COVID. Some lost their lives. Further, there was and is no way of reliably sorting those who are vulnerable to COVID-related disability or death from those who are resilient.

We take risks when we make assumptions about a new disease, relying too heavily on what has been true for other pandemic pathogens. Over and over again, making assumptions about the behavior of a virus and making promises that ultimately cannot be kept have proven to be tactical errors. The herd immunity theory is but one early example with fateful consequences, though it still holds considerable sway over U.S. health policy.

As 2020 dragged on, President Trump's tensions with his CDC and his top medical experts intensified until he resorted to sniping at Anthony Fauci, director of the National Institute of Allergy and Infectious Diseases, and Deborah Birx, the White House coronavirus response coordinator. Trump brought Dr. Scott Atlas on as an adviser, despite the fact that Atlas was neither an epidemiologist nor an infectious disease specialist, but a neuroradiologist. Given the friction and the partial muzzling of public health leaders, there was no unified federal initiative against COVID: There was a tug of war instead.

On the positive side, however, it would be the Trump administration's Operation Warp Speed, designed to accelerate the development of a vaccine, that turned the tables on the virus in the U.S. and began to save lives. Operation Warp Speed provides a useful model for the future.

The COVID Crisis Group tells the origin story of Operation Warp Speed, an idea that began to take shape quite early, and of the convoluted path it took to gain a hearing, in Chapter 5 of *Lessons from the COVID War*: "Federal Crisis Management Collapses; Operation Warp Speed Begins."[35] Though the idea did not originate with Trump or his inner circle, when Alex Azar, then Secretary of the HHS, was sold on the idea and sold Jared Kushner on it, Kushner took the idea to Trump, and the president embraced it. A vaccine produced more quickly than most people thought possible, ahead of the November election, would be a critical weapon against the pandemic and an impressive victory that the Trump administration could rightly claim. Operation Warp Speed succeeded in producing effective vaccines in a time frame few had imagined possible.

Successful models for public-private partnerships, whether for creating COVID tests in South Korea or for creating new vaccines in the U.S., are tools to carry forward and to improve upon so that partnerships can be activated promptly and managed effectively from development to implementation and distribution. By the end of 2020, the FDA had given emergency use authorizations to both Pfizer-BioNTech's and Moderna's mRNA vaccines, which built upon mRNA vaccine research dating back to the 1990s.

Solving for the vaccines' swift distribution was another matter. By the end of 2020, of the 20 million doses allocated, 14 million had been distributed to states, but only 2.8 million shots had been administered.[36] In January of 2021, the incoming Biden administration faced the challenge of ramping up vaccine production and getting vaccines into Americans' arms quickly in order to prevent further severe disease and death. By March 10, 2021, according to the CDC, nearly 10% of Americans had been fully vaccinated (with two doses).[37] The administration met its goal of administering 100 million doses in 100 days 42 days ahead of the original goal. Demand would outstrip supply, though, in May of 2021, when all adults became eligible to be vaccinated.

Vaccine production and distribution would prove to be challenges that yielded to expertise and effort. A third challenge, convincing the vast majority Americans to get shots, would prove to be far more difficult and finally a battle lost.

The anti-vaccine movement made much over the relatively small risks that the vaccines posed compared to the much greater risks of infection with COVID-19, especially for the unvaccinated. Unpleasant vaccine side effects, especially lingering ones, have limited some people's willingness to get subsequent shots. Distrust of government (especially from Trump followers disgruntled over the outcome of the 2020 election) and distrust of pharmaceutical companies' profit motives influenced some not to be vaccinated.

By November of 2021, as reported by the Kaiser Family Foundation, a marked gap in vaccine acceptance had emerged along partisan lines. Sixty percent of those who remained unvaccinated were Republicans, while Democrats and independents each represented 17% of the unvaccinated.[38]

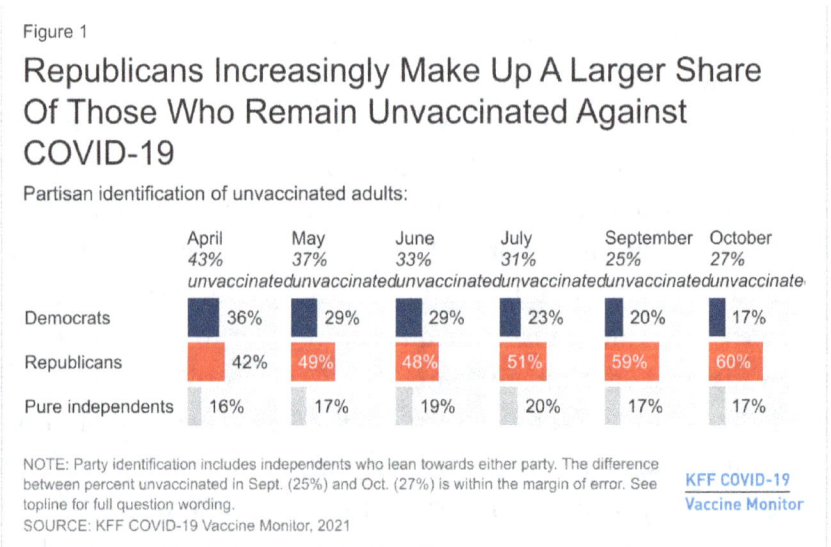

Figure 1

Republicans Increasingly Make Up A Larger Share Of Those Who Remain Unvaccinated Against COVID-19

Partisan identification of unvaccinated adults:

	April 43% unvaccinated	May 37% unvaccinated	June 33% unvaccinated	July 31% unvaccinated	September 25% unvaccinated	October 27% unvaccinate
Democrats	36%	29%	29%	23%	20%	17%
Republicans	42%	49%	48%	51%	59%	60%
Pure independents	16%	17%	19%	20%	17%	17%

NOTE: Party identification includes independents who lean towards either party. The difference between percent vaccinated in Sept. (25%) and Oct. (27%) is within the margin of error. See topline for full question wording.
SOURCE: KFF COVID-19 Vaccine Monitor, 2021

KFF COVID-19 Vaccine Monitor

Figure 18.1 Republicans increasingly make up a larger share of those who remain unvaccinated against COVID-19, KFF COVID-19 Vaccine Monitor (2021), https://www.kff.org/coronavirus-COVID-19/poll-finding/importance-of-partisanship-predicting-vaccination-status/.

Opting out of vaccination was a choice that would cost more lives among Trump voters than among Democrats, as multiple studies have shown.[39] But vaccination was not the only factor. Even before vaccines were available, behavioral choices based on both economic circumstances and ideology impacted outcomes. President Trump's efforts to minimize fear of the virus in order to boost the economy worked among his supporters especially, but at a cost, as people opted out of behaviors that would have reduced their risk.[40]

Early on, the Biden administration mandated COVID vaccinations and masks where that was possible. Courts upheld vaccine mandates in healthcare settings during the pandemic emergency, but the Supreme Court overturned the Biden administration's mandate that employees of larger companies and institutions be vaccinated or else mask and undergo regular testing, deeming the policy to be overreach. Courts upheld the vaccine mandate for members of the armed forces, but Section 525 of the 2023 National Defense Authorization Act required the Secretary of Defense to rescind the COVID-19 vaccination mandate for those serving in the military.[41] For the first time in American history (all the way back to Washington's decision to inoculate his troops against smallpox), the U.S. Congress chose to curb the power of the military to make a call as to what measures could best protect the operational readiness of the U.S. armed forces.

COVID vaccine mandates, including the one imposed by the U.S. Department of Defense, crumbled not only because of rising anti-vaccination resistance but also because COVID vaccines, it turned out, offer diminishing protection over time. Trust levels in the vaccines' value sank. It did not help that the Biden administration initially touted the vaccines' early success in preventing infection, setting public expectations too high. A high level of protection against infection was a bonus that did not last, given the long march of new variants capable of immune escape. The costly communications misstep was another case of overpromising based on an assumption that did not pan out as new variants emerged. The measure of protection that the vaccines offered against serious illness and death, which declined over time, now seemed to many not enough to make getting the shots and dealing with possible side effects worthwhile.

Further, since proof of vaccination was initially touted as a ticket to discontinue masking (setting up circumstances in which masking would be impossible to enforce in many public settings), masking as a common practice soon fell by the wayside in the United States. Some conservative states moved to outlaw both mask mandates and vaccination requirements.[42] After the ending of the public health emergency, in many places masking is no longer practiced even in healthcare settings, where medically vulnerable people must access care, risking a COVID infection, or else risk foregoing care. The rush to get "back to normal" has left many vulnerable people behind.

There is, four years into the age of COVID, no dialogue about win-win solutions for both those who want to carry on with their lives as if it were still 2019 and those who must continue to be careful — or else risk their lives. There is only a push-pull from opposing perspectives. (It is not hard to imagine options. Could there, for example, not be designated days and times — mornings, for this to work — when immunocompromised patients could go to their doctors' office knowing that every person in the building had masked before entering and that every waiting and exam room benefitted from air filtration sufficient to produce five air exchanges per hour?)

The politicization of the pandemic has profoundly influenced the course of the COVID-19 pandemic in the United States and will impact U.S. preparedness for the next surge of COVID infections or the next pandemic because of animated opposition, now at the level of state and federal governance, to the tools of mitigation and to the funding of public health.

At the end of January 2023, the House, with its new Republican majority, voted to declare the COVID national emergency over. The Senate followed suit at the end of March; and, in early April, President Biden reluctantly signed the Republican-backed measure, ending the COVID emergency effective May 11. Congress's failure to extend funding for COVID tests, treatments, vaccines, and enhanced surveillance led to the rollback of the U.S. COVID response, whatever the virus might still hold in store for the nation. Access to testing, vaccines, and treatments has become harder for the uninsured, though the CDC worked with federally qualified clinics and some pharmacies to provide free vaccines through its Bridge Access Program, designed to ensure that COVID vaccines are available at no cost to the 30% of Americans who are uninsured or underinsured, through August of 2024.[43] The contentious debt ceiling deal, agreed under duress in July

2023, clawed back $27 billion in COVID funding that had not yet been spent. That amount included $391 million from the earmarks to support states and schools, $1 billion from efforts to address fraud, and more than $13 billion from the CDC and FDA for purposes such as distributing vaccines and helping strained pharmaceutical supply chains to recover.[44]

The CDC's capability to perform surveillance has taken a hit. Wastewater surveillance is what remains to afford advance warning of new variants spreading, but that surveillance is limited to particular sewersheds unevenly scattered across the country, as the CDC's COVID Data Tracker map of wastewater sampling sites makes clear, with 89% of existing sites currently reporting as of August 2024.

Current SARS-CoV-2 Virus Levels in Wastewater by Site, United States
Time Period: Jul 08, 2024 – Jul 22, 2024

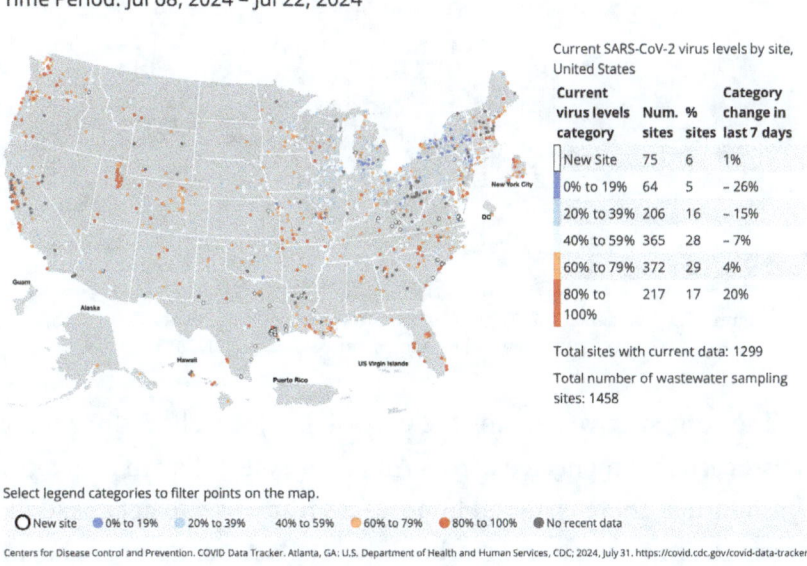

Current SARS-CoV-2 virus levels by site, United States

Current virus levels category	Num. sites	% sites	Category change in last 7 days
New Site	75	6	1%
0% to 19%	64	5	– 26%
20% to 39%	206	16	– 15%
40% to 59%	365	28	– 7%
60% to 79%	372	29	4%
80% to 100%	217	17	20%

Total sites with current data: 1299

Total number of wastewater sampling sites: 1458

Select legend categories to filter points on the map.

○ New site ● 0% to 19% ● 20% to 39% ● 40% to 59% ● 60% to 79% ● 80% to 100% ● No recent data

Centers for Disease Control and Prevention. COVID Data Tracker. Atlanta, GA: U.S. Department of Health and Human Services, CDC; 2024, July 31. https://covid.cdc.gov/covid-data-tracker

Figure 18.2 Current SARS-CoV-2 Virus Levels in Wastewater by Site, Time Period: Jul. 08, 2024 – Jul. 22, 2024, U.S. CDC COVID Data Tracker, retrieved July 31, 2024.

States are no longer reporting test positivity rates or case numbers: there is too little reported testing happening to track precisely what is going on. Instead, the CDC reports emergency room visits, hospitalizations, and deaths — all lagging indicators (by several weeks) of a COVID surge. We do know that there is an enormous gap between what testing catches and the actual prevalence of COVID in a given locale, and we know this from wastewater data where it is collected. As an example, in the chart below, the Santa Clara County Public Health Department in California compares its COVID testing data to the story that wastewater surveillance details for the City of San Jose.

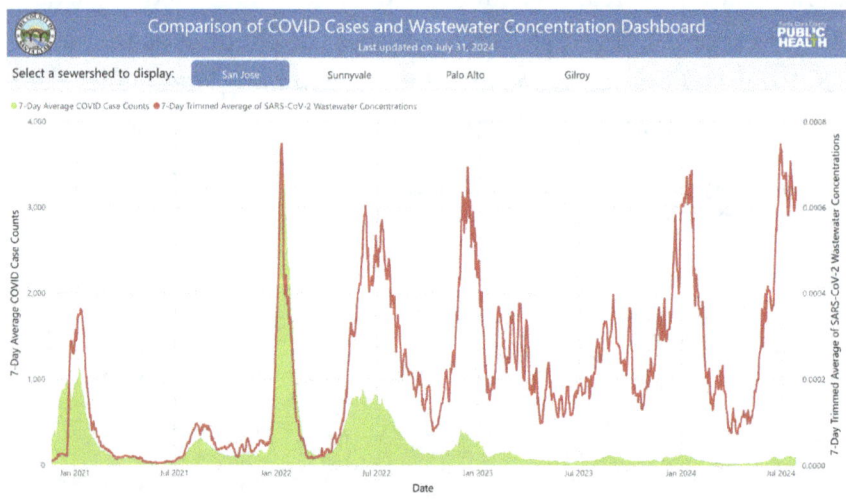

Figure 18.3 Comparison of COVID Cases and Wastewater Concentration Dashboard, Santa Clara County Public Health, retrieved August 31, 2023.

The comparative data for the City of San Jose tells a story that is almost certainly replicated across America, except that, in many local communities, there is no red line and no ready way to get ahead of a surge and limit its impact on schools, workplaces, and human health. In pragmatic terms, surveillance across the country has been reduced by 90%.[45]

As SARS-CoV-2 continues to mutate, often-reported estimates of the prevalence of variants circulating in the U.S. reflect data the CDC reported in 2023 from only three regions. In August of 2024, only HHS regions 2, 8, and 9 were reporting the minimum of 300 sequences required for a Nowcast estimate. The rest of the country was a vast gray blank on the Nowcast map. It is hard to imagine any army fighting a war effectively against a still-active enemy with so little surveillance. There is not better surveillance because there is not money for better surveillance, and that dearth of money is a matter of governance and specifically the responsibility of the U.S. Congress.

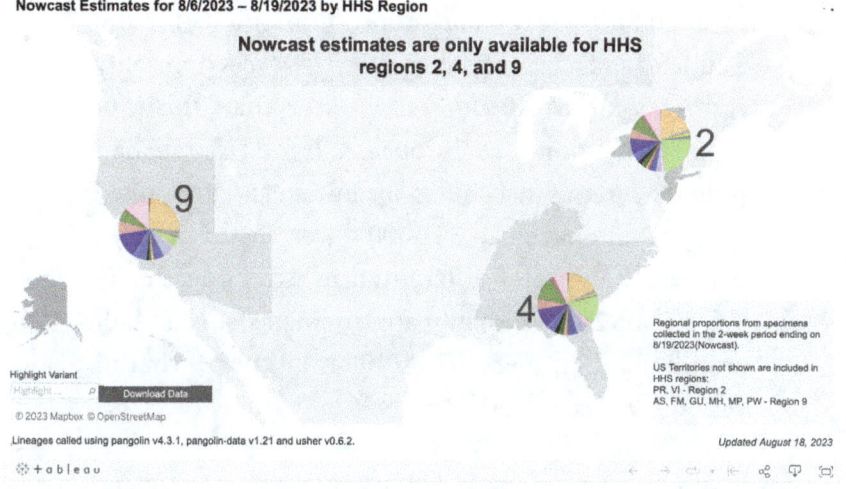

Nowcast Estimates for 8/6/2023 – 8/19/2023 by HHS Region

Figure 18.4 Nowcast Estimate for 8/6/2023 – 8/89/2023 by HHS Region, Centers for Disease Control and Prevention, "Variant Proportions," Data Tracker, Atlanta, GA, U.S. Department of Health and Human Services, CDC, August 29, 2023, https://COVID.cdc.gov/COVID-data-tracker/#variant-proportions.

We cannot say precisely what the future holds as of the writing of this book, but we do know the SARS-CoV-2 virus will continue to churn out variants that will continue to infect us until we find and deploy the means to defend ourselves. And history assures us that other pandemics lie before us.

Given the sum of governance choices and all other factors, how have COVID outcomes to date in the United States compared with outcomes in other countries? As of November of 2021, the Institute for Health Metrics and Evaluation (IHME) found that India ranked highest in cumulative total COVID deaths, with an estimate of more than 2,800,000; and the U.S. ranked second, with 925,000, followed by Brazil, the Russian Federation, and Mexico.[46]

In *Lessons from the COVID War*, the COVID Crisis Group compared the performance of the U.S. with that of European countries as a group. They observed stark contrasts:

> In 2020 and 2021, using common methods for the estimates and adjusting for age, the U.S. excess mortality rate was about 40 percent higher than the rate monitored among the Europeans. If the U.S. rate had been the same as that among the Europeans, the United States would have had 391,000 fewer deaths in those two years; the total differential in excess deaths by the end of 2022 probably approximates at least half a million. Then there are all the multiples of that in serious illness and other costs.[47]

Interestingly, U.S. relative performance actually deteriorated in the fall of 2020 and spring of 2021, as COVID and responses such as masking and then vaccination were politicized. Whereas in the spring and summer of 2020, excess mortality in Europe was 29% lower than excess mortality in the U.S., in the fall of 2020 and the spring of 2021, that margin widened to 51%. The COVID Crisis Group points to the riskier behavioral choices many made in the U.S., driven in part by the politicization of pandemic perceptions and response.[48]

Thomas J. Bollyky, Isabella Turilli, and Emma Castro, writing for the Council on Foreign Relations in August of 2023, usefully point out that outcomes varied by state as widely as if the 50 states were not jurisdictions in one country but disparate nations instead:

For most of the pandemic, New Hampshire, Vermont, and Washington posted COVID-19 death rates comparable to those in Denmark, Germany, or Switzerland, while mortality rates from the virus in Arizona and Mississippi rival those in the world's three worst-performing countries during that same period: Bulgaria, Peru, and Russia. Even after accounting for the relevant biological factors in this pandemic — variation in the age of state populations and in the local rates of diabetes, obesity, and other exacerbating health conditions — there is still a nearly fourfold difference between COVID-19 death rates in the best- and worst-performing U.S. states.[49]

They note that the battles against pandemic disease are always won or lost "in the local trenches." In the U.S., that dynamic was intensified when the Trump White House abdicated its own federal leadership role in policy and guidance and left the conduct of the COVID war up to individual states.[50] Bollyky, Turilli, and Castro concluded that variations in mortality outcomes among states reflect a picture much larger than that painted by policy decisions such as mandates or the lack thereof. Mortality rates also reflected "social, economic, and racial disparities" that made some groups more vulnerable, along with how states had addressed those disparities prior to the pandemic, and how they addressed them during the pandemic.[51]

New Hampshire, which scored second highest on their health metric, deployed vax vans and set up a mass vaccination site at the New Hampshire Motor Speedway among other venues popular among its conservative citizens, expedited testing and treatments in nursing homes, leaned on telehealth solutions, and strategized with the private sector to ensure that medical supplies were shared across the state and that hospitals shared the heavy patient load. New Hampshire was, of course, not alone in doing these things to optimally serve its population. It also had the advantages of a low poverty rate, quality healthcare accessible to many because of the high percentage of New Hampshire residents who enjoy health insurance, and high interpersonal trust.[52]

Bollyky, Turilli, and Castro note that, of the 10 states that scored highest on the health metric they used, six had Democratic governors and four had Republican ones. It was during the Delta wave, when vaccinations lagged among political conservatives and mitigations were crumbling, that living in one state versus another entailed more risk versus less.[53] During that period, living in a poorly performing state versus a better-performing state did feel tantamount to living in a different country, with a significantly higher risk attached.

Should a particularly deadly variant drive a surge today, we might expect less divergent outcomes because we see less divergent behavioral choices and a national choice to unilaterally disarm against the virus that causes COVID. The United States is hardly alone in adopting that stance; and we are finding that many Americans have become inured to the higher risk of illness, disability, and death than they faced pre-COVID. Perhaps it is instructive to remember that a century of rapidly lengthening lifespans and lower health risks actually stands out as a brief exception to millennia of human experience as the easy prey of infectious disease. Perhaps a measure of fatalism is knit into our evolutionary biology, even though we have now developed tools that can empower us against infectious disease should we choose to invest in them and use them.

The second metric that Bollyky, Turilli, and Castro employed to judge the performance of states during the pandemic was a combined score for economic and educational performance. On that metric (which relied on states' gross GDP and fourth graders' test scores), the top-performing states' leadership skewed Republican rather than Democratic. Only Illinois, Kansas, Kentucky, Rhode Island, Washington, and Wisconsin, among states with Democratic governors, even made it into the top half. Levels of concern about infection — less concern in the case of Republican-leaning states and more in the case of Democratic leaning ones — seem to have been a determining factor even more important than mandates or a lack of them were.[54]

It behooves policy makers and the public to understand, however, that there are multiple ways to lessen levels of a population's concern about illness, disability, and death during a pandemic. One way was the way President Trump chose to do it, by downplaying a real threat when he knew that threat was serious.[55] Lowering the level of fear worked to spur many people to revert to familiar behaviors that boosted the economy, even at risk of their health. Many people could also be forced back to work by economic necessity, and policy makers determined that keeping that necessity in place would drive many low-wage essential workers back to their jobs despite the risks they were forced to incur.

But there has always been another way to alleviate concern, and that is to make workplaces safer and schools safer and to provide people the information they need to make decisions about their own risk. Making it safer for people to do the things they need to do and the things they want to do dials down the deterrent to economic activity that fear constitutes. People want to work. People do not want to cook at home on an everlasting and incessant basis. People want to go to the dentist safely and access healthcare safely and send their children to school safely. Ensuring that shared air is not laden with viruses is one obvious way to help, reducing exposure to COVID and its cousins, SARS and MERS; influenza; human rhinovirus; and RSV — all afflictions most of us would be happy to do without.[56]

The United States and other countries around the world have faced bracing lessons in the dynamics that govern the seesaw of societal and political support for pandemic response and mitigation. Both the most constructive and the most politically expedient way to ride that seesaw would be to bring it into balance using win-win approaches for all stakeholders. To make sometimes necessary mitigations less jarring and painful, it pays to reduce the "ask" those mitigations make of people insofar as that is possible.

Optimal air filtration and ventilation of public spaces, for example, go a long way in that direction and make spaces safer for people who are more vulnerable, as a real-world air filtration "road test" in a British hospital's makeshift COVID ward found. With an adequately capable HEPA filtration device in place, the hospital found no detectable virus in the air. If the device was turned off for a time, infectious levels of SARS-CoV-2 were detected again.[57] In the U.S., where any masking requirement is likely to precipitate vociferous protests in many places, cleaning the air is a win-win because it asks nothing of those who breathe and yet it lowers risk significantly for everyone, including not only those intent on "face freedom" as a human right but also those whose health status or age makes them particularly vulnerable to COVID. The choices of a few (or the vast majority) to remain unmasked will be far less likely to dictate outcomes for others.

Just as important, ongoing adequately funded surveillance pinpoints when measures may need to be taken in local communities because of rising cases and risk, and surveillance also indicates when they can be dialed back. In a virulent pandemic, good local surveillance can shorten the time that more burdensome mitigations are in place because it indicates when infections have dropped to the point that it is reasonably safe to relax precautions.

Vaccines tweaked to protect against new variants and made available in a timely manner can enable people to better protect themselves against severe illness, disability, or death, all outcomes that were ongoing in 2023 when a late summer surge outpaced the race to produce updated COVID boosters in the United States. As the vaccines were approved and became available in September of that year, a Reuters/ Ipsos poll found that some 30% of Americans still considered them dangerous (a testament to the persuasive power of misinformation and disinformation as opposed to the actual level of risk, which is very, very small); and willingness to roll up a sleeve for shots still varied by political orientation. While only 34% of Republicans planned to get a COVID booster, 77% of Democrats did.[58] That figure constitutes more than an opinion poll to shrug off with an "Oh well"; it is a predictor of which populations will experience relatively heavier burdens of serious disease, death, and long-term health impacts — all outcomes that the boosters make significantly less likely. And it has implications for the size of the labor force.

Governance, whether effective or ineffective, dramatically impacted every country's health and economic outcomes during COVID-19. With the future in mind, we have distilled observations about what strategies make for effective versus ineffective pandemic governance. These are not political in nature because, as we have seen, both U.S. political parties are quite capable of choosing, for expediency's sake, strategies that afford a pandemic pathogen more opportunities to infect, to disrupt, to drive up costs, and to whittle the size of the labor force that is well enough to work. The first column provides a template for governance that limits and manages pandemic shocks such that they are less likely to knock nations to their knees; in other words, governance that buffers citizens, essential systems, and economies against the worst damage that a pandemic pathogen can do. The second column extrapolates and observes governance strategies (or lapses) that fail to optimally protect. The table represents a distillation of insights drawn most heavily, though not exclusively, from the vast expertise of the COVID Crisis Group in their book, *Lessons from the Covid War*, which we highly recommend.[59]

Effective Pandemic Governance vs. Ineffective Pandemic Governance

Governance that leads to optimal outcomes	Governance that leads to poor outcomes
Recognizes that infectious diseases can threaten national security as surely as human enemies can.	Fails to recognize the gravity of potential pandemic threats.
Keeps infectious disease surveillance systems in place and in use. These incorporate every jurisdiction and facilitate the gathering of statewide and nationwide anonymized data. Uses timely data to respond effectively to outbreaks and to inform decisions at local and regional levels.	Scrambles to create surveillance systems on the fly and then neglects them when an emergency is perceived to be over. Fails to systematically collect anonymized health data on a national level from every jurisdiction. Loses opportunities to learn and to act in a timely manner. Prefers flying blind to understanding prevalence and impacts.
Engages in international cooperation and information sharing.	Eschews international cooperation and information sharing.
Correctly identifies the pathogen as a primary adversary that must be countered.	Targets political adversaries while neglecting to effectively lead the battle against a pathogen that infects and kills.
Puts the national pandemic response and the production of essentials on war footing.	Fails to recognize that a war against a pathogen requires a stance and response just as a war against a human enemy would.

Governance that leads to optimal outcomes	Governance that leads to poor outcomes
Coordinates a national response in partnership with states/regions/provinces.	Engenders conflict, politicization, and competition for resources by abdicating a national leadership role in pandemic response.
Forges public/private partnerships and learns from what works, creating templates for future collaborations. Owns "the problems" of pandemic governance while partnering with the private sector in solving them.	Fails to create effective public/private partnerships or hands "the problem" over to the private sector to solve, abdicating crucial governance roles and thus failing to cultivate know-how and the human infrastructure of effective governmental pandemic response.
Maintains preparedness and "operational readiness" in terms of resources, capacity, staff, and expertise. Conducts drills, rather than merely creating and pointing to plans.	Neglects preparedness efforts. Plans do not reflect operational readiness — a stockpile of necessary supplies for ready response, clarity with regard to responsibilities and roles and process, adequate expertise in place, and drill and practice.
Invests in vaccine research and technologies that ensure rapid development of effective vaccines when a new pathogen arises. (The COVID Crisis Group suggests "vaccine libraries," 263.)	Funds vaccine research on a reactive rather than proactive basis.

Governance that leads to optimal outcomes	Governance that leads to poor outcomes
Has functioning community health systems in place so that people are connected with healthcare, use it, and have trusted relationships with healthcare providers.	Maintains a system in which uninsured and underinsured citizens have limited connections with the healthcare system. (In the U.S., 40% avoiding accessing healthcare because of cost.)
Implements a whole-of-government initiative to support, retain, grow, and protect the nation's vital healthcare workforce, recognizing that an effective healthcare system is a matter of national and economic security.	Fails to act as an overworked and undervalued healthcare labor force continues to hemorrhage workers, leaving everyone who needs medical care at greater risk.
Implements policy and guidelines designed to ensure that citizens, including the immunocompromised and ill, can access healthcare safely, using effective infection control strategies in healthcare settings on an ongoing basis. Policy supports widespread and ongoing availability of telemedicine.	Fails to ensure that the ill and/or immunocompromised can access healthcare safely. Provides guidance and infection-control standards that do not provide optimal real-world protection against infection in healthcare settings.
Relies on best available information from authoritative sources as it emerges.	Relies on questionable information from questionable sources, misinformation, disinformation, outdated information, or wishful thinking.

Governance that leads to optimal outcomes	Governance that leads to poor outcomes
Equips citizens to recognize disinformation and effectively communicates reliable information.	Fails to effectively counter misinformation and disinformation.
Provides practical, timely guidance for citizens, schools, and healthcare providers.	Practical guidance may come late and be inadequate to protect. It may fail to acknowledge the implications of emerging data in a timely manner.
Governs and surveilles risky biological research to minimize risk.	Maintains lax policy and oversight with regard to risky biological research.
Coordinates efforts of jurisdictions to create a "central nervous system" for tracking, sharing, and analyzing data, and for providing guidance. Maintains both a big, accurate picture at a national level and the "zoomable" detail needed for local decision-making. (COVID Crisis Group, 267.)	Data is siloed and fragmented in various jurisdictions, with incomplete and/or inaccurate or delayed reporting so that no big, clear picture is available at a national level. Data may cease to be collected when it is still relevant.
Mitigates extreme inequalities to safeguard the wellbeing of all members of a society and the functioning of the economy, which relies on essential workers.	Neglects or even structurally contributes to extreme inequalities, such that some groups (essential workers earning low wages, working in unprotected conditions, and living in crowded housing, for instance) remain extremely vulnerable during a pandemic emergency.

Governance that leads to optimal outcomes	Governance that leads to poor outcomes
Learns the enemy — the pandemic pathogen — swiftly and creates guidance, policy, incentives, and financial support for implementing mitigations that impede the transmission of pandemic pathogens in schools, workplaces, healthcare settings, and other public spaces. Thereby effectively minimizes the degree to which a pandemic pathogen disrupts lives, educations, economic activity, and the long-term capacity of the labor force.	Makes one of two errors, both of which reflect a failure to learn and to act effectively: (1) "Locks down" economic activity and disrupts education for an extended period without doing the "homework" required to reopen with minimized risk, both impairing an economy and ensuring a surge of disease when a lockdown cannot be maintained. This error ensures an extended economic shock and a disease shock. (2) Downplays risk and mandates "normality" without acting effectively to reduce risk and make workplaces, schools, healthcare settings, and other public spaces safe, resulting in more infections, disability, and death, which may impact the labor force over decades.

Table 18.1 Effective Pandemic Governance vs. Ineffective Pandemic Governance

Around the world, a number of countries managed to keep their economies functioning even as they curbed infections and deaths. Taiwan and South Korea are examples, taking GDP hits of only -0.6% and -3.0% respectively in the second quarter of 2020 (as compared with the U.S.'s -9.5% that quarter), with their comparatively strong performance in the recovery period boosted by chip demand and interest in AI. It is that combination of economic and health outcomes that marks effective pandemic governance and reflects a cohesive societal response.

Countries that heed the lessons writ large by COVID-19 will minimize the continuing erosion of human health and labor force capacity that emerging COVID variants impose going forward. Countries that do not heed those lessons will continue to see deaths and cases of disability mount. They will be poorly prepared for future pandemics, and the pandemic shocks they endure will be more severe, along with the longer-term economic implications of those shocks.

It seems hard now for many Americans to grasp the scope of the loss of life that COVID has caused in the U.S. Frontline healthcare workers shoulder traumatic memories of caring for the sick and dying, as do those who dealt with the many dead. Those whose loved ones died have weathered enormous personal loss. But during the COVID pandemic, Americans did not see death wagons come around to pick up bodies from homes where people had died, as happened in past pandemics. They did not see victims who fell dead in the street from septicemic plague, as happened during the Black Death, or from a cytokine storm precipitated by H1N1 influenza, as happened a century ago. Life is different now. Though the number of pandemic deaths at home ticked upward, people's lives mostly slipped away in hospitals. Funerals were, for a time, small, family-only affairs. Morgue trucks, when they were needed, were nondescript and parked out back, behind city hospitals. Nursing homes closed, and when they opened again to visitors, familiar faces were missing, and sections of facilities stood empty. There is much that many people did not witness, and we all have great difficulty imagining numbers as individual lives lost.

In the United States, visitors to Washington, DC, see multiple monuments dedicated to U.S. soldiers who have died in wars fought over the nation's history. The Vietnam Memorial, inscribed with the names of more than 58,000 dead, stretches 493 feet and 6 inches. If a memorial of the same design were constructed to remember all Americans who have died of COVID, as tallied by the John Hopkins Coronavirus dashboard until it closed down on March 10, 2023, and if that memorial began alongside where the Vietnam Memorial stands at an easy walking distance from the Lincoln Memorial, the nation's COVID-19 Memorial Wall would stretch from the Vietnam War Memorial past Constitution Gardens, the World War II Memorial, and the Washington Monument. It would not stop there. It would extend far down the National Mall, past the Museum of African American History, the Museum of American History, and the Museum of Natural History on the left and the Smithsonian and the National Air and Space Museum on the right, all the way to 4th Street, a block away from Union Square and the grounds of the United States Capitol. And even there, the memorial would not be finished, because the COVID death toll continues to rise. There would be several feet of wall to add every week to hold hundreds of new names. As total U.S. deaths approached 1.2 million, a July 8, 2024, post from BNO News reminds us of the reality four years into the pandemic: "This marks the 225th week in a row with more than 400 new COVID deaths in the U.S."[60] Perhaps if this memorial wall were a physical reality rather than merely a mental exercise in grasping the scope of our COVID losses, and perhaps if our lawmakers had to walk past its black, mirror-like expanse every day into the Capitol Building, governance defending the nation's people and its economic interests against pandemic pathogens might be more in keeping with the scope of the threat.

---

1. "News Scan for Dec 31, 2019," *CIDRAP*, December 31, 2019, https://www.cidrap.umn.edu/COVID-19/news-scan-dec-31-2019; Muyi Xiao, Isabelle Qian, Tracy Wen Liu, and Chris Buckley, "How a Chinese Doctor Who Warned of COVID-19 Spent His Final Days," *New York Times,* October 6, 2022, https://www.nytimes.com/2022/10/06/world/asia/COVID-china-doctor-li-wenliang.html.

2. "Global Health Security Index: Building Collective Action and Accountability," *Nuclear Threat Initiative*, Johns Hopkins Bloomberg School of Public Health, October 2019, https://www.ghsindex.org/wp-content/uploads/2019/10/2019-Global-Health-Security-Index.pdf.

3. Ian Bremmer, "The Best Global Responses to the COVID-19 Pandemic, 1 Year Later," *TIME*, updated February 23, 2021, originally published June 12, 2020, https://time.

com/5851633/best-global-responses-COVID-19/; Cynthia Cox and Krutika Amin, "COVID-19 is the Number One Cause of Death in the U.S. in Early 2021," KFF, February 22, 2021, https://www.kff.org/coronavirus-COVID-19/issue-brief/COVID-19-is-the-number-one-cause-of-death-in-the-u-s-in-early-2021/.

4. "COVID-19 Dashboard," Johns Hopkins Coronavirus Resource Center, Johns Hopkins University Medicine, March 10, 2023, https://coronavirus.jhu.edu/map.html.

5. "Cases and Mortality by Country, Johns Hopkins Coronavirus Resource Center, https://coronavirus.jhu.edu/data/mortality.

6. Jennifer Tolbert, Patrick Drake, and Anthony Damico, "Key Facts about the Uninsured Population," KFF, December 19, 2022, https://www.kff.org/uninsured/issue-brief/key-facts-about-the-uninsured-population/.

7. Megan Brenan, "Record High in U.S. Put Off Medical Care Due to Cost in 2022," GALLUP, January 17, 2023, https://news.gallup.com/poll/468053/record-high-put-off-medical-care-due-cost-2022.aspx.

8. Selena Simmons-Duffin, "Texas Medicaid dropped more than 500,000 enrollees in one month," Shots: Healthcare News from NPR, NPR, updated August 3, 2023, https://www.npr.org/sections/health-shots/2023/08/03/1191416312/texas-medicaid-drops-500k-enrollees-rate-of-82-percent.

9. Max Cohen, "Georgia governor sues to stop Atlanta mask mandate," Politico, July 17, 2020, https://www.politico.com/news/2020/07/16/georgia-mayors-brian-kemp-face-masks-366497.

10. Kevin Breuninger and Spencer Kimball, "Supreme Court blocks Biden COVID vaccine mandate for businesses, allows health-care worker rule," CNBC, January 13, 2022, https://www.cnbc.com/2022/01/13/supreme-court-ruling-biden-COVID-vaccine-mandates.html.

11. COVID Crisis Group, Lessons from the COVID War: An Investigative Report (New York: Public Affairs, 2023), 58–59.

12. Ed Pilkington and Tom McCarthy, "The missing six weeks: how Trump failed the biggest test of his life," The Guardian, March 28, 2020, https://www.theguardian.com/us-news/2020/mar/28/trump-coronavirus-politics-us-health-disaster.

13. Peter Whoriskey and Neena Satija, "How U.S. coronavirus testing stalled: Flawed tests, red tape and resistance to using the millions of tests produced by the WHO," Washington Post, March 16, 2020, https://www.washingtonpost.com/business/2020/03/16/cdc-who-coronavirus-tests/.

14. "Lab Advisory: FDA Guidance to Develop Novel Molecular Diagnostic Tests for SARS-CoV-2," Centers for Disease Control and Prevention, March 2, 2020, https://www.cdc.gov/locs/2020/fda_guidance_to_develop_novel_molecular_diagnostic_tests_for_sars-cov-2.html.

15. Michael Lewis, The Premonition: A Pandemic Story (New York: W.W. Norton, 2021), 252. Kindle Edition.

16. COVID Crisis Group, Lessons from the COVID War, 112–113.

17. Jon Swaine, Robert O'Harrow Jr., and Aaron C. Davis, "Before pandemic, Trump's stockpile chief put focus on biodefense. An old client benefited," Washington Post, May 4, 2020, https://www.washingtonpost.com/investigations/before-pandemic-trumps-stockpile-chief-put-focus-on-biodefense-an-old-client-benefited/2020/05/04/d3c2b010-84dd-11ea-878a-86477a724bdb_story.html.

18. COVID Crisis Group, *Lessons from the COVID War,* 112.

19. "U.S. Bioterrorism Threats," C-SPAN, October 18, 2011, https://www.c-span.org/video/?302149-1/us-bioterrorism-threats.

20. Lena Sun, "CDC to cut by 80 percent efforts to prevent global disease outbreak," *Washington Post,* February 1, 2018, https://www.washingtonpost.com/news/to-your-health/wp/2018/02/01/cdc-to-cut-by-80-percent-efforts-to-prevent-global-disease-outbreak/.

21. COVID Crisis Group, *Lessons from the COVID War,* 27.

22. Michael Penn, "Statistics Say Large Pandemics Are More Likely Than We Thought," Duke Global Health Institute, August 23, 2021, https://globalhealth.duke.edu/news/statistics-say-large-pandemics-are-more-likely-we-thought; Marco Marani, Gabriel G. Katul, William K. Pan, and Anthony J. Parolar, "Intensity and frequency of extreme novel epidemics," *PNAS* 118, no. 35 (August 2021): e2105482118, https://www.pnas.org/doi/10.1073/pnas.2105482118.

23. Monika Evstatieva, "U.S. Companies Shifted To Make N95 Respirators During COVID. Now, They're Struggling," Morning Edition, NPR, June 25, 2021, https://www.npr.org/2021/06/25/1009858893/u-s-companies-shifted-to-make-n95-respirators-during-COVID-now-theyre-struggling.

24. Jane Spencer and Christina Jewett, "12 Months of Trauma: More Than 3,600 U.S. Health Workers Died in COVID's First Year," Lost on the Frontline, KFF Health News, April 8, 2021, https://kffhealthnews.org/news/article/us-health-workers-deaths-COVID-lost-on-the-frontline/.

25. Ariana Eunjung Cha and Laurie McGinley, "Who gets a shot at life if hospitals run short of ventilators?" *Washington Post,* April 7, 2020, https://www.washingtonpost.com/health/2020/04/07/ventilators-rationing-coronavirus-hospitals/.

26. David Welna, "Trump Invokes A Cold War Relic, The Defense Production Act, For Coronavirus Shortages," NPR, March 18, 2020, https://www.npr.org/2020/03/18/818069722/trump-invokes-a-cold-war-relic-the-defense-production-act-for-coronavirus-shorta.

27. Kristen Korosec, "GM, Ford wrap up ventilator production and shift back to auto business," *TechCrunch*, September 1, 2020, https://techcrunch.com/2020/09/01/gm-ford-wrap-up-ventilator-production-and-shift-back-to-auto-business/.

28. Tom Inglesby and J. Stephen Morrison, "Building the CDC the Country Needs," CSIS Commission on Strengthening America's Health Security, Center for Strategic and International Studies, January 2023, https://csis-website-prod.s3.amazonaws.com/s3fs-public/publication/230112_Morrison_Building_CDC.pdf.

29. Inglesby and Morrison, "Building the CDC the Country Needs," 3.

30. Emily Peck, "The missing workers who are never coming back," Axios, December 16, 2022, https://www.axios.com/2022/12/16/the-missing-workers-who-are-never-coming-back.

31. Inglesby and Morrison, "Building the CDC the Country Needs ," 26.

32. Ximena Bustillo and Tamara Keith, "Debt limit deal claws back unspent COVID relief money," NPR, May 31, 2023, https://www.npr.org/2023/05/31/1178996725/debt-ceiling-deal-unspent-COVID-relief-money-democrats-republicans.

33. COVID Crisis Group, *Lessons from the COVID War: An Investigative Report,* New York: PublicAffairs, Hachette Book Group, 2023, 164–166. Kindle Edition

34. Martin Kulldorff, Sunetra Gupta, and Jay Battacharya, "Great Barrington Declaration," October 5, 2020, https://gbdeclaration.org.

35. COVID Crisis Group, *Lessons from the COVID War* , 128–136.

36. "A Timeline of COVID-19 Developments in 2020," *AJMC*, Jan 1, 2021, https://www.ajmc.com/view/a-timeline-of-COVID19-developments-in-2020.

37. "A Timeline of COVID-19 Vaccine Developments in 2021," *AJMC*, June 3, 2021, https://www.ajmc.com/view/a-timeline-of-COVID-19-vaccine-developments-in-2021.

38. Ashley Kirzinger, Audrey Kearney, Liz Hamel, and Mollyann Brodie, "KFF COVID-19 Vaccine Monitor: The Increasing Importance of Partisanship in Predicting COVID-19 Vaccination Status," KFF, Nov. 16, 2021, https://www.kff.org/coronavirus-COVID-19/poll-finding/importance-of-partisanship-predicting-vaccination-status/.

39. Fernanda Ferreira, Ed., "Evidence suggests that political partisanship is associated with higher COVID-19 mortality rates among Republicans compared to Democrats," *Health Feedback*, Nov. 5, 2022, https://healthfeedback.org/claimreview/evidence-suggests-political-partisanship-associated-with-higher-COVID-19-mortality-rates-among-republicans-compared-to-democrats/; Wallace, Jacob, Goldsmith-Pinkham, Jacob and Schwartz, Jason. 2022. "Excess Death Rates for Republicans and Democrats During the COVID-19 Pandemic." Working Paper 30512, National Bureau of Economic Research, https://www.nber.org/papers/w30512.

40. Jingjing Gao and Benjamin J. Radford, "Death by political party: The relationship between COVID-19 deaths and political party affiliation in the United States," *World Medical & Health Policy* 13, no. 2 (May 2021): 224–249, reprinted by NIH, https://www.ncbi.nlm.nih.gov/pmc/articles/PMC8242603/.

41. "Army rescinds COVID-19 vaccination requirements," U.S. Army Public Affairs, February 24, 2023, https://www.army.mil/article/264274/army_rescinds_COVID_19_vaccination_requirements.

42. Hannah Mitchell, "12 states banning COVID-19 vaccine mandates & how they affect healthcare workers," Becker's Hospital Review, October 12, 2021, https://www.beckershospitalreview.com/workforce/11-states-banning-COVID-19-vaccine-mandates-how-it-affects-healthcare-workers.html; Jenni Fink, "Mandating Masks Is Banned in These States Despite Updated CDC Guidance," *Newsweek*, July 28, 2021, https://www.newsweek.com/mandating-masks-banned-these-states-despite-updated-cdc-guidance-1613976.

43. "CDC's Bridge Access Program," Centers for Disease Control and Prevention, last accessed June 11, 2024, https://www.cdc.gov/vaccines/programs/bridge/index.html.

44. Ximena Bustillo and Tamara Keith, "Debt limit deal claws back unspent COVID relief money," NPR, May 31, 2023, https://www.npr.org/2023/05/31/1178996725/debt-ceiling-deal-unspent-COVID-relief-money-democrats-republicans.

45. Katelyn Jetelina, "BA.2.86 update," Your Local Epidemiologist, September 5, 2023, https://yourlocalepidemiologist.substack.com/p/ba286-update.

46. Maja Pašović, Katherine Leach-Kemon, Christopher Troeger, Theo Vos, and Rafael Lozano, "Countries Hit Hardest by COVID-19," Think Global Health, November 17, 2021, https://www.thinkglobalhealth.org/article/countries-hit-hardest-COVID-19.

47. COVID Crisis Group, *Lessons from the COVID War,* 14–15.

48. COVID Crisis Group, *Lessons from the COVID War,* 171–172.

49. Thomas J. Bollyky, Isabella Turilli, and Emma Castro, "Judging How U.S. States Performed in the COVID-19 Pandemic Depends on the Metric," Council on Foreign Relations Global Health Program, July 13, 2023, https://www.cfr.org/article/judging-how-us-states-performed-COVID-19-pandemic-depends-metric#chapter-title-0-2.

50. Bollyky, et al., "Judging."

51. Bollyky, et al., "Judging."

52. Bollyky, et al., "Judging."

53. Bollyky, et al., "Judging."

54. Bollyky, et al., "Judging."

55. Dareh Gregorian, "Trump told Bob Woodward he knew in February that COVID-19 was 'deadly stuff' but wanted to 'play it down,'" NBC News, Sept. 9, 2020, https://www.nbcnews.com/politics/donald-trump/trump-told-bob-woodward-he-knew-february-COVID-19-was-n1239658.

56. Chia C. Wang, Kimberly A. Prather, Josué Sznitman, Jose L. Jimenez, Seema S. Lakdawala, Zeynep Tufekci, Linsey C. Marr, "Airborne transmission of respiratory viruses," *Science* 373, no. 6558 (August 2021), https://www.science.org/doi/10.1126/science.abd9149.

57. "Air filter significantly reduces presence of airborne SARS-CoV-2 in COVID-19 wards," *Research News*, University of Cambridge, November 16, 2021, https://www.cam.ac.uk/research/news/air-filter-significantly-reduces-presence-of-airborne-sars-cov-2-in-COVID-19-wards.

58. Ahmed Aboulenein and Jason Lange, "Half of Americans interested in getting updated COVID shot, Reuters/Ipsos poll shows," Reuters, September 15, 2023, https://www.reuters.com/world/us/half-americans-interested-getting-updated-COVID-shot-reutersipsos-poll-2023-09-15/.

59. As we developed this table, we began by capturing insights from the COVID Crisis Group, *Lessons from the COVID War,* especially but not exclusively the "Strategic Lessons" portion of Chapter 11, "America the Competent?" Other sources included Tom Inglesby and J. Stephen Morrison, "Building the CDC the Country Needs," and the OECD's "First lessons from government evaluations of COVID-19 responses: A synthesis," OECD, January 21, 2022, https://www.oecd-ilibrary.org/governance/first-lessons-from-government-evaluations-of-covid-19-responses-a-synthesis_483507d6-en. Insights from reading other works, such as Michael Lewis's *Premonition,* from listening to numerous podcasts from Michael Osterholm and other experts, following the news, and engaging in conversations over the first three years of the pandemic were no doubt also swirling around in our heads along with our own observations and contributed to our synthesis here.

60. "U.S. COVID update (July 7): Cases rise for 5th week in a row," BNO News, July 7, 2024, https://bnonews.com/index.php/2024/07/us-covid-update-july-7/

Chapter 19

Pandemic Lesson 7:
Pandemics Impact Governance

Just as governance and politics shape the course of pandemics, pandemics drive political change. A pandemic is not a happy-making time in any society. Wherever wedges in societies exist, pandemics drive those wedges deeper.[1] Divisions and discontent have political ramifications. When death rates are high and the level of public concern is high, there is greater support for public health mitigations, as there was early in 2020. Strong leadership that protects lives garners support. On the other hand, the perceived failure of a government and its leaders to competently protect human lives and human health will drive political change.

In a working paper published by the nonpartisan Peterson Institute for International Economics, Marcus Noland and Eva Yiwen Zhang calculated the impact that the pandemic and the Trump administration's handling of it had on the outcome of the 2020 U.S. presidential election. They found that, had there been no pandemic, Trump would have won. Had the pandemic's impact been 30% less severe in the U.S., Joe Biden would have won the popular vote, but Trump would have won the electoral vote because Arizona, Georgia, Pennsylvania, and Wisconsin would have flipped to Trump. Had the pandemic's impact been 20% less severe in the U.S., the election would have ended in an electoral tie, throwing the election into the House of Representatives.[2] In 2021, in the days before Joe Biden was inaugurated as America's 46th president, Trump's own chief pollster, Tony Fabrizio, compiled a post-election analysis based on exit polling in 10 key states. Fabrizio found that Trump suffered two liabilities — first, the perception that he was less than honest and trustworthy and, second, the perception that he had bungled the response to the pandemic.[3]

In Brazil, President Jair Bolsonaro's widely condemned pandemic leadership and the country's heavy COVID death toll likewise factored into that politician's defeat. Disapproval of Bolsonaro's handling of the pandemic was so intense that, in October of 2021, ahead of the 2022 election, a Brazilian Senate committee recommended that Bolsonaro be charged with crimes against humanity because of the heavy loss of life that resulted from his handling of the pandemic, though charges were later withdrawn.[4]

But there is a tipping point, too, as death rates and hospitalization rates subside and people become accustomed to a new risk landscape (or as many are successfully led to underestimate an actual threat). Pandemic fatigue sets in. Think of a seesaw. When the threat of death and severe disease loom heavy and large, closures and wearing masks seem a burden smaller than fear and grief, so more people are willing to go along with public health mitigations that minimize spread of a pathogen and save lives. The seesaw (or balance) tips hard to preserve life, even though the measures are jarring. Governance that results in high mortality and suffering will lose support.

Then, as months pass and circumstances change (a lull happens; a vaccine is developed and distributed; treatments that work are found), the onerous burden of supervising children's education at home, the psychological price and the learning losses, the ongoing disruption of ordinary life and work, and even the minor hassle of masking all loom larger and larger in comparison to the health risk. The longer mitigations disrupt the familiar, the more burdensome they feel to many. There is a tipping point, and the seesaw shifts.

In the case of the U.S., the seesaw received an extra push by a president who minimized a threat he knew was real and by misinformation and disinformation. Pandemic fatigue was genuine, but it was also cultivated and amplified, in part to reduce fear and spur a return to behaviors that would boost the economy whether or not the country had done its homework to make those behaviors safer again.

Whereas before, governance that failed to protect lives lost support, at the tipping point, governance that maintains stringent measures sees support erode. People recalculate priorities, and they want their lives back. In the U.S., where individual liberty is celebrated even at the expense of collective good, "freedom" and "rights" become rallying cries. Many conclude that politicians and public health officials are overreaching and must be replaced or otherwise disempowered. Call it pandemic fatigue or call it reactance — when enough voters feel it keenly, many politicians shift policy rather than ensuring that they will lose the next election.

The calculations that drive perceptions and votes differ, of course, on an individual basis. But if a shift in perspectives is broad enough, strong leadership in the fight against a pathogen loses support. Bills to fund the fight against disease come to face strong opposition. The seesaw of national priorities tips hard and bangs into the ground. That is where U.S. governance is as this book is written. The result is not a balanced, constructive approach to solving the pandemic-related problems of evolving variants, adequate surveillance, funding for vaccines and treatments, and their accessibility for all.

The tipping point is assuredly a political one, and it is best captured in the memo from Impact Research that changed the COVID leadership strategy of the Biden administration. Leadership became followship; and, in part, what policy began to reflect was public opinion shaped by misinformation and disinformation.[5] Was this course —

near unilateral disarmament against the virus that causes COVID-19 — the best one? We do not expect it to stand the test of time. As the CDC's HICPAC committee proposed accepting as guidance the fantasy that (cheaper) surgical masks can provide the same significant protection that N95s do in healthcare settings, Gregg Gonsalves, an epidemiologist and associate professor at the Yale School of Public Health, wrote in response:

> The Biden administration has made a political choice — not a scientific or public health one — to downgrade the national response to COVID-19. Included in this is the reticence or outright avoidance of mentioning masking even as cases rise in the U.S. The CDC director, in talking about this late increase in COVID cases, bends over backward to mention hand-washing, but not N95s. Without question, N95s offer individuals protection against infection, and leaving out that fact is a disservice and an abdication of duty.[6]

In 2024 a visitor to the CDC website during the late summer COVID surge would find the topic of COVID-19 relegated to the listing of health topics from A–Z. The CDC lists, in addition to the perennial advice to wash our hands, a recommendation to "Take steps for cleaner air," which is hyperlinked to another page that recommends taking measures to improve ventilation and air filtration indoors to the tune of five air exchanges per hour. Near the bottom of the COVID-19 page, under "Additional Prevention Strategies," the CDC notes that "Wearing a mask and putting distance between yourself and others can help lower the risk of COVID-19 transmission." The word *mask* is hyperlinked to a page on masks that features a photo of a man wearing a procedural mask rather than a far more effective N-95 respirator, though, several paragraphs in, the relative effectiveness of various types of masks is discussed. Scientifically valid information about how people can protect themselves and those they love was by this time reflected in CDC guidance, but website architecture did not foreground the information even during a time when many Americans were falling ill with COVID yet again, and the country watched a COVID-positive President Biden board Air Force One unmasked. The message deemed politically acceptable was dual: "COVID is still here, but we are over COVID."

In 2021 and 2022, opposition to public health measures found its way into a surge of legislation at the state level, aimed at curbing the authority of public health officials and governors. These bills trimmed emergency powers at the state or local level, placed limits on how long public health emergencies can last, reined in governors' powers to mandate mitigations (as in Kentucky, Michigan, and Ohio), outlawed or limited closures of businesses, and banned mask and vaccine mandates. Such legislation depended heavily on the premise that state governments possess primary authority over public health policy, ensuring that questions of where local public health authority ends and state authority begins, and of where state authority ends and federal authority begins, will be litigated in the courts for some time to come. The fact is, however, that maintaining biosecurity against any highly pathogenic pandemic will always be a matter of national and economic security.[7]

Ironically, responses to the COVID-19 pandemic have actually weakened the capacity of the United States to defend itself against infectious disease threats in the future. Given laws that restrict public health measures designed to limit dire consequences, the risk of devastating outcomes with medium- and long-term economic implications from pandemic shocks rises sharply.

At all levels of governance, leaders face enormous challenges and almost certain repercussions when pandemics occur. Leadership is shaped by discontent, even in undemocratic countries with strong central governments. The world watched that happen even in China, as Xi Jinping's doomed "zero COVID" policy was finally abandoned in the face of political unrest. Xi's hand was forced, and the policy was dropped despite the fact that China had not yet vaccinated vast swathes of its population, despite the time it had bought in which to get that done.

Even success on one front can become a political liability on the other, as New Zealand Prime Minister Jacinda Arden found when fatigue with pandemic restrictions, and especially with vaccine mandates, met with enough resistance that Arden became a target for discontent. Once widely praised for New Zealand's coronavirus response, which was estimated in 2020 to have saved 80,000 lives, Arden chose in early 2023 not to seek reelection. She noted, "I know what this job takes, and I know that I no longer have enough in the tank to do it justice. It is that simple." Reflecting on the crises that unfolded during her six years in office, she observed,

> It's one thing to lead your country in peace times, it's another to lead them through crisis. There's a greater weight of responsibility, a greater vulnerability amongst the people, and so in many ways, I think that will be what sticks with me. I had the privilege of being alongside New Zealand during crisis, and they placed their faith in me.[8]

The COVID pandemic made many leaders at all levels of governance political targets for change. As ever, pandemic shocks have a way of spurring changes in governance, whether for better or for worse.

---

1.   Kat Devlin, Moira Fagan, and Aidan Connaughton, "People in Advanced Economies Say Their Society Is More Divided Than Before Pandemic," Pew Research, June 23, 2021,

https://www.pewresearch.org/global/2021/06/23/people-in-advanced-economies-say-their-society-is-more-divided-than-before-pandemic/.

2.   Noland, Marcus and Zhang (2021), "COVID-19 and the 2020 U.S. presidential election: Did the pandemic cost Donald Trump reelection?" Working Paper 21-3, Peterson Institute for International Economics, https://www.piie.com/publications/working-papers/COVID-19-and-2020-us-presidential-election-did-pandemic-cost-donald.

3.   Alex Isenstadt, "Trump pollster's campaign autopsy paints damning picture of defeat," POLITICO, February 1, 2021, https://www.politico.com/news/2021/02/01/trump-campaign-autopsy-paints-damning-picture-of-defeat-464636.

4.   "Brazil senators recommend President Jair Bolsonaro face charges over COVID," CNBC, October 26, 2021, https://www.cnbc.com/2021/10/27/brazil-senators-recommend-jair-bolsonaro-face-charges-over-COVID.html.

5.   Molly Murphy and Brian Stryker, "Taking the Win over COVID-19," IMPACT Research, February 24, 2022, posted at Punchbowl News, https://punchbowl.news/wp-content/uploads/IMPACT-COVID-positioning-strategy-memo.pdf.

6.   Judy Stone, "Where Have All the Masks Gone?" *Forbes*, September 7, 2023, https://www.forbes.com/sites/judystone/2023/09/07/where-have-all-the-masks-gone/.

7.   James G. Hodge, "COVID-19's Repercussions on Public Health Policy and Law in the United States," Think Global Health, May 3, 2022, https://www.thinkglobalhealth.org/article/COVID-19s-repercussions-public-health-policy-and-law-united-states.

8.   Nick Perry, "New Zealand's Jacinda Ardern, an icon to many, to step down," AP News, January 19, 2023, https://apnews.com/article/politics-new-zealand-government-COVID-jacinda-ardern-0e6d8eedd96f94aab07eeb0c37164591.

Chapter 20

Pandemic Lesson 8:
A Pandemic Is a Learning Opportunity Either Squandered or Seized

With the COVID pandemic, we saw a political debate around what mattered most — protecting people against infection or protecting the economy. On the one hand, disease, disability, and death claimed loved ones' lives and eroded human capital. We learned how to measure the "excess deaths" and the COVID disabled in the workforce. On the other hand, it became clear that our complex and globally interdependent economy could not cease functioning. Lives and the means to live them depend on its functioning.

There was a middle way; however, we failed to realize it. We could have overhauled ventilation and air filtration in all public spaces, especially all schools. We could have chosen vaccination of greater numbers of people by accepting the small risks of vaccination over the far greater risks of infection. We could have explained that vaccines are imperfect protection against a rapidly mutating virus, but death and sickness are worse. We could have designated shopping days and hours for vulnerable and older people. We could have explained that their COVID risk level means that they need to mask when COVID is surging, and they need others around them to do the same. We could

The Fed and the Flu: Parsing Pandemic Economic Shocks

have maintained masking in medical facilities, where people need to seek care and some of the people who need that care most are now avoiding it because of the COVID risk. The response would have been based on the mechanism by which the virus spread — through the air, particularly in poorly ventilated indoor spaces.

None of these measures needed to become the focus of misinformation, but because of the species that we are and the choices that key influencers made early in the pandemic, they have. We could have carried on with our economic activities more safely than we did. Pandemics through history demonstrate that we and our governments are not always logical. History demonstrates how we fail to make data-based choices.

Are we capable of better? Yes. We have solved for other types of disease risk. Drinking from clean(er) water sources ensures that we do not have deadly cholera epidemics. Mass vaccination wiped out smallpox and has largely beaten back polio risk. Vaccination reduced childhood diseases that kept child mortality high for millennia. Children today do not commonly die of whooping cough (though that illness is making a comeback after childhood vaccination rates faltered during the pandemic).[1] Most children do not risk paralysis or death from polio. Most children do not encounter mumps. Most children avoid measles, but slipping rates of vaccination are increasing the number of measles outbreaks, too.[2]

We vaccinate our pets against rabies so we do not witness a reprisal of the plot of *Old Yeller*. Whether on farms or in cities, we endeavor to keep populations of rats in check so we do not see outbreaks of bubonic plague. New York City now has a "rat czar" to lead the city's battle against resourceful, disease-carrying rats. We wash our hands after using the bathroom and teach our children to do the same. Good hygiene habits and waste management help to protect us against typhoid fever caused by the bacterium *Salmonella typhi*. We disinfect surfaces in our homes and workplaces. Measures like these, along

436

with the development of vaccines and evidence-based treatments for the ills that plague us, have dramatically lengthened human lifespans.

But we have not yet adequately curbed the spread of pathogens that waft through the air, whether in large droplets alone or in the form of aerosols, too. We have not conquered influenza or coronaviruses, whether the pesky common cold, SARS, MERS, or SARS-CoV-2. There is work yet to be done. Discounting or ignoring that work will not serve us well since ever-mutating influenza viruses and coronaviruses can be highly pathogenic in humans. Solving for these threats involves both ensuring cleaner air, especially indoors, and developing vaccines that provide broader and more lasting protection. Cleaner air will also help to prevent transmission of tuberculosis, measles, chickenpox, pertussis (whooping cough), polio, and RSV.

Each pandemic we endure is a learning opportunity. Each is an invitation to prepare for another that might be as bad or worse. Preparation can help us to save lives and manage to keep a complex global economy running. Those two objectives are not, in fact, opposed to each other: They are intertwined (and integral to our wellbeing and long-term success). Furthermore, the higher the pathogenicity of a pandemic virus, the more deeply intertwined we find them to be. Should we not heed the lessons of COVID and the lessons of pandemics stretching back to antiquity, we may find ourselves paying a far higher price for avoidable missteps.

---

1. Mark Johnson and Sabrina Malhi, "Whooping cough cases double in the U.S., a potential legacy of the pandemic," *Washington Post,* June 6, 2024, https://www.washingtonpost.com/health/2024/06/06/whooping-cough-cases-rising/.
2. "Measles Cases and Outbreaks," CDC, updated June 27, 2024, https://www.cdc.gov/measles/data-research/index.html.

PART 5:

A U.S. Pandemic Chart Book

by Mike Englund

An Introduction from David Kotok

Mike Englund of Action Economics contributed to this book the following superb assemblage of graphic depictions of the various economic and financial elements in play during the COVID-19 shock period and its aftermath.

I have known Mike Englund for decades. We have been colleagues together at various economic organizations, including the National Association for Business Economics. His service with Action Economics I know both as a friend and as a subscriber. I have been a paid subscriber to Action Economics for many years and have used his materials in my business career and found them very helpful. What I like about Mike Englund's work is that he strives to set aside political biases and tries his best, with his colleagues, to portray an economic series — of which he has many, as we can see by this assemblage of charts — in a politically neutral way. Mike's great skill is to present facts and data and do so with clarity and consistency and allow readers to draw their own conclusions. It is an invaluable addition to this book to be able to have Mike Englund contributing this extensive collection of charts to depict the economic and financial effects of the pandemic economic shock before, during, and on the exit side of this global event.

What we have been saying throughout this book is that epidemics and pandemics (*plagues,* as the biblical term was used) create economic shocks. We have examined that reality in antiquity and in more modern times, and then in the last century with the Federal Reserve and monetary policy and its implications. When we look through these charts, we see the degree of volatility in the shock that hit elements and sectors of the economy and the financial markets.

Mike Englund's final chart (Figure 26.6), depicting total borrowed and nonborrowed reserves, captures the Fed's reaction function to the pandemic. We have discussed elsewhere in the book the study by economists Oscar Jordà, Sanjay Singh, and Alan Taylor, published by the San Francisco Fed at the beginning of the pandemic in 2020, and how that study outlined the economic impacts of 19 epidemics over the course of 800 years, based upon European and American history. In every case, there was a financial shock, and the implications of the shock were reflected in the interest rates and often the monetary policy at the time. We also see evidence of pandemic economic shocks and responses in ancient Greece and Rome, Europe in the Middle Ages, and the entire planet in the COVID-19 era.

Under no circumstances in our examination of history, covering 3,500 years, could we find an event where a large and deadly epidemic, pandemic, or plague occurred without economic consequences. The charts that follow depict changes in savings rates and changes in economic activity. We see financial responses, and these charts show some of the reaction function in the COVID-19 pandemic.

Mike Englund's report follows. It contains 58 graphs of U.S. economic data over the 2017–2022 period that summarize the impact of the pandemic and the ensuing policy response on the economy. This is the American COVID economic shock story, depicted graphically. It rhymes with the experiences of other countries and their economies around the world during COVID, and it rhymes with 3,500 years of human history.

Chapter 21

GDP and Components

The GDP and component data provide a useful overview of the macroeconomic effects of the pandemic, via the initial lockdowns and later three stimulus packages, alongside a severe easing of monetary policy that included a drop in interest rates to zero, an expanded QE, and newly developed credit market channels, before the start of a sharp monetary policy reversal in 2022.

For GDP and final sales, lockdowns initially depressed output more than sales, and sales were then quickly lifted by the first of three stimulus packages, the CARES Act. As such, GDP fell sharply in Q2 of 2020; sales fell by less; and inventories were sharply depleted. Producers were unable to keep up with demand through the rest of 2020 and most of 2021, so the inventory build-back process really did not start until late 2021.

Figure 21.1 Real GDP and Final Sales vs Pre-2008 Trend
(Data source: U.S. Bureau of Economic Analysis)

Because of the large and rapid U.S. policy response, U.S. GDP fell by less in Q2 of 2020 than was seen in most industrialized countries and rebounded more sharply than in most countries through Q3 and beyond. Real and nominal GDP exceeded the prior peaks by Q1 of 2021.

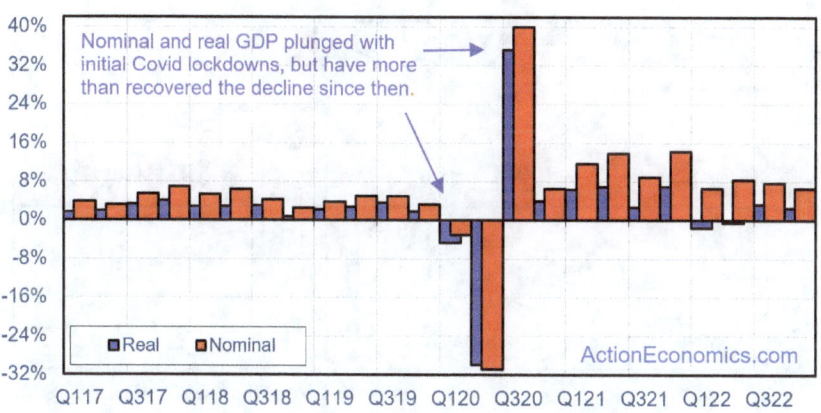

Figure 21.2 Nominal and Real GDP Growth
(Data source: U.S. Bureau of Economic Analysis)

The economy was supported throughout the pandemic by an excess of demand relative to supply, as stimulus packages were huge. Final sales bounced sharply in Q3 of 2020 and continued to post solid quarterly gains in nominal terms through 2021. Surging prices by 2022 left a weaker path for "real" spending, but firms consistently posted large nominal sales gains.

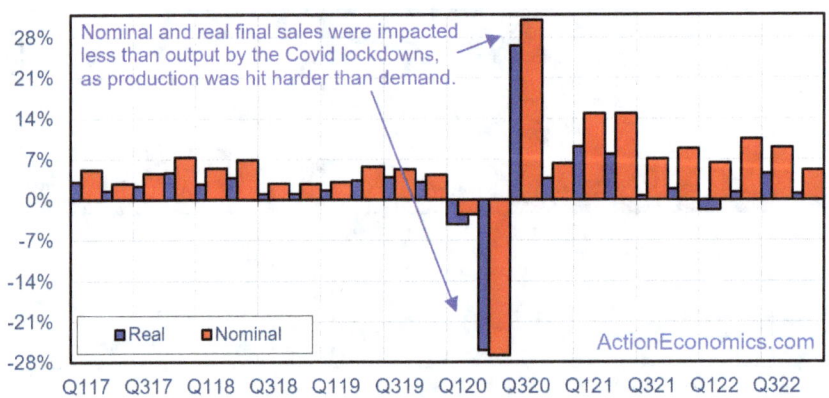

Figure 21.3 Nominal and Real Final Sales Growth
(Data source: U.S. Bureau of Economic Analysis)

The inventory liquidation of $279.1 bln in Q2 of 2020 marked a record decline; and though we had a modest rebuild of inventories in the ensuing two quarters with the initial rebound in imports, inventories resumed liquidation through Q3 of 2021 before producers were finally able to restock through the remainder of 2021 and 2022.

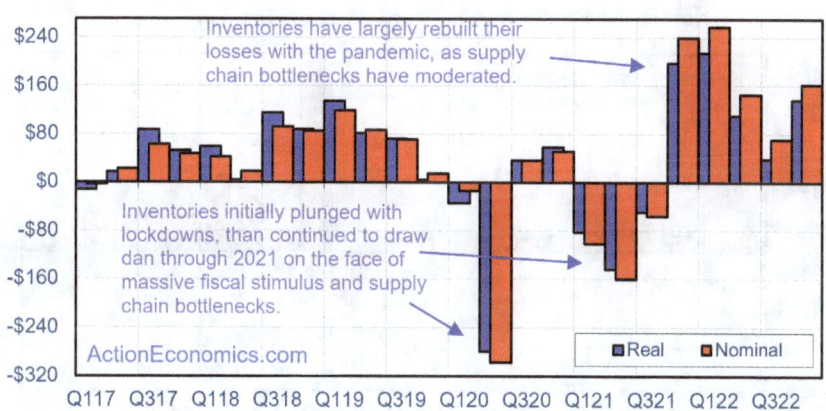

Figure 21.4 Nominal and Real Private Inventory Accumulation
(Data source: U.S. Bureau of Economic Analysis)

Consumption in the U.S. initially fell in March and April of 2020 but rebounded sharply in May and June with stimulus payments, as was later seen in January and March of 2021 with the second and third rounds of stimulus. Nominal consumption exceeded its pre-pandemic peak by January of 2021, while "real" consumption beat its prior peak by March of 2021.

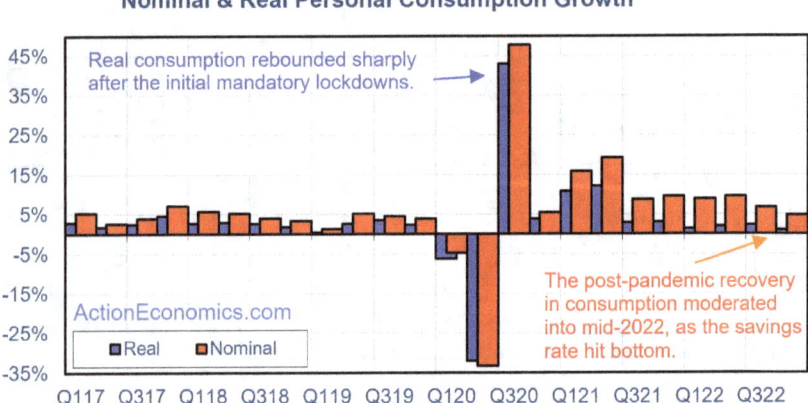

Figure 21.5 Nominal and Real Personal Consumption Growth
(Data source: U.S. Bureau of Economic Analysis)

Nonresidential fixed investment rebounded sharply after the initial hit from lockdowns, led by massive gains for equipment spending and investment in intellectual property. Investment in structures mostly fell through Q3 of 2022, with huge headwinds in large urban areas, though investment did boom for some segments of the commercial sector, such as warehousing.

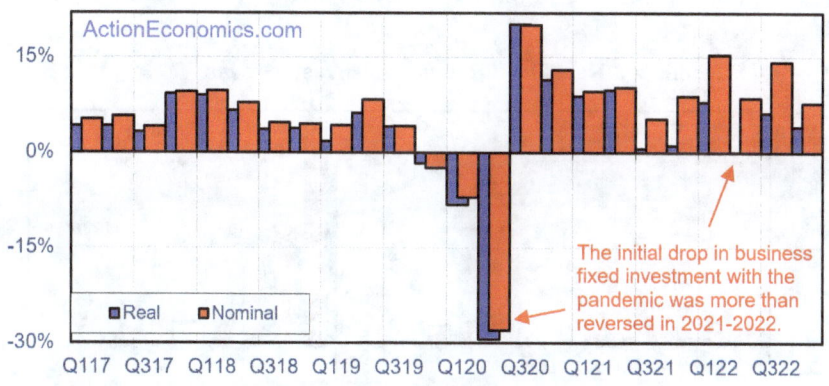

Figure 21.6 Nominal and Real Fixed Nonresidential Investment Growth (Data source: U.S. Bureau of Economic Analysis)

The residential construction sector faced brief disruptive effects with lockdowns in Q2 of 2020 but quickly rebounded to capacity constraints for materials, skilled labor, and buildable land. Pre-sales of homes have remained robust, and new home construction continued through Q2 of 2022, when headwinds from soaring mortgage rates kicked in. The GDP aggregate includes sales commissions, and the plunge in existing home sales with soaring rates sharply depressed this GDP component in 2022.

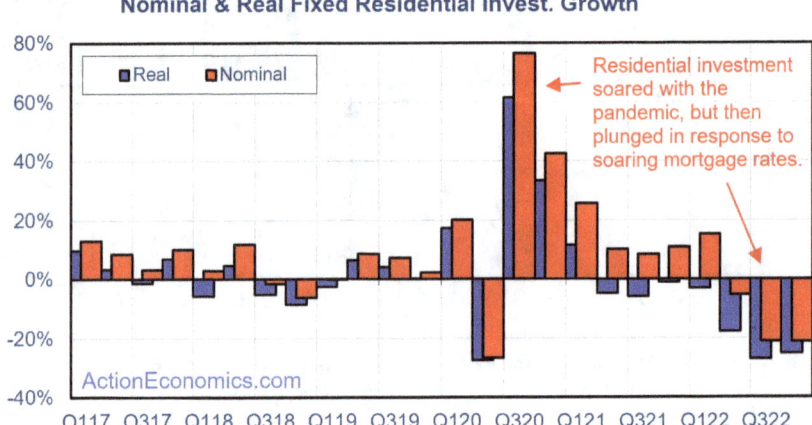

Figure 21.7 Nominal and Real Fixed Residential Investment Growth
(Data source: U.S. Bureau of Economic Analysis)

Exports fell sharply with global lockdowns and were slow to recover given the extensions of lockdowns for much longer periods in most industrialized countries than was seen in the U.S.

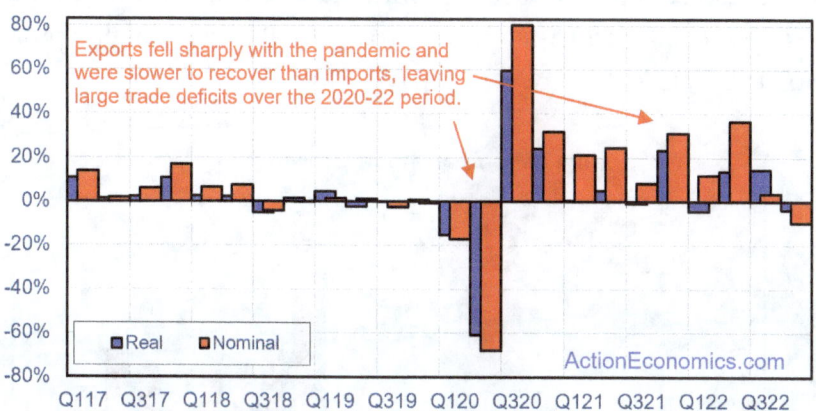

Figure 21.8 Nominal and Real Export Growth
(Data source: U.S. Bureau of Economic Analysis)

Imports fell sharply with March 2020 lockdowns but rebounded sharply when U.S. lockdowns were largely eliminated outside of major urban centers in May and June. Soaring imports into Q3 and Q4 of that year allowed inventories to rebuild modestly in those two quarters before resuming their downtrend with the second and third stimulus packages, combined with port constraints that became highly problematic by late 2021.

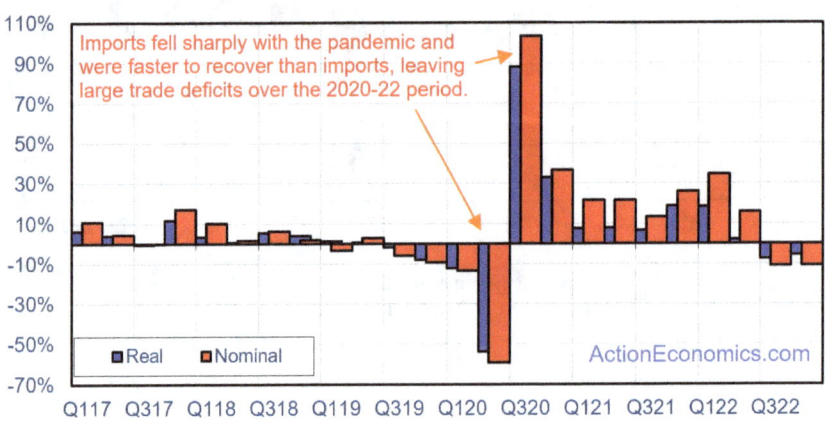

Figure 21.9 Nominal and Real Import Growth
(Data source: U.S. Bureau of Economic Analysis)

An imports recovery that was larger and faster than the exports recovery prompted a massive widening in the U.S. net export deficit, as also measured by the current account balance, to all-time wide gaps.

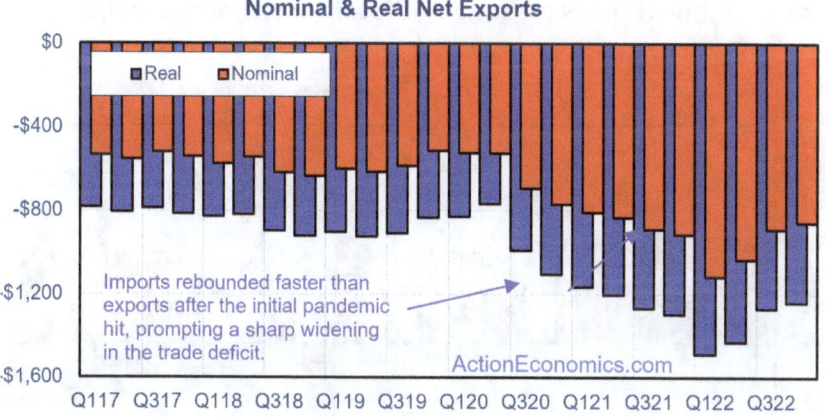

Figure 21.10 Nominal and Real Net Exports
(Data source: U.S. Bureau of Economic Analysis)

Though government spending soared with the three stimulus packages, government "purchases," which is the government component of GDP, rose only modestly, as most government spending occurred via transfer payments. These transfers did prevent what would otherwise have been big declines for state and local government purchases.

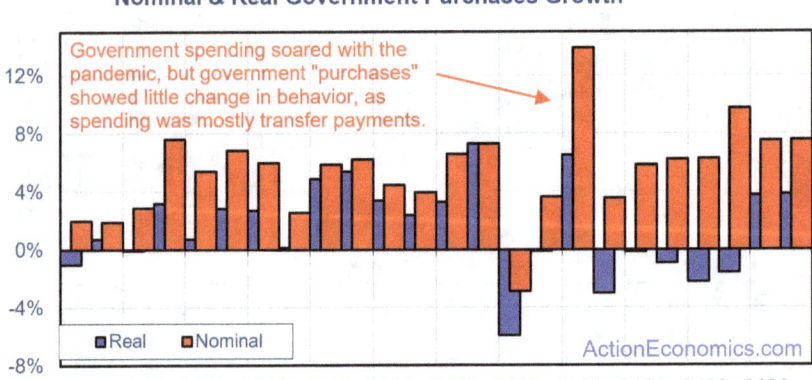

Figure 21.11 Nominal and Real Government Purchases Growth
(Data source: U.S. Bureau of Economic Analysis)

The combination of massive stimulus spending, including PPP loans, and supply constraints that lifted monopoly power for the providers of goods and services allowed a steep climb in the ratio of corporate profits to national income.

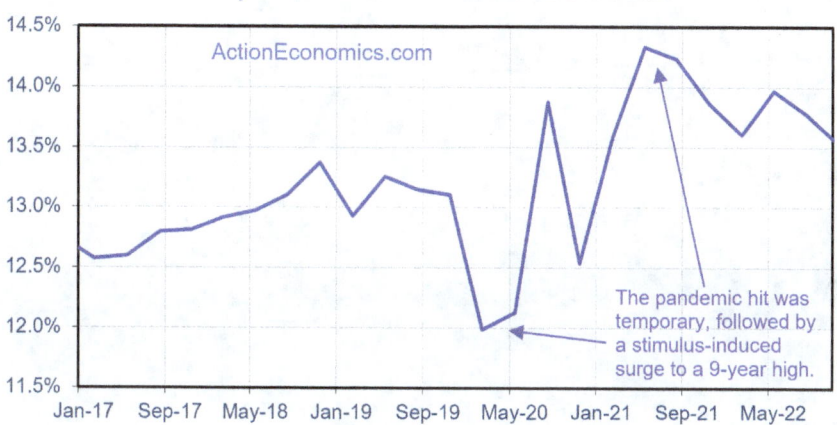

Figure 21.12 Corporate Profits as a Percent of National Income
(Data source: U.S. Bureau of Economic Analysis)

Chapter 22

Housing and Construction

Housing starts and permits fell in March and April of 2020 with lockdowns but quickly soared to capacity constraints by Q4 of 2020. Starts under construction moderated slightly in April and May of 2020 but then climbed persistently at their capacity constraint through a peak in October of 2022 that marked a lofty 49-year high.

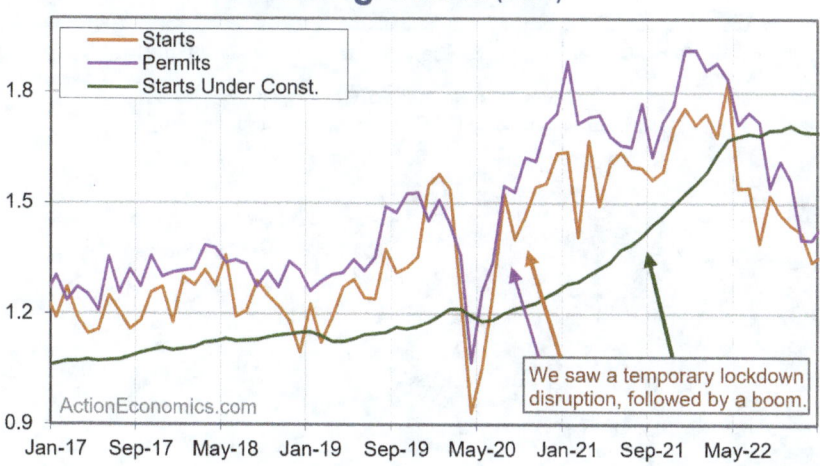

Figure 22.1 Housing Starts
(Data source: Department of Commerce, U.S. Census Bureau)

The post-lockdown boom in starts was spread across regions but was smallest in the West, likely due to zoning and building restrictions that are particularly severe in California.

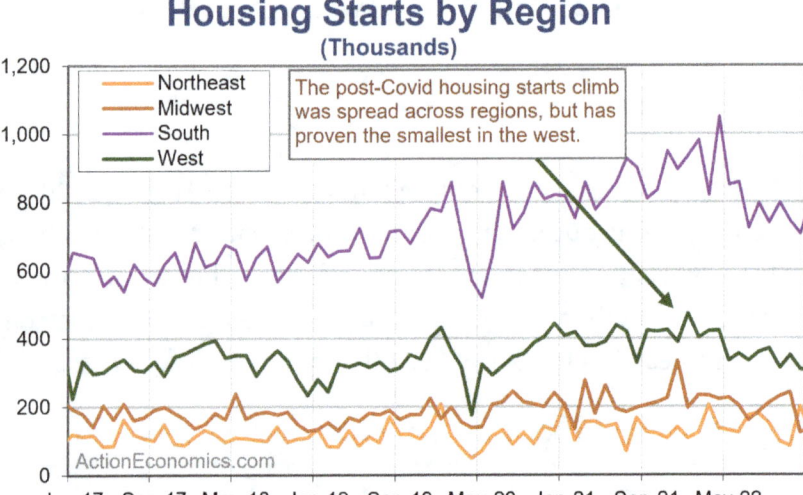

Figure 22.2 Housing Starts by Region
(Data source: Department of Commerce, U.S. Census Bureau)

Because of material and labor shortages, home completions were unable to keep up with the building boom, though they continued to climb steadily through 2022 despite soaring mortgage rates as builders played "catch-up." New-home sales, including pre-sales, soared in 2020 to unsustainable levels, and then we saw a pullback into 2021–22. These sales will be supported going forward as completions bring new product to market.

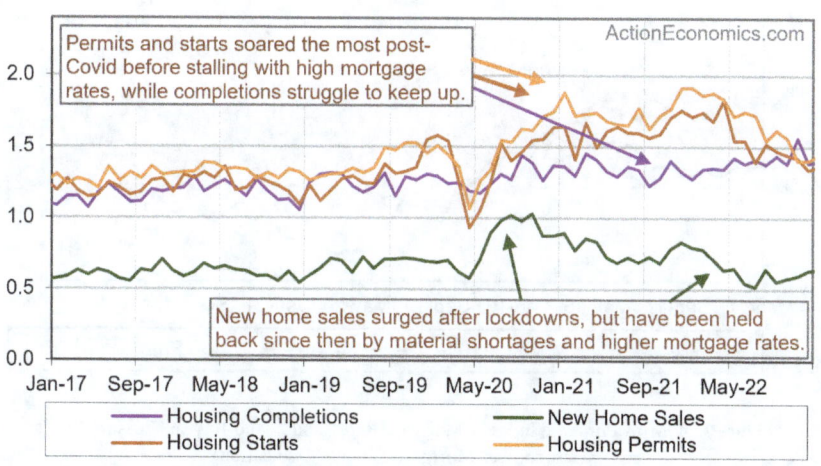

Figure 22.3 New Home Sales and Completions
(Data source: Department of Commerce, U.S. Census Bureau)

The MBA Purchase Index has been an important predictor of sales activity through the erratic pandemic period, with powerful gains through the period of near-zero policy rates; but there were sharp declines when mortgage rates surged as existing-home sales transactions were disrupted.

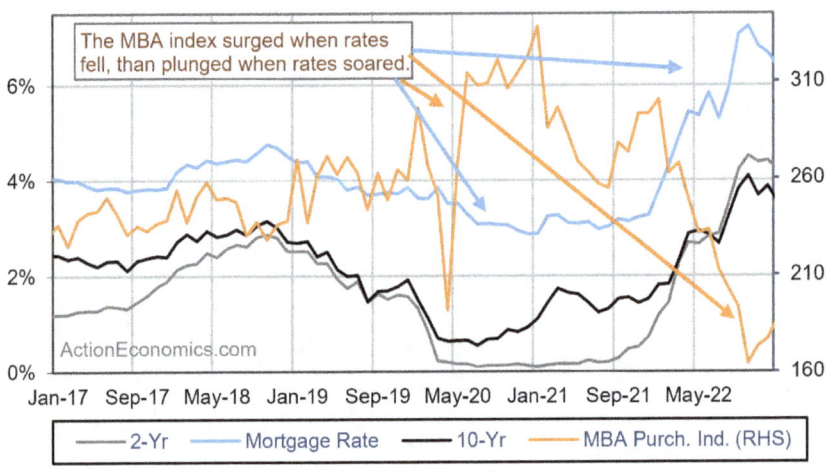

Figure 22.4 MBA Purchase Index vs Mortgage Rates, and 2- and 10-year Treasury Yields (Data source: Mortgage Bankers Association)

Both existing and pending home sales were massively hit by soaring mortgage rates, as the percentage of households that could qualify for a mortgage plunged and existing-home owners became unwilling to relinquish their homes and associated low-rate mortgages.

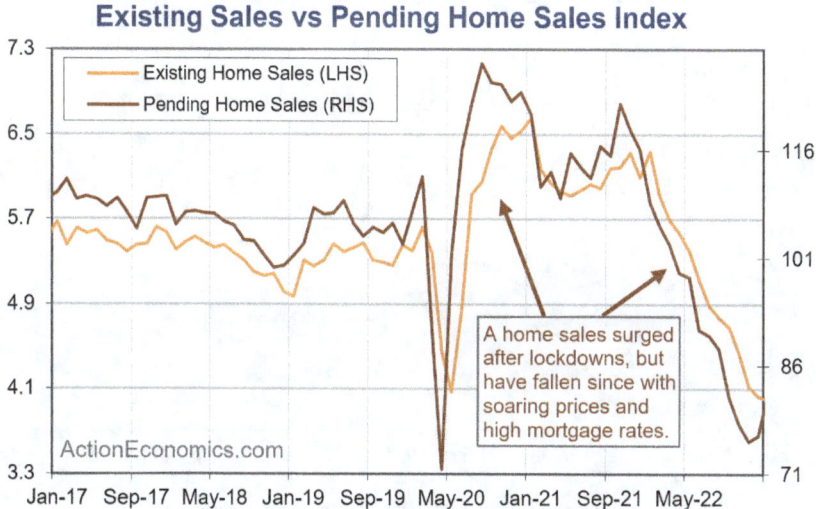

Figure 22.5 Existing Sales vs Pending Home Sales Index
(Data source: National Association of Realtors)

Household reluctance to sell homes was evident in the "months of supply" gauge for single-family homes, which set a deep new all-time low in January of 2022.

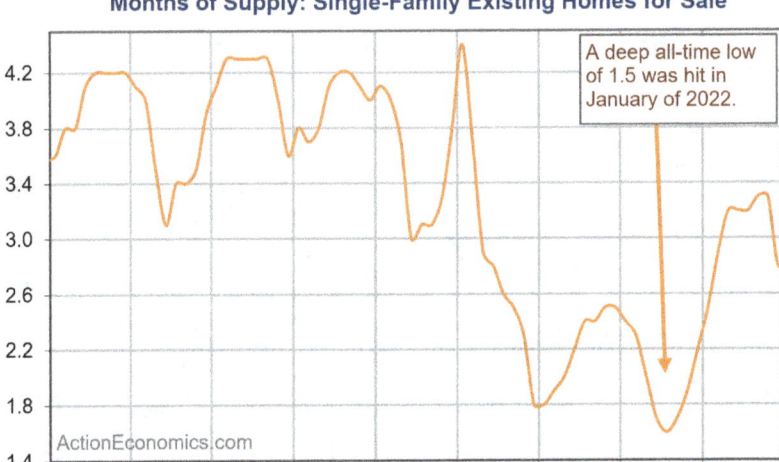

Figure 22.6 Months of Supply: Single-Family Existing Homes for Sale
(Data source: National Association of Realtors)

Through the period of low mortgage rates and severe supply constraints, home prices soared to lofty record highs in mid-2022 before a modest pullback afterward.

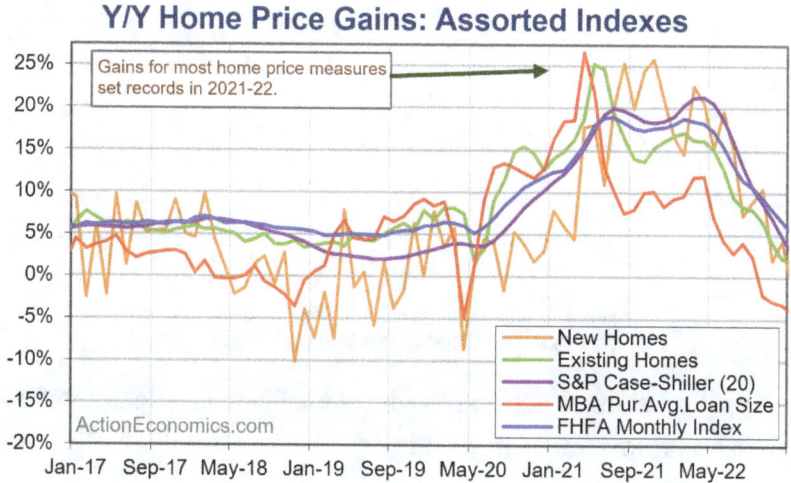

Figure 22.7 Y/Y Home Price Gains: Assorted Indices
(Data sources: Department of Commerce, U.S. Census Bureau;
National Association of Realtors; S&P Global; Dow Jones Indexes;
Mortgage Bankers Association; Federal Housing Finance Agency)

Prices soared across all regions but rose to particularly high levels in the West, where starts and permits grew the least.

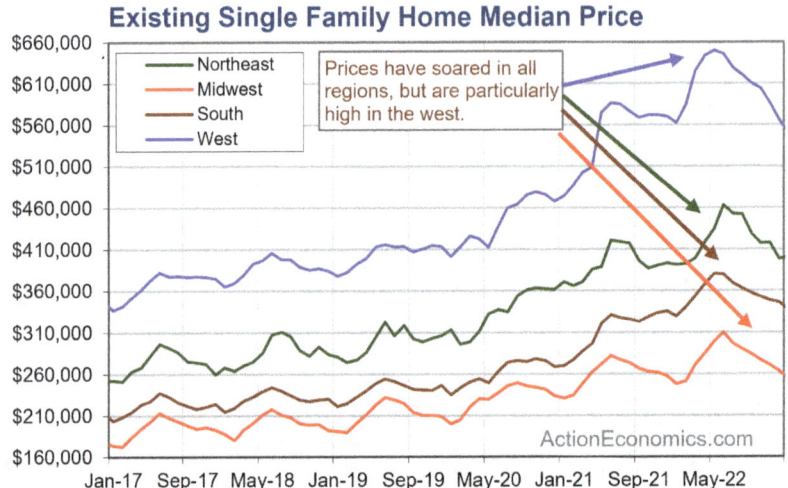

Figure 22.8 Existing Single Family Home Median Price
(Data source: National Association of Realtors)

New-home construction rose dramatically from a lockdown low to a peak in mid-2022 before falling.

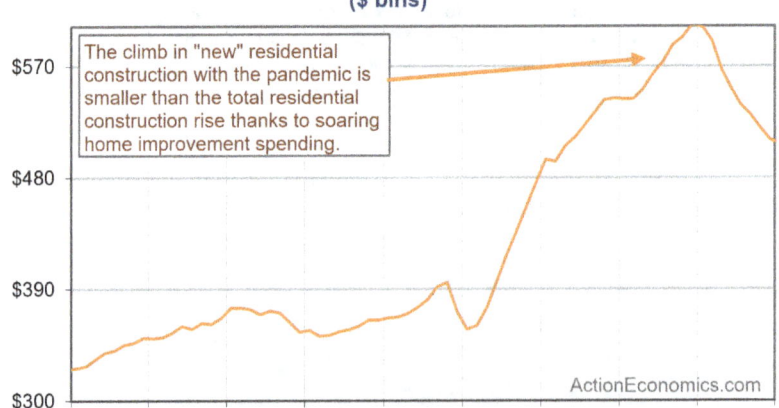

Figure 22.9 Private New Residential Construction
(Data source: Department of Commerce, U.S. Census Bureau)

Home improvement spending posted solid growth through the early lockdowns in 2020 and continued to grow at a robust pace through a mid-2022 peak before moderating. Some of the boom, and ensuing moderation, likely reflected a similar pattern of booming construction material prices through mid-2022, and a pullback afterwards.

Figure 22.10 Private Residential Home Improvement Construction
(Data source: Department of Commerce, U.S. Census Bureau)

Nonresidential construction fell through 2020 despite the boom in other construction aggregates but then grew modestly in 2021 and accelerated sharply into the end of 2022.

Figure 22.11 Private Nonresidential Construction
(Data source: Department of Commerce, U.S. Census Bureau)

Chapter 23

Factory Activity and Inventories

The factory sector has posted rapid capacity-constrained growth since a collapse of activity in Q2 2020, but broken supply chains prevented a full recovery, and the sector has struggled to reach fresh highs. The industrial production index, for instance, rose to a high in October of 2022 that was still 0.5% below its peak level in August of 2018; and this measure then moderated into the end of 2022.

Figure 23.1 U.S. Industrial Production Index
(Data source: U.S. Federal Reserve Board G.17 Release)

Capacity utilization rose to an 18-year high of 80.8% in September of 2022 from its all-time low of 64.6% in April of 2020, leaving the measure just above the 80.4% prior peak in August and September of 2018.

U.S. Capacity Utilization

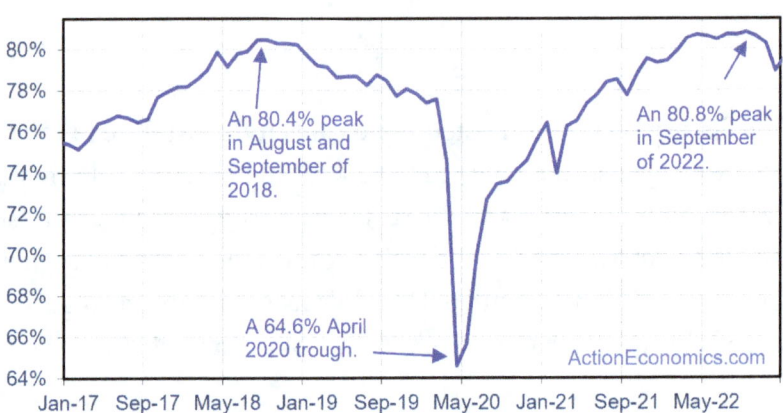

Figure 23.2 U.S. Capacity Utilization
(Data source: U.S. Federal Reserve Board G.17 Release)

Durable goods orders ex-transportation soared dramatically after an initial plunge with lockdowns in April of 2020 that marked a 10th consecutive monthly decline. Then a string of all-time highs ended in August of 2022 before a modest pullback.

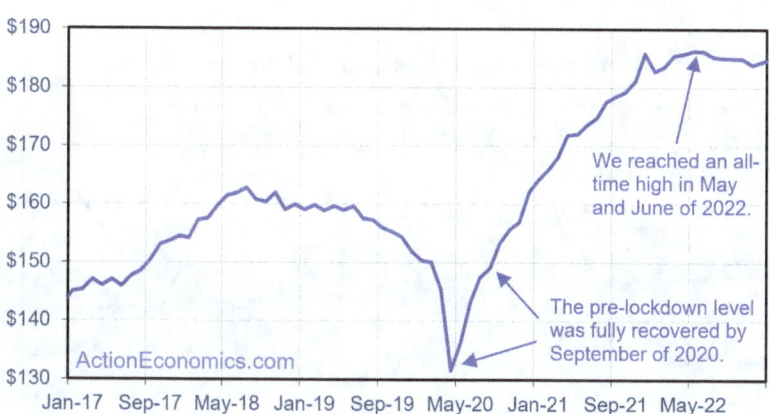

Figure 23.3 U.S. Durable Goods Orders Ex-Transportation
(Data source: Department of Commerce, U.S. Census Bureau)

The mining sector faced a particularly dramatic plunge in April and May of 2020, as mining companies suddenly expected massive gluts of most mined materials. A gradual recovery nevertheless began for the sector mid-2020 that extended to a temporary peak in September of 2022 and a later peak in January of 2023 that was still well below prior highs.

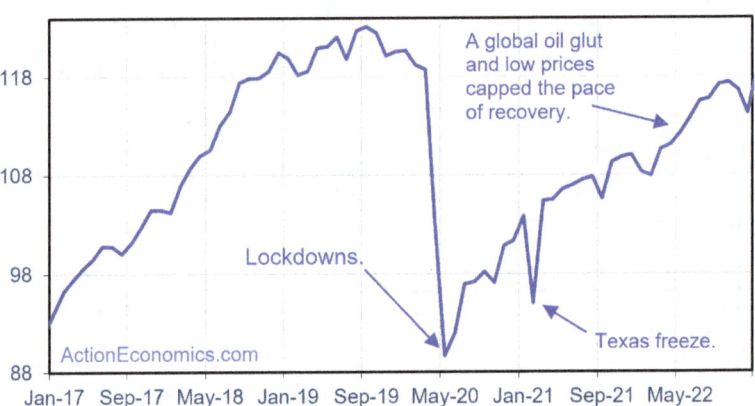

Figure 23.4 U.S. Mining Component of Industrial Production
(Data source: U.S. Federal Reserve Board G.17 Release)

The U.S. aircraft sector faced a massive setback before the pandemic with the second 737 Max crash in early 2019 that initiated a freeze of 737 aircraft production at Boeing. A further drop for the sector was nevertheless seen with lockdowns in March and April of 2020 before a gradual claw-back through mid-2022 and an accelerated pace of improvement since then.

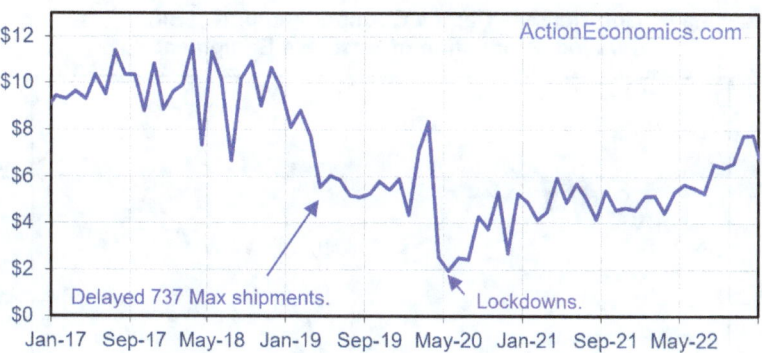

Figure 23.5 U.S. Aircraft and Parts Shipments
(Data source: Department of Commerce, U.S. Census Bureau)

The nondefense capital goods shipments component of the monthly durable goods series plunged in April of 2020 but posted a robust recovery afterward, as businesses purchased equipment rapidly as they struggled to regain output levels. Domestic equipment production, as gauged by the business equipment component of industrial production, recovered less dramatically, as the demand was partly met by a sharply widening trade deficit in capital goods.

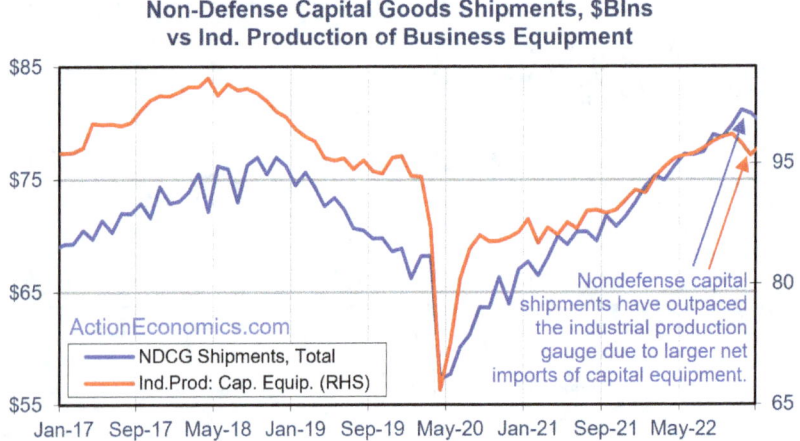

Figure 23.6 Nondefense Capital Goods Shipments vs Industrial Production of Business Equipment
(Data sources: Department of Commerce, U.S. Census Bureau;
U.S. Federal Reserve Board G.17 Release)

Business inventory-to-sales (I/S) ratios surged with lockdowns as the denominator plunged but then fell dramatically into late 2020 as stimulus spending boosted demand, while supply chain disruptions limited supply. The shelves were cleared, and businesses spent the 2021–22 period in sometimes futile attempts to restock. The vehicle sector had a supply imbalance that extended well beyond 2022.

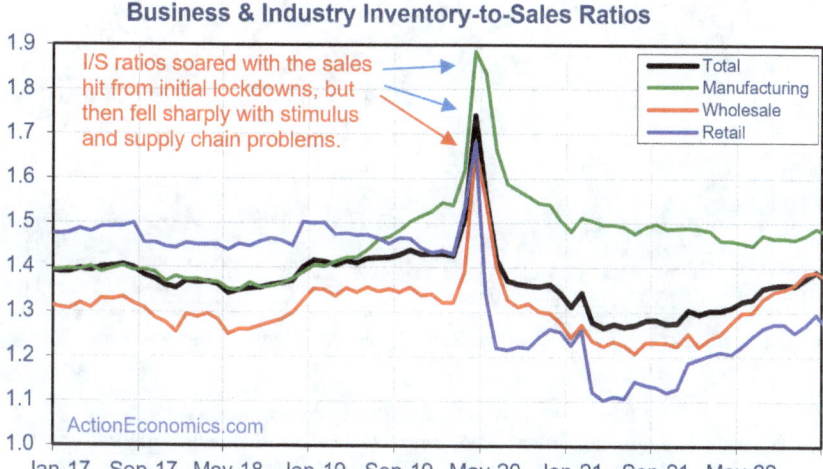

Figure 23.7 Business and Industry Inventory-to-Sales Ratios (Data source: Department of Commerce, U.S. Census Bureau)

The various producer sentiment measures set record lows in April of 2020 before a climb to record highs for most measures in November of 2021. We have seen a steady pullback in these measures since then.

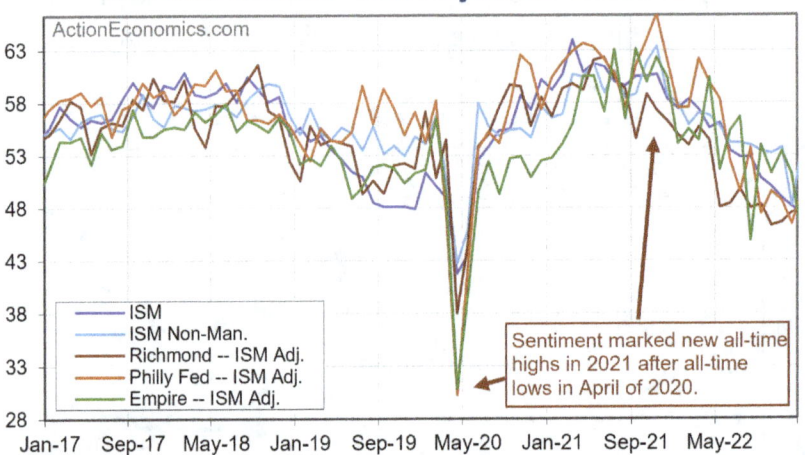

Figure 23.8 ISM and Related "ISM Adjusted" Indexes
(Data sources: ISM Institute of Supply Management, U.S. Federal Reserve Bank of Richmond, U.S. Federal Reserve Bank of Philadelphia, U.S. Federal Reserve Bank of New York)

Gyrations in the income and consumption data through the pandemic period almost entirely reflected the impact of the three massive stimulus packages. We saw a modest income drop in March of 2020 before a massive income surge in April of 2020. Sustained transfer payments kept income elevated below peak April levels until later spikes with stimulus in January and March of 2021. We faced fiscal-cliff income declines starting in late 2021, with particularly big hits in September of 2021 and January of 2022. Consumption followed income with a lag.

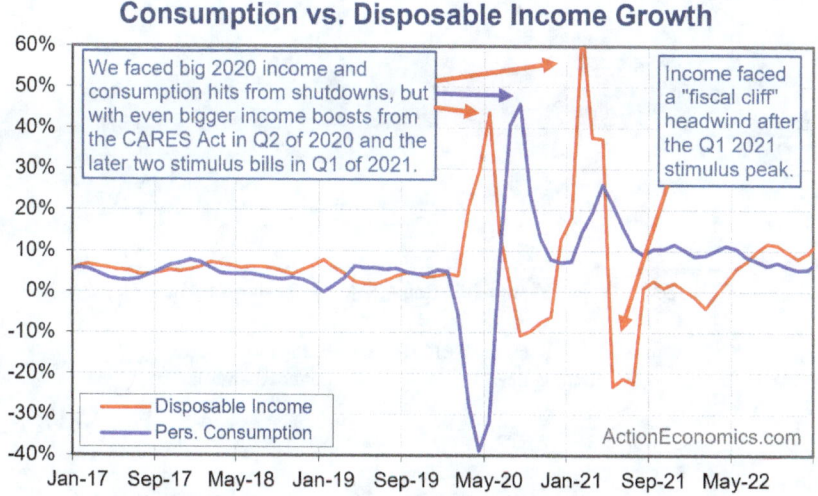

Figure 23.9 Consumption vs. Disposable Income Growth
(Data source: U.S. Bureau of Economic Analysis)

The massive income spikes with each stimulus package prompted large savings rate spikes and then unwound as households took their time spending the extra income. This process seemed to end, in aggregate, in June of 2022, when the savings rate bottomed at a 17-year low of 2.7%.

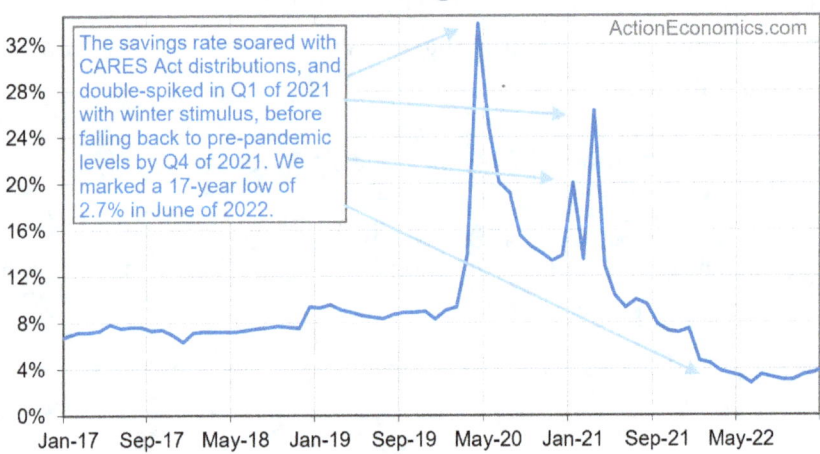

The Savings Rate

The savings rate soared with CARES Act distributions, and double-spiked in Q1 of 2021 with winter stimulus, before falling back to pre-pandemic levels by Q4 of 2021. We marked a 17-year low of 2.7% in June of 2022.

ActionEconomics.com

Figure 23.10 The Savings Rate
(Data source: U.S. Bureau of Economic Analysis)

The vehicle sector provides a good example of industries where the initial hit from lockdowns over the March–May period was followed by an inability to recoup prior production levels despite robust demand for vehicles. Even by the end of 2022, inventories of popular models were still lean, and prices for both new and used vehicles were quite elevated.

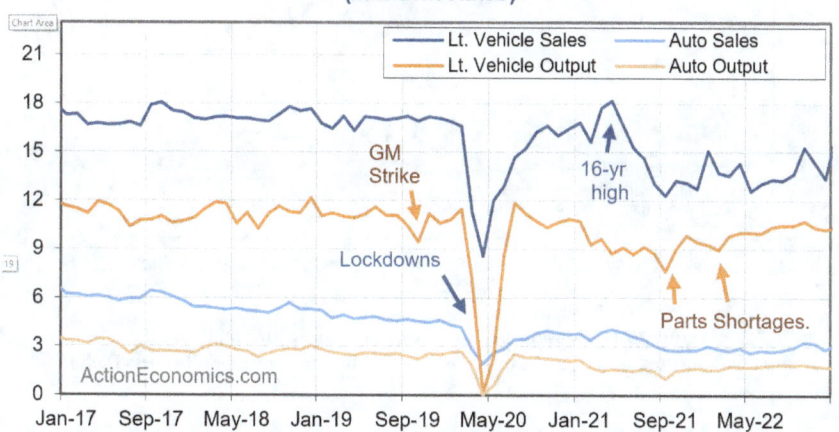

Figure 23.11 Vehicle Sales and Output
(Data source: Bloomberg Finance, LP)

The consumer confidence measures were sharply depressed by the start of the pandemic before a steep climb for the Conference Board's measure and the IBD/TIPP measure to historically high levels by mid-2021 but a smaller improvement for Michigan sentiment. Confidence then fell to a trough in mid-2022 and climbed modestly afterward.

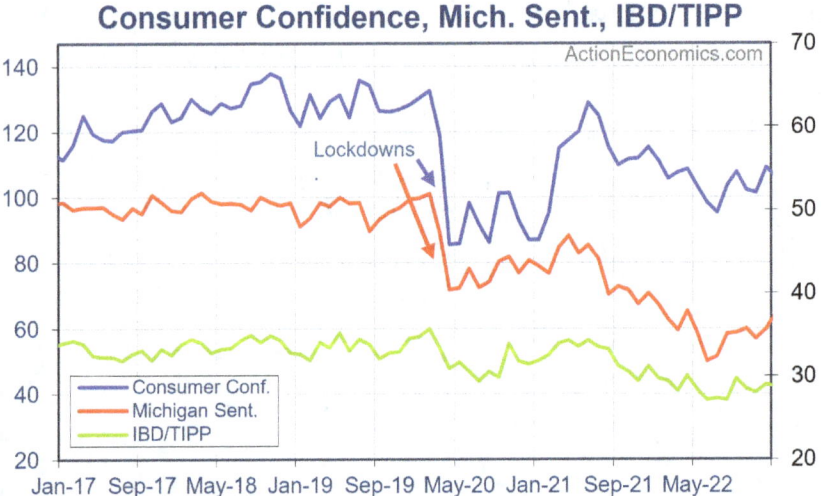

Figure 23.12 Consumer Confidence, Michigan Sentiment, IBD/TIPP
(Data sources: Conference Board, University of Michigan, Investor's Business Daily)

Chapter 24

Labor Market

The labor market data revealed massive declines for both employment levels and the labor force at the start of the pandemic, and only gradual recoveries for each measure afterward. Nonfarm payrolls took until June of 2022 to reach their pre-pandemic peak, while civilian employment took until December of 2022. The labor force took until a temporary overshoot in August of 2022 and a later, more permanent overshoot in December of 2022.

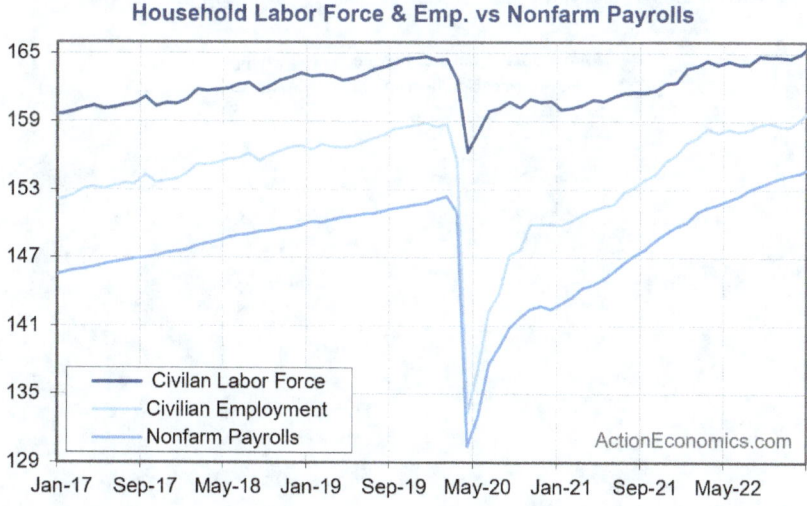

Figure 24.1 Household Labor Force and Employment vs. Nonfarm Payrolls
(Data source: U.S. Bureau of Labor Statistics)

The plunge and rebound for employment were greater, in percentage terms, for private payrolls than for government payrolls.

Figure 24.2 Total and Private Payroll Changes
(Data source: U.S. Bureau of Labor Statistics)

The hours-worked index in the monthly employment report fell more sharply than GDP did with lockdowns and recovered with a long lag, leaving a boom in productivity early in the pandemic that was not reversed until 2022.

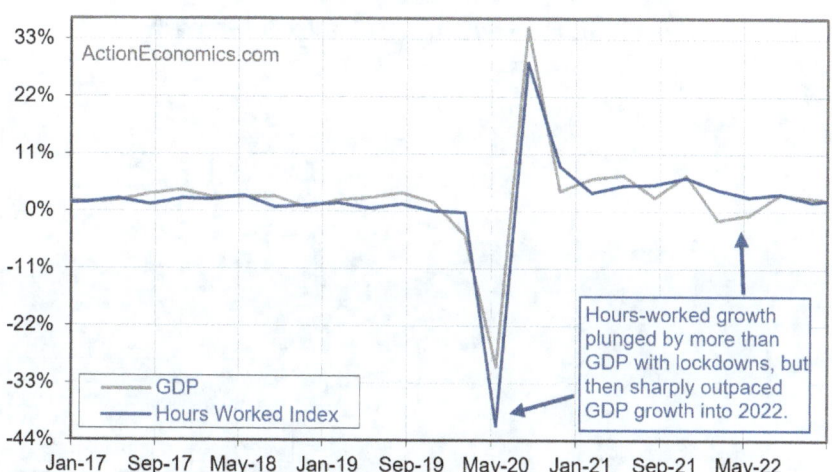

Figure 24.3 Real GDP vs. Hours Worked Growth
(Data sources: U.S. Bureau of Labor Statistics, U.S. Bureau of Economic Analysis)

Payrolls fell more sharply than either hours worked or GDP at the start of the pandemic and then largely reversed this hit through 2022. Essentially, managers faced a reduced pool of employees starting in 2020, so they did the work themselves. These employees gradually returned to work through 2022.

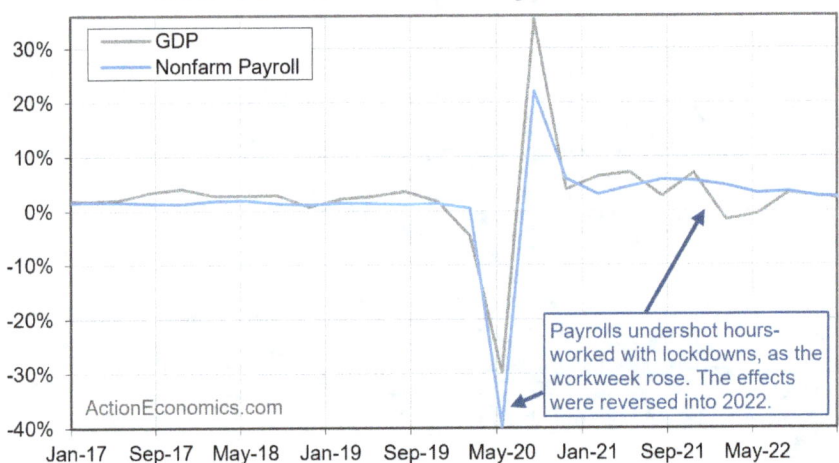

Real GDP vs Nonfarm Payroll Growth

Figure 24.4 Real GDP vs. Nonfarm Payroll Growth
(Data sources: U.S. Bureau of Labor Statistics, U.S. Bureau of Economic Analysis)

The work week had the opposite pattern from payrolls, with a sharp boost at the start of the pandemic and an unwind that was concentrated in 2022.

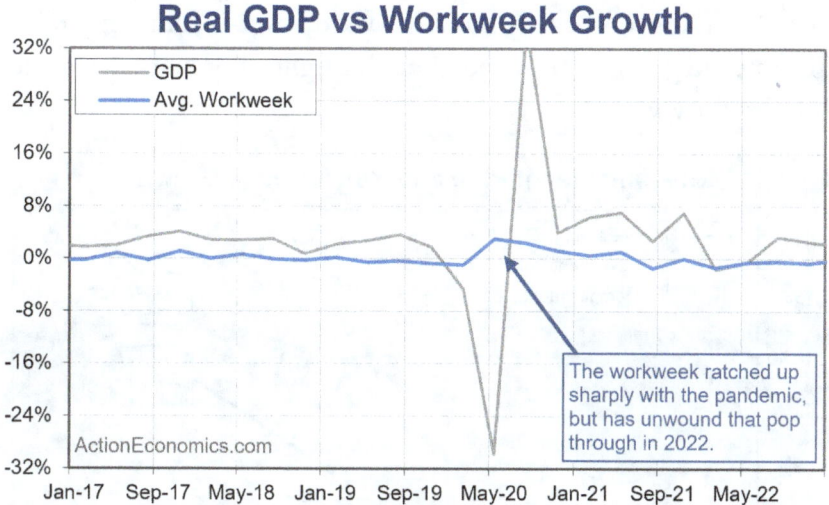

Figure 24.5 Real GDP vs. Workweek Growth
(Data sources: U.S. Bureau of Labor Statistics, U.S. Bureau of Economic Analysis)

The unemployment rate spiked to a record high of 14.75% in April of 2020, but then gradually unwound to reach a low of 3.43% in January that marked a 54-year low last undershot with a 3.39% rate in May of 1969. Average hourly earnings spiked with the jobless surge, as the exit of workers was heavily skewed toward lower-income employees. The rate did gradually unwind, though a tight labor market provided support for y/y gains.

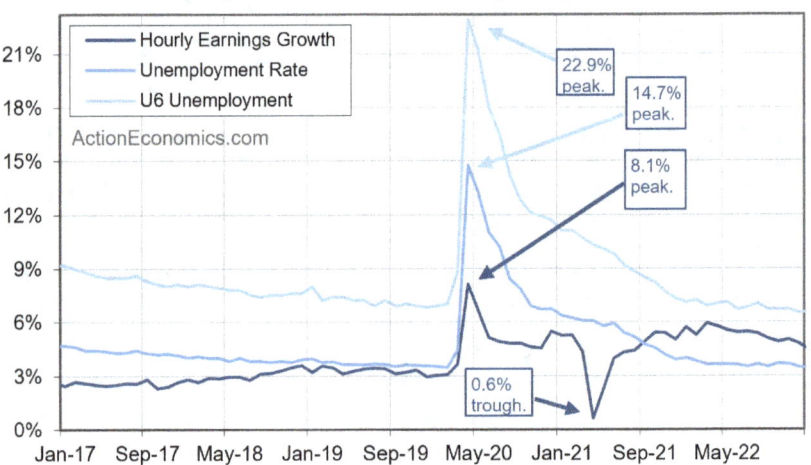

Figure 24.6 Unemployment Rate and Hourly Wage Growth
(Data source: U.S. Bureau of Labor Statistics)

Productivity posted robust increases of 2.2% in 2021, 4.5% in 2020, 2.0% in 2019, and 1.4% in 2018 that marked the four biggest increases since 2010, followed by a 1.7% drop in 2022 that marked the largest decline in history for a series extending back to 1947.

Figure 24.7 Nonfarm Productivity Growth: Quarterly vs. Year/Year
(Data source: U.S. Bureau of Labor Statistics)

The Fed used to cite a 1%–2% inflation "comfort zone," which morphed into a 2% target, and then an average-inflation-targeting process with a 2% average rate as an objective. Throughout, the Fed seemed quite comfortable with its inflation-targeting efforts — until early 2021, when a steep uptrend in y/y inflation rates began that reached remarkable heights around mid-2022. The climb left the ugliest inflation backdrop since the Volcker era.

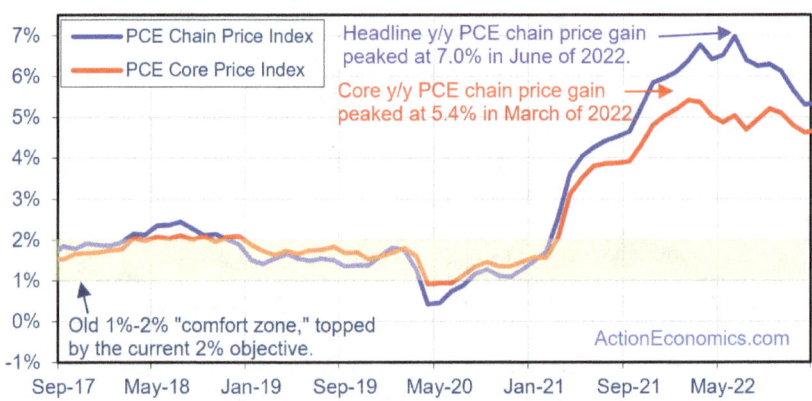

Figure 24.8 U.S. PCE Chain Price Index, vs. Core, Y/Y Growth
(Data source: U.S. Bureau of Economic Analysis)

The rise in core rates was particularly problematic, as the Fed could claim that the commodity price boom with supply chain bottlenecks would likely reverse course. Core price gains could become more persistent.

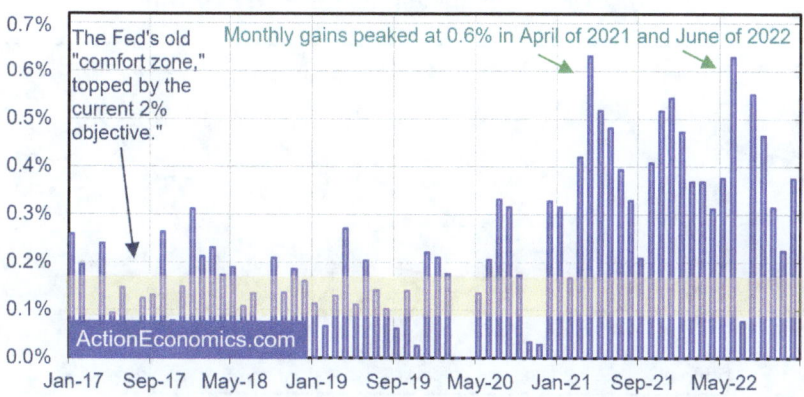

Figure 24.9 PCE Core Chain Price Gains vs. "Comfort Zone"
(Data source: U.S. Bureau of Economic Analysis)

The Fed prefers the PCE chain price indexes, though the markets put weight on CPI as well; and the inflation climb for this measure in 2022 was even bigger. The gap between PCE and CPI inflation widened in 2022.

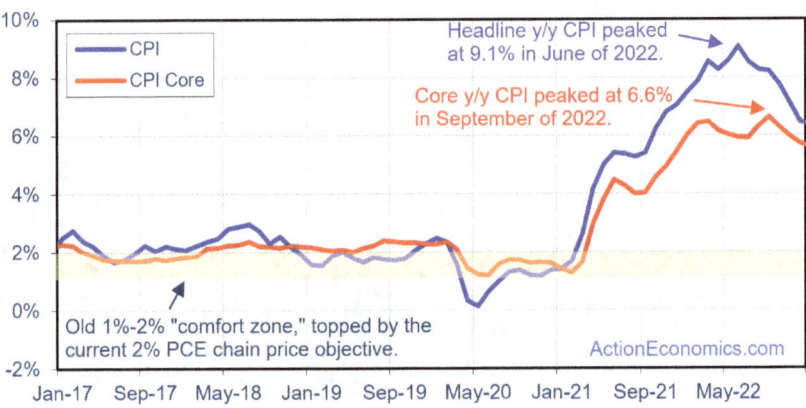

Figure 24.10 U.S. CPI Headline vs. Core, Y/Y Growth
(Data source: U.S. Bureau of Labor Statistics)

The average hourly earnings data through the pandemic were hard to interpret, given that those figures are sensitive to the composition of jobs and most job loss was for lower-paying jobs. The Employment Cost Index (ECI) is free from this distortion, and it is clear from this measure that wage inflation began to accelerate sharply in Q1 of 2021, with an updraft for benefit costs beginning around mid-2021.

Figure 24.11 Growth in the ECI and Components, Y/Y
(Data source: U.S. Bureau of Labor Statistics)

The trade price indexes initially fell sharply over the February to April period, with an earlier hit from lockdowns than for other domestic measures because of the earlier start for the pandemic in Asia and Europe, and also because of a surge in the dollar from February to April. After the initial drop, however, trade prices soared through mid-2022, fueled by massive stimulus globally and supply chain bottlenecks that created scarcities in many internationally traded commodities.

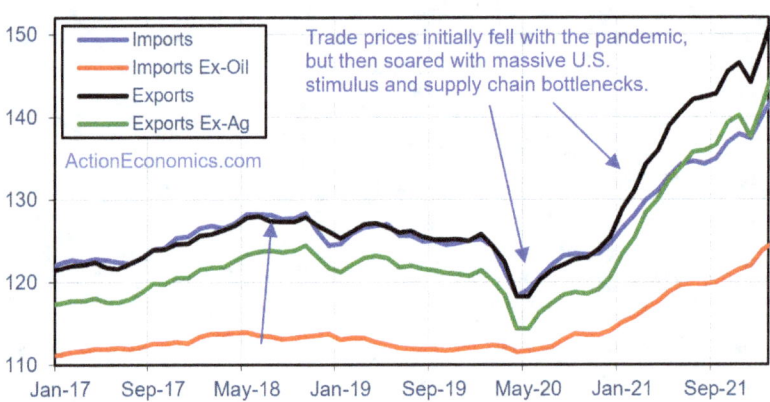

Figure 24.12 Merchandise Import and Export Prices
(Data source: Bureau of Labor Statistics)

Oil prices can be a useful weather vane for the global demand outlook, and here we saw a plunge in prices to a bottom in May of 2020, with futures prices going negative as traders feared they needed to take delivery. Oil prices then climbed sharply to a peak in July of 2022, as the U.S. and global recovery proved more rapid than most had expected, while oil exploration and drilling fell short of its usual cyclical bounce.

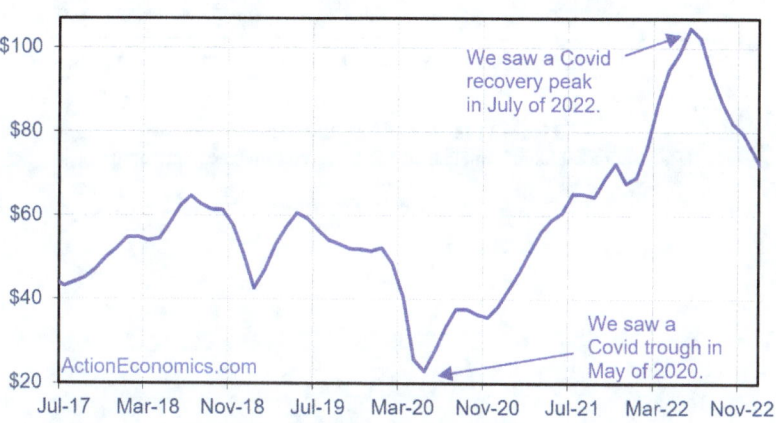

Figure 24.13 U.S. Oil Import Price, $/bbl Monthly Average
(Data source: Department of Commerce, U.S. Census Bureau)

A broad array of commodity prices went through a similar bust-boom cycle, with an extra lift in the first half of 2022 from the war in Ukraine.

CRB and Ag-Price Indexes

Figure 24.14 CRB and Ag-Price Indexes
(Data sources: Bloomberg Finance, LP; U.S. Department of Agriculture)

Chapter 25

Financial Market Values

A t the start of the pandemic, the Fed adopted a path of maximum easing, famously coining the phrase "We aren't even going to think about thinking about raising rates" as a way to establish a credible pre-commitment to a path of ZIRP and QE for the foreseeable future. The fed funds rate target was cut to 0%–0.25% in March of 2020 and remained there until March of 2022, before a steady climb to a 4.25%–4.50% by December of 2022 and later to 5.25%–5.50% by July of 2023. Market yields moved accordingly.

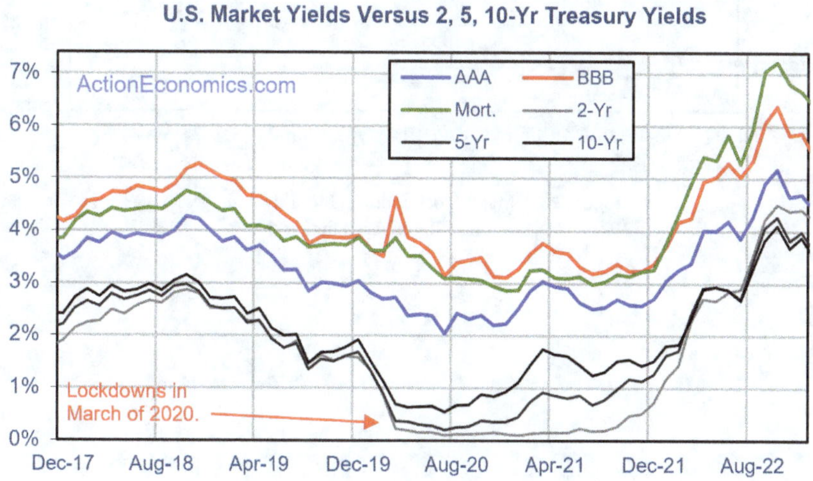

U.S. Market Yields Versus 2, 5, 10-Yr Treasury Yields

Figure 25.1 U.S. Market Yields vs. 2-,5-,10-Year Treasury Yields
(Data sources: U.S. Federal Reserve Board H.15 Release; Bloomberg Finance, LP)

Stock market values initially fell with the pandemic and lockdowns, which might be seen as intuitive; but they quickly reversed course and soared alongside rate cuts, a surging Fed balance sheet, and the announcement of the size and key components of the CARES Act. Shortages would translate to greater monopoly pricing power, and zero interest rates meant higher present values for growth stocks, where returns are skewed to later years.

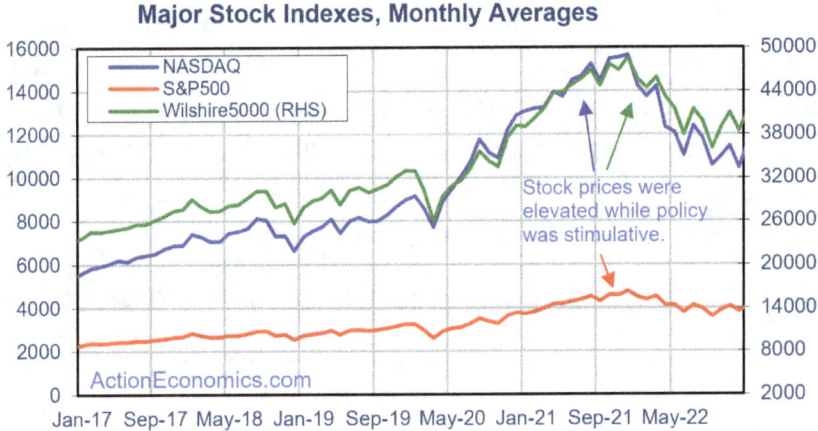

Figure 25.2 Major Stock Indexes, Monthly Averages
(Data source: Bloomberg Finance, LP)

The dollar initially surged over the February–April period of 2020 but then fell to a bottom in May of 2021, likely due to the accommodative policy backdrop. The dollar then climbed to a lofty peak in October of 2022 as inflation soared and the Fed switched from an aggressive easing strategy to an aggressive tightening path, with a strong verbal commitment to defeating inflation despite expectations of deteriorating economic and labor market conditions.

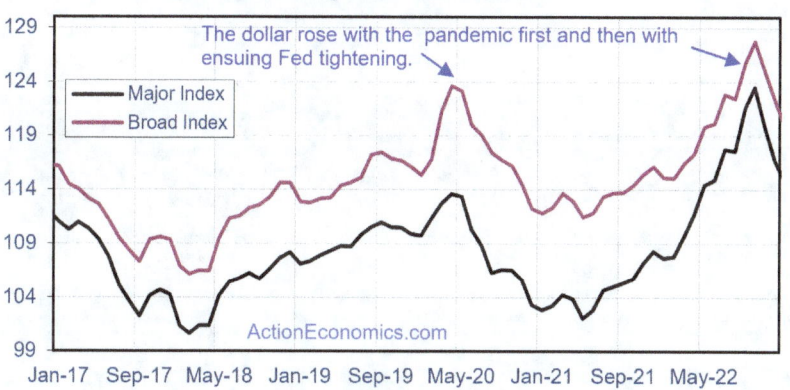

Figure 25.3 FRB Trade-Weighted Dollar Indexes
(Data source: U.S. Federal Reserve Board H.10 Release)

Chapter 26

Household, Bank, and Fed Balance Sheets

The monetary and fiscal policy response to the pandemic provided a powerful boost for household balance sheets, despite headwinds from the pandemic itself, which could be seen via stock price declines over the three months of Q1 2020. Household asset values fell at a 17% pace in Q1 of 2020 before soaring at a 27% rate in Q2 of 2020 to a new all-time high. We saw growth of 10%–27% in each of the seven quarters through Q4 of 2021.

The Fed's emerging inflation problem became evident in early 2022; and the steep rate climb, combined with QT and the fiscal cliff, meant an end to the pandemic lift for asset values.

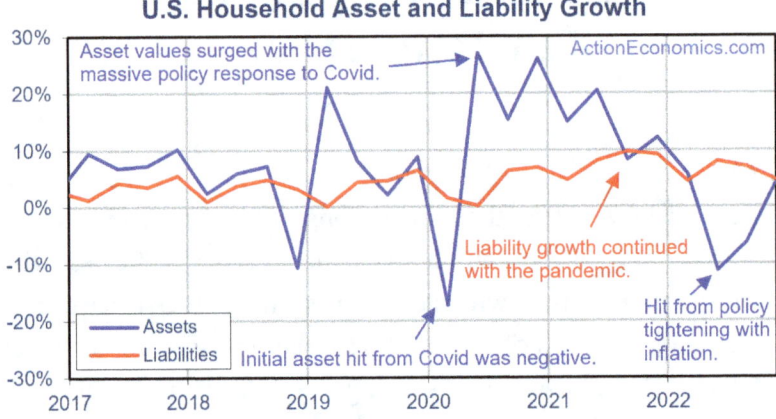

Figure 26.1 U.S. Household Asset and Liability Growth
(Data source: U.S. Federal Reserve Board Z.1 Release)

Household liability growth was fairly steady through the period, so the boom-bust pattern for asset values meant a similar boom-bust pattern for household net worth, which rose 37% over the eight quarters through Q1 of 2022. Net worth fell sharply in Q2 and Q3 of 2022, though it bounced into Q4 of 2022 with moderating y/y inflation rates and a drop-back in bond yields.

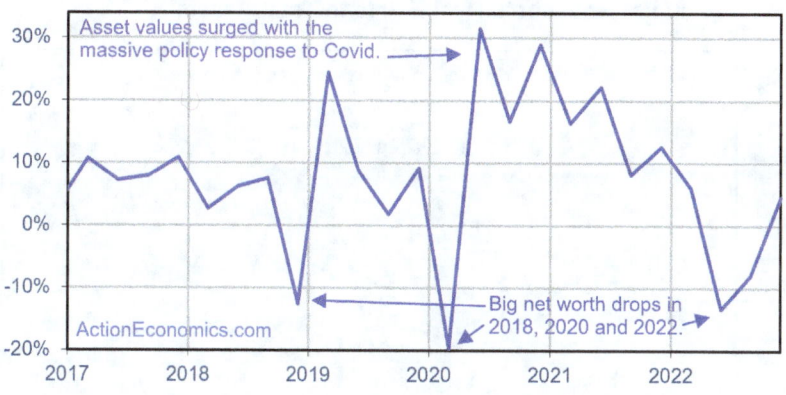

Figure 26.2 Nominal Growth in U.S. Household Net Worth
(Data source: U.S. Federal Reserve Board Z.1 Release)

The ratio of household real estate holdings to total assets received a big boost with the pandemic. The ratio initially popped from a 25% pre-pandemic level to 27% in Q1 of 2020 due to the temporary stock price pullback, before falling back to the 25% area over the four quarters ending in mid-2021. We then saw a steep climb to 29% by mid-2022 where the ratio has remained, though the expected pullback in home prices in 2023 will likely trim the rise.

Figure 26.3 Ratio of Household Real Estate to Total Assets
(Data source: U.S. Federal Reserve Board Z.1 Release)

The Fed's aggressive easing strategy limited the initial financial market disruptions that might have been expected in early 2020, and y/y growth in overall bank credit was fairly stable through the period. Commercial and industrial loans surged with the initial lockdowns as businesses drew from their lines of credit, reaching a 30% y/y gain in May of 2020 before falling to a trough of -16% in May of 2021 due to the hard comparison. Bank real estate loan growth eased modestly into 2021 before rebounding into 2022. Overall, though, total bank credit grew at a solid 8% rate over the 2019–2022 period.

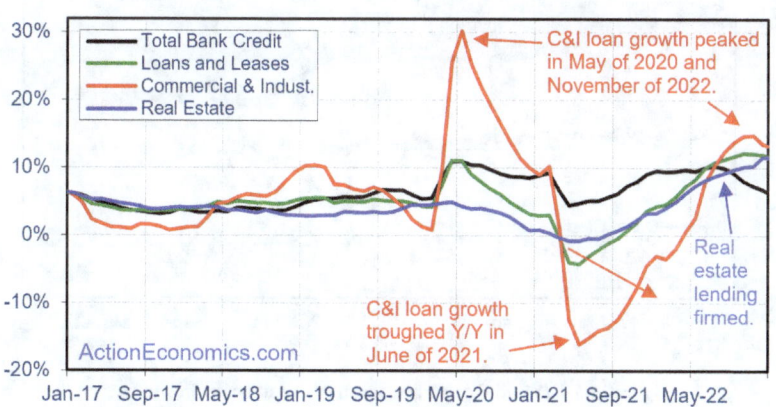

Figure 26.4 Total Y/Y Bank Credit and Component Growth
(Data source: U.S. Federal Reserve Board H.8 Release)

Consumer spending initially fell with lockdowns in early 2020, and consumer credit moderated initially as well, though by a much smaller amount. No doubt some households depended on credit cards, with the drop in employment. But, on net, consumer credit moderated through Q1 of 2021 despite explosive gains in spending that were likely due to the three massive stimulus packages that largely financed these transactions.

Y/Y & Qtrly Consumer Credit Loan Growth vs Y/Y Consumption Spending Growth

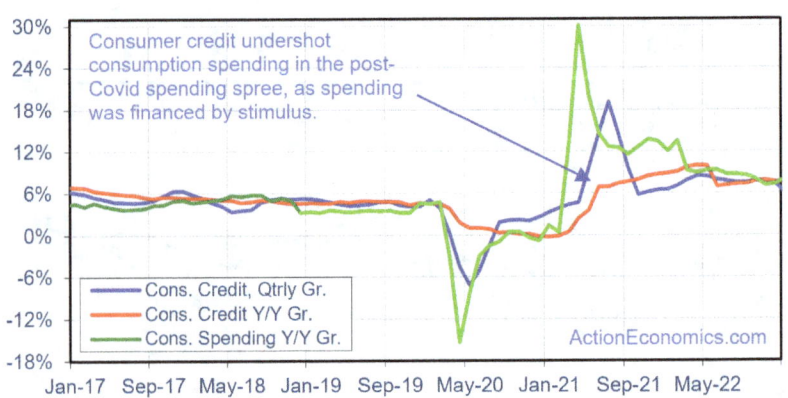

Figure 26.5 Y/Y and Quarterly Consumer Credit Loan Growth vs. Y/Y Consumption Spending Growth
(Data sources: U.S. Federal Reserve Board H.15 Release, U.S. Bureau of Economic Analysis)

The Fed's balance sheet soared in early 2020, with large initial asset purchases followed by ongoing QE, which continued through March of 2022, though total reserves peaked in October of 2021 before an unwind of repo market activity allowed the reserve base to moderate.

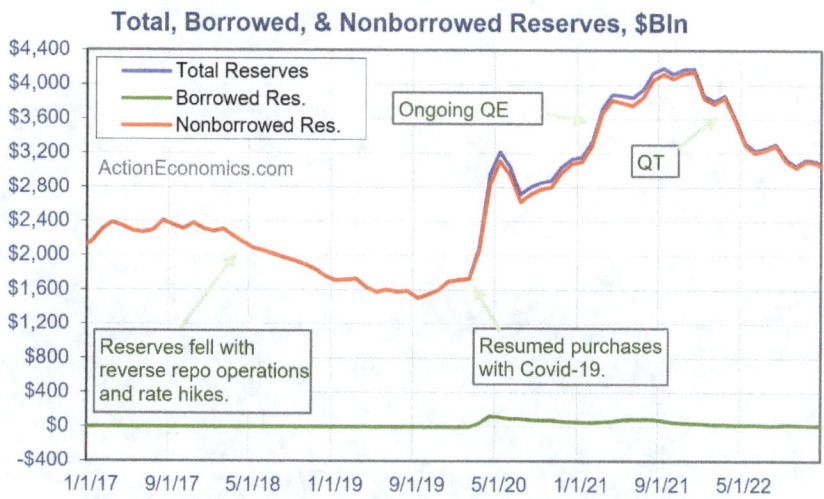

Figure 26.6 Total, Borrowed, and Nonborrowed Reserves
(Data source: FRED economic data, St. Louis Federal Reserve)

Conclusion

The stories of pandemic shocks across the centuries share common elements. Depending on their severity, pandemics and large epidemics disrupt lives and, for a time, normal economic activity. They kill people; people are therefore missing from the economy. In the case of COVID-19, among those missing from the workforce are COVID survivors who have been temporarily or permanently disabled by long COVID. But the capital structure of survivors remains, whether an empty building or farmland in antiquity or some manufacturing or service activity, though the value of these assets may be altered during and after a pandemic shock. When a society loses people and keeps the capital structure, the economics shift. The wealth that was accumulated remains and is redistributed among the remaining people, so some survivors are wealthier. During the COVID pandemic, many people inherited wealth or property from someone who died. One of the outcomes we see is that the wealthier segment of the population increased their wealth.[1] On the other hand, others faced financial hardship because a wage earner in a family perished or because a supply-chain-related job evaporated for a time or because long COVID resulted in disability, eroding productivity and earnings.

Corporate profits fell during the shutdown when COVID hit in 2020 but were boosted by stimulus assistance that cushioned the shock. The reopening and recovery found corporations raising prices to cover higher costs and then a bit more, showing profits that partly reflected both stimulus assistance and rock-bottom interest rates on borrowing.[2] However, some small businesses that were not able to access stimulus assistance early on suffered deeply and perhaps failed, inspiring a second round of assistance. There was an enormous churn as a spike in business closures was followed with a spike in new business creation.[3]

We know from history that the least productive elements in an economy are the ones that fall by the wayside after a pandemic. After the Black Death the least productive agricultural fields in Europe were left to lie fallow because there were not as many people demanding the food that would be produced in those fields. What did the farmer do? The farmer did not plant the field that produced less but did plant the fertile fields that produced more. Hence, the farmer's productivity rose.

What do we see when savings are redistributed and we have fewer people because the people are either dead or, in the case of COVID-19, long COVID-disabled, and the weakest productive assets are allowed to lie fallow? We see a population with higher productivity in certain areas, assisted, sooner or later, by innovations spurred by the labor shortfall. When an economy achieves that higher productivity, inflation from the pandemic shock subsides because, by definition, rising productivity diminishes inflationary pressures.

We have also seen shocks to labor costs and wages. Why? The pandemic claimed the lives of skilled workers whose expertise and contributions had to be replaced, and long COVID has partly or completely sidelined many others. COVID-19's impact on the labor force was exacerbated when people did not take precautions, as we have seen in the data about sickness, deaths, and higher hospitalization rates in political jurisdictions where the government's activities discouraged — or failed to encourage — behaviors that would have lowered the risk of infection, serious illness, and death. We see that reality reflected in the economic charts. Wages rose when jobs went unfilled, until workers could be found to fill them.

And what are we seeing now, in 2025 and beyond? We are still seeing lingering impacts of the pandemic, though always in concert with other developments. We see them portrayed in charts, and we see them in the outlook for the future. In the United States we had two years of declining life expectancy after COVID struck. We had essentially no population growth. We are exiting the COVID-19 shock, but the population of long COVID-disabled people is measurable in the millions; and while perhaps half recover, others find themselves newly afflicted with long COVID after multiple infections.

We have had to navigate the prolonged attenuation of an inflation spike that was initially generated by the pandemic shock but now reflects subsequent shocks, too, including two wars. In a 2024 working paper, Ben Bernanke and Olivier Blanchard parse its causes as follows:

> The pandemic-era inflation in the United States was initially the result of a series of adverse relative price shocks and sectoral shortages, each of which had a strong but largely transient effect on inflation. The labor market had little effect on inflation early on, but increased tightness eventually produced limited but sustained pressure on inflation. As the effects of relative price shocks and shortages stabilized or reversed, inflation declined, and the role of labor market tightness became increasingly important, suggesting that some slowing of activity might be necessary to get U.S. inflation all the way back to target.[4]

Bernanke and Blanchard broadened a 2023 study of pandemic-era inflation to include 10 more countries, with parallel findings:

In sum, early on, the sharp inflation experienced by most countries was accounted for by shocks directly and indirectly affecting price levels, including rising commodity prices, shortages of specific goods, and, in some cases, reduced labor supply. Labor markets became tight almost everywhere but played almost no role in the inflation takeoff. However, the inflation effects of tight labor markets are persistent, so that, as the shocks to prices (e.g., for energy and food) have reversed, the wage pressures from hot labor markets have become a more important source of inflation. In most countries, traversing the last mile back to central bank inflation targets will likely require bringing labor markets into better balance by reducing vacancy-unemployment ratios.[5]

Where COVID-19 is concerned, the medium-term post-pandemic period that Jordà, Taylor, and Singh studied stretches decades into the future. The period will be shaped not only by the coronavirus pandemic that erupted globally in 2020 but also by regional conflicts that are also proxy wars, the politics of nations, the monetary policies of the world's central banks, an AI revolution and other innovations, climate change impacts, and very possibly another pandemic. We have a war in Europe, a war in the Middle East, geopolitical tensions worldwide, and uncertainty about our internal political construction, with deep political divisions and cultural conflicts tearing at the fabric and functionality of our system. All of these factors have economic implications.

That said, whatever succeeding decades look like, the pressures that a pandemic asserts (with their intensity varying according to the burden of mortality and disability that a particular pathogen imposes) on human psyches, societies, governments, and economies seem now familiar and consistent. We — along with the Federal Reserve — know more now about what to expect and perhaps about how best to manage pandemic economic shocks and their aftermath. When we look at the history of pandemics and epidemics, we find in many cases that they coincided, within short periods of time — maybe a few years, and maybe contemporaneously — with the same characteristic developments. Whether in Athens during the plague and the Peloponnesian War, or World War I with the Spanish flu pandemic and its aftermath, or today, history repeats itself.

Our study of 3,500 years of history shows that the initial economic shocks from pandemics are indeed transient, with the duration of their impacts directly tied to the magnitude of mortality, to the frequency and duration of subsequent outbreaks, and to the resourcefulness of survivors who carry on. Pandemic mitigations, especially to the extent that they can safely enable continuity of economic activity, drive stronger, quicker, fuller recoveries from pandemic economic shocks. A pandemic economic shock may encompass just a few years; but certainly, if a pandemic pathogen strikes again and again over a longer period, as bubonic plague did, disrupting economic activity and eroding populations, its economic impacts continue for longer because it delivers not one but an extended series of shocks.

The COVID shock is still young. Barring a new, significantly more virulent variant (please note that we cannot rule one out), we have segued to a new normal with COVID in our midst. COVID currently claims tens of thousands of lives a year in the United States rather than hundreds of thousands, and a succession of variants that shows no sign of slowing still drives illnesses, worker absences, and both short- and long-term impacts on health. The official end of the pandemic emergency in 2023 did not mark the end of COVID-19's impacts on human health or their economic implications. SARS-CoV-2 continues to mutate, such that new variants cause new surges when they change enough so that populations lack sufficient immunity to fend them off. Epidemiologist Katelyn Jetelina reminds us why it is that our immunity to a new COVID infection wanes substantially four months or so after a vaccination:

> SARS-CoV-2 continues to mutate — about two times faster than the flu. It's normal to update vaccines when the virus mutates quickly. For example, we update vaccines for flu (which changes ~annually), but we don't update vaccines for measles (which hasn't mutated in a meaningful way for decades).[6]

Regardless of what the virus is doing, people have, for the most part, succumbed to pandemic fatigue, many assuming they must finally be protected by prior infections and/or vaccinations; and they have dropped precautions. (It is an old story — we can point to the same pattern after the second wave of the 1918 H1N1 pandemic, preceding a deadly third wave.) The abandonment of precautions makes them — and all of us — more vulnerable to new variants now. In the war against microbes that cause disease, human beings look for first opportunities to lay down their arms, while certain viruses continually and industriously better their opportunities to infect and reproduce, ever on the offensive.

Given what we know at this point, we expect that studies undertaken a lifetime from now will document COVID's impacts across an entire generation, with economic costs and necessary labor-force adaptations spanning decades. We will not see a return to the world of 2019. An economy that has recovered from a pandemic will still differ from what it might otherwise have been. Still, populations and economies regroup after pandemics, sometimes with impressive resilience. We speed economic recoveries following pandemic shocks by being ever prepared to mitigate the worst harms that pandemics can do, protecting people (including essential workers) from disease transmission even as we protect continuity of essential economic activity, and cultivating sources of economic resilience. Further, the vital role of central bank policy in an effective response to a pandemic economic shock has become clear during the COVID–19 pandemic, which has now afforded the U.S. Federal Reserve and other modern central banks globally a wealth of data and experience to draw upon for the future.

As we conclude our study inspired by the work of Jordà, Singh, and Taylor, the risk of another pandemic, especially one driven by H5N1 avian flu, appears to be rising as that virus evolves to more efficiently infect various mammals, including dairy cattle and other species that people interact with closely. The virus, as Dr. Michael Osterholm of CIDRAP reminds us, still lacks a mutation that would enable it to readily infect people via respiratory transmission, though it can infect human eyes, which have the same receptors that birds and cows and other species currently being infected do.[7] Beyond H5N1 flu, pandemic risks in general are rising in a crowded world with a changing and more volatile climate and fewer places for wild things to live and be without close contact with humans. The World Health Organization currently lists more than 30 "priority pathogens" considered to be capable of causing the next pandemic.[8] And it has, as of August 2024, declared mpox a public health emergency of international concern.[9]

More than anything, most people who have just lived through a pandemic long to put that trauma behind them; and our politicians have mirrored that public sentiment in rhetoric and policy, rushing to curtail the response to COVID and undermining our pandemic preparedness going forward. But circumstances press us to learn assiduously from pandemics past, including the one we have just lived through. How long we have before the next pandemic is unpredictable, and the next one may prove more devastating than the last. In the meantime, our preparations, surveillance, research, and vaccine development have yet to be scaled and paced to adequately prepare us for the threat of a new pandemic. (In the case of flu, that is going to mean improving the effectiveness of our influenza vaccine technology — seasonal flu vaccines today offer quite limited protection against serious illness.[10]) It behooves us to act on the realization that the epilogue to one pandemic story is always the prologue to the next.

---

1. Molly Kinder, Katie Bach, and Laura Stateler, "Profits and the Pandemic: As Shareholder Wealth Soared, Workers Were Left Behind," Brookings, April 21, 2022. https://www.brookings.edu/articles/profits-and-the-pandemic-as-shareholder-wealth-soared-workers-were-left-behind/.

2. Beradino Palazzo, "Corporate Profits in the Aftermath of COVID-19," FEDS Notes, Board of Governors of the Federal Reserve System, September 8, 2023. https://www.federalreserve.gov/econres/notes/feds-notes/corporate-profits-in-the-aftermath-of-covid-19-20230908.html#:~:text=The%20large%20increase%20in%20profitability,after%20the%20Global%20Financial%20Crisis.

3. Ryan A. Decker and John Haltwanger, "Business Entry and Exit in the COVID-19 Pandemic: A Preliminary Look at Official Data," FEDS Notes, Board of Governors of the Federal Reserve System, May 6, 2022. https://www.federalreserve.gov/econres/notes/feds-notes/business-entry-and-exit-in-the-covid-19-pandemic-a-preliminary-look-at-official-data-20220506.html.

4. Ben Bernanke and Olivier Blanchard, "An Analysis of Pandemic-Era Inflation in 11 Economies," Working Paper 24-11, Peterson Institute for International Economics, May 2024. https://www.piie.com/sites/default/files/2024-05/wp24-11.pdf.

5. Bernanke and Blanchard, "An Analysis of Pandemic-Era Inflation in 11 Economies."

6. Katelyn Jetelina, "Expect an updated COVID-19 Vaccine This Fall: Cliff Notes from FDA's Vaccine Meeting for Fall 2024," Your Local Epidemiologist, Substack, June 6, 2024. https://yourlocalepidemiologist.substack.com/p/expect-an-updated-covid-19-vaccine

7. Michael Osterholm, "Episode 160: The H5N1 Response," Osterholm Update, CIDRAP, June 27, 2024, https://www.cidrap.umn.edu/avian-influenza-bird-flu/episode-160-h5n1-response.

8. Smriti Mallapaty and Nature Magazine, "These Pathogens Could Spark the Next Pandemic, Scientists Warn," Scientific American, August 6, 2024, https://www.scientificamerican.com/article/these-pathogens-could-spark-the-next-pandemic-scientists-warn/.

9. "WHO Director-General declares mpox outbreak a public health emergency of international concern," news release, World Health Organization, August 14, 2024, https://www.who.int/news/item/14-08-2024-who-director-general-declares-mpox-outbreak-a-public-health-emergency-of-international-concern.

10. Michael Osterholm, "Episode 160: The H5N1 Response."

Acknowledgments

B ooks happen with a lot of help and support. I and my co-authors wish first to acknowledge the three distinguished authors of the San Francisco Federal Reserve Bank working paper, "Longer-Run Economic Consequences of Pandemics"; it is their work that inspired the writing of this book. They are as follows:

> Òscar Jordà, senior policy advisor in econometrics, macroeconomics, and monetary economics for the Federal Reserve Bank of San Francisco and a UC Davis professor of economics,

> Sanjay R. Singh, senior economist at the Federal Reserve Bank of San Francisco and assistant professor of economics at UC Davis,

> Alan M. Taylor, a former visiting scholar at the Federal Reserve Bank of San Francisco, distinguished professor emeritus at UC Davis, and currently a professor in the School of International and Public Affairs at Columbia University.

We also wish to acknowledge Global Interdependence Center colleagues and particularly the College of Central Bankers. The organization's member fellows and advisory board colleagues originated many ideas as this book progressed; often those ideas arose out of various GIC presentations and webinars.

We also wish to acknowledge the shareholders, directors, executive management, and staff of Cumberland Advisors for their support. All business activity proceeded unabated during the writing of this book.

Ed Cohen and Ray Perez helped me, early on, with sections on antiquity — we must acknowledge them and thank them. We would also like to thank journalist and historian Mary Ellen Gilliland for her assistance with research on Colorado and specifically Summit County during the 1918 H1N1 pandemic. Barry Ritholtz was a staunch supporter of this effort and kindly utilized a Masters in Business podcast for advance discussion of this book. More friends and colleagues than we can name here have, in various discussions at Camp Kotok, NBEIC, and in personal conversations, offered helpful comments, general support, and suggestions along the way as this book has taken shape.

To our collective acknowledgments, I would like to add personal thanks to the team that made this book happen. Elizabeth and Charley Sweet helped enormously with the project; it couldn't have been completed without them. Elizabeth and I worked together, month in and month out, to fully develop the vision for the book, which I had spent many hours mapping in early drafts. Charley read our drafts, organized Mike's charts, and assisted me as I maintained the flow of writing for Cumberland Advisors. Tristan Erwin contributed extensive research and drafted historical background for the chapters on epidemics and pandemics from antiquity through the medieval period in Part 2 of the book. Mike Englund of Action Economics created our pandemic chart book in Part 5, capturing for readers' exploration a catalog of economic impacts that resulted as the COVID-19 pandemic and pandemic responses unfolded.

Finally, a special acknowledgment goes to my partner Christine Schlesinger, who has offered unwavering support, patience, love, and encouragement while enduring this four-year journey of book creation with me.

Index

A page number in italics refers to a figure or a table. A page number followed by "n" and a number refers to an endnote.

About the Authors

David R. Kotok

 David Kotok co-founded Cumberland Advisors in 1973 and during his career served as its Chief Investment Officer, CEO, and Board Chairman. David's articles and financial market commentaries have appeared in the *New York Times,* the *Wall Street Journal, Barron's,* and other publications. He is a contributor or source to Bloomberg, Yahoo, CNN, Reuters, *USA Today,* and other media. He holds a B.S. in economics from the Wharton School of the University of Pennsylvania, an M.S. in organizational dynamics from the School of Arts and Sciences at the University of Pennsylvania, and an M.A. in philosophy from the University of Pennsylvania.

David has authored or co-authored four books, including *From Bear to Bull with ETFs* (now in its second edition) and *Adventures in Muniland.*

He has also written three monograph pamphlets. The first of these is "Lessons from Thucydides," which details information asymmetries and their implications for investors and world affairs. The second is "Zika," a work that compiles David's research, interviews, and personal experience concerning the Zika virus and its potential for serious damage in the way of health and monetary costs. The expense for individuals can be devastating; and in the case of governments, ballooning health budgets may affect municipal bond ratings. The third is

"Yield Curve Control – The story of ZIRP and NIRP." The yield curve is usually defined as the range of yields on Treasury securities from three-month Treasury bills to 30-year Treasury bonds. David's narrative and graphics tell the story of ZIRP (zero interest rate policy) and NIRP (negative interest rate policy) and explore what happens when central banks use YCC to control interest rates along some portion of the yield curve.

David has served as Program Chairman and as a director of the Global Interdependence Center (GIC), www.interdependence.org/, whose mission is to encourage the expansion of global dialogue and free trade in order to improve cooperation and understanding among nation states, with the goal of reducing international conflicts and improving worldwide living standards. David chaired its Central Banking Series and organized a five-continent dialogue held in Cape Town, Hong Kong, Hanoi, Milan, Paris, Philadelphia, Prague, Rome, Santiago, Shanghai, Singapore, Tallinn, and Zambia (Livingstone). He has received the Global Citizen Award from GIC for his efforts and serves on the advisory board to GIC's College of Central Bankers. In conjunction with GIC, David organizes fishing retreats, primarily in Maine, that are affectionately known as "Camp Kotok" by friends and many in the financial press. More about those retreats can be found at www.cumber.com/about/camp-kotok and at David's personal website, www.davidkotok.com/.

Michael R. Englund

Michael Englund (Mike) has been Principal Director and Chief Economist for Action Economics, LLC, since 2004. Previously, he was the Chief Economist for MMS International, where he worked for over twenty years, pioneering the early stages of the real-time commentary industry. Mike took on numerous initiatives to expand the breadth and depth of the MMS Treasury product over that period and worked closely on the development and original launch of the MMS Currency product. For just over a decade ending in 2002, MMS International was owned by Standard & Poor's, where Mike held the title of Chief Market Economist for Standard and Poor's and where he served on the Standard and Poor's Forecast Council.

Dr. Englund has a Ph.D. in economics and an M.A. in statistics from the University of California at Berkeley. He also spent a year studying at the London School of Economics and has a B.A. in economics from Middlebury College. In addition, Mike previously was on the Board of Directors for the National Association of Business Economics, was Chair of the NABE Financial Roundtable, and was President of the San Francisco Chapter of the NABE.

Tristan J. Erwin

Tristan Erwin earned his B.A. in history from the University of North Georgia in 2020 and pursues his passion for historical research at every opportunity. He believes that "Only by knowing our past can we began to understand the present, and only by understanding the present can we begin to glimpse the future." Tristan works as an account manager representing a large software company that serves the life sciences industry. His next history-related project is a sourcebook of ancient texts written about the Celts.

Elizabeth J. Sweet

A former English teacher, Elizabeth Sweet has worked since 2012 as a copy editor, researcher, and writer with a variety of clients, mostly in the financial industry. In the 2000s, when the threat of an H5N1 pandemic first loomed, she collaborated with others at the grassroots level and internationally to promote pandemic preparedness. She holds an M.A.

in English from Duke University and a B.A. in English from the College of William and Mary.

www.ingramcontent.com/pod-product-compliance
Lightning Source LLC
Chambersburg PA
CBHW060756120626
46557CB00001B/2